The Structure of Sociological Theory

THE DORSEY SERIES IN SOCIOLOGY

EDITOR   ROBIN M. WILLIAMS, JR.   *Cornell University*

The Structure of Sociological Theory

JONATHAN H. TURNER
University of California
Riverside

 1974

THE DORSEY PRESS   *Homewood, Illinois   60430*

Irwin-Dorsey International   Arundel, Sussex   BN18 9AB
Irwin-Dorsey Limited   Georgetown, Ontario   L7G 4B3

First Printing, January 1974
Second Printing, June 1974
Third Printing, November 1974
Fourth Printing, March 1975
Fifth Printing, November 1975
Sixth Printing, January 1976

ISBN 0-256-01540-6
Library of Congress Catalog Card No. 73–89117
Printed in the United States of America

To Sandy

Preface

In this volume I have sought to analyze the historical roots and contemporary profile of the four dominant paradigms of sociological theorizing: functionalism, conflict theory, interactionism, and exchange theory. I have also attempted, in the last chapter, to introduce the reader to the ethnomethodological alternative to these dominant paradigms.

There are several points of emphasis running through my analysis. Appreciation of these can perhaps make each chapter more readable. First, social theory must ultimately address the Hobbesian "problem of order": How and why is society possible? Phrased more scientifically this problem becomes one of discerning the conditions under which different social processes and patterns of social organization are likely to occur.

Second, in addressing this fundamental problem all social theory reveals—sometimes only implicitly—certain characteristics. All theories present a substantive "image" of society, of what the world is "really" like. All theories consider certain causal relations more important than others. All theories imply certain methodological strategies. And all theories reveal key propositions. In reviewing sociology's dominant paradigms, I have attempted to highlight these characteristics.

Third, I have sought to analyze social theory from the criteria of science. This analysis has not involved a mechanical comparison of each theory with the canons of scientific protocol. Such an exercise is sterile and futile, since all social theory can be found deficient in these terms. Rather, I have addressed a more meaningful set of questions: What *potential* does a theory offer for eventual conversion into scientific theory? What must be done to realize this potential?

And fourth, in Chapter 16, I outline some of the basic issues that social theory has ignored. Only after the detailed exposition and analysis of sociology's dominant paradigms can these issues be exposed. I offer my assessment of these issues with the hope that they will stimulate conceptual effort in some long neglected, and yet critical, areas.

ACKNOWLEDGMENTS

The particular form of theoretical analysis in this book is the result of my fortunate exposure to a few distinguished scholars. Each might consider my analysis of social theory to violate his preferences; and yet, the pages to follow represent a mixture of learning experiences with a diverse group of teachers. While each will be horrified with some aspects of my analysis, I would nevertheless like to acknowledge my long-standing debt to them. Tomatsu Shibutani taught me the importance of phrasing arguments propositionally, but I am afraid he will be somewhat dismayed by my analysis of interactionism. Walter Buckley first exposed me to the broad range of sociological theory, but will disagree with my portrayal of functional theory. Donald R. Cressey first emphasized that in "science" one should state arguments succinctly and not waste time pontificating on issues; I have always tried to follow this dictum, but I suspect I will always have a tendency to embellish discussion. Robin M. Williams, Jr., reaffirmed Professor Shibutani's earlier concern with stating arguments propositionally, while expanding the conceptual base first laid by Professor Buckley. To William Friedland, who reinforced Professor Cressey's dictum, I owe a no-nonsense desire to get to the guts of a conceptual perspective.

I would also like to thank Robin Williams—the Sociology Series editor for The Dorsey Press—for engaging in two separate line by line reviews of the manuscript during its various stages of development. Supplementing these two reviews have been the perceptive and face-saving comments of Professors Everett K. Wilson and Jerald T. Hage. I appreciate their critical remarks.

In preparing a manuscript, many embarrassing details are overlooked by the author. I would like to thank my typist and editor, Clara Dean, who despite all my efforts to the contrary produced an intelligible manuscript.

January 1974   J. H. TURNER

Contents

Political Machines in America. Problems in Merton's Paradigm and Protocol. Merton's Functional Strategy: An Overview.

1

Sociological Theorizing

SOCIOLOGICAL THEORY AND THE PROBLEM OF ORDER

In a now-famous passage, the 17th-century social philosopher, Thomas Hobbes, proclaimed the natural state of human society to be one of "continual fear, and danger of violent death; and the life of man, solitary, poor, nasty, brutish, and short."[1] Left to themselves, humans were viewed by Hobbes as continually in pursuit of power and profit and as governed primarily by motives of self-interest. In light of this situation and its potential for generating a social world of perpetual war and strife, Hobbes was led to ask: How can some semblance of social order and organization be created and maintained?

While few contemporary sociologists would accept his assumptions about the natural state of man, Hobbes can be given credit for touching upon the most fundamental question facing sociological theorizing: How and why is society possible? To phrase this question, or "the problem of order" as it has become known, it is not necessary to impute motives to men in their natural state, nor is it essential to view the natural social order as an incessant war of every man against every other man. Rather, it is only necessary to display a curiosity about how patterns of social organization are created, maintained, and changed.

This curiosity about the "problem of order" has been translated into a large number of specific theoretical questions concerning how and why such units as groups, aggregations, organizations, institutions, and whole societies reveal certain patterns of organizations and internal social processes. At the most general level, ignoring for the moment the differences in the units of organization and processes studied by various theorists, sociological theory can be identified as the

---

[1] Thomas Hobbes, *Leviathan* (New York: Macmillan Co., 1947); originally published in 1651.

1

attempt to explain *processes of institutionalization and de-institutionalization.* Through what basic processes are various types of social structure, in all their diverse forms, built up, maintained, changed, and broken down? Whether investigation focuses on a small face-to-face group, a restless crowd or mob, a large and complex organization, or an entire society, sociological theory is concerned with the conditions under which certain processes and patterns of structure are likely to occur.

To analyze the structure of social theory therefore requires the examination of the general perspectives that seek to explain the varied and complex processes of institutionalization and de-institutionalization. While there are many specific social theories pertaining to particular types of structures and processes, the chapters that follow will examine only the more general paradigms in sociology which address the problem of institutionalization. Specific theories are, in large part, a variant of one of these more general orientations; and thus it is appropriate that an overview of the structure of sociology's general theoretical perspectives should come before the analysis of its many special and delimited theories. For this reason, only the more general answers to the "problem of order" so forcefully asserted by Thomas Hobbes in the 17th century will be explored.

WHAT IS THEORY?

To conclude that sociology's general theoretical perspectives address the problem of order does not reveal just what theory is or how it can provide an answer to this problem. Theorizing can be viewed as the means by which the intellectual activity known as "science" realizes its three principal goals: (1) to classify and organize events in the world so that they can be placed into perspective; (2) to explain the causes of past events and predict when, where, and how future events will occur; and (3) to offer an intuitively pleasing sense of "understanding" why and how events should occur.

In striving to achieve these goals, social theory should reveal several basic elements or building blocks:[2] (1) concepts, (2) variables, (3) statements, and (4) formats. While there are many divergent claims about what theory is, or should be, these four elements are common to all of them. An understanding of what each represents is thus the first step in the analysis of social theory.

---

[2] Among several fine introductory works on the nature of scientific theory, the discussion in this chapter draws heavily upon Paul Davidson Reynolds' excellent, *A Primer in Theory Construction* (New York: Bobbs-Merrill Co., 1971). For other readable introductory works, see Arthur L. Stinchcombe, *Constructing Social Theories* (New York: Harcourt, Brace, & World, 1968), pp. 3–56; Karl R. Popper, *The Logic of Scientific Discovery* (New York: Harper & Row, 1959); David Willer and Murray Webster, Jr., "Theoretical Concepts and Observables," *American Sociological Review* 35 (August 1970): 748–57; Hans Zetterberg, *On Theory and Verification in Sociology,* 3d ed. (Totowa, N.J.: Bedminister Press, 1965).

Concepts as the Basic Building Blocks of Theory. Theories are built from concepts. Most generally, concepts denote or point to phenomena; in so doing they isolate features of the world which are considered, for the moment at hand, important. For example, notions of atoms, protons, neutrons, and the like are concepts, pointing to and isolating phenomena for certain analytical purposes. Familiar sociological concepts would include group, formal organization, power, stratification, interaction, norm, role, status, and socialization. Each term is a concept that embraces aspects of the social world which are considered essential for a particular analytical purpose.

Concepts that are useful in building theory have a special characteristic: they strive to communicate a uniform meaning to all those who use them. However, since concepts are frequently expressed with the words of everyday language, it is difficult to avoid words that connote varied meanings—and hence point to different phenomena—for different groups of scientists. It is for this reason that many concepts in science are expressed in technical or more "neutral" languages, such as the symbols of mathematics. In sociology, however, expression of concepts in such special languages is sometimes not only impossible, but also undesirable; hence, the verbal symbols used to develop a concept must be defined as precisely as is possible in order that they point to the same phenomena for all investigators.[3] While "perfect consensus" may never be attained with conventional language, a body of theory rests on the premise that scientists will do their best to define concepts unambiguously. Not to do so, or to give up because the task is difficult, is to invite conceptual chaos and thereby to preclude the accumulation of theoretical knowledge.

Concepts in science can display different degrees of *abstractness*. Some concepts pertain to concrete phenomena at specific times and locations. Other more abstract concepts point to phenomena that are not related to concrete times or locations. For example, in the context of small-group research, *concrete concepts* would refer to the persistent interactions of particular individuals, whereas an *abstract* conceptualization of such phenomena might refer to those general properties of face-to-face groups which are not tied to particular individuals interacting at a specified time and location. Abstract concepts are thus not tied to a specific context, whereas concrete concepts are. In building theory, abstract concepts are crucial, because they transcend particular events or situations and point to the common properties of similar events and situations. The importance of abstractness can perhaps be illustrated by the fact that people watched apples fall from trees for centuries, but real understanding of this phenomenon came

---

[3] The issue of defining the symbols employed in a concept is, of course, much more complex. For a quick review of the issues, see Reynolds, *Primer in Theory Construction*, pp. 45–48. For a more technical discussion, see Carl G. Hempel, *Fundamentals of Concept Formation in Empirical Science* (Chicago: University of Chicago Press, 1952).

only with the more abstract concept of gravity, which allowed for many similar occurrences to be visualized and incorporated into a theoretical statement that explained much more than why apples should fall from trees.

Abstractness poses a problem: How is it possible to attach abstract concepts to the ongoing, everyday world of events? While it is essential that many of the concepts of theory transcend specific times and places, it is equally critical that there be procedures for making these abstract concepts relevant to observable situations and occurrences. After all, the utility of an abstract concept can only be demonstrated when the concept is brought to bear on some specific empirical problem encountered by investigators; otherwise, concepts remain detached from the very processes they are supposed to help investigators understand. For this reason, abstract concepts should be accompanied by a series of statements known as *operational definitions*, which are sets of procedural instructions telling investigators how to go about discerning phenomena in the real world which are denoted by an abstract concept. It is thus through these kinds of definitions that the problem of how to relate abstract concepts to empirical events is resolved. For highly abstract concepts embracing a wide spectrum of empirical phenomena, it is usually necessary to have a large number of operational definitions—each one describing procedures for discerning a particular situation or event encompassed by the concept. In fact, the more operational definitions attached to an abstract concept, the more likely is the concept to serve many different investigators seeking to comprehend the complex operation of events in the empirical world.

In sum, then, concepts are the building blocks of theory. Of particular importance for theory are the more abstract concepts that are not tied to particular temporal and spatial settings. Yet, such concepts must specify procedures, through the vehicle of operational definitions, for their application to concrete events in the world.

Variables as an Important Type of Concept. When used to build theory, two general types of concepts can be distinguished:[4] (1) those that simply label phenomena and (2) those that refer to phenomena that differ in degree. Concepts that merely label phenomena would include such commonly employed abstractions as "dog," "cat," "group," "social class," "star," and the like. When stated in this way, none of these concepts reveal the ways in which the phenomena they denote vary in terms of properties such as size, weight, density, velocity, cohesiveness, or any of the many criteria used to inform investigators about differences in degree among phenomena. It is for this reason that scientific theory typically utilizes concepts that refer to the *variable properties* of such phenomena

---

[4] Reynolds, *Primer in Theory Construction*, p. 57; see also Stinchcombe, *Constructing Social Theories*, pp. 38–47 for a discussion of how concepts not only point to variable properties of phenomena, but to the interaction effects of interrelated phenomena.

as dogs, cats, groups, social classes, and stars. These kinds of concepts allow investigators to distinguish different events and situations from each other in terms of the degree to which they reveal some important property, such as size, weight, density, cohesiveness, and the like. For example, to note that an aggregate of people is a "group" does not indicate what type of group it is or how it compares with other groups in terms of such criteria as size, differentiation, and cohesiveness. Thus, the concepts of scientific theory should denote the *variable* features of the empirical world they describe. For, indeed, to understand, explain, and predict events requires that scientists visualize how measurable variation in one phenomenon can cause or produce measurable variation in another. However, this transformation of concepts into full-blown theory requires their incorporation into theoretical statements.

Theoretical Statements. Theories are concepts organized into groups of statements. These statements can be organized into several different forms, but at the core of all theory is the systematic incorporation of concepts into statements that describe the "real world." Generally, there are two kinds of theoretical statements: (1) existence statements and (2) relational statements.[5] *Existence statements* indicate when and where in the world instances of a particular concept exist. Such statements usually take the form: under Condition$_1$, C_2, C_3, . . . , C_n, concept x will be evident. For example, if there are two or more individuals in an interaction (C_1), if they can talk face to face (C_2), if they can all derive impressions of each other (C_3), if the interaction persists for 15 minutes or more (C_4), then a small, face-to-face group (concept x) can be said to exist.[6] Some existence statements can be more complex and anticipate when and where two concepts, x and y, will occur and perhaps vary together in some determinative way. For instance, under conditions C_1, C_2, C_3, and C_4 listed above, plus the assignment of a task (C_5), a small group (x) will display a distinct leadership structure (y). This latter kind of statement is a *relational statement* between two concepts, x and y.

Relational statements represent a critical feature of theory, for only by stating the relationships between or among concepts is prediction, explanation, and understanding of events in the world possible. Relational statements bring together concepts, denoting variable properties of phenomena, and begin to pave the way for visualizing how one variable may be "caused" by another. Some relational statements stop short of proclaiming that variations in one phenomenon cause variations in another and are therefore termed *associational*. These statements merely state that variations in phenomena are correlated, but do not indicate that they are causally related. Other relational statements, and these are

---

5 Reynolds, *Primer in Theory Construction,* p. 67.

6 Example adopted from ibid., p. 68.

the heart of theory, are *causal;* that is, one set of variable properties denoted by one concept is seen as causing the occurrence of other variable properties denoted by another concept.[7]

Whether associational or causal, relational statements will vary in the abstractness of their constituent concepts. Some remain highly abstract, others point to concrete phenomena in time and space. In the construction of theory, abstract theoretical statements usually encompass—in varying patterns and forms—a group of concrete statements. One reason for this is that most theoretical concepts are likely to have several operational definitions. Thus, when abstract concepts become incorporated into theoretical statements, the multiple operational definitions beget multiple operational statements, which in turn can beget several concrete statements about particular events in specified times and locations. The end result of this proliferation is that the sets of abstract statements, if well formulated, will encompass the generalizing implications of lower-order statements.

In sum, concepts that are useful for building theory are incorporated into statements that depict relationships among phenomena in the "real world." These statements can be existence or relational statements, both crucial to building theory. Causal relational statements are of particular importance for theory because they indicate that variation in the referent of one concept can account for variation in another.

The Form of Theory.   Theoretical statements may be organized into a number of different formats.[8] While many arguments for and against different formats can be made, it is more appropriate here simply to argue that theoretical statements should be *systematically organized* in accordance with logical rules of the theorist's choosing.[9] The systematic organization of theoretical statements, however, should attempt to meet the goals of science enumerated earlier: (*a*) Each format should employ abstract concepts that allow for the classification phenomena in the world; (*b*) each format should contain existence and relational statements, especially of the causal variety, which enable the causes of events to be determined; and (*c*) each format should offer a basis for an "intuitive

---

[7] Causal statements can usually take two different forms: (1) deterministic or (2) probabilistic. A deterministic statement takes the form: Under conditions $C_1, C_2, C_3, \ldots, C_n$, if x occurs, then y will occur. Few causal statements in sociology can be phrased this way. Rather, they are phrased probabilistically: Under conditions $C_1, C_2, C_3, \ldots, C_n$, if x occurs then y will occur with P probability. For example, in a small, face-to-face group assigned a task, a definitive leadership structure will occur 40 percent of the time.

[8] For readable discussions of these various formats, see Reynolds, *Primer in Theory Construction*, pp. 83–114; Zetterberg, *Theory and Verification in Sociology*, pp. 87–113; Herbert M. Blalock, Jr., *Theory Construction, from Verbal to Mathematical Formulations* (Englewood Cliffs, N.J.: Prentice-Hall, Inc., 1969).

[9] For an exposition of my preferences, see the brief appendix on the forms of theory at the end of the chapter.

understanding" of why given events occur and of what is involved in their occurrences.

There is probably no more difficult task in the building of theories than providing for the systematic organization of statements so that they meet these goals. In sociology there are a great many important abstract statements, as well as empirical generalizations capable of being converted into theoretical statements, but their organization into logically rigorous formats has proven very difficult. At this juncture, it is too time consuming to list the reasons why these difficulties exist, and it is not helpful to indict the discipline for failing to be more systematic; rather, it is more useful simply to note how the challenge of the task may be met. As the substantive perspectives of subsequent chapters unfold, an effort will be made to assess the extent to which the theoretical statements are amenable to incorporation into more systematic formats; and, equally important, some general and tentative suggestions for how such systematic formats should be constructed will be offered.

Unless theoretical statements can be ordered systematically, they cannot be efficiently tested; for, without some sense of the interrelationships among statements, each and every statement would have to be tested independently. But when statements are organized, bearing clear-cut relations with one another, the testing of a few crucial statements can shed light on the plausibility of other statements.

The formats of scientific theory lend themselves to testing only to the extent that certain of their constituent statements are phrased in such a way that they *can be* refuted with empirical investigation. Hypotheses must be vulnerable. It is this concern with *disproving* the key statements of a format that distinguishes science from other kinds of idea systems; for if statements cannot be disproven, "theory" is simply a self-maintaining body of statements which bears little relationship, except in their framers' minds, to real phenomena.[10] In order for theory

---

[10] There is a growing conviction among some sociologists that "science" is much like any other thought system in that it is devoted to sustaining a particular vision, among a community of individuals called scientists, of what is "really real." "Science" simply provides one interesting way of constructing and maintaining a vision of reality, but there are other, equally "valid" views among different communities of individuals. Obviously, this book does not accept this argument, but will close with a chapter on the "ethnomethodological" alternative to current varieties of sociological theory (see chap. 17). For some interesting explorations of the issues, see Edward A. Tiryakian, "Existential Phenomenology and the Sociological Tradition," *American Sociological Review* 30 (October 1965): 674–88; J. C. McKinney, "Typification, Typologies, and Sociological Theory," *Social Forces* 48 (September 1969): 1–11; Alfred Schutz, "Concept and Theory Formation in the Social Sciences," *Journal of Philosophy* 51 (April 1954): 257–73; Harold Garfinkel, *Studies in Ethnomethodology* (Englewood Cliffs, N.J.: Prentice-Hall, Inc., 1967); George Psathas, "Ethnomethods and Phenomenology," *Social Research* 35 (September 1968): 500–520; Don H. Zimmerman and Melvin Pollner, "The Everyday World as a Phenomenon," in *Understanding Everyday Life*, ed. J. D. Douglas (Chicago: Aldine Publishing Co., 1970), pp. 80–103; and Don H. Zimmerman and D. Lawrence Wieder, "Ethnomethodology and the Problem of Order," in *Understanding Everyday Life*, ed. J. D. Douglas (Chicago: Aldine Publishing Co., 1970), pp. 285–95.

to provide ways of ordering, explaining, and understanding events, those statements that do not help achieve the goals of science must be eliminated. By successively eliminating incorrect statements, those that survive attempts at refutation offer, for the present at least, the most accurate picture of the real world. Although having one's theory refuted may cause professional stigma, refutations are crucial to theory building. It is somewhat disheartening, therefore, that some scientists appear to live in fear of such refutation. For, in the ideal scientific process, just the opposite should be the case, as Karl Popper has emphasized:[11]

> Refutations have often been regarded as establishing the failure of a scientist, or at least of his theory. It should be stressed that this is an inductive error. Every refutation should be regarded as a great success; not merely as a success of the scientist who refuted the theory, but also of the scientist who created the refuted theory and who thus in the first instance suggested, if only indirectly, the refuting experiment.

Even statements that survive refutation, and hence bring professional prestige to their framers, are never fully "proven," for it is always possible that the next empirical test could disprove them. Yet, if statements consistently survive empirical tests, they have high credibility and are likely to be at the core of a theoretical body of knowledge. In social science, it is these highly credible statements that will offer the best comprehension of the conditions under which patterns of social organization emerge, persist, change, and break down. Thus, the testing and interrelating of such statements constitutes a strategy for answering scientifically the question of how and why processes of institutionalization should occur and take the form they do.

SOCIOLOGICAL THEORY

One of the simplest, but most fruitless, enterprises in sociology is to play a game called *criticize-the-discipline*. One variant of this game is to list the general features of proper scientific theory, as done briefly above, and then to examine critically a particular theoretical perspective in sociology. A certain result always is to find the perspective in question sadly deficient, which is what the *critic-of-the-discipline* usually wants anyway. This game takes little skill and always produces the same results; and yet it continues as a favorite sport among sociologists.

Any analysis of sociological theory should begin with a blunt admission that, from the perspective of ideal scientific theory, sociological theorizing has a long way to go. Such a confession is not meant to imply that *all* theory in sociology is so lacking; indeed, some of the specific theoretical perspectives of sociology

---

[11] Karl R. Popper, *Conjectures and Refutations* (New York: Basic Books, 1962), p. 243.

can be converted rather easily into a proper theoretical format. Still, the most general theoretical paradigms that have guided sociological theorizing on processes of institutionalization will be found wanting by those playing *criticize-the-discipline*.

An important and appropriate concern in an analysis of dominant theoretical perspectives is: In what ways do these perspectives deviate from scientific formulations? But this obvious question should be followed quickly by more important ones, infrequently asked: What can be done about these inadequacies? Potentially, can they be corrected? What should be the general direction of remedies? Assuming that current theoretical perspectives are not going to be converted immediately into ideal theory—and this indeed is a safe assumption—what strategies are possible for making such conversions in the long run?

As soon as the question becomes one of potential for theory building, critical analysis must move beyond the mechanical comparison of a particular theoretical perspective with the canons of scientific theory. While such comparisons cannot be ignored, their polemical intent often gets in the way of the productive analysis of a particular conceptual perspective.

THEORETICAL PERSPECTIVES IN SOCIOLOGY

Much of what is labeled sociological theory is, in reality, only a loose clustering of implicit assumptions, inadequately defined concepts, and a few vague and logically disconnected propositions. Sometimes assumptions are stated explicitly and serve to inspire abstract theoretical statements containing well-defined concepts, but most sociological theory constitutes a verbal "image of society" rather than a rigorously constructed set of theoretical statements organized into a logically coherent format. Thus, a great deal of so-called theory is really a general "perspective" or "orientation" for looking at various features of the process of institutionalization, which, if all goes well, can be eventually translated into true scientific theory.

The fact that there are many such perspectives in sociology poses problems of exposition; and these problems, in turn, are compounded by the fact that the perspectives blend one into another, sometimes rendering it difficult to analyze them separately. The initial solution to this dilemma is to limit arbitrarily the number of perspectives covered and, at the same time, to act as if they were separable. Accordingly, only four general sociological perspectives or orientations are covered in the sections to follow: (1) functional "theory," (2) conflict "theory," (3) interactionism and role "theory," and (4) exchange "theory."

The quotations around the word "theory" above do not represent an indictment, but again, a recognition of current inadequacies of sociological theory. These four perspectives have been selected for a number of reasons: (1) It is felt that they are the most general perspectives in sociology, which underlie most specific perspectives in the field. (2) These perspectives are also the most widespread and influential—the subjects of much analytical elaboration and, of course, inevitable criticism by both constructive critics and those playing *criticize-the-discipline*. (3) Each of these perspectives, at various times, has been proclaimed by its more exuberant proponents as the only one that could take sociology out of its theoretical difficulties. Therefore, each must be considered in a book attempting to assess the structure of sociological theorizing.

APPENDIX: PREFERABLE FORMS OF THEORETICAL STATEMENTS

Theoretical statements can be organized into several types of formats. Only two of these forms are considered here, primarily because they are considered to offer the most utility in building sociological theory. One form is termed *axiomatic;* the other has been labeled the *causal process* form.[12]

The axiomatic organization of theoretical statements takes, in general, this form: First, it contains a set of concepts that have operational definitions. Some of the concepts are highly abstract; others, more concrete. Second, there is always a set of existence statements that describe those situations in which concepts and relational statements apply. These existence statements make up what is usually called the *scope conditions* of the theory. Third, and most nearly unique to the axiomatic format, relational statements are stated in a hierarchical order. At the top of the hierarchy are *axioms,* or a group of highly abstract statements, from which *all* other theoretical statements are derived. These latter statements are usually called *propositions* and are logically derived in accordance with varying rules from the more abstract axioms. The selection of axioms is, in reality, a somewhat arbitrary matter, but usually they are selected with these criteria in mind: (*a*) The axioms should be consistent with one another, although they do not have to be logically interrelated; (*b*) axioms should be highly abstract; (*c*) they should state *causal* relationships among abstract concepts; (*d*) these causal relationships should be "lawlike" in that the more concrete propositions derived from them have not been disproved by empirical investigation; and (*e*) the axioms should have an "intuitive" plausibility in that their truth appears "self-evident."

The end result of tight conformity to axiomatic principles is an inventory or

---

[12] These labels have had fairly standard meaning among those concerned with the forms of theory construction. The utility of the axiomatic form in sociology has been urged by many, including Zetterberg (*Theory and Verification in Sociology*) and George C. Homans ("Sociological Theory,") in *Handbook of Sociology*, ed. E. Faris [Chicago: Rand McNally, 1964], and *The Nature of Social Science* [New York: Harcourt, Brace & World, 1967]. The causal process form has been recently urged by Reynolds (*Primer in Theory Construction*) and Buckley (*Sociology and Modern Systems Theory* [Englewood Cliffs, N.J.: Prentice-Hall, Inc., 1967], particularly pp. 62–81).

set of interrelated propositions, each derivable from at least one axiom and usually more abstract propositions. There are several advantages to this form of theory construction:[13] First, highly abstract concepts, encompassing a broad range of related phenomena, can be employed. These abstract concepts do not have to be *directly* measurable, since they arc logically tied to more specific and measurable propositions, which, when empirically tested, can *indirectly* subject the more abstract propositions and the axioms to empirical tests. Thus, by virtue of this logical interrelatedness of the propositions and axioms, research can be more efficient since the failure to refute a particular proposition lends credence to other propositions and to the axioms. Second, the use of a logical system to derive propositions from abstract axioms can generate many interesting propositions that point to previously unknown or unanticipated relationships among social phenomena.

The *causal process* form of theory construction takes a somewhat different form: First, like axiomatic theory, it contains both abstract and concrete concepts, with appropriate operational definitions. Second, and again much like axiomatic theory, it reveals a set of existence statements that establish the scope conditions of the causal statements. Third, and unlike axiomatic theory, the causal process form presents a set of causal statements describing the effect of one variable on another without establishing a strict hierarchical ordering of the statements. Rather, causal processes are considered of equal importance, although, clearly, some independent variables are recognized to have more impact on dependent variables than others. Thus, while axiomatic formats will resemble hierarchies of statements emanating from the axioms, the causal process format will resemble a flow diagram that charts the interactions among selected variables.

These two formats share two common features that allow them to meet the goals of science discussed earlier: (1) Each format employs abstract concepts that make possible the classification and categorization of social phenomena. Typologies are necessary to order the world so that it is comprehensible; and each form of theory does this necessary analytical work adequately. (2) Each form of organization posits causal relationships among variables and, in doing so, allows for the explanation of past events and the prediction of future events.

However, the causal process format may allow for more "understanding"—the third goal of science—of events than would the axiomatic form. While axiomatically arranged propositions explain and predict events through logical derivations, the exact *causal chains* involved in these derivations are not always clear. To provide "understanding of the world," it has been argued that the causal chains—whether direct, indirect, mutual, cybernetic, or teleological—need to be sorted

---

[13] Reynolds, *Primer in Theory Construction*, p. 96.

out by theory.[14] Quite frequently, axiomatic statements can be converted to a causal process form and thereby provide a "sense of understanding" of events in the real world. But sometimes such conversion is not possible; and thus it is presumed that the causal process format is superior.

SUGGESTED READINGS

Blalock, Herbert M. *Theory Construction.* Englewood Cliffs, N.J.: Prentice-Hall, Inc., 1969.

Dubin, Robert. *Theory Building.* New York: Free Press, 1969.

Gibbs, Jack. *Sociological Theory Construction.* Hinsdale, Ill.: Dryden Press, 1972.

Kaplan, Abraham. *The Conduct of Inquiry.* San Francisco: Chandler Publishing Co., 1964.

McCain, Carvin, and Segal, Erwin M. *The Game of Science.* Belmont, Calif.: Wadsworth Publishing Co., 1969.

Mullins, Nicholas C. *The Art of Theory: Construction and Use.* New York: Harper & Row, 1971.

Nagel, Ernest. *The Structure of Science,* New York: Harcourt, Brace & World, 1961.

Popper, Karl R. *The Logic of Scientific Discovery.* New York: Harper & Row, 1959.

———. *Conjectures and Refutations.* New York: Basic Books, 1962.

Reynolds, Paul Davidson. *A Primer in Theory Construction,* New York: Bobbs-Merrill Co., 1971.

Rudner, Richard S. *Philosophy of Social Science.* Englewood Cliffs, N.J.: Prentice-Hall, Inc., 1966.

Stinchcombe, Arthur L. *Constructing Social Theories.* New York: Harcourt, Brace & World, 1968.

Willer, David, and Webster, Murray, Jr. "Theoretical Concepts and Observables." *American Sociological Review* 35 (August 1970): 748–56.

Zetterberg, Hans. *On Theory and Verification in Sociology.* 3d ed. Totowa, N.J.: Bedminister Press, 1965.

---

[14] This position has been taken by a number of prominent authors, including Joseph Berger, Bernard P. Cohen, J. Laurie Snell, and Morris Zelditch, Jr. (*Types of Formalization in Small-Group Research* [Boston: Houghton Mifflin Co., 1962], pp. 67–100); Blalock (*Theory Construction,* pp. 100–140); Buckley (*Sociology and Modern Systems Theory,* pp. 67–105); and Reynolds (*Primer in Theory Construction,* pp. 107–11).

Part I

Functional Theories

2

Early Functionalism

FUNCTIONALISM AND THE ORGANISMIC ANALOGY

During the 19th century, the utilitarian doctrines of British classical economics were increasingly being called into question by social thinkers on the European continent. No longer was man to be viewed at a rational and calculating entrepreneur in a free, open, unregulated, and competitive marketplace. Nor was the doctrine of the "invisible hand of order" considered a very adequate explanation of how social organization could emerge out of free and unbridled competition among individuals. Although utilitarianism remained a prominent social doctrine for the entire 19th century, the first generation of French sociologists had ceased to accept the assumption that social order would automatically be forthcoming if only free competition among individuals were left intact.

The disenchantment with utilitarianism was aided in France, and to a lesser extent in all of continental Europe, by the disruptive social changes wrought by industrialization and urbanization. Coupled with the political instability of the late 18th century, as revealed most dramatically by the violent French Revolution, early-19th-century social thinkers in France displayed a profound concern with the problems of maintaining the social order. While each was to phrase the question somewhat differently, social thinkers began to ask seriously: Why and how is society possible?

Whether in France or elsewhere in Europe, the answer to this fundamental question was to be shaped by events occurring in the biological sciences. It was in the 19th century that biological discoveries were to alter significantly the social and intellectual climate of the times. For example, as many of the mysteries of the human body were being unfolded, the last vestiges of mysticism surrounding the body's functioning were being laid to rest. The diversity of the animal species was finally being systematically recorded under the long-standing classification procedures outlined by the Swedish biologist Carolus Linnaeus. And most importantly, conceptions of evolution, culminating in the theories of Wallace and Darwin, were stimulating great intellectual and social controversy.

Since it was in this social and intellectual milieu that sociology as a self-conscious discipline was born, it is not surprising that conceptions of social order were influenced by the preoccupation with biology. As the nominal founder of sociology in the early 19th century, the French thinker August Comte launched, in an effort to comprehend why and how society was possible, a mode of analysis that can be termed the "organismic" interpretation of society.[1] For Comte, society was conceptualized as a type of organism and was to be viewed through the prism of biological conceptions of structure and function. While there were acknowledged differences between social and biological organisms, the 19th century's exuberant acceptance of the new biological discoveries and theories often caused thinkers to underemphasize these differences. For example, in one of his frequent moments of overstatement, in his *Polity* Comte was moved to proclaim that families were the basic social cells, social forces were the essential social tissues, the state and city were the social organs, and the nations of the world were the analogues of organismic systems in biology.[2]

Much of the tendency for overstatement in Comte's work stems from the fact that he was reacting to the chaotic aftermath of the French Revolution and to the utilitarian slant in the doctrines of the then-prominent British social thinker Herbert Spencer. Yet, even Spencer became enamored of the mood of the times, for, by the late 19th century, Spencer like Comte was moved to proclaim that "society is *like* an organism." However, unlike other thinkers who had made this organismic analogy, Spencer went on to list systematically the ways in which society could be viewed as analogous to an organism:

1. Both society and organisms can be distinguished from inorganic matter, for both grow and develop.
2. In both society and organisms an increase in size means an increase in complexity and differentiation.
3. In both, a progressive differentiation in structure is accompanied by a differentiation in function.
4. In both, parts of the whole are interdependent with a change in one part affecting other parts.

---

[1] Comte's first organic doctrines can be found in *Philosophie positive*, vol. 10, pp. 430–98. For a summary of Comte's organicism, see Howard Becker and Harry Elmer Barnes, *Social Thought from Lore to Science* (New York: Dover Publications, 1952), 2: 572–75. It should be emphasized that Comte was not the first social thinker to view society in organic terms. On the contrary, organic analogizing goes at least as far back as Aristotle and Plato, as Comte was quick to point out. But it was Comte who reevoked the organismic analogy in the last century.

[2] Comte, *Polity*, vol. 2, pp. 241–42, taken from Becker and Barnes, *Social Thought*, p. 573.

5. In both, each part of the whole is also a micro society or organism in and of itself.
6. And in both organisms and societies, the life of the whole can be destroyed but the parts will live on for a while.[3]

While Spencer was initially cautious in emphasizing that such statements were *analogies*, his followers, such as Paul von Lilienfield and René Worms, moved from mere analogies to visualizing society not as just *like* an organism, but as an actual living organism. Apparently carried away by such assertions, these followers of Spencer were inspired to view society as the highest form of organism on a somewhat contrived phylogenetic "scale." This extreme organicism was perhaps inevitable in light of the mood of the times, but an equally important influence was Spencer's unfortunate inclination to forget the distinction he had made between analogy and reality.

While many of the extremes of the organismic analogy had been rejected by the latter part of the 19th century, the conception of society as an organism introduced three assumptions that began to typify sociological functionalism: First, social reality is visualized as a *system*. Second, the processes of a system can only be understood in terms of the *interrelatedness* of its parts. And third, like an organism, a system is *bounded*, with certain processes operating to maintain both its integrity and its boundaries. Stated in this minimal form, these assumptions would appear necessary for a proper understanding of social structures and processes. However, because these basic functionalist tenets were inspired by the organismic analogy, many additional and questionable biological concepts "slipped in the back door" as sociologists developed theoretical schemes. In fact, much of the century-old debate over functionalism stems from the implicit organicism accompanying this conceptual perspective. Depending on whose schema is under scrutiny, the number of implicit organismic assumptions has varied.

In the most *extreme* form, functional theorizing began to include the following conceptions: (1) Society as a bounded system is self-regulating, tending toward homeostasis and equilibrium. (2) As a self-maintaining system, similar to an organism, society perhaps has certain basic needs or requisites, which must be met if survival is to ensue, if homeostasis is to be preserved, or if equilibrium is to be maintained. (3) Sociological analysis of a self-maintaining system with needs and requisites should therefore focus on the function of parts in meeting system needs and hence maintaining equilibrium and homeostasis. (4) In systems with needs, it is probable that certain types of structures *must* exist to ensure

---

[3] Herbert Spencer, *The Social Organism* (1860) Herbert Spencer, *Principles of Sociology*, vol. 1, pt. 2, chap. 2. As Spencer clearly notes, "the permanent relations among the parts of a society *are analogous* to the permanent relations among parts of a living body" (Spencer's italics); see also, Becker and Barnes, *Social Thought*, p. 680.

survival/homeostasis/equilibrium. While perhaps several alternative structures can exist to fulfill the same need, a delimited range of necessary alternative structures exists to fulfill any system need.

These assumptions have often persisted and have been the subject of much of the debate over functionalism.[4] Organisms display homeostatic tendencies, but do societies? Organisms might reveal stable sets of survival requisites or needs, but do societies? Organisms may display interrelated parts that must exist to meet system needs, but is this a viable assumption for societies? These questions have persisted for close to a century, as can be seen from the more self-conscious formulations of functionalism by Émile Durkheim, Bronislaw Malinowski, and A. R. Radcliffe-Brown —the titular founders of functionalism.

FUNCTIONALISM AND ÉMILE DURKHEIM

As the inheritor of a long French tradition of social thought, especially Comte's organicism, it is not surprising that Émile Durkheim's early works were heavily infused with organismic terminology. While his major work, *The Division of Labor in Society,* was sharply critical of Herbert Spencer, many of Durkheim's formulations were clearly influenced by the 19th-century intellectual preoccupation with biology.[5] Aside from the extensive use of biologically inspired terms, Durkheim's basic assumptions reflected those of the organicists: (1) Society was to be viewed as an entity in itself that could be distinguished from, and was not reducible to, its constituent parts. In conceiving of society as a reality, *sui generis,* Durkheim in effect gave analytical priority to the social whole. (2) While such an emphasis by itself did not necessarily reflect organismic inclinations, Durkheim, in giving causal priority to the whole, viewed system parts as fulfilling basic functions, needs, or requisites of that whole. (3) The frequent use of the notion "functional needs" is buttressed by Durkheim's conceptualization of social systems in terms of "normal" and "pathological" states. Such formulations, at the very least, connote the view that social systems have needs that must be fulfilled if "abnormal" states are to be avoided. (4) In viewing systems as normal and pathological, as well as in terms of functions, there is the additional inference that systems have equilibrium points around which normal functioning occurs.

---

[4] It should be emphasized that many of the critics of functional analysis have assumed that the concepts of "equilibrium" and "homeostasis" *necessarily* connote a vision of the social world as unchanging and static. This interpretation is incorrect, for notions of equilibrium can also provide an analytical reference point for observing instances of change and disequilibrium. Thus, there is no logical reason for assuming that the concept of equilibrium allows only a static image of the social world. Critics sometimes appear to talk as if there were such a logical compulsion.

[5] Émile Durkheim, *The Division of Labor in Society* (New York: MacMillan Co., 1933), bk. 1 (originally published in 1893). Durkheim tended to ignore the fact that Spencer wore several "intellectual hats." He reacted to Spencer's advocacy of utilitarianism, seemingly ignoring the similarity between Spencer's organismic analogy and his own organic formulations.

Durkheim recognized all of these dangers and explicitly tried to deal with several of them. First, he was clearly aware of the dangers of teleological analysis —of implying that some future consequence of an event causes that very event to occur. Thus, he warns that the causes of a phenomenon must be distinguished from the ends it serves:

> When, then, the explanation of a social phenomenon is undertaken, we must seek separately the efficient cause which produces it and the function it fulfills. We use the word "function" in preference to "end" or "purpose," precisely because social phenomena do not generally exist for the useful results they produce.[6]

Thus, despite giving analytical priority to the whole, and in viewing parts as having consequences for certain "normal" states, and hence meeting system requisites, Durkheim remained aware of the dangers of asserting that all systems have "purpose" and that the need to maintain the whole causes the existence of its constituent parts. Yet, Durkheim's insistence that the function of a part for the social whole always be examined sometimes led him, and certainly many of his followers, into questionable teleological reasoning. For example, even when distinguishing "cause" and "function" in his major methodological statement, he leaves room for an illegitimate teleological interpretation: "Consequently, to explain a social fact it is not enough to show the cause on which it depends; we must also, at least in most cases, show its function *in the establishment* of social order" (italics added).[7] In this summary phrase, the words "the establishment of," could connote that the existence of system parts can be explained only by the whole, or "social order," which they function to maintain. From this view, it is only a short step to outright teleology: The social fact is caused by the needs of the social order that the fact fulfills. Such theoretical statements do not necessarily have to be illegitimate, for it is conceivable that a social system could be "programmed" to meet certain "needs" or designated "ends" and thereby have the capacity to cause variations in cultural items or "social facts" in order to meet these needs or ends. But if such a system is being described by an analyst, it is necessary to document how the system is programed and how it operates to cause variations in "social facts" to meet needs or ends. As the above quote illustrates, Durkheim did not have this kind of system in mind when he formulated his particular brand of functional analysis; thus, he did not wish to state his arguments teleologically.

Despite his warnings to the contrary, Durkheim appears to have taken this short step into teleological reasoning in his substantive works. In his first major work on the division of labor, Durkheim went to great lengths to distinguish between cause (increased moral density) and function (integration of society).

---

[6] Émile Durkheim, *The Rules of Sociological Method* (Glencoe, Ill.: Free Press, 1938), p. 96.
[7] Ibid., p. 97.

However, as Cohen indicates,[8] the causal statements often become fused with functional statements. The argument runs, very generally, something like this: Moral density leads to competition, which threatens the social order, which, in turn, leads to the specialization of tasks, mutual interdependence, and increased willingness to accept the morality of mutual obligation. This transition to a new social order is not made consciously, or by "unconscious wisdom," but because division of labor is necessary to restore the order that "unbridled competition might otherwise destroy."[9] Hence, the impression is left that the "threat" or the need for social order "causes" the division of labor. Such reasoning can be construed as an illegitimate teleology, since the consequence of the division of labor—the social order—is the implied cause of the division of labor. At the very least, then, cause and function are not kept as analytically separate as Durkheim so often insisted.[10]

Similarly, Cohen argues further,[11] Durkheim's analysis of the origins and nature of religion slips into teleological reasoning: Society constrains its members, while providing them with the cultural resources necessary to be creative; primitive men are vaguely aware of the constraining force of society, but are incapable of stating such dependency despite a *need* to do so; therefore, they choose some object to represent society and their collective attitudes toward it. By virtue of representing the social (moral) order, these symbols become sacred; and, as they become the central focus of ritual activity, they arouse and sustain group sentiments and hence social solidarity. Such a "theory" thus relies on the notion of "need" in men to express their vague awareness of the social constraints on them and on the assumption that such a need has beneficial consequences for "normal" social functioning, that is, social solidarity. The teleology occurs at the individual level, a need to express; or if this imputation of purpose is not accepted, then a social need for solidarity causes religion. Thus, the emergence of religion, and its maintenance, is not explained by prior antecedent conditions, or carefully documented causal chains, but by the purpose of the activity for meeting either individual and/or group "needs."

---

[8] *Modern Social Theory* by Percy S. Cohen, (c) 1968 by Percy S. Cohen, Basic Books, Inc., Publishers, New York, pp. 35–37. Whether the line of argument presented here is "true" is debatable. But the very fact that it is a "debatable topic" would indicate that perhaps there was some disparity between what Durkheim said and what he did when actually analyzing social facts.

[9] Ibid., p. 35.

[10] There are ways out of this causal analysis, if one can impute some additional assumptions to Durkheim's analysis. First, competition must occur under conditions of scarcity of resources (perhaps caused by increased moral density). Second, a law of economic utility must be invoked. Third, it must be assumed that actors are motivated to avoid "unbridled competition" (an "individualistic" assumption, which, at this point in his writing, Durkheim might not accept). With these assumptions, the division of labor can be "explained," for now the explanation involves a legitimate teleology (the assumption that actors are motivated to avoid competition).

[11] Cohen, *Modern Social Theory*, p. 36.

In sum, then, despite Durkheim's warnings about illegitimate teleology, he often appears to waver on the brink of the very traps he wished to avoid. The reason for this failing can probably be traced to the organismic assumptions built into his form of sociological analysis. In taking a strong sociologistic position on the question of emergent properties—that is, on the irreducibility of the whole to its individual parts—Durkheim saved sociology from the naïve psychology and anthropology of his day.[12] However, in supplementing this emphasis on the social whole with organismic assumptions of "function," "requisite," "need," and "normality/pathology," Durkheim helped weld organismic principles to sociological theory for nearly three quarters of a century. The brilliance of his analysis of substantive topics, as well as the suggestive features of his analytical work, made a "functional" mode of analysis highly appealing to subsequent generations of sociologists and anthropologists.

FUNCTIONALISM AND THE ANTHROPOLOGICAL TRADITION

Functionalism as a well-articulated conceptual perspective emerged in the 20th century with the writings of two anthropologists, Bronislaw Malinowski[13] and A. R. Radcliffe-Brown.[14] Each of these thinkers was heavily influenced by the organicism of Durkheim, as well as by their own field studies among primitive societies. Despite the similarities in their intellectual backgrounds, however, the conceptual perspectives developed by Malinowski and Radcliffe-Brown revealed a considerable number of dissimilarities.

While Radcliffe-Brown disavowed the label *functionalism* in favor of *structuralism*, his perspective was more thorough than Malinowski's and was therefore to guide a generation of functional analysis in anthropology. Recognizing that "the concept of function applied to human societies is based on an analogy between social life and organic life" and that "the first systematic formulation of the concept as applying to the strictly scientific study of society was performed by Durkheim,"[15] Radcliffe-Brown tried to indicate how some of the problems of organismic analogizing might be overcome.

For Radcliffe-Brown, the most serious problem with functionalism was the

---

[12] Robert N. Nisbet, *Émile Durkheim* (Englewood Cliffs, N.J.: Prentice-Hall, Inc., 1965), pp. 9–102.

[13] For basic references on Malinowski's functionalism, see these works: Malinawski, "Anthropology," *Encyclopedia Britannica*, supp., vol. 1 (London and New York, 1936); Malinowski, supp., vol. 1 *A Scientific Theory of Culture* (Chapel Hill: University of Carolina Press, 1944); Malinowski, *Magic, Science, and Religion and Other Essays* (Glencoe, Ill.: Free Press, 1948).

[14] For basic references on Radcliffe-Brown's functionalism, see his "Structure and Function in Primitive Society," *American Anthropologist* 37 (July–September 1935): 58–72; *Structure and Function in Primitive Society* (Glencoe, Ill.: Free Press, 1952); and *The Andaman Islanders* (Glencoe, Ill.: Free Press, 1948).

[15] Radcliffe-Brown, "Structure and Function in Primitive Society," p. 68.

tendency for analysis to appear teleological. Noting that Durkheim's definition of function pertained to the way in which a part fulfills system "needs," he emphasized that, in order to avoid the teleological implications of such analysis, it would be necessary to "substitute for the term 'needs' the term 'necessary condition of existence.' " In doing so, he felt that no universal human or societal needs would be postulated; rather, the question of which conditions were necessary for survival would be an empirical one, an issue that would have to be discovered for each given social system. Furthermore, in recognizing the diversity of conditions necessary for the survival of different systems, analysis would avoid asserting that every item of a culture must have a function and that items in different cultures must have the same function.

Once the dangers of illegitimate teleology were recognized, functional, or, to use his term, *structural,* analysis could legitimately proceed from several assumptions: (1) One necessary condition for survival of a society is minimal integration of its parts; (2) the term *function* refers to those processes that maintain this necessary integration or solidarity; (3) thus, in each society structural features can be shown to contribute to the maintenance of necessary solidarity. In such an analytical approach, social structure and the conditions necessary for its survival are irreducible. In a vein similar to that of Durkheim, Radcliffe-Brown saw society as a reality in and of itself. For this reason he was usually led to visualize cultural items, such as kinship rules and religious rituals, as explicable in terms of social structure—particularly its "need" for solidarity and integration. For example, in analyzing a lineage system, Radcliffe-Brown would first assume that some minimal degree of solidarity must exist in the system. Processes associated with lineage systems would then be assessed in terms of their consequences for maintaining this solidarity. The conclusion to be reached was that lineage systems provided a systematic way of adjudicating conflict in societies where families owned land, because such a system specified who had the right to land and through which side of the family it would always pass. In doing so, the integration of the economic system—landed estates owned by families—is explained.[16]

This form of analysis poses a number of problems that have continued to haunt functional theorists. While Radcliffe-Brown admits that "functional unity [integration] of a social system is, of course, a hypothesis," he fails to specify the analytical criteria for assessing just how much or how little functional unity is necessary for system survival, to say nothing of specifying the operations necessary for testing this hypothesis. As subsequent commentators were to discover, without some analytical criteria for determining what is and what is not minimal functional integration and societal survival, the hypothesis cannot be tested, even

---

[16] Radcliffe-Brown, *Structure and Function in Primitive Society,* pp. 31–50. For a secondary analysis of this example, see Arthur L. Stinchcombe, "Specious Generality and Functional Theory," *American Sociological Review* 26 (December 1961): 929–30.

in principle. Thus, what is typically done is to assume that the existing system encountered by the investigator at a particular point in time is minimally integrated and surviving, because it exists and persists. Without carefully documenting how various cultural items promote instances both of integration and malintegration of the social whole, such a strategy can reduce the hypothesis of functional unity to a tautology: If one can find a system to study, then it must be minimally integrated; therefore, lineages that are a part of that system must promote this integration. To discover the contrary would be difficult, since the system, by virtue of being a system, is already composed of integrated parts, such as a lineage system. There is a non sequitur in this reasoning, since it is quite possible to view a cultural item like a lineage system as having both integrative and malintegrative (and other) consequences for the social whole. In his actual ethnographic descriptions, Radcliffe-Brown often slips inadvertently into a pattern of circular reasoning in which the fact of a system's existence requires that its existing parts, such as a lineage system, be viewed as contributing to the system's existence.

Assuming integration and then assessing the contribution of individual parts to the integrated whole leads to an additional analytical problem. Such a mode of analysis implies that the causes of a particular structure, for example lineages, lie in the system's needs for integration (most likely an illegitimate teleology).

Radcliffe-Brown would, of course, have denied these conclusions. His awareness of the dangers of illegitimate teleology would have seemingly eliminated the implication that the needs of a system cause the emergence of its parts, while his repeated assertions that the notion of function "does not require the dogmatic assertion that everything in the life of every community has a function"[17] should have led to a rejection of tautological reasoning. However, much like Durkheim, what Radcliffe-Brown asserted analytically was frequently not practiced in the concrete analysis of substantive systems. Such lapses were not intended, but appeared to be difficult to avoid when functional "needs," functional integration, and "equilibrium" were his operating assumptions.[18]

Thus, while Radcliffe-Brown displayed an admirable awareness of the dangers of organicism[19]—especially of the problem of illegitimate teleology and the hypothetical nature of notions of solidarity—he all too often slipped into a

---

[17] See, for example, Radcliffe-Brown, "Structure and Function in Primitive Society."

[18] A perceptive critic of an early draft of this manuscript provided an interesting way to visualize the problems of tautology:

    When do you have a surviving social system?
    When certain survival requisites are met.
    How do you know when certain survival requisites are met?
    When you have a surviving social system.

[19] Don Martindale, The Nature and Types of Sociological Theory (Boston: Houghton-Mifflin Co., 1960), p. 459.

pattern of questionable teleological reasoning. Forgetting that integration was only a "working hypothesis," he opened his analysis to problems of tautology. Such problems were persistent in Durkheim's analysis; and despite his attempts to the contrary, their spectre haunted even Radcliffe-Brown's insightful essays and ethnographies.

Many of Radcliffe-Brown's reasoned theoretical statements were responses to the assertions of Malinowski—the first to apply the title *functionalism* to organismic forms of analysis. While Radcliffe-Brown was prone to fall unintentionally into the pitfalls of organicism, Malinowski appeared to plunge headlong into them. Malinowski's conceptual perspective was built around the dogmatic assertion that cultural items exist to fulfill basic human and cultural needs: "The functional view of culture insists therefore upon the principle that in every type of civilization, every custom, material object, idea and belief fulfills some vital function, has some task to accomplish, represents an indispensable part within a working whole."[20] Such a position can easily become teleological, for the impression is left that cultural items exist (i.e., are caused) by the needs of the system and/or its members.

Probably the most distinctive aspect of Malinowski's functionalism was its reductionistic tendencies. His analytical scheme starts with an emphasis on such individual human needs as food, shelter, and reproduction. To meet these needs, organization of human populations into groups and communities is necessary, as is the creation of cultural symbols to regulate such organization. In turn, the creation of patterns of social organization and culture gives rise to additional needs, which must be met by other, more elaborate forms of social organization and culture. By such reasoning, it is possible to visualize several types of requisites shaping culture: (1) those that are biologically based; (2) acquired psychological needs; and (3) derivative needs that are necessary to maintain the culture and patterns of social organization which originally met basic biological and acquired psychological needs. Thus, the impression is left that structures arise in response to a number of different types of requisites: biological, psychological, and cultural. By visualizing culture as meeting several "layers" of such requisites, Malinowski could employ reductionist argument to explain the existence and persistence of any structure in a society. If such a structure does not meet cultural requisites, it may be said to meet psychological ones; and, if it cannot be linked to either of these types, it may be said to meet biological needs. It was perhaps this ability to shift levels of requisites that allowed Malinowski to proclaim so confidently that any cultural item *must* have some "task to accomplish . . . within a working whole."

Such reasoning is not only teleological—the item emerges to meet the end

---

[20] Malinowski, "Anthropology," p. 132.

it fulfills—it is also tautological in that any cultural item exists to meet a need of the cultural whole, while the cultural whole exists to meet biological and psychological needs. Such circular reasoning appears inevitable once teleological reasoning is compounded by reductionist assumptions. As will be evident, it is to the credit of modern functionalists that such teleological reductionism was not adopted.

THE EMERGENCE OF FUNCTIONALISM: AN OVERVIEW

With its roots in the organicism of the early 19th century, functionalism is the oldest and, until recently, the dominant conceptual perspective in sociology. The organicism of Comte and later that of Spencer and Durkheim clearly influenced the first functional anthropologists—Malinowski and Radcliffe-Brown—who, in turn, with Durkheim's timeless analysis, helped shape the more modern functional perspectives.

In emphasizing the contribution of sociocultural items to the maintenance of a more inclusive systemic whole, early functional theorists often conceptualized social "needs" or "requisites." The most extreme formulation of this position was that of Malinowski, in which all cultural items were viewed as meeting one of various levels of needs or requisites: biological, psychological, and sociocultural. More tempered in their statements and more aware of the problems in postulating social "needs" were Émile Durkheim and A. R. Radcliffe-Brown, who implicitly "hypothesized" the requisite for social integration, but who also recognized that needs for integration do not necessarily cause the processes and structures leading to such integration. For them, it was important to analyze separately the causes and functions of a sociocultural item, since the causes of an item could be unrelated to its function in the systemic whole. However, despite their awareness of this fact, in their analyses of actual phenomena both Durkheim and Radcliffe-Brown lapsed into assertions that the need for integration caused a particular event—say, for example, the emergence of a particular type of lineage system or the division of labor.

This tendency for their theoretical statements to blur the distinction between cause and function created two related problems in the analyses of Durkheim and Radcliffe-Brown: those of tautology and illegitimate teleology. To say that a structural item, such as the division of labor, emerges because of the need for social integration is a teleological assertion, for an end state—social integration—is presumed to cause the event—the division of labor—which brings about this very end state. Such a statement is not necessarily illegitimate, since, indeed, the social world is rife with systemic wholes that initiate and regulate the very structures and processes maintaining them. However, to assert that the need for integration is the cause of the division of labor is probably an illegitimate teleology, since to make the teleology legitimate would require some documentation of the causal chain of events through which needs for integration operate to produce a division of labor. Without such documentation, the statement is vague and theoretically vacuous. Assumptions of system "needs" and "requisites" also create problems of tautology, for, unless clear-cut and independent criteria can be established to determine when a system requisite is fulfilled, or not fulfilled, theoretical statements become circular: A surviving system is meeting its survival needs; the system under study is surviving; a sociocultural item is a part of this system; therefore, it is likely that this item is meeting the system's needs. Such statements are true by definition, since no independent criteria exist for assessing when a requisite is met and whether a given item meets these criteria. To stretch Durkheim's analysis for purposes of illustration, without clear criteria for determining what constitutes "integration" and what levels of "integration" denote a "surviving" system, the statement that the division of labor meets an existing system's needs for integration must be true by definition, since the system exists and is therefore surviving and the division of labor is its most conspicuous integrative structure.

In looking back on the theoretical efforts of early functionalists, then, the legacy of their analytical work can be summarized as follows:[21]

1. The social world was viewed in systemic terms. For the most part, such systems were considered to have needs and requisites that had to be met to assure survival.
2. Despite their concern with evolution, thinkers tended to view systems with needs and requisites as having "normal" and "pathological" states— thus connoting system equilibrium and homeostasis.
3. When viewed as a system, the social world was seen as composed of mutually interrelated parts; the analysis of these interrelated parts focused on how they fulfilled requisites of systemic wholes and, hence, maintained system normality or equilibrium.
4. By typically viewing interrelated parts in relation to the maintenance of a systemic whole, causal analysis frequently became vague, lapsing into tautologies and illegitimate teleologies.

Much of contemporary functionalism has attempted to incorporate the suggestiveness of early functional analysis—especially the conception of "system" as composed of interrelated parts. At the same time, current forms of functional

---

[21] For a more thorough analysis of the historical legacy of functionalism, see Don Martindale's *Nature and Types of Sociological Theory* and his "Limits of and Alternatives to Functionalism in Sociology," in *Functionalism in the Social Sciences*, American Academy of Political and Social Science Monograph, no. 5 (Philadelphia, 1965), pp. 144–62; see also in this monograph, Ivan Whitaker, "The Nature and Value of Functionalism in Sociology," Ibid., pp. 127–43.

theorizing have tried to cope with the analytical problems of teleology and tautology, which Durkheim and Radcliffe-Brown so unsuccessfully tried to avoid. In borrowing the organicism of the 19th century and in attempting to exploit conceptually the utility of viewing system parts as having implications for the operation of systemic wholes, modern functionalism provided early sociological theorizing with a unified conceptual perspective. However, the adequacy of this perspective has increasingly been called into question in recent decades, for as will be discovered throughout this book, such questioning has often led to excessively polemical and counterproductive debates in sociology. On the positive side, however, the controversy over functional theorizing has also stimulated attempts to expand upon old conceptual perspectives and to develop new perspectives as alternatives to what are perceived to be the inadequacies of functionalism.

Without this sometimes heated dialogue, a book on theory in sociology might be short, since there would be little diversity among perspectives. The intensity of the debate over functionalism has divided the field into various "theoretical camps," which, while overlapping to some extent, do allow demarcation of several major theoretical perspectives and their respective proponents. Two figures have emerged to expound the utility of the functionalist perspective: Talcott Parsons and Robert K. Merton, who are discussed in chapters 3 and 4, respectively. Thinkers who question the functionalist approach are treated in subsequent sections.

3

Functional Imperativism:
Talcott Parsons[1]

In 1937, Talcott Parsons published his first major work, *The Structure of Social Action*.[2] With exhaustive and detailed scholarship seldom equaled in sociological works, Parsons delineated the strengths and weaknesses of prominent thinkers in three main intellectual traditions: utilitarianism, positivism, and idealism. In this review, Parsons indicated how key assumptions and concepts from these three traditions could be synthesized to form a more adequate conceptual base for subsequent sociological theorizing. Emerging from this effort was not only a substantive vision of social phenomena, which was to become the subject of heated controversy, but also a unique strategy for building sociological theory.

In reviewing Parson's contribution to sociological theorizing, it is necessary to remain attuned to the interplay between Parsons's initial substantive vision of social life and the strategy he advocated for conceptualizing this vision. Out of this interplay has proliferated a "general theory of action" which, while constantly supplemented over the last four decades, has never become conceptually disassociated from the analytical base first laid in *The Structure of Social*

---

[1] While few appear to agree with all aspects of "Parsonian theory," rarely has anyone quarreled with the assertion that he has been the dominant sociological figure of this century. For documentation of Parsons's influence, see Robert W. Friedrichs, *A Sociology of Sociology* (New York: Free Press, 1970); and Alvin W. Gouldner, *The Coming Crisis of Western Sociology* (New York: Basic Books, 1970).

[2] Talcott Parsons, *The Structure of Social Action* (New York: McGraw-Hill Book Co., 1937); the most recent paperback edition (New York: Free Press, 1968) will be used in subsequent footnotes.

Action. The developmental continuity in action theory over several decades is perhaps one of its most distinguishing features.[3] To appreciate how such an intellectual feat has been possible requires an understanding of Parsons's faithful adherence to a somewhat unique conception of how to build sociological theory.

THE PARSONIAN STRATEGY FOR BUILDING SOCIOLOGICAL THEORY

In *The Structure of Social Action,* Parsons advocated an "analytical realism" in building sociological theory. Theory in sociology must utilize a limited number of important concepts that "adequately 'grasp' aspects of the objective external world. . . . These concepts correspond not to concrete phenomena, but to elements in them which are analytically separable from other elements."[4] Thus, theory must, first of all, involve the development of concepts that abstract from empirical reality, in all its diversity and confusion, common analytical elements. In this way, concepts will isolate phenomena from their imbeddedness in the complex relations that go to make up social reality.

The unique feature of Parsons's "analytical realism" was his insistence on how these abstract concepts are to be employed in sociological analysis. Parsons did not advocate the immediate incorporation of these concepts into theoretical statements, but rather, their use to develop a "generalized system of concepts." This use of abstract concepts would involve the ordering of concepts into a coherent whole that would reflect the important features of the "real world." What is sought is an ordering of concepts into analytical systems that grasp the salient and systemic features of the universe without being overwhelmed by empirical details. As such, theory should initially resemble an elaborate classification and categorization of social phenomena that reflects significant features in the organization of these social phenomena.

However, Parsons had more than mere classification in mind, for he was advocating the priority of developing systems of concepts over systems of propositions. Concepts in theory should not be incorporated into propositions prematurely. They must first be ordered into analytical systems that are isomorphic with the systemic coherence of reality; then, if one is so inclined, operational defini-

---

[3] It has been emphasized again and again that such continuity does not exist in Parsons's work. For the most often quoted source of this position, see Joseph F. Scott, "The Changing Foundations of the Parsonian Action Scheme," *American Sociological Review* 28 (October 1969): 716–35. This position is held to be incorrect in the analysis to follow. In addition to the present discussion, *see* also Jonathan H. Turner and Leonard Beeghley, "Current Folklore in the Criticisms of Parsonian Action Theory," *Sociological Inquiry,* forthcoming 1974. See also, Parsons's reply and comments on this article, ibid.

[4] Parsons, *Structure of Social Action,* p. 730.

tions can be devised and the concepts can be incorporated into true theoretical statements.

Thus, only after systemic coherence among abstract concepts has been achieved is it fruitful to begin the job of constructing true theory, for propositional inventories of existence, associational, and causal statements cannot hope to capture the "realness" of the social world until conceptual classification of the systemic nature of the universe is performed. This position thus advocated a *strategy* for theory building in sociology; and it is only after this strategy is comprehended that Parsons's subsequent theoretical and substantive work makes sense, since throughout his intellectual career—from *Structure of Social Action* to the present—Parsons has adhered to this *strategy* for building sociological theory.[5]

THE PARSONIAN IMAGE OF SOCIAL ORGANIZATION

Parsons's strategy for theory building maintains a clear-cut ontological position: The social universe displays systemic features that must be captured by a parallel ordering of abstract concepts. Curiously, the substantive implications of this strategy for viewing the world as composed of systems were recessive in *The Structure of Social Action*. Much more conspicuous were assumptions about the "voluntaristic" nature of the social world.

The "voluntaristic theory of action" represented for Parsons a synthesis of the useful assumptions and concepts of utilitarianism, positivism, and idealism. In reviewing the thought of classical economists, Parsons noted the excessivenesses of their utilitarian conceptualization of unregulated and atomistic men in a free and competitive marketplace rationally attempting to choose those actions that would maximize their profits in their transactions with others. Such a formulation of the social order presented for Parsons a number of critical problems: Did humans always behave rationally? Were they indeed free and unregulated? How was order possible in an unregulated and competitive system? Yet, Parsons saw as fruitful several features of utilitarian thought, especially the concern with actors as seeking goals (or profits) and the emphasis on the choice-making capacities of men who weighed alternative lines of action. Stated in this minimal form, Parsons felt that the utilitarian heritage could indeed continue to inform sociological theorizing. In a similar critical stance, Parsons rejected the extreme formulations of radical positivists, who tended to view the social world in terms of observable cause-and-effect relationships among physical phenomena and, as a result, to ignore the complex symbolic functionings of the human mind.

---

[5] See Parsons, ibid., especially pp. 3–43, 727–76. For an excellent secondary analysis of Parsons's position and why it does not appeal to the critics, see Enno Schwanenberg, "The Two Problems of Order in Parsons' Theory: An Analysis from Within," *Social Forces* 49 (June 1971): 569–81.

Furthermore, Parsons saw the emphasis on observable cause-and-effect relationships as too easily encouraging a sequence of infinite reductionism: groups were reduced to the causal relationships of their individual members; individuals were reducible to the cause-and-effect relationships of their physiological processes; these were reducible to physicochemical relationships, and so on, down to the most basic cause-and-effect connections among particles of physical matter. Nevertheless, despite these extremes, radical positivism did draw attention to the physical parameters of social life and to the deterministic impact of these parameters on much—but, of course, not all—social organization. Finally, in assessing idealism, Parsons saw as useful their conceptions of "Ideas" as also circumscribing both individual and social processes, although all too frequently these "ideas" were seen as detached from the ongoing social life they were supposed to regulate.

The scholarship in Parsons's analysis of these traditions cannot be recaptured, but perhaps more important than the details of his analysis is the weaving of selected concepts from each of these traditions into a "voluntaristic theory of action." For it is at this starting point that, in accordance with his theory-building strategy, Parsons began to construct a functional theory of social organization. In this initial formulation, he conceptualizes voluntarism as the subjective decision-making processes of individual actors, but he views such decisions as the partial outcome of certain kinds of constraints, both normative and situational. Voluntaristic action therefore involves these basic elements: (1) an *actor*, who, at this point in Parsons's thinking, is an individual person; (2) the actor is viewed as *goal seeking;* (3) the actor is also in possession of alternative *means* to achieve the goals; (4) the actor is confronted with a variety of *situational conditions*, such as his own biological makeup and heredity as well as various external ecological constraints, which influence the selection of goals and means; (5) the actor is seen to be governed by values, norms, and other ideas in that these ideas influence what is considered a goal and what means are selected to achieve it; thus, (6) action involves the *actor's making subjective decisions about the means to achieve goals*, all of which are *constrained by ideas* and *situational conditions*. This conceptualization of "voluntarism" is represented diagrammatically in Figure 3–1.

The processes diagrammed in Figure 3–1 are often termed the *unit act*, with social action involving a succession of such unit acts by one or more actors. Parsons appears to have chosen to focus on such basic units of action for at least two reasons: (1) He felt it necessary to synthesize the historical legacy of social thought—from social philosophy and classical economics to early sociological theory— concerning the most basic social process, especially when dissected into its most elementary components. (2) Given his position on what theory should be, it is clear that the first analytical task in the development of sociological theory was to isolate conceptually the systemic features of the most basic unit from which more complex processes and structures were built.

FIGURE 3–1

The Units of Voluntaristic Action

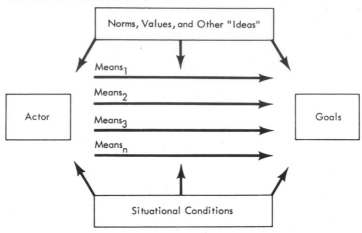

Once these basic tasks were completed, Parsons appears to have asked: How are unit acts connected to each other and how can this connectedness be conceptually represented? Indeed, near the end of *The Structure of Social Action,* he recognized that "any atomistic system that deals only with properties identifiable in the unit act . . . will of necessity fail to treat these latter elements adequately and be indeterminate as applied to complex systems."[6] However, only the barest hints of what was to come were evident in those closing pages.

Yet, perhaps only through the wisdom of hindsight, Parsons did offer several clues about the features of these "more complex" systems. Most notable, near the close of this first work, he emphasized that "the concept of action points again to the *organic* property of action systems" (italics added).[7] Buttressed by the ontology of his strategy for building theory—that is, the development of systems of concepts that mirror reality—it is clear what he intended to do: develop a conceptual scheme that captured the systemic essence of social reality.

By 1945, eight years after he published *The Structure of Social Action,* Parsons became more explicit about the form this analysis should take: "The structure of social systems cannot be derived directly from the actor-situation frame of reference. It requires *functional* analysis of the complications introduced by the interaction of a plurality of actors" (italics added).[8] More significantly, this functional analysis should allow notions of "needs" to enter: "The functional

---

6 Parsons, *Structure of Social Action,* pp. 748–49.

7 Ibid., p. 745.

8 Talcott Parsons, "The Present Position and Prospect of Systemic Theory in Sociology," *Essays in Sociological Theory* (New York: Free Press, 1949), p. 229.

needs of social integration and the conditions necessary for the functioning of a plurality of actors as a 'unit' system sufficiently well integrated to exist as such impose others."[9] Starting from these assumptions, which bear a close resemblance to those of Durkheim and Radcliffe-Brown, Parsons began to develop a complex functional scheme.

THE EARLY SYSTEMS OF ACTION

The transition from the analysis of discrete unit acts to systems of action appears to have occurred in a series of conceptual elaborations: (1) Unit acts are not emitted in a social vacuum—as was clearly recognized in *The Structure of Social Action*. (2) Rather, unit acts occur in a social context, a context in which an actor occupies a status and enacts normatively prescribed role behaviors. (3) Status-roles are not unrelated, but, in fact, are connected to each other in various types of systems. (4) Unit acts must therefore be viewed from the perspective of *systems of interaction*, in which action is now seen as patterns of role enactments by actors. (5) These interaction systems comprised of a plurality of actors occupying statuses and enacting normatively prescribed roles are viewed as comprising a *social* system.

However, as can be recalled from *The Structure of Social Action*, the "structure of action" involves more than normatively prescribed behaviors. First, action involves individual decision making in the pursuit of goals. Second, values and other ideas circumscribe the actor's decision making in the pursuit of goals. Third, situational conditions, such as heredity and features of the physical environment, further constrain action.

These components of action also began to be viewed in a systemic context, leading Parsons at first to postulate one additional system of action, the *personality*, which would encompass the systemic interrelations among needs and decision-making capacities of actors enacting roles in the social system. At this early stage in the transition from the analysis of unit acts to systems of action, neither culture nor the organic and physical features of action were viewed as systems. However, *cultural patterns* figured prominently in the analysis in that they were seen as underlying both the normative structure of the social system and the need dispositions and decision-making processes of the personality system.[10] But given Parsons's commitment to developing analytical schemes that captured the connected coherence of reality and given this new commitment to analytically

---

[9] Ibid.

[10] However, even at this early stage Parsons frequently talked as if culture were a system, anticipating the later conceptualization of culture as a true system. For a comparison of the different emphases, see, first, Talcott Parsons, *Toward a General Theory of Action* (New York: Harper & Row, 1951), pp. 20–23, and then, Talcott Parsons, *Societies: Evolutionary and Comparative Perspectives* (Englewood Cliffs, N.J.: Prentice-Hall, Inc., 1966).

separating the components of the unit act into discrete systems of action, he soon began to visualize culture in systemic terms. And somewhat later the physical features of organisms, such as heredity and other biological processes, were also seen as a separable system of action.

As a sociologist, Parsons recognized that his main theoretical concern involved the analysis of social systems. Thus, his second book, appearing some fourteen years after *The Structure of Social Action*, was appropriately entitled *The Social System*.[11] It was in this book that the analytical distinctions among social and personality systems, as well as cultural patterns, were first analyzed in detail. Since much of the subsequent development of "action theory" is an elaboration of this analysis, it is perhaps wise to pause and examine this work in detail.

Parsons's *The Social System*

Analyzing social systems involves developing a system of concepts that, first of all, captures the systemic features of society at all its diverse levels and, second, points to the nodes of articulation among personality systems, social systems, and cultural patterns.

To capture conceptually the systemic features of culture, society, and personality, Parsons wastes little time in introducing notions of functional requisites for each of these basic components of action. Such requisites pertain not only to the internal problems of the action components, but also to their articulation with one another. Following both Durkheim's and Radcliffe-Brown's lead, he views *integration* within and among the two action systems and the cultural patterns as a basic survival requisite. Since the social system is his major topic, Parsons is concerned with the integration within the social system itself and between the social system and the cultural patterns, on the one hand, and between the social system and the personality system, on the other. In order for such integration to occur, at least two functional requisites must be met:

1. A social system must have "a sufficient proportion of its component actors adequately motivated to act in accordance with the requirements of its role system."[12]
2. Social systems must avoid "commitment to cultural patterns which either fail to define a minimum of order or which place impossible demands on people and thereby generate deviance and conflict."[13]

Having made explicit the incorporation of requisites, which in later works are expanded and made even more prominent, Parsons then attempts to develop a

---

[11] Talcott Parsons, *The Social System* (New York: Free Press, 1951).

[12] Ibid., p. 27.

[13] Ibid., pp. 27–28.

conceptual scheme that reflects the systemic interconnectedness of social systems, although he later returns to the integrative problems posed by the articulation of culture and the personality system with the social system. Crucial to this conceptualization of the social system is the concept of *institutionalization*, which refers to relatively stable patterns of interaction among actors in statuses. Such patterns are normatively regulated and infused with cultural patterns. This infusing of values can occur in two ways: First, norms regulating role behaviors can reflect the general values and beliefs of culture. Second, cultural values and other patterns can become internalized in the personality system and, hence, affect that system's need structure, which, in turn, determines an actor's willingness to enact roles in the social system.

Parsons views institutionalization as both a process and a structure. It is significant that he initially discusses the *process of institutionalization* and only then refers to it as a structure—a fact that is often ignored by critics who contend that action theory is overly structural. As a process, institutionalization can be typified in this way: (1) Actors who are variously oriented enter into situations where they must interact. (2) The way actors are oriented is a reflection of their need structure and how this need structure has been altered by the internalization of cultural patterns. (3) Through specific interaction processes—which are not clearly specified, but which by implication include role taking, role bargaining, and exchange—norms emerge as actors adjust their orientations to each other. (4) Such norms emerge as a way of adjusting the orientations of actors to each other, but, at the same time, they are circumscribed by general cultural patterns. (5) In turn, these norms regulate subsequent interaction, giving it stability. It is through such a process that institutionalized patterns are created, maintained, and altered.

As interactions become institutionalized, a "social system" can be said to exist. While Parsons has typically been concerned with whole societies, a social system is not necessarily a whole society, for indeed any organized pattern of interaction, whether a micro or macro form, is termed a "social system." When focusing on total societies, or large parts of them that are composed of several of these interrelated clusters of institutionalized roles, Parsons frequently refers to the constituent social systems as *subsystems*.

In sum, then, institutionalization is the process through which social structure is built up and maintained. Institutionalized clusters of roles—or, to phrase it differently, stabilized patterns of interaction—comprise a social system. When the given social system is large and is composed of many interrelated institutions, these institutions are typically viewed as subsystems. A total society may be defined as one large system composed of interrelated institutions. At all times, for analytical purposes, it is necessary to remember that a social system is circumscribed by cultural patterns and infused with personality systems.

In his commitment to the development of concepts that reflected the properties of all action systems, Parsons was led to a set of concepts denoting some of the variable properties of these systems. Termed *pattern variables*, they allowed for the categorization of the modes of orientation in personality systems, the value patterns of culture, and the normative requirements in social systems.[14] The variables were phrased in terms of polar dichotomies, which, depending upon the system under analysis, would allow for a rough categorization of decisions by actors, the value orientations of culture, or the normative demands on status roles.[15]

1. *Affectivity–affective neutrality* concerns the amount of emotion or affect that is appropriate in a given interaction situation. Should a great deal or little affect be expressed?
2. *Diffuseness-specificity* denotes the issue of how far reaching obligations in an interaction situation are to be. Should the obligations be narrow and specific or should they be extensive and diffuse?
3. *Universalism-particularism* points to the problem of whether evaluation and judgment of others in an interaction situation is to employ standardized and agreed-upon criteria or subjective standards. Should evaluation be performed in terms of objective, universalistic criteria or in terms of more subjective, particularistic standards?
4. *Achievement-ascription* deals with the issue of how to assess an actor, whether in terms of performance or on the basis of inborn qualities, such as sex, age, race, and family status. Should an actor treat another on the basis of achievements or ascriptive qualities that are unrelated to performance?
5. *Self-collectivity* denotes the extent to which action is to be oriented to self-interest and individual goals or to group interests and goals. Should an actor consider his personal or self-related goals over those of the group or larger collectivity in which he is involved?

Some of these concepts, such as self-collectivity, have been dropped from the action scheme, while others, such as universalism-particularism have assumed greater importance. But the intent of the pattern variables has remained the same: to categorize dichotomies of decisions, normative demands, and value orientations. However, in *The Social System*, Parsons is inclined to view them as value orientations that circumscribe the norms of the social system and the decisions of the personality system. Thus, the patterns of the two true systems of action—personality and social—are a reflection of the dominant patterns of value orientations in culture. This implicit emphasis on the impact of cultural

---

[14] Ibid., pp. 48–50.

[15] These pattern variables were developed in collaboration with Edward Shils and were elaborated upon in *Toward a General Theory of Action*, pp. 48, 76–98, 203–4, 183–89.

patterns on regulating and controlling other systems of action was to become more explicit in later work—as will be discussed shortly.

However, for the present, it is evident that Parsons has woven a complex conceptual system that emphasizes the process of institutionalization of interaction into stabilized patterns called social systems, which are penetrated by personality and circumscribed by culture. The profile of institutionalized norms, of decisions by actors in roles, and of cultural value orientations can be typified in terms of concepts, called the pattern variables, that capture the variable properties in each of these components of action.

Having built this analytical edifice, Parsons returns to a question first raised in *The Structure of Social Action*, which has guided all his subsequent theoretical formulations: How do social systems survive? More specifically, why do institutionalized patterns of interaction persist? This question again raises the issue of system imperatives or requisites, for Parsons is asking how systems resolve their integrative problems. The "answer" to this question is provided by the elaboration of additional concepts that point to the ways personality systems and culture are integrated into the social system, thereby providing assurance of some degree of normative coherence and a minimal amount of commitment by actors to conform to norms and play roles. In developing concepts of this kind, Parsons begins to weight his analysis in the direction of an ontology that stresses the equilibrating tendencies of social systems.

Just how are personality systems integrated into the social system, thereby promoting equilibrium? At the most abstract level, Parsons conceptualizes two "mechanisms" that integrate the personality into the social system, mechanisms of socialization and mechanisms of social control. It is through the operation of these mechanisms that personality systems become structured such that they are compatible with the structure of social systems.

In abstract terms, *socialization mechanisms* are seen by Parsons as the means through which cultural patterns—values, beliefs, language, and other symbols —are internalized into the personality system, thereby circumscribing the latter's need structure. It is through this process that actors are made willing to deposit motivational energy in roles (thereby willing to conform to norms) and are given the interpersonal and other skills necessary for playing roles. Another function of socialization mechanisms is to provide stable and secure interpersonal ties that alleviate much of the strain, anxiety, and tension associated with acquiring "proper" motives and skills.

Mechanisms of social control involve those ways in which status roles are organized in social systems to reduce strain and deviance. There are numerous specific contol mechanisms, including (*a*) institutionalization, which makes role expectations clear and unambiguous, while segregating in time and space contradictory expectations; (*b*) interpersonal sanctions and gestures, which actors subtly employ to mutually sanction conformity; (*c*) ritual activities, in which actors act out symbolically sources of strain that could prove disruptive, and which at the same time reinforce dominant cultural patterns; (*d*) safety-value structures, in which pervasive "deviant" propensities are segregated in time and space from "normal" institutional patterns; (*e*) reintegration structures, which are specifically charged with coping with and bringing back into line deviant tendencies; and, finally, (*f*) the institutionalization into some sectors of a system the capacity to use force and coercion.

These two mechanisms are thus viewed as resolving one of the most persistent integrative problems (read *requisites*) facing social systems. The other major integrative problem facing social systems concerns how cultural patterns contribute to the maintenance of social order and equilibrium. Again at the most abstract level, Parsons visualizes two ways in which this occurs: (*a*) Some components of culture, such as language, are basic "resources" necessary for interaction to occur. Without symbolic resources, communication and hence interaction would not be possible. Thus, by providing common "resources" for all actors, interaction is made possible by culture. (*b*) A related but still separable influence of culture on interaction is exerted through the substance of "ideas" contained in cultural patterns (values, beliefs, ideology, etc.). These ideas can provide actors with common viewpoints, personal ontologies, or, to borrow from W. I. Thomas, a common "definition of the situation." These "common meanings" (to use G. H. Mead's term) allow interaction to proceed smoothly with minimal disruption.

Naturally, Parsons acknowledges that the mechanisms of socialization and social control are not always successful, hence allowing deviance and social change to occur. But it is clear that the concepts developed here in *The Social System* weight analysis in the direction of looking for processes that maintain the integration and, by implication, the equilibrium of social systems. The subsequent developments of "action theory" represent an attempt to expand upon the basic analytical scheme of *The Social System*, while trying to accommodate some of the critics' charges of a static and conservative conceptual bias (see later section). The critics of action theory have not been silenced, but some interesting elaborations of the scheme have occurred in the two decades following Parsons's first explicitly functional work.

ELABORATION OF SYSTEM REQUISITES

Shortly after the publication of *The Social System*, Parsons, in collaboration with Robert Bales and Edward Shils, published *Working Papers in the Theory of Action.*[16] It was in this work that conceptions of functional imperatives came

---

[16] Talcott Parsons, Robert F. Bales, and Edward A. Shils, *Working Papers in the Theory of Action* (Glencoe, Ill.: Free Press, 1953).

to dominate the general theory of action; and by 1956, with Parsons and Neil Smelser's publication of *Economy and Society*,[17] the functions of structures for meeting system requisites were well "institutionalized" into action theory.

During this period, systems of action were conceptualized to have four survival problems, or requisites: adaptation, goal attainment, integration, and latency. *Adaptation* involves the problem of securing from the environment sufficient facilities and then distributing these facilities throughout the system. *Goal attainment* refers to the problem of establishing priorities among system goals and mobilizing system resources for their attainment. *Integration* denotes the problem of coordinating and maintaining viable interrelationships among system units. *Latency* embraces two related problems: pattern maintenance and tension management. Pattern maintenance pertains to the problem of how to insure that actors in the social system display the "appropriate" characteristics (motives, needs, role-playing skills, etc.). Tension management concerns the problem of dealing with the internal tensions and strains of actors in the social system.

All of these requisites were implicit in *The Social System*, but they tended to be viewed under the general problem of integration. Yet, in the discussion of integration within and between action systems in *The Social System*, "problems" of securing facilities (adaptation), allocation and goal seeking (goal attainment), socialization and social control (latency) were conspicuous. The development of the four functional requisites—abbreviated A, G, I, and L—is thus not so much a radical departure from earlier works, but an elaboration of concepts clearly evident in *The Social System*.

However, with the introduction of A, G, I, L, there is a subtle shift away from the analysis of structures to the analysis of functions. Structures are now viewed *explicitly* in terms of their functional consequences for resolving the four problems. Interrelationships among specific structures are now analyzed in terms of how their interchanges affect the requisites that each must meet. In fact, Parsons now views every system and subsystem as having to resolve the problems of A, G, I, and L. Diagrammatically, this view of the social system is represented in Figure 3–2.

As is evident from Figure 3–2, any system or subsystem can be divided into four sectors, each denoting a survival problem—whether A, G, I, or L. Thus, a total society has to resolve the problems of A, G, I, L; but so does each of its constituent subsystems, as is illustrated for the adaptation sector in Figure 3–2. Thus, as is depicted in the adaptation sector of Figure 3–2, all systems at any system level, whether large or small, must resolve the four system requisites of A, G, I, L.

Of critical analytical importance in this scheme are the interchanges among

---

[17] Talcott Parsons and Neil J. Smelser, *Economy and Society* (New York: Free Press, 1956).

FIGURE 3–2

The Functional View of Social Systems

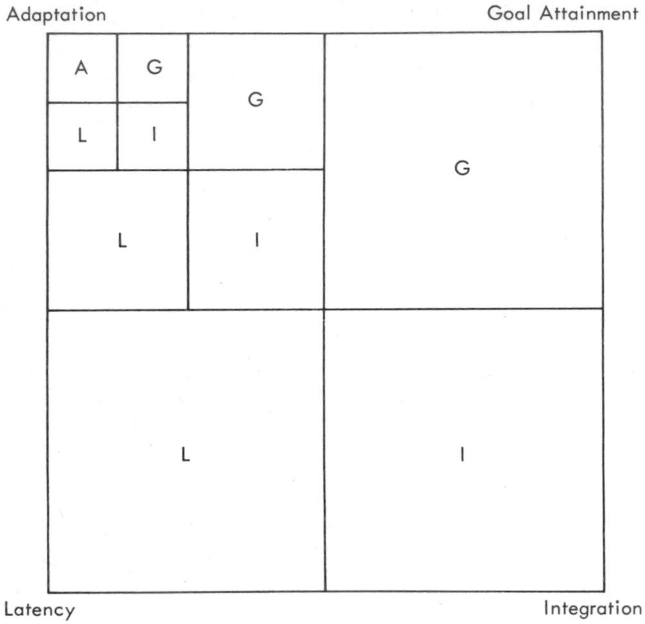

systems and subsystems, for it is difficult to comprehend the functioning of a designated social system without examining the interchanges among its A, G, I, and L sectors, especially as these interchanges are affected by exchanges among constituent subsystems and other systems in the environment. In turn, the functioning of a designated subsystem cannot be understood without examining internal interchanges among its adaptive, goal attainment, integrative, and latency sectors, especially as these interchanges are influenced by exchanges with other subsystems and the more inclusive system of which it is a subsystem. Thus at this juncture, as important interchanges among the functional sectors of systems and subsystems are outlined, the Parsonian scheme now begins to resemble an elaborate mapping operation.

THE INFORMATIONAL HIERARCHY OF CONTROL

Toward the end of the 1950s, Parsons turned attention toward interrelationships *among* (rather than within) what were then four distinct action systems: culture, social structure, personality, and organism. In many ways, this concern represented an odyssey back to the analysis of the basic components of the "unit act" outlined in *The Structure of Social Action*. But now, each element of the unit act was a full-fledged action system, each confronting four functional problems to resolve: adaptation, goal attainment, integration, and latency. Furthermore, while individual decision making was still a part of action as personalities adjusted to the normative demands of status-roles in the social system, the analytical emphasis had shifted to the input-output connections among the four action systems.

It is at this juncture[18] that Parsons begins to visualize an overall action system, with culture, social structure, personality, and organism comprising its constituent subsystems. Each of these subsystems is seen as fulfilling one of the four system requisites—A, G, I, L—of the overall action system. The organism is considered to be the subsystem having the most consequences for resolving adaptive problems, since it is ultimately through this system that environmental resources are made available to the other action subsystems. As the goal-seeking and decision-making system, personality is considered to have primary consequences for resolving goal-attainment problems. As an organized network of status-norms integrating the patterns of the cultural system and the needs of personality systems, the social system is viewed as the major integrative subsystem of the general action system. As the repository of symbolic content of interaction, the cultural system is considered to have primary consequences for managing tensions of actors and assuring that the proper symbolic resources are available to assure the maintenance of institutional patterns (latency).

After viewing each action system as a subsystem of a more inclusive, overall action system, Parsons begins to explore the interrelations among the four subsystems. What emerges is a hierarchy of informational controls, with culture informationally circumscribing the social system, social structure informationally regulating the personality system, and personality informationally regulating the organismic system. For example, cultural value orientations would be seen as circumscribing or limiting the range of variation in the norms of the social system; in turn, these norms, as translated into expectations on actors playing roles, would be viewed as limiting the kinds of motives and decision-making processes in personality systems; these features of the personality system would then be seen as circumscribing biochemical processes in the organism. Conversely, each system in the hierarchy is also viewed as providing the "energic conditions" necessary for action at the next higher system. That is, the organism provides the energy necessary for the personality system, the personality system provides the energic conditions for the social system, and the organization of personality

[18] Talcott Parsons, "An Approach to Psychological Theory in Terms of the Theory of Action," in *Psychology: A Science*, ed. S. Koch, vol. 3 (New York: McGraw-Hill Book Co., 1958), pp. 612–711. By 1961, these ideas were even more clearly formulated; see Talcott Parsons, "An Outline of the Social System," in *Theories of Society*, ed. T. Parsons, E. Shils, K. D. Naegele, and J. R. Pitts (New York: Free Press, 1961), pp. 30–38. See also Jackson Toby, "Parsons' Theory of Social Evolution," *Contemporary Sociology* 1 (September 1972): 395–401.

systems into a social system provides the conditions necessary for a cultural system. Thus, the input-output relations among action systems are reciprocal, with systems exchanging information and energy. Systems high in information circumscribe the utilization of energy at the next lower system level, while each lower system provides the conditions and facilities necessary for action in the next higher system. This scheme has been termed a *cybernetic hierarchy* and is diagrammatically represented in Figure 3–3.

FIGURE 3–3

The Cybernetic Hierarchy of Control

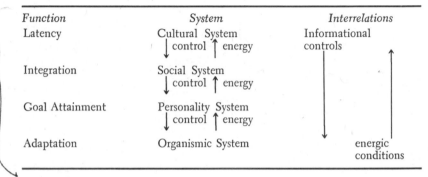

Function	System	Interrelations
Latency	Cultural System ↓ control ↑ energy	Informational controls
Integration	Social System ↓ control ↑ energy	
Goal Attainment	Personality System ↓ control ↑ energy	
Adaptation	Organismic System	energic conditions

GENERALIZED MEDIA OF EXCHANGE

In the last two decades, Parsons has maintained his interest in the intra- and intersystemic relationships of the four action systems. Although he has yet to develop the concepts fully, he has begun to view these inter- and intrasystemic relationships in terms of "generalized symbolic media of exchange."[19] In any interchange, generalized media are employed—for example, money is used in the economy to facilitate the buying and selling of goods. What typifies these generalized media, such as money, is that they are really symbolic modes of communication. The money is not worth much by itself; its "value" is evident only in terms of what it "says" symbolically in an exchange relationship.

Thus, what Parsons proposes is that the links among action components are ultimately informational. This means that transactions are mediated by symbols. Parsons's emphasis on information is consistent with the development of the idea of a cybernetic hierarchy of control. Informational exchanges, or cybernetic

---

[19] Parsons's writings on this topic are vague and incomplete, but see Talcott Parsons, "On the Concept of Political Power," *Proceedings of the American Philosophical Society* 107 (June 1963): 232–62; Talcott Parsons, "On the Concept of Influence," *Public Opinion Quarterly* 27 (Spring 1963): 37–62; and Talcott Parsons, "Some Problems of General Theory," in *Theoretical Sociology: Perspectives and Developments*, eds. J. C. McKinney and E. A. Tiryakian (New York: Appleton-Century-Crofts, 1970), pp. 28–68. See also Parsons's forthcoming work on the American university.

controls, are seen as operating in at least three ways: First, the interchanges or exchanges *among* the four subsystems of the overall action system are carried out by means of different types of symbolic media, that is, money, power, influence, or commitments. Second, the interchanges *within* any of the four action systems are also carried out by means of distinctive symbolic media. This determination of media by functional requisites will hold equally whether within a particular action system or among the four general systems of action. Finally, the system requisites of adaptation (A), goal attainment (G), integration (I), and latency (L) are thought to determine the type of generalized symbolic media used in an inter- or intra-systemic exchange.

Within the social system, the adaptive sector utilizes money as the medium of exchange with the other three sectors; the goal-attainment sector employs power—the capacity to induce conformity—as its principal medium of exchange; the integrative sector of a social system relies upon influence—the capacity to persuade; and the latency sector uses commitments—apparently, the capacity to be loyal. The analysis of interchanges of specific structures within social systems should thus focus on the input-output exchanges utilizing different symbolic media.

Among the subsystems of the overall action system, a similar analysis of the symbolic media used in exchanges should be undertaken, but, as yet, Parsons has not clearly described the nature of these media.[20] What he appears to be approaching is a conceptual scheme for analyzing the basic types of symbolic media, or information, linking systems in the cybernetic hierarchy of control (see Figure 3-3).[21]

PARSONS ON SOCIAL CHANGE

In the last decade Parsons has become increasingly concerned with social change. Built into the cybernetic hierarchy of control is a conceptual scheme for classifying the locus of such social change. What Parsons visualizes is that the information-energic interchanges among action systems provide the potential for change within or between the action systems. One source of change may be excesses in either information or energy in the exchange among action systems, which, in turn, alter the informational or energic outputs across systems and within any system. For example, excesses of motivation (energy) would have consequences for the enactment of roles, and perhaps ultimately for the reorgani-

---

[20] For his first attempt at a statement, see Parsons, "Some Problems of General Theory," pp. 61–68. This discussion is so vague and tentative that it is wise to defer interpretation until Parsons makes more explicit his concepts.

[21] For a more readable discussion of these "generalized media," see T. S. Turner, "Parsons' Concept of Generalized Media of Social Interaction and its Relevance for Social Anthropology," *Sociological Inquiry* 38 (Spring 1968): 121–34.

zation of these roles, of the normative structure, and eventually of cultural value orientations.[22] Another source of change comes from an insufficient supply of either energy or information, again causing external and internal readjustments in the structure of action systems. For example, value (informational) conflict would cause normative conflict (or anomie), which, in turn, would have consequences for the personality and organismic systems. Thus, inherent in the cybernetic hierarchy of control are concepts that point to the sources of both stasis and change.[23]

To augment this new macro emphasis on change, Parsons has become interested in utilizing the action scheme to analyze social evolution in historical societies. In this context, it is of some importance that the first line of *The Structure of Social Action* posed a simple question: "Who now reads Spencer?" Parsons then answered the question by delineating some of the reasons why Spencer's evolutionary doctrine had been so thoroughly rejected by 1937. Now, after some 35 years, Parsons has chosen to reexamine the issue of societal evolution which he so easily dismissed in the beginning.

Drawing heavily not only from Spencer,[24] but also from Durkheim's[25] insights into societal development, Parsons proposes that the processes of evolution display the following elements:

1. Increasing differentiation of system units into patterns of functional interdependence,
2. Establishment of new principles and mechanisms of integration in differentiating systems, and
3. Increasing survival capacity of differentiated systems in relation to the environment.

From the perspective of action theory, evolution therefore involves: (*a*) increasing differentiation of the personality, social, cultural, and organismic systems from one another; (*b*) increasing differentiation within each of these four action subsystems; (*c*) escalating problems of integration and the emergence of new integrative

---

[22] There are several bodies of empirical literature that bear on this example. McClelland's work on the achievement motive as initiating economic development in modernizing societies is perhaps the most conspicuous example; see David C. McClelland, *The Achieving Society* (New York: Free Press, 1961).

[23] For a fuller discussion, see Alvin L. Jacobson, "Talcott Parsons: A Theoretical and Empirical Analysis of Social Change and Conflict," in *Institutions and Social Exchange: The Sociologies of Talcott Parsons and George C. Homans*, ed. H. Turk and R. L. Simpson (Indianapolis: Bobbs-Merrill Co., 1970).

[24] Herbert Spencer, *First Principles*, vol. 1, 5th ed. (New York: A. L. Burt, 1880), pp. 107–483.

[25] Émile Durkheim, *The Division of Labor in Society* (New York: Free Press, 1933) (first published in 1893).

structures; and (d) the upgrading of the survival capacity of each action subsystem, as well as of the overall action system, to its environment.[26]

Parsons then embarks on an ambitious effort in two short volumes[27] to outline the pattern of evolution in historical systems through primitive, intermediate, and modern stages.[28] In contrast with *The Social System*, where he stressed the problem of integration between social systems and personality, Parsons draws attention in his evolutionary model to the *inter* and *intra* differentiation of the cultural and social systems and to the resulting integrative problems. In fact, each stage of evolution is seen as reflecting a new set of integrative problems between society and culture as each of these systems has become both more internally differentiated and increasingly differentiated from the other. Thus, the concern with the issues of integration within and among action systems, so evident in earlier works, has not been abandoned, but has been applied to the analysis of specific historical processes.

While Parsons is vague about the causes of evolutionary change, he apparently views evolution as guided by the cybernetic hierarchy of controls, especially the informational component. In his concern for documenting how integrative problems of the differentiating social and cultural systems have been resolved in the evolution of historical systems, the informational hierarchy is regarded as crucial, because the regulation of societal processes of differentiation must be accompanied by legitimation from cultural patterns (information). Without such informational control, movement to the next stage of development in an evolutionary sequence[29] will be inhibited.

Thus, the analysis of social change represents an attempt to use the analytical tools of the "general theory of action." What is of interest in this effort is that Parsons develops many propositions about the sequences of change and the processes that will inhibit or accelerate the unfolding of these evolutionary sequences. It is of more than passing interest that preliminary tests of these propositions indicate that, on the whole, they have a great deal of credence.[30]

It might be argued from such preliminary "success" that vindication of the strategy for developing sociological theory as first expounded in *The Structure*

[26] Parsons, *Societies*.

[27] Ibid., and Talcott Parsons, *The System of Modern Societies* (Englewood Cliffs, N.J.: Prentice-Hall, Inc., 1971.

[28] The general stages of development were first outlined in Talcott Parsons, "Evolutionary Universals in Society," *American Sociological Review* 29 (June 1964): 339–57.

[29] It should be emphasized that Parsons does not advocate a strict unilineal pattern of evolution. Rather, he is attempting to point to *continuities* in patterns of social change—a tack that left him open to criticism by those who would point to the discontinuities in social change.

[30] See Gary L. Buck and Alvin L. Jacobson, "Social Evolution and Structural-Functional Analysis: An Empirical Test," *American Sociological Review* 33 (June 1968): 343–55; A. L. Jacobson, "Talcott Parsons: Theoretical and Empirical Analysis."

of Social Action has occurred. As will be recalled, Parsons has steadfastly urged that sociological theory first develop systems of concepts for classifying the social world, and only then attempt to construct bodies of propositions. Perhaps, after 30 years of developing a system of concepts for depicting social action, Parsons felt it was time to employ that system to develop an inventory of propositions.

However, the recent emphasis on social change and the ability of Parsons to use his "theory of action" to generate testable propositions have not silenced his critics. In fact, functionalism has consistently provoked controversy, primarily because the very utility of any form of functional theorizing has been increasingly called into question. It is not surprising, then, that the critics periodically resurrect the same analytical problems first raised by Durkheim and Radcliffe-Brown to indict Parsons's scheme in particular and all forms of functionalism in general.

PERSISTENT CRITICISMS OF PARSONIAN FUNCTIONALISM

Criticisms of Parsons's Image of Society

By the early 1960s a number of critics had begun to question whether Parsons's emerging "system of concepts" corresponded to events in the "real" world. Such a line of criticism is significant because the Parsonian strategy assumes that it is necessary to elaborate a system of concepts that "adequately grasp" salient features of the social world, from which propositions can eventually be derived. Assertions that the maturing system of concepts inadequately mirrors features of actual social systems represent a fundamental challenge to the strategy and substance of Parsons's form of functional theorizing.

Ralf Dahrendorf[31]—the subject of chapter 6—codified this growing body of criticism when he likened functionalism to a "utopia." Much like prominent portrayals of social utopias of the past, Dahrendorf asserted, Parsons's concepts point to a world that (*a*) reveals no developmental history, (*b*) evidences only consensus over values and norms, (*c*) displays a high degree of integration among its components, and (*d*) reveals only mechanisms that preserve the "status quo." Such an image of society is utopian, because there appears little possibility that ubiquitous phenomena like deviance, conflict, and change could occur.

While the evidence marshaled to support these assertions is minimal, it is not difficult to visualize the source of the critics' dismay. With the publication of *The Social System*, the critics seem to charge, Parsons becomes overly concerned

---

[31] Ralf Dahrendorf, "Out of Utopia: Toward a Reorientation of Sociological Analysis," *American Journal of Sociology* 64 (September 1958): 115–27. This polemic echoed the earlier assessments by others, including David Lockwood ("Some Remarks on 'The Social System,'" *British Journal of Sociology* 7 [June 1950]: 134–46), C. Wright Mills (*The Sociological Imagination* [New York: Oxford University Press, 1959], pp. 44–49), and Lewis Coser (*The Functions of Social Conflict* [New York: Free Press, 1956], pp. 1–10).

with the integration of social systems. In a vein similar to Radcliffe-Brown and Durkheim, the emphasis on the "need" or "requisite" for integration in social systems leads, in the critics' eyes, to a disproportionate concern with those processes in social systems that meet this need for integration. In *The Social System*, this concern with integration is evidenced by the tendency to assume, for analytical purposes, a system that is in "equilibrium." From this starting point, analysis "must" then focus on the elaboration of concepts promoting integration and equilibrium. For example, the extended discussion of institutionalization describes the processes whereby structure is built up, with relatively scant mention of concepts denoting the breakdown and change of institutionalized patterns. To compound this omission, a discussion of how institutionalized patterns are maintained by the "mechanisms" of socialization and social control is launched. For the critics, too much emphasis is place upon how socialization assures the internalization of values and the alleviation of strains among actors and how mechanisms of social control reduce the potential for malintegration and deviance. When deviance and change are discussed, the critics contend, they are viewed as residual or, in a way reminiscent of Durkheim, as "pathological." In fact, deviance, conflict, and change are so "alien" to the scheme that the social equilibrium is considered to constitute, in Parsons's words, a "first law of social inertia."

The subsequent expansion of concepts denoting four system requisites—adaptation, goal attainment, integration, and latency—has further horrified the critics, for now system processes become almost exclusively viewed in terms of their consequences for meeting an extended list of system needs. In all this concern for the consequences of processes for meeting needs, how is it, the critics ask, that deviance, conflict, and change are to be conceptualized?[32] Are they merely "pathological" events that occur on those rare occasions when system needs are not met? Or, in reality, are not these phenomena pervasive features of social systems, which are "inadequately grasped" by the proliferating system of concepts?

The elaboration of the informational hierarchy of control among the overall systems of action and its use to analyze social *change* has still not silenced the critics, for the only type of change that is conceptualized is "evolution," as opposed to "revolution" and other forms of violent disruption in social systems. Much like that of Durkheim and Spencer, Parsons's view of change involves a "progressive" differentiation and integration, with the inexorable progress of societal development delayed from time to time by a failure to integrate the differentiating cultural and social systems.

Is this line of criticism accurate or justified? In Parsons's defense, it has been

---

[32] Leslie Sklair, "The Fate of the Functional Requisites in Parsonian Sociology," *British Journal of Sociology* 21 (March 1970): 30–42.

argued that most of the major concepts in action theory do not preclude the analysis of deviance, conflict, and change. In fact, the concept of institutionalization would logically lead to the analysis of instances in which interaction resulted not only in stabilized patterns, but also in various types of unstable interaction networks. Similarly, the mechanisms of social control would seemingly alert one to instances in which they fail to operate effectively. Furthermore, conceptualization of system requisites does not preclude, in any logical and empirical sense, the analysis of events that disrupt social systems. In fact, notions of what is necessary for survival in a system can actually alert investigators to those processes that prevent full resolution of requisites.[33] Additionally, the subsequent elaboration of the action scheme underscores the amenability of its concepts to the analysis of deviance, dissensus, malintegration, and change. For example, the conceptualization of the four action systems—the organismic, personality, social, and cultural—as an informational hierarchy of control has allowed Parsons to conceptualize deviance (a failure to informationally regulate the energy of the personality system), dissensus over values and malintegration of social systems (contradictory and/or inadequate informational controls), and societal development (the increasing differentiation and integration of normative and cultural controls).[34]

Thus, what appears to have disturbed the critics are the *connotations* of equilibrium, stasis, control, consensus, and order which they *perceive* in Parsons's work.[35] For *them*, Parsons has not dealt adequately with problems they consider important: change, conflict, and deviance. But for *others*, Parsons has provided concepts that can conceptualize adequately these phenomena. What emerges from this fact is that the issue of whether Parsons has put sociological theorizing into a "utopia" cannot be resolved by arguments over the substantive connotations of his theoretical perspective, since for different groups of theorists a scheme as abstract and complex as Parsons's will connote different images of society. This conclusion suggests that it is perhaps futile to debate the connotations of Parsons's concepts, for such debates boil down to whose image of society is consid-

---

[33] Percy Cohen, *Modern Social Theory* (New York: Basic Books, 1968); Kingsley Davis, "The Myth of Functional Analysis as a Special Method in Sociology and Anthropology," *American Sociological Review* 24 (December 1959): 757–72.

[34] For examples of Parsons's treatment of these diverse topics, see Parsons, "An Approach to Psychological Theory," *Societies,* and *System of Modern Societies.*

[35] Perhaps the most recent and scholarly attempt to document the reasons behind these "problems" in Parsonian action theory is provided by Alvin Gouldner in *The Coming Crisis of Western Sociology* (New York: Basic Books, 1970). However, John K. Rhoads in "On Gouldner's Crisis of Western Sociology," *American Journal of Sociology* 78 (July 1972): 136–54, emphasizes that Gouldner has perceived what he wants to perceive in Parsons's work, ignoring those passages that would connote just the opposite of stasis, control, consensus, and order. See also Rhoads, "Reply to Gouldner," *American Journal of Sociology* 78 (May 1973): 1493–96, which was written in response to Gouldner's defense of his position (Alvin Gouldner, "For Sociology: 'Varieties of Political Expression' Revisited," *American Journal of Sociology* 78 [March 1973]: 1063–93, particularly pp. 1083–93).

ered most isomorphic with a particular perception of reality. The only way such debates can be resolved is to address a more theoretical question: Will the propositions about reality inspired by a particular conceptual scheme stand attempts at their refutation? To argue over the connotations of concepts is to perpetuate the argument,[36] whereas to address the issue of what kinds of propositions are likely to be generated by a particular analytical scheme offers more theoretical payoff. Thus, whether Parsons's analytical scheme connotes a conservative, static, or utopian view of the world is, at present, a pseudoissue; the theoretically interesting questions revolve around the kinds of propositions the scheme can potentially yield.

The Logical Adequacy of Parsons's Systems of Concepts

Supplementing the substantive criticisms of Parsons's scheme have been a number of questions about Parsons's success in executing his own strategy of developing a "system of concepts," regardless of its isomorphism with the "real" world. These questions revolve around the issues: Is the Parsons action scheme "theory"? Does Parsons bring into line what he does with what he says is good theory?

With regard to the first query, the question is usually phrased rhetorically, since favorite sport among sociologists has been to criticize Parsonian action "theory" from an axiomatic conception of what theory should be.[37] To argue that Parsons does not supply a deductive set of theoretical statements, and hence does not engage in what the critic calls "true" theory, is not only to state the obvious, but to ignore Parsons's strategy for theory building. Since for Parsons inventories of logically interrelated propositions should come after the development of a conceptual inventory, or system of concepts, it does little to note that Parsons does not do the very thing he says he will not do. Rather, it is more fruitful to examine Parsons's scheme from his own perspective of what theory should be, and thereby offer a tentative answer to the second query. Such an assessment would include answers to at least three specific questions: (1) How clear are the abstract concepts of the schema? (2) How are they linked to form a system of concepts? (3) And can this system of concepts potentially generate in the long run inventories of propositions that can build scientific theory?

---

[36] For a recent attempt to perpetuate the argument, see Desmond Ellis, "The Hobbesian Problem of Order: A Critical Appraisal of the Normative Solution," *American Sociological Review* 36 (August 1971): 692–703.

[37] George Homans has long played this game; for example, see his "Sociological Theory" in *Handbook of Sociology*, ed. E. Faris (Chicago: Rand-McNally, 1964). For a more sophisticated assessment of Parsonian theory employing this tactic, see Austin T. Turk, "On the Parsonian Approach to Theory Construction," *Sociological Quarterly* 8 (Winter 1967): 37–49.

How Clear Are Abstract Concepts?   Parsons clearly has made a commitment to employing highly abstract concepts capable of denoting a wide range of social phenomena. Notions of institutionalization, the pattern variables, culture, personality, society, the cybernetic hierarchy of control, mechanisms of social control and socialization, and the functional imperatives of adaptation, goal attainment, integration, and latency all document the abstractness of his concepts. One criticism of such concept formation revolves around the apparent unwillingness to provide *formal* operational definitions that tie these concepts to concrete empirical events or to other rigorously defined abstract concepts. While such concepts have been used in many descriptive essays on a wide variety of concrete phenomena, from the American school classroom to political processes in Nazi Germany, there is still no precise way to climb down the abstraction ladder to concrete events. Without even operational clues, it is difficult to determine whether these concepts would be useful in generating an "analytical realism," since to employ vague concepts to erect a conceptual edifice could lead to a schema reflecting not so much the real world, but the logical imperatives of the schema or the whims of its framer's intellect.[38]

How Are Concepts Linked?   In his commitment to developing systems of concepts, Parsons has tended to link concepts to one another in several ways:[39] (1) Concepts frequently overlap so that elements of one concept embrace elements of phenomena denoted by another; (2) concepts are connotatively associated, in that the definition of one is phrased so as to evoke the definition of another; and (3) concepts are often linked through cross-tabulation in such a way that two independently defined dimensions or axes imply additional concepts when intersected with one another. While such a system of linking concepts suffers from lack of logical rigor, the resulting analytical edifice compels investigators examining one feature of a system to examine other related features. As such, the scheme provides a "check list"[40] for the description of the interrelatedness of social phenomena. However, such vague links among concepts can do little more than alert investigators to systemic features of the world, since they cannot indicate precisely how and in what ways the concepts, and hence events of the real world, are connected. Without clear definitions of concepts and without systematic derivations of concepts from one another, the action scheme

[38] This statement is not meant to imply that other investigators have not tried to operationalize Parsons's concepts. His concepts have stimulated considerable empirical research, but Parsons *himself* has not helped investigators come down the abstraction ladder. Nor do the empirical studies using his concepts seem to have moved Parsons to revise and reformulate his theoretical edifice. Thus, while Parsons's scheme is suggestive and while it has stimulated attempts at operationalization and research, a gap between action theory and the research it inspires remains, with the former stimulating the latter, but with the latter having little impact on the former.

[39] Robin M. Williams, Jr., "The Sociological Theory of Talcott Parsons," in *The Social Theories of Talcott Parsons*, ed. M. Black (Englewood Cliffs, N.J.: Prentice-Hall, Inc. 1961), p. 92.

[40] Ibid., p. 94.

can perhaps be better typified as *bundles* rather than systems of concepts, for, in a true system of concepts, the overlaps, gaps, and vague associations among concepts in action theory would not be allowed. Thus, what is needed to be consistent with Parsons's strategy for building systems of concepts is more meticulous attention to both independently defining abstract concepts and pointing to their nodes articulation (perhaps through the elucidation of additional concepts).

Potentially, Can the Scheme Generate True Theoretical Statements? At the heart of the Parsonian strategy for theory building is the presumption that the development of systems of concepts is the first step on the road to generating logically related theoretical statements. From Parsons's failure to follow his own strategy for concept formation and linkage, it can be questioned whether such vague bundles of concepts can generate propositions of the type: under C_1, C_2, C_3, C_n, x causes variation in y. This is not to argue that Parsons does not develop such propositions; indeed he does in his work on evolution, where each stage of evolution sets the conditions $(C_1, C_2, C_3, \ldots, C_n)$ under which variations in other phenomena (x) cause a new stage of evolution (y) to emerge.[41] However, these testable[42] propositions make minimal use of action-theoretic concepts; rather, the propositions appear to be induced from Parsons's extensive knowledge of events in historical societies and then reconciled with the general theory of action. The most conspicuous concepts are the pattern variables and the informational hierarchy of control, which are used to denote different cultural and normative patterns at each stage of evolution, but the rest of the action schema appears almost superfluous. Naturally, it can be argued that the total action schema sensitized Parsons to some processes and not others in the evolutionary development of historical societies. Such is no doubt the case, but there are no explicit statements about the process of derivation from Parsons's "bundles" of concepts to causal theoretical statements about evolution. Without these explicit statements, the scheme is only useful when intellectually internalized, thereby becoming a kind of conceptual gestalt that allows the intellectual convert to "action theory" to perceive the patterning of the social world.

Thus, while Parsons cannot be faulted for not constructing the kind of theory advocated by those concerned with building axiomatic formats, his failure to execute the strategy he has so consistently championed for close to four decades can be considered one of the serious shortcomings of action theory. Although suggestive "bundles" of concepts have been developed and although these concepts appear to have inspired the construction of theoretical statements, it is unclear how the latter were derived from the former. In fact, it often appears

---

[41] See Parsons, "Evolutionary Universals," *Societies*, and *System of Modern Societies*.

[42] See Buck and Jacobson, "Social Evolution and Structural-Functional Analysis"; and Jacobson, "Talcott Parsons."

that Parsons abandons the action scheme when addressing empirical events. Or, if the elements of action theory are retained, Parsons frequently seems to be caught reconciling in an ex post facto fashion his theoretical statements with his formal analytical scheme. Just whether either or both of these practices are intended is unclear, which is, of course, the very problem with the current execution of the strategy: Without a rigorous *system* of concepts, with *clear* definitions, it is difficult to understand how the scheme is to be used, except intuitively, in generating either theoretical statements or empirical hypotheses. The fact that the scheme has "inspired" both theoretical and empirical statements is a testimony to its suggestiveness. But it would seem critical that Parsons begin to document just *how* and through what logical steps these theoretical and empirical statements are forthcoming, for, without this necessary information, Parsonian action theory remains an interesting, and perhaps even inspirational, conglomerate of suggestive concepts—a state of affairs that is inconsistent with Parsons's avowed strategy for building theory.

The Logical Criticisms of Imperativism

The problems of illegitimate teleology and tautology have consumed a considerable amount of the literature on functionalism.[43] For the most part, this literature holds that since assumptions of needs and requisites are so prominent in functional theorizing, theoretical statements will too frequently lapse into illegitimate teleologies and tautologies. Typically, conspicuous examples of the functional works of Durkheim, Radcliffe-Brown, and Malinowski are cited to confirm the truth of this assertion, but, by implication, the efforts of contemporary functionalists are similarly indicted—otherwise, the criticisms would not be worth the considerable efforts devoted to making them. To the extent that this indirect indictment of Parsons's functional imperativism can be sustained, it can

---

[43] For analyses of the logic of functionalist inquiry, see R. B. Braithwaite, *Scientific Explanation* (New York: Harper Bros., 1953), chaps. 9 and 10; Carl G. Hempel, "The Logic of Functional Analysis" in *Symposium on Sociological Theory*, ed. L. Gross (New York: Harper & Row, 1959), pp. 271–307; Percy S. Cohen, *Modern Social Theory* (New York: Basic Books, 1968), pp. 58–64; Francesca Cancian, "Functional Analysis of Change," *American Sociological Review* 25 (December 1960): 818–27; S. F. Nadel, *Foundations of Social Anthropology* (Glencoe, Ill.: The Free Press, 1951), pp. 373–78; Ernest Nagel, "Teleological Explanation and Teleological Systems," in *Readings in the Philosophy of Science*, ed. H. Feigl and M. Broadbeck (New York: Harper & Bros., 1953), pp. 537–58; Phillip Ronald Dore, "Function and Cause," *American Sociological Review* 26 (December 1961): 843–53; Charles J. Erasmus, "Obviating the Functions of Functionalism," *Social Forces* 45 (March 1967): 319–28; Harry C. Bredemeier, "The Methodology of Functionalism," *American Sociological Review* 20 (April 1955): 173–80; Bernard Barber, "Structural-Functional Analysis: Some Problems and Misunderstandings," *American Sociological Review* 21 (April 1956): 129–35; Robert K. Merton, *Social Theory and Social Structure* (Glencoe, Ill.: Free Press, 1957), pp. 44–61; Arthur L. Stinchcombe, *Constructing Social Theories* (New York: Harcourt, Brace & World, 1968), pp. 80–116; Hans Zetterberg, *On Theory and Verification in Sociology* (Totowa, N.J.: Bedminister Press, 1965), pp. 74–79.

be considered to represent a serious criticism. For Parsons's strategy for theory building has revolved around the assumption that his system of concepts can generate testable systems of propositions that account for events in the empirical world. But if such a conceptual system inspires illegitimate teleologies and tautologous propositions, then its utility as a strategy for building sociological theory can be called into question.

   The Issue of Teleology.   Parsons has always considered "action" to be goal directed—whether it is a single "unit act" or the complex informational and energic interchanges among the organismic, personality, social, and cultural systems. Thus, Parsons's conceptualization of "goal attainment" as a basic system requisite would make inevitable teleological propositions, since for Parsons much social action can only be understood in terms of the ends it is designed to serve. Such propositions, however, are often considered to be vague, for to assess the goal-attainment consequences of a particular process can frequently be used as a way to obscure the specific causal chains whereby goal-attainment sectors in a system activate processes to meet specified end states. Yet, when looking closely at the Parsonian legacy, it is clear that in his many essays and formal theoretical statements he has been vitally concerned with just how, and through what processes, system processes are activated to meet goal states. For example, Parson's various works on how political systems strive to legitimate themselves are filled with both analytical and descriptive accounts of how the processes—such as patterns of socialization[44] in educational and kinship institutions—are activated to meet goal-attainment requisites.[45] While the empirical adequacy of this discussion can be questioned, Parsons's analysis does not present illegitimate teleologies, for his work reveals a clear concern for documenting the causal chains involved in activating processes designed to meet various end states.

   It is perhaps the other three requisites—adaptation, integration, and latency—which would seemingly pose a more serious problem of illegitimate teleology. Critics would argue that to analyze structures and processes in terms of their functions for these three system needs compels analysts to state their propositions teleologically, when in fact the processes so described may not be goal directed

   [44] See, for example, Talcott Parsons, *Family, Socialization and Interaction Process* (New York: Free Press, 1955); Talcott Parsons, "Social Structure and the Development of Personality," *Psychiatry* 34 (November 1958): 321–40; Talcott Parsons, "The School Class as a Social System," *Harvard Educational Review*, vol. 54 (Fall 1959): 487–99; Talcott Parsons, "The Link between Character and Society," in *Culture and Social Character*, ed. S. M. Lipset and L. Lowenthal (New York: Free Press, 1961); Talcott Parsons, "Youth in the Context of American Society," *Daedalus*, vol. 28 (Winter 1961); Talcott Parsons, "Comment on Dennis Wrong's 'The Over-socialized Conception of Man,'" *Psychoanalysis and Psychoanalytic Review*, vol. 10 (Summer 1962): 322–34; and Talcott Parsons, *Social Structure and Personality* (New York: Free Press, 1964).

   [45] For example, see Talcott Parsons, "Authority, Legitimation and Political Action" in *Authority*, ed. C. J. Friedrich (Cambridge, Mass.: Harvard University Press, 1958); Parsons, "On the Concept of Power"; and Talcott Parsons, "The Political Aspect of Structure and Process," in *Varieties of Political Theory*, ed. David Easton (Englewood Cliffs, N.J.: Prentice-Hall, Inc., 1966).

or teleological. Logically, as several commentators have pointed out, teleological phrasing of propositions in the absence of clear-cut goal-attainment processes does not necessarily make the proposition illegitimate, for at least two reasons.

1. Nagel[46] has argued that phrasing statements in a teleological fashion is merely a shorthand way of stating the same causal relationship nonteleologically. For example, to argue that the relief of anxiety (an end state) is the "latency function" of religion (a present phenomenon) can be rephrased nonteleologically without loss of asserted content: under conditions $C_1, C_2, C_3, \ldots, C_n$, religion (concept x) causes reduction of group anxiety (concept y). Such a form is quite acceptable in that it involves existence and relational statements: Under $C_1, C_2, \ldots, C_n$, variations in x cause variations in y. However, other authors have contended that such transposition is not always possible, because the existence statements so necessary to such conversion are absent from the statements of functionalists such as Parsons. Without necessary existence statements, to assert that the function of religion is to reduce group anxiety can be interpreted to mean that the latency needs of the group for low levels of anxiety cause the emergence of religion. This most likely constitutes an illegitimate teleology, since little information is provided about the nature of the "latency purposes" of the given system and the specific causal chains involved in keeping the system in pursuit of its latency goals. Or, if teleology is not intended, then the statement is simply vague, offering none of the necessary information that would allow its conversion to a nonteleological form. As Nadel was led to conclude: "To pronounce at once upon the ultimate functions subserved by social facts is to short-circuit explanation and reduce it to generalities which, so prematurely stated, have little significance."[47]

However, a careful review of Parsons's work reveals many insightful essays on the processes and mechanisms whereby various system requisites are maintained. This fact mitigates the severity of the critics' charges, for such descriptions do specify conditions under which requisites are met by specific parts of the more inclusive system. However, the fact that Parsons frequently describes these processes in essays that are not systematically tied to his more formal conceptualizations of action theory makes the conversion of teleological statements into nonteleological form somewhat difficult. Such conversion would require considerable synthesis of the conceptual scheme with Parsons's more discursive essays on a wide variety of system processes. Despite the fact that Parsons has neglected this important task, such synthesis is possible—thus throwing into doubt the assertion that Parsons has, in principle, "short-circuited explanation." Rather, Parsons has merely failed to realize the full explanatory power of a more rigorous attempt

---

[46] Nagel, "Teleological Explanation and Teleological Systems."
[47] Nadel, *Foundations of Social Anthropology*, p. 375.

to link his formal theory of action to his more discursive essays on a wide range of empirical events. For example, Parsons's[48] analytical discussion of how inputs from the latency sector of appropriately skilled (socialized) labor into the adaptive sector, or economy, of a social system would be greatly supplemented by a more systematic linking of his numerous essays on socialization[49] to these analytical statements. If such a task were more seriously undertaken, even critics such as Nadel would have difficulty asserting that Parsons's use of system requisites such as adaptation had allowed him to "short circuit" a full causal explanation.

2. Perhaps the most significant defense of Parsons's tendency to phrase propositions teleologically comes from the fact that such propositions point to *reverse causal chains* that are typical of many social phenomena.[50] By emphasizing that the function served by a structure in maintaining the needs of the whole could *cause* the emergence of that structure, Parsons's functional imperativism forces analysis to be attuned to those causal processes involved in the *initial selection*, from the infinite variety of possible social structures, of only certain types of structures. The *persistence over time* of these selected structures can also be explained by the needs and/or equilibrium states of the whole: Those structures having consequences for meeting needs and/or maintaining an equilibrium have a "selective advantage" over those that do not. Such statements need *not* be illegitimate teleologies, for it is quite possible for the systemic whole to exist *prior in time* to the structures that emerge and persist to maintain that whole.

For example, Parsons's analysis of the evolution of legal systems and their impact on the transition to a "modern" system of societies represents the use of such a reverse causal chain. Legal residues (codified, secular codes) of previous cultures—most notably Greece—came to have a "selective advantage" in subsequent societies, because they allowed for the secular legitimation of the political system, while at the same time regulating diverse institutional spheres, such as the economy, family, and religion.[51]

Furthermore, it is not even necessary to impute purpose to the systemic whole. Just as in the biophysical world ecological and population balances are maintained by nonpurposive selective processes (for example, predators increase until they eat themselves out of food, and then decrease until the food supply regenerates itself), so social wholes can maintain themselves in a state of equilibrium or meet the imperatives necessary for survival.

This line of argument has led Stinchcombe to summarize:

---

[48] See, for example, Parsons and Smelser, *Economy and Society;* Talcott Parsons, "Some Reflections on the Institutional Framework of Economic Development," *The Challenge of Development: A Symposium* (Jerusalem: The Hebrew University, 1958).

[49] See n. 44.

[50] Stinchcombe, *Constructing Social Theories,* pp. 87–93.

[51] For the details of what is obviously a more complex argument, see Parsons, *Societies,* pp. 95–115, and *System of Modern Societies.*

Functional explanations are thus complex forms of causal theories. They involve causal connections among . . . variables as with a special causal priority of the consequences of activity in total explanation. There has been a good deal of philosophical confusion about such explanations, mainly due to the theorist's lack of imagination in realizing the variety of reverse causal processes which can select behavior or structures according to their consequences.[52]

The above considerations would lead to some tentative conclusion about Parsons's scheme and the issue of teleology: (1) The scheme has always been teleological, from the initial conceptualization of unit acts to the four-function paradigm embracing the concept of goal attainment. (2) Contrary to the opinion of his detractors, most of Parsons's theoretical statements can be converted into nonteleological form, such that relevant statements about the conditions under which x varies with y can be discerned. (3) Parsons's work is filled with discussions on the mechanisms and processes through which specific end states or requisites of a system are met. (4) Parsons's work is replete with reverse causal chains in which a systemic whole existing prior in time to the emergence of subsystems causes the perpetuation of a subsystem because of its selective advantages in meeting problems faced by the systemic whole.

Most of the criticisms outlining the dangers of illegitimate teleology in functional theorizing have drawn examples from early functional anthropology, where it is relatively easy to expose the questionable teleologies of thinkers such as Malinowski and Radcliffe-Brown. But it is difficult to see how Parsons's notion of system requisites has led him to this same trap, thus allowing the defenders of the action-theoretic strategy to challenge the critics to find conspicuous instances in Parsons's work where there is an illegitimate teleology.

The Issue of Tautology.   Parsons's conceptualization of four system requisites—adaptation, goal attainment, integration, and latency—is based on the assumption that if these requisites are not met "survival" of the system is threatened. However, when employing this assumption, it is necessary to know what level of failure in meeting each of these requisites is necessary to pronounce a crisis of survival. How does one determine when adaptive needs are not being met? Goal attainment needs? Integrative requisites? And latency needs? Unless there is some way to determine what constitutes the survival and nonsurvival of a system, propositions documenting the contribution of items for meeting survival requisites become tautologous: The item meets survival needs of the system because the system exists and, therefore, must be surviving. Thus, to phrase propositions with regard to system requisites of adaptation, goal attainment, integration, and latency, Parsons would have to provide either of two types of

---

[52] Stinchcombe, *Constructing Social Theories*, p. 100.

information: (1) evidence on a "nonsurviving" system where a particular item did not exist; or (2) specific criteria as to what constitutes survival and nonsurvival in various types and classes of social systems. Without this kind of information, propositions employing notions of requisites are likely to be untestable, even in principle; therefore, they are not likely to be very useful in building sociological theory.

Parsons's solution to this problem has not been elegant, for he has been unable to provide clear criteria specifying the minimal levels of adaptation, goal attainment, integration, and latency necessary for system survival. At times, however, Parsons has accumulated "evidence" of systems that did not meet certain requisites and therefore did not "survive." For example, in his recent analysis of social evolution, he is able to discern, at least to his satisfaction, when certain requisites for evolutionary development were not met, since it is relatively "easy" to establish that in a given historical period a system ceased to evolve. For instance, in his discussion of why Greece and Israel failed to move beyond what he termed the "advanced intermediate" stage of evolution, he postulated that certain integrative requisites had not been met—namely, the codification of universalistic norms (legal codes) that legitimated the political (goal attainment) system, while insulating other institutional spheres (such as family, religion, economy) from each other.[53] This kind of analysis would seemingly denote some of the important structural and cultural components necessary for meeting various requisites for adaptation, goal attainment, integration, and latency in historical and, by inference, contemporary societies at different levels of development. The absence of these conponents, Parsons implies, would indicate that these systems are not meeting requisites for further development. However, requisites for further development are not quite the same as those for survival, although a failure to meet requisites for the next stage of evolution gives some indication of what is minimally necessary for survival of systems at this next stage. Thus, while Parsons has obviated at least some of the problems of tautology in his extensive use of system requisites, his "solution" is not likely to silence the critics—perhaps with some justification.

The Theoretical Utility of Survival Imperatives. Considering the problems of tautology created by using the concept of requisites, it may be asked: What do requisites add to Parson's theoretical scheme and to the analysis of specific events? And why does he continue to use the concept? For the detractors of imperativism, it would appear possible to document the conditions under which events influence each other in systemic wholes without dragging in notions of survival requisites. In fact, as the critics might observe, Parsons often appears

---

[53] Parsons, *Societies*, pp. 69–115.

to abandon reference to system requisites when discussing concrete empirical events, causing one to ponder why the requisites are retained in his more formal conceptual edifice.

An answer to such queries can only be tentative, but Parsons appears to retain the requisites for strategic reasons: to provide crude and rough criteria for distinguishing "important" from "unimportant" social processes. Parsons's entire intellectual career has been spent elaborating the complex systems of interrelationships among the basic "unit acts" he first described in *The Structure of Social Action.* The more the system of concepts has been brought to bear on increasingly complex patterns of organization among unit acts, the more Parsons has relied upon the requisites to sort out what processes in these complex patterns of interaction will help explain the most "variance." Thus, Parsons's imperatives constitute not so much a metaphysical entity, but a yardstick for distinguishing what is "crucial" from "not crucial" among the vast number of potential processes in social systems. Despite the fact that Parsons is unable to specify exact criteria for assessing whether adaptive, goal-attainment, integrative, and latency needs are being met, he appears to be able to use these somewhat vaguely conceptualized requisites to assess the theoretical significance of concrete social phenomena. To the extent that Parsons has employed the requisites in his many essays, the widely acknowledged insightfulness of these essays, which even the critics do not deny, can perhaps justify his continued use of the requisites to assess social phenomena.

Furthermore, as Parsons would seemingly argue, the requisites can be particularly useful in studying complex empirical systems, since for empirical systems it may be possible to specify more precisely criteria necessary for their survival. With these criteria, it is then possible to distinguish significant from less significant social processes in these systems, thereby assuring more insightful explanations. It appears, then, that despite some of the logical problems created by their retention, Parsons feels that the strategic value of the requisites in explaining social processes in social systems will more than compensate for the logical difficulties so frequently stressed by the critics.

TALCOTT PARSONS: AN OVERVIEW

The "theory of action" as it has unfolded over the last decades reveals an enormous amount of continuity—starting with the basic unit act and proliferating into the cybernetic hierarchy of control among the systems of action. Such continuity is the outgrowth of Parsons's particular view of how theory in sociology should be constructed, for he has consistently advocated the priority of systems of concepts over systems of propositions. The latter can only be useful when the former task is sufficiently completed.

Both the substantive vision of the world connoted by Parsons's concepts and the logical problems imputed to the scheme have stimulated widespread criticism of his functional perspective. In fact, it is unlikely that other forms of sociological theorizing can be understood unless the revulsion of many critics for the perspective is appreciated. As will become evident in subsequent chapters, other theoretical perspectives in sociology typically begin with a rejection of Parsonian functionalism and then proceed to build what is considered a more desirable alternative. In fact, Parsons appears to have become "the straw man" of sociological theorizing, for no "theory" is now considered adequate unless it has performed the necessary ritual of rejecting functional imperativism.

Before examining this ritual and the alternative theoretical perspectives it has stimulated, an examination of an alternative form of functionalism—the structural perspective advocated by Robert K. Merton—will be undertaken. In a more reasoned way than most of Parsons's other critics, Merton has attempted to formulate a functional strategy that corrects for some of the substantive and logical problems imputed to functional imperativism.

REPRESENTATIVE READINGS

Parsons, Talcott. *The Structure of Social Action.* New York: Free Press, 1968; original edition: New York: McGraw-Hill Book Co., 1937.

———. *The Social System.* New York: Free Press, 1951.

Parsons, Talcott; Bales, R. F.; and Shils, E. A. *Working Papers in the Theory of Action.* Glencoe, Ill.: Free Press, 1953.

Parsons, Talcott. "An Approach to Psychological Theory in Terms of the Theory of Action," in *Psychology: A Science,* edited by S. Koch, vol. 3. New York: McGraw-Hill Book Co., 1958.

———. "An Outline of the Social System" in *Theories of Society,* edited by T. Parsons et al. New York: Free Press, 1961.

———. *Societies: Evolutionary and Comparative Perspectives.* Englewood Cliffs, N.J.: Prentice-Hall, 1966.

———. "Some Problems of General Theory," in *Theoretical Sociology: Perspectives and Developments,* edited by J. C. McKinney and E. A. Tiryakian. New York: Appleton-Century-Crofts, 1970.

———. *The System of Modern Societies.* Englewood Cliffs, N.J.: Prentice-Hall, Inc. 1971.

4

Functional Structuralism:
Robert K. Merton

THEORIES OF THE MIDDLE RANGE

Just as Talcott Parsons was beginning to embrace a form of functional imperativism,[1] Robert K. Merton launched a critique of Parsons's functional strategy for building sociological theory.[2] At the heart of this criticism was Merton's contention that Parsons's concern for developing an all-encompassing system of concepts would prove both futile and sterile: To search for "a total system of sociological theory, in which observations about every aspect of social behavior, organization, and change promptly find their preordained place, has the same exhilarating challenge and the same small promise as those many all-encompassing philosophical systems which have fallen into deserved disuse."[3]

For Merton, such grand theoretical schemes are premature, for the theoretical and empirical groundwork necessary for their completion has not been performed. Just as Einsteinian theory did not emerge without a long cumulative research foundation and theoretical legacy, so sociological theory will have to wait

---

[1] As will be recalled, Parsons in 1945 began to conceptualize unit acts in systemic terms and began to visualize such systems in terms of requisites. See Talcott Parsons, "The Present Position and Prospects of Systemic Theory in Sociology," *Essays in Sociological Theory* (New York: Free Press, 1949).

[2] Robert K. Merton, "Discussion of Parsons' 'The Position of Sociological Theory'," *American Sociological Review* 13 (April 1948): 164–68.

[3] Ibid. Most of Merton's significant essays on functionalism have been included, and frequently expanded upon, in Robert K. Merton, *Social Theory and Social Structure* (New York: Free Press, 1949). Quotation taken from pages 45 of the 1968 edition of this classic work. Most subsequent references will be made to the articles incorporated into this book.

for its Einstein, primarily because "it has not yet found its Kepler—to say nothing of its Newton, Laplace, Gibbs, Maxwell or Planck."[4]

In the absence of this foundation, what passes for sociological theory, in Merton's critical eye, consists of "general orientations toward data, suggesting types of variables which theorists must somehow take into account, rather than clearly formulated, verifiable statements of relationships between specified variables."[5] Strategies advocated by those such as Parsons are not really "theory," but "philosophical systems," with "their varied suggestiveness, their architectonic splendor, and their sterility."[6] However, to pursue the opposite strategy of constructing inventories of low-level empirical propositions will prove equally sterile, thus suggesting to Merton the need for "theories of the middle range" in sociology.

Theories of the middle range offer more theoretical promise than grand theory, because they are couched at a lower level of abstraction, revealing clearly defined and operationalized concepts that are incorporated into statements of co-variance for a limited range of phenomena. While middle range theories are abstract, they are also connected to the empirical world, thus encouraging the research so necessary for the clarification of concepts and reformulation of theoretical generalizations. Without this interplay between theory and research, theoretical schemes will remain suggestive congeries of concepts, which are incapable of being refuted, while, on the other hand, empirical research will remain unsystematic, disjointed, and of little utility in expanding a body of sociological knowledge. Thus, by following a middle-range strategy, the concepts and propositions of sociological theory will become more tightly organized as theoretically focused empirical research forces clarification, elaboration, and reformulation of the concepts and propositions of each middle-range theory.

From this growing clarity in theories directed at a limited range of phenomena and supported by empirical research can eventually come the more encompassing theoretical schemes. In fact, for Merton, while it is necessary to concentrate energies on the construction of limited theories that inspire research, theorists must also be concerned with "consolidating the special theories into a more general set of concepts and mutually consistent propositions."[7] The special theories of sociology must therefore be formulated with an eye toward what they can offer more general sociological theorizing. However, just how these middle-range theories should be formulated to facilitate their eventual consolidation into a more general theory poses a difficult analytical problem, for which Merton has a ready solution: A form of functionalism should be utilized in formulating the

---

[4] Merton, *Social Theory and Social Structure*, p. 47.

[5] Ibid., p. 52.

[6] Ibid., p. 51.

[7] Merton, *Social Theory and Social Structure* (1957), p. 10.

theories of the middle range. Such functional theorizing is to take the form of a "paradigm" that would allow for both the easy specification and elaboration of relevant concepts, while encouraging systematic revision and reformulation as empirical findings would dictate. Conceived in this way, functionalism became for Merton a *method* for building not only theories of the middle range[8] but also the grand theoretical schemes that would someday subsume such theories of the middle range. Thus, in a vein similar to Parsons, functionalism for Merton represents a strategy for ordering concepts and for sorting out "significant" from "insignificant" social processes. But, unlike Parsons's strategy, Merton's functional strategy requires first the formulation of a body of middle-range theories. Only when this groundwork has been laid should a functional protocol be used to construct more abstract theoretical systems.

MERTON'S "PARADIGM" FOR FUNCTIONAL ANALYSIS

As with most commentators on functional analysis, Merton begins his discussion with a review of the mistakes of early functionalists, particularly the anthropologists Malinowski and Radcliffe-Brown.[9] Part of the reason for this assessment of the anthropological tradition stems from the fact that Merton's paradigm was first published in 1949,[10] when these anthropologists were still prominent figures in the social sciences. But the fact that this section of Merton's introduction to his paradigm has remained intact through two subsequent editions indicates his current concern that contemporary functionalism faces the same problems that early anthropologists failed to resolve. Generally, Merton views functional theorizing as potentially revealing—if only implicitly—three questionable postulates: (1) the functional unity of social systems, (2) the functional universality of social items, and (3) the indispensibility of functional items for social systems.

The Functional Unity Postulate. As can be recalled from chapter 2, Radcliffe-Brown in following Durkheim's lead frequently transformed the "hypothesis" that social systems reveal social integration into a necessary "requisite" or "need" for social survival. While it is difficult to argue that human societies do not possess some degree of integration—for otherwise they would not be systems—Merton views the degree of integration in a system as an issue to be empirically determined. To assume, however subtly, that a high degree of func-

---

[8] M. J. Mulkay (*Functionalism, Exchange and Theoretical Strategy* [New York: Schocken Books, 1971], pp. 98–99) argues a similar position, although he places less emphasis on Merton's concern for eventually building grand theory with his functional protocol.

[9] Robert K. Merton, "Manifest and Latent Functions," in *Social Theory and Social Structure* (1968), pp. 74–91.

[10] See Robert K. Merton, *Social Theory and Social Structure* (Glencoe, Ill.: Free Press, 1949), pp. 45–61.

tional unity must exist in a social system is to define away the important theoretical and empirical questions: What levels of integration exist for different systems? What various types of integration can be discerned? Are varying degrees of integration evident for different segments of a system? And, most importantly, what variety of processes lead to different levels, forms, and types of integration for different spheres of social systems? For Merton, to begin analysis with the postulate of "functional unity" or integration of the social whole can divert attention away from not only these questions, but also the varied and "disparate consequences of a given social or cultural item (usage, belief, behavior pattern, institutions) for diverse social groups and for individual members of these groups."[11]

Underlying this discussion of the functional unity imputed to systemic wholes is an implicit criticism of Parsons's early concern with social integration. As will be recalled, Parsons first postulated only one requisite in his early functional work:[12] the need for integration. Later, this postulate was to be expanded into three additional functional requisites for adaptation, goal attainment, and latency. But Parsons's functionalism appears to have begun with the same concerns evident in Durkheim's and Radcliffe-Brown's work, leading Merton to question the "heuristic value" of an assumption that can divert attention away from important theoretical and empirical questions. Thus, in the place of the postulate of functional unity should be an emphasis on varying types, forms, levels, and spheres of social integration and the varying consequences of the existence of items for specified segments of social systems. In this way, Merton begins to direct functional analysis away from concern with total systems toward an emphasis on how different patterns of social organization within more inclusive social systems are created, maintained, and changed not only by the requisites of the total system but also by interaction among sociocultural items within systemic wholes.

The Issue of Functional Universality. One result of an emphasis on functional unity was that some early anthropologists assumed that if a social item existed in an ongoing system, it must therefore have had positive consequences for the integration of the social system. This assumption tended to result in tautologous statements of the form: A system exists; an item is a part of the system; therefore, the item is positively functional for the maintenance of the system. In its most extreme form, Malinowski extended this form of reasoning to the point of asserting that "every custom, material object, idea and belief fulfills some vital function." To Merton, such an assumption was perhaps understandable in light of the fact that Malinowski was reacting to the view advanced

---

[11] Merton, *Social Theory and Social Structure* (1968), pp. 81–82.

[12] See Parsons, "Present Position and Prospects of Systemic Theory," and Talcott Parsons, *The Social System* (Glencoe, Ill.: Free Press, 1951).

by some anthropologists at the turn of the century that social "customs" could not be explained by their present utility, but rather, they could only be viewed as "survivals" of a culture's past history. Yet, Merton's analysis of Malinowski's excessive reaction to the now-discredited "historical reconstruction" school of anthropology has been retained to serve as a warning to contemporary functional theorizing, which might in more subtle form allow conceptions of "needs" and "requisites" to so skew analysis that only the positive functions of items for meeting these needs are analyzed.

For Merton, however, if an examination of empirical systems is undertaken, it is clear that there is a wider range of empirical possibilities. First, items may be not only positively functional for a system or another system item, but also dysfunctional for either particular items or the systemic whole. Second, some consequences, whether functional or dysfunctional, are intended and recognized by system incumbents and are thus "manifest," whereas other consequences are not intended or recognized and are therefore "latent." Thus, in contrast with the assertions of Malinowski and others such as Radcliffe-Brown who unwittingly fell into the same tautologous trap, Merton proposes the analysis of diverse consequences or functions of sociocultural items—whether positive or negative, manifest or latent—"for individuals, for sub-groups, and for the more inclusive social structure and culture."[13] In turn, the analysis of varied consequences requires the calculation of a "net balance of consequences" of items for each other and more inclusive systems. In this way, Merton visualizes contemporary functional analysis as compensating for the excesses of earlier forms of analysis by focusing on the crucial types of consequences of sociocultural items for each other and, if analysis dictates, for the social whole.

The Issue of Indispensability. Merton views Malinowski's assertion that every cultural item "fulfills *some vital function,* has some task to accomplish, represents an *indispensable part* within a working whole" as simply an extreme statement of two interrelated issues in functional analysis: (*a*) Do social systems have functional requisites or needs that must be fulfilled? (*b*) Are there certain crucial structures that are indispensable for fulfilling these functions?

In response to the first question, Merton provides a tentative yes, but with an important qualification: The functional requisites must be established empirically for specific systems. For actual groups or whole societies it is possible to ascertain the "conditions necessary for their survival," and it is of theoretical importance to determine which structures, through what specific processes, have consequences for these conditions. But to assume a system of universal requisites —as Parsons does—adds little to theoretical analysis, since to stress that certain

---

[13] Merton, *Social Theory and Social Structure* (1968), p. 84.

functions must be met in all systems simply leads observers to describe processes in social systems which meet these requisites. Such descriptions, Merton contends, can be done without the excess baggage of system requisites, for it is more desirable to describe cultural patterns and then assess their various consequences in meeting the specific needs of various segments of concrete empirical systems.

Merton's answer to the second question is emphatic: Empirical evidence makes the assertion that only certain structures can fulfill system requisites obviously false. Examination of the empirical world reveals quite clearly that "alternative structures" can exist to fulfill basically the same requisites in both similar and diverse systems. This fact leads Merton to postulate the importance in functional analysis of concern with various types of "functional alternatives," or "functional equivalents," and "functional substitutes" within social systems. In this way, functional analysis would not view as indispensable the social items of a system and thereby would avoid the tautologous trap of assuming that items must exist to assure the continued existence of a system. Furthermore, in looking for "functional alternatives," analytical attention would be drawn to questions about the "range" of items that could serve as functional equivalents. If these questions are to be answered adequately, analysts should then determine why a particular item was selected from a range of possible alternatives, leading to questions about the "structural context" and "structural limits" that might circumscribe the range of alternatives and account for the emergence of one item over another. For Merton, examination of these interrelated questions would thus facilitate the separate analysis of the causes and consequences of structural items. By asking why one particular structure instead of various alternatives had emerged, analysts would not forget to document the specific processes leading to an item's emergence as separate from its functional consequences. In this way, the danger of assuming that items must exist to fulfill system needs would be avoided.

In looking back at Merton's criticisms of traditional anthropological reasoning, and by implication that of some contemporary functionalists, it is evident that much of his assessment of these three "functional postulates" involves the destruction of "straw men," for the mistakes of Malinowski and Radcliffe-Brown were well understood even in 1949 when Merton's discussion was first published. Yet, in destroying his "straw men" Merton was led to formulate alternative postulates, which advocated a concern for the multiple consequences of sociocultural items for each other and for more inclusive social wholes, without a priori assumptions of functional needs or imperatives. Rather, functional analysis must specify (a) the social patterns under consideration, whether a systemic whole or some subpart; (b) the various types of consequences of these patterns for empirically established survival requisites; and (c) the processes whereby some patterns rather than others come to exist and have the various consequences for each other and for systemic wholes.[14]

With this form of functional analysis, Merton has sought to provide "the minumum set of concepts with which the sociologist must operate in order to carry through an adequate functional analysis."[15] In doing so, Merton hopes that this strategy will allow sociological analysis to avoid some of the mistaken postulates and assumptions of previous attempts to use a functional strategy. While the functional imperativism of Parsons is only briefly assessed in Merton's proposals, it appears that he is stressing the need for an alternative form of functional analysis in which there is less concern with total systems and abstract statements of system requisites. Instead, to build "theories of the middle range," it is necessary to focus attention on the mutual and varied consequences of specified system parts for each other and for systemic wholes. While these parts and systemic wholes have conditions necessary for their survival, these conditions must be empirically established, for only through a clear understanding of the actual requisites of a concrete system can the "needs" of social structures provide a useful set of criteria for assessing the consequences, or functions, of social items. Furthermore, while the analysis of consequences of items is the unique feature of functional analysis, it is also necessary to delineate the causal processes that have resulted in a particular item having a specified set of consequences for other items and systemic wholes. To assure adherence to this form of structural analysis, Merton went so far as to outline a set of procedures for executing the general guidelines of his "functional paradigm."

A PROTOCOL FOR EXECUTING FUNCTIONAL ANALYSIS

To ascertain the causes and consequences of particular structures and processes, Merton insists that functional analysis begin with "sheer description" of the activities of individuals and groups under study. In describing the patterns of interaction and activity among units under investigation, it will be possible to discern clearly the social items to be subjected to functional analysis. Such descriptions can also provide "a major clue to the functions performed" by such patterned activity; but, in order for these functions to become more evident, additional steps are necessary.

The first of these steps is for investigators to indicate the principal alternatives that are excluded by the dominance of a particular pattern. Such description of

---

[14] Merton's actual paradigm is more extensive than the above listing, but this description summarizes the thrust of his functional strategy. For the complete paradigm, see Merton, *Social Theory and Social Structure* (1968), pp. 104–9.

[15] Ibid., p. 109.

the excluded alternatives provides an indication of the "structural context" from which an observed patterned first emerged and is now maintained—thereby offering further clues about the functions, or consequences, the item might have for other items and perhaps for the systemic whole. The second analytical step beyond sheer description involves an assessment of the "meaning," or mental and emotional significance, of the activity for members of the group. Description of these meanings may offer some indication of the motives behind the activities of the individuals involved, and thereby shed some tentative light on the "manifest" functions of an activity. These descriptions require a fourth analytical step of discerning "some array of motives for conformity or for deviation" among participants, but these motives must not be confused with either the objective description of the pattern or the subsequent assessment of the functions served by the pattern. Yet, by understanding the configuration of motives for conformity and deviation among actors, an assessment of the psychological "needs" served (or not served) by a pattern can be understood—offering an additional clue to the various functions of the pattern under investigation.

But focusing on the meanings and motives of those involved in an activity can skew analysis away from unintended or latent consequences of the activity. Thus, a final analytical step involves the description of how the patterns under investigation reveal regularities not recognized by participants, but which appear to have consequences for both the individuals involved and other central patterns or regularities in the system. In this way, analysis will be attuned to the "latent" functions of an item.

By following each of these steps, Merton assumes that it will be possible to assess the "net balance of consequences" of the pattern under investigation, as well as to determine some of the independent causes of the item. These steps assure that a proper functional inquiry will ensue, because postulates of functional unity, assumptions of survival requisites, and convictions about indispensible parts do not precede the analysis of social structures and processes. On the contrary, attention is drawn only to observable patterns of activity, the structural context in which the focal pattern emerged and persists in the face of potential alternatives, the meaning of these patterns for actors involved, the actors' motives for conformity and deviation, and the implications of the particular pattern for unrecognized needs of individuals and other items in the social system. Thus, with this kind of preliminary work, functional analysis will avoid the logical and empirical problems of previous forms of functionalism and thereby provide an understanding of the causes and consequences of system parts for each other and for more inclusive system units.[16]

---

[16] Ibid., p. 136.

An Illustration of Merton's Protocol: Political Machines in America

Merton's paradigm and protocol for constructing functional theories of the middle range are remarkably free of statements about individual and system needs or requisites. In his protocol statements, Merton appears to prefer to approach the question of the needs and requisites fulfilled by a particular item only *after* description of (*a*) the item in question, (*b*) the structural context in which the item survives, and (*c*) its meaning for the individuals involved. With this information, it is then possible to establish both the manifest and latent functions of an item, as well as the "net balance" of functions and dysfunctions of the item for varied segments of a social system. Unfortunately, the implied sequencing of functional analysis is not always performed by Merton, presumably for at least two reasons. First, in selecting an established structure in a system for analysis, the investigator usually assumes that the item persists because it is fulfilling some need. As will be evident, Merton *begins* (as opposed to concludes) with this assumption in his analysis of political machines—thus leaving him to conclude that "structure affects function and function affects structure." When description of items begins with an implicit assumption of their functions for fulfilling needs, then it is more likely that the description will be performed in a way assuring confirmation of the implicit assumption. Second, in analyzing the structural context of an item and assessing why it emerges and persists over alternative items, it is necessary to have some preconception of the functions served by an item in order to know why it fulfills a set of needs "better" than would various alternatives. Otherwise, it would be difficult to determine what potential alternatives could exist to "substitute" for the present item.

For at least these two reasons, then, execution of Merton's strategy is difficult, as becomes evident in his analysis of American political machines. Much like that of his anthropological "straw men," such as Radcliffe-Brown, Merton's recognition of the necessity for analyzing separately the "causes" and "functions" of structural items is not as evident in his actual account of empirical events.

Merton begins his analysis of American political machines with the simple question: "How do they manage to continue in operation?"[17] Following this interesting question is an assumption reminiscent of Malinowski's functional analysis:

> Preceding from the functional view, therefore, that we should *ordinarily* (not invariably) expect persistent social patterns and social structures to perform positive functions *which are at the time not fulfilled by other patterns and structures,* the thought occurs that perhaps this publicly maligned organization is, *under present conditions,* satisfying basic latent functions. [Italics in original][18]

[17] Ibid., p. 125.
[18] Ibid., pp. 125–26.

In this passage, the fact that the word "ordinarily" is qualified by the parenthetical phrase "not invariably" is perhaps enough to allow Merton to escape the
change of tautology: If an item persists in a surviving system, it must therefore
have positive functions. Yet, Merton seems to be saying that if an enduring item
does not fulfill "manifest" functions, then it fulfills "latent" functions, leading
one to recall Malinowski's dictum that "every custom, material object, idea and
belief fulfills some vital function, has some task to accomplish." For Merton, this
assumption becomes translated into the dictum that social items that do not fulfill
manifest functions must fulfill latent ones; and, as is added in a footnote, if the
item has dysfunctions for some segments of the population, its persistence implies
that it *ordinarily* must have positive functions for meeting the needs of other
segments.

In fairness to Merton's suggestive analysis of political machines, it should be
emphasized that he was offering this analysis only as an illustration of the usefulness of the distinction between "manifest" and "latent" functions. It was not
intended as a full explication of his functional paradigm or protocol, but only
as an example of how attention to "latent" functions can provide new insights
into the operation of political machines. However, it would appear that Merton's
commitment to a clear protocol was not enough to preclude an inadvertent
lapse—so typical of earlier functionalists—into the postulates of "universality of
functions" and "functional indispensibility." Thus, Merton appears to begin his
concrete analysis with a set of postulates that he earlier had gone to great lengths
to discredit, resulting in this central assumption:

> The key structural function of the Boss is to organize, centralize and maintain in
> good working condition "the scattered fragments of power" which are at present
> dispersed through our political organization. By this centralization of political
> power, *the boss can satisfy the needs of diverse subgroups* in the larger community
> which are not adequately satisfied by legally devised and culturally approved social
> structures.[19]

For Merton, political machines emerge in the "structural context" of a system
in which power is decentralized to the extent that it cannot be mobilized to meet
the needs of significant segments of the population. The causal processes by
which machines arise in this power vacuum to pick up the "scattered fragments
of power" involve a sequence of events in which political machines are seen as
able to satisfy the "needs" of diverse groups more effectively than "legally devised
and culturally approved social structures." Logically, this form of analysis is not
necessarily tautologous or an illegitimate teleology—as some critics might charge
—because Merton appears to be asserting that political machines at one time
had a selective advantage over alternative structures in meeting *prior* needs of

---

[19] Ibid., p. 126.

certain segments in a system. This kind of "reverse causal chain," to use Stinch-combe's term,[20] is a legitimate form of causal analysis, since the system needs are seen as existing *prior in time* to the events they cause—in this instance the emergence of political machines in the American social structure. Furthermore, it is not necessary to impute purposes—although at times purpose is certainly involved—to the segments of the system affected by the machines, since a political machine may be seen as a chance event that had a selective advantage over alternatives in a spiraling process similar to that which is typical of the expansions and contradictions of predator populations that grow rapidly until they eat themselves out of prey. Clearly, the emergence of a political machine is both a purposive and nonpurposive process in which the machine meets the prior needs of a population, which has signaled to the leaders or the "bosses" of the machine the efficacy of their expanded pursuits (purpose) in meeting its needs. Eventually, in a spiraling process of this nature, the original needs of the population which caused the emergence and expansion of political machines and big city bosses may recede in causal significance as the needs of the well-estab-lished political machine cause, in a reverse causal process, certain activities that have little consequence (or perhaps a dysfunctional consequence) for the needs of the population that initially caused the machine's emergence.

This kind of causal argument appears to be Merton's intent, but, unfortu-nately, his overriding concern with discerning the functions of the political machines obscures this necessary causal analysis, for, as he is prone to remark, "whatever its specific historical origins, the political machine persists as an ap-paratus for satisfying unfulfilled needs of diverse groups in the population."[21] By bypassing these specific causal chains involved in the emergence of the political machine in America, Merton is left with the relatively simple and ad hoc task of cross-tabulating the "needs" of a population and the activities of the political machine that fulfill them.

For example, the political machine fulfills the needs of deprived classes by providing vital services through the local neighborhood ward heeler, including "food baskets and jobs, legal and extra-legal advice, setting to rights minor scrapes with the law, helping the bright poor boy to a political scholarship in a local college, looking after the bereaved," and so on. The political machine, according to Merton, can provide these services more effectively than various alternatives, such as welfare agencies, settlement houses, legal aid clinics, and the like, because it offers these services in a personal way through the neighborhood ward heeler with a minimum of questions, red tape, and abuse to people's self-respect. For other populations, such as the business community, the political machines pro-

---

[20] Arthur L. Stinchcombe, *Constructing Social Theories* (New York: Harcourt, Brace and World, 1968), p. 100.

[21] Merton, *Social Theory and Social Structure* (1968), p. 127.

vide another set of needed services—namely, political regulation and control of unbridled competition among corporations and businesses without undue governmental interference in the specific operations of economic enterprises. By virtue of controlling various public agencies and bureaus, the big city boss can rationalize and organize relations among economic organizations, while, at the same time, preventing too much governmental scrutiny into their various illegal activities. The political machine can perform this function more effectively than legal governmental alternatives because it recognizes the need of economic organizations for both regulation and noninterference in certain activities. In contrast, legally constituted government agencies would recognize only the former need—thus giving the political machine a selective advance over legally constituted government. Similarly, the political machine can organize and rationalize illegal economic enterprises concerned with providing illicit services, including gambling, drugs, and prostitution, whereas legally constituted governmental agencies cannot condone, to say nothing of organizing, this kind of prevalent activity. Thus, for both legal and illegal businesses, the political machine provides "protection" by assuring a stable marketplace, high profits, and selective governmental regulation. Finally, for another population—notably the deprived—the political machine provides opportunities for social mobility in a society where monetary success is a strong cultural value, but where actual opportunities for such success are closed to many deprived groups. Thus, by opening the doors to social mobility for members of deprived groups who do not have "legitimate" opportunities, the political machine meets the needs of the deprived, while, at the same time, assuring itself of loyal, committed, and grateful personnel.

PROBLEMS IN MERTON'S PARADIGM AND PROTOCOL

Merton's functional explanation of the persistence of political machines has considerable plausibility, for, indeed, the existence of political machines in America was correlated with a relatively ineffective federal establishment, deprived urban masses, high demand for illegal services, and high degrees of economic competition. But most of Merton's account is simply a statement of correlation, dressed in functional assumptions about how the needs of "diverse subgroups" led to the emergence and persistence of political machines in America. As is obvious, statements of correlation are not causal statements. To the extent that it simply notes the correlation between social "needs" and political machines, Merton's analysis will be of little utility in building theoretical statements of the form: under C_1, C_2, C_3, . . . , C_m, x causes variation in y. There are many *implied* causal chains in Merton's analysis, but his failure to make them explicit detracts from his analysis. As was emphasized in chapter 2, Durkheim's concrete analysis of the division of labor lapsed into statements implying, at the very least, that the "need for social order" caused the division of labor.[22] Without explicit causal statements about how the need for order caused the division of labor, the analysis constituted an illegitimate teleology.

The difficulties that these "founders" of functionalism had in separating "cause" and "function" were clearly recognized by Merton and, presumably, served as the impetus to his insightful explication of a paradigm and protocol for functional analysis. Yet, much like his predecessors, Merton abandons the very protocol that would keep "cause" and "function" separated. Merton indicates that the emergence and persistence of political machines occur in response to needs, without documenting very precisely the causal chains through which "needs" cause the emergence and persistence of an event.

Merton also appears to fall into the problems of tautology so evident in Malinowski's functional analysis. By assuming that "ordinarily" persistent structures serve positive functions for meeting the needs of some segment of the population, Merton indicates that if an item persists in an existing system, then it is functional (perhaps only latent) for some groups. It is somewhat surprising that Merton falls back onto this postulate, since he went to such great lengths to sound the warning against just this assumption. Yet, Merton's analysis of political machines does not start with a description of the phenomenon, nor does he initially address the structural context in which it exists, but rather, Merton begins with the assumption that political machines exist to fulfill a function—if not a manifest function, then a latent one.

This criticism of Merton's analysis of a concrete phenomenon does not mean that, with more specification of causal processes, charges of tautology and illegitimate teleology could be avoided. Indeed, with more specification of the "historical origins" of the political machines and of the "feedback" processes between political machines, on the one hand, and the segments of the population they serve, on the other, Merton's account could be rephased in less suspicious causal terms. This fact leads to an important question: Why did Merton fail to specify the causal chains that would make less suspicious his propositions? One answer to this question is simply that Merton offered this account of political machines only as an illustration of the utility in the concept of "latent" functions. As an illustration, the account would naturally be brief and not involve a thorough explication of the emergence of political machines in America. Merton's awareness of the problems inherent in previous functional analysis would lend credence to this argument, for how could he fall into the very traps that he sought to avoid?

However, Durkheim's and Radcliffe-Brown's similar failure to avoid completely the logical problems they clearly understood raises the more fundamental question: Is there something about functional analysis that encourages theorists

---

[22] Emile Durkheim, *The Rules of the Sociological Method* (Glencoe, Ill.: Free Press, 1938), p. 96.

to "short-circuit" causal explanation? Logically, there is no reason why functional explanation must be tautologous or constitute an illegitimate teleology. In point of fact, much functional analysis does seem to confuse "causes" and "function," or at least fail to clarify the causes of phenomena—whether the author be Durkheim, Radcliffe-Brown, Parsons, or Merton. Why should this be so? The answer seems to reside in the conceptualization of "needs," "requisites," or "imperatives." Once these concepts become analytically conspicuous, some authors have difficulty in sorting out just how causal processes operate independently of the needs they fulfill, or, if teleological processes are seen to occur, distinguishing just which processes are teleological and which are nonteleological.

A great deal of causal analysis in sociology is vague, for knowledge about how events cause each other is, to state the obvious, incomplete. When combined with what inevitably must be vague causal statements, given the state of the discipline, notions of system needs and requisites compound the difficulties in constructing causal statements, since to be vague on how systemic or individual needs relate to particular sets of events increases the probability that statements will become illegitimate (or, at least, unspecified) teleologies and/or tautologies.

With further specification of causal chains, such statements will recede, but there always remains the danger that some theorists will remain satisfied with tautologous and teleological explanations, primarily because they often sound pleasing and appear to explain phenomena. Merton's account of the persistence of political machines is a good example of an intuitively pleasing set of statements that lacks the rigor necessary for scientific theory in sociology. To the extent that Merton's strategy can allow the luxury of abandoning an explicit protocol in order to engage in a suggestive but causally inadequate form of explanation, then the critics will have ample reason to question the utility of Merton's paradigm and protocol.

MERTON'S FUNCTIONAL STRATEGY: AN OVERVIEW

Merton has occupied a unique position in sociological theorizing. His tempered and reasoned statements have typically resolved intellectually stagnating controversies in the field. For example, his advocacy of theories of the "middle range" quelled a vigorous debate between theoretically and empirically inclined sociologists by reasserting the efficacy of empirically oriented theory and theoretically oriented research.

Similarly, Merton's functional paradigm and protocol were explicated to deal with the growing body of criticism of functional theorizing. By pointing to the logical problems inherent in certain functional postulates, Merton's paradigm was viewed as providing an alternative form of functional analysis which avoided these problems. The uncritical acceptance of this paradigm attests to Merton's seemingly charismatic capacity to "resolve" issues. However, as reasoned and as appealing as his argument appears, it does not obviate the very theoretical problems it was explicitly designed to resolve. In fact, Merton's own analysis of political machines, for all its insight and intuitive appeal, does not conform to the dictates of his protocol, leading critics to wonder why it is that functional analysis keeps slipping back into certain long-standing problems.

On the surface, Merton's paradigm and protocol appear to guide investigators to the interconnections and mutual consequences of structures. Theoretical statements on the nature of these interconnections among diverse system units constitute one of the principal goals of sociological theory, but imperativist assumptions of individual and system needs often appear to have diverted analytical attention away from documentation of the precise causal connections among systemically related phenomena. As Merton's analysis illustrates, the mere cross-tabulation of one item, such as the existence of political machines, with need states imputed to another item, such as the "needs" of new immigrants in the large city, is sometimes performed in lieu of more precise causal statements about the relations between the two phenomena.

This situation, however, need not automatically ensue from functional analysis, even one in which concepts of system and individual needs figure prominently. Cross-tabulation can suggest a further theoretical question: What causal linkages would account for the fact that phenomena are capable of being cross-tabulated? In sorting out these linkages, the problems of imperativist assumptions recede. In fact, as long as there is commitment to go beyond cross-tabulation and construct causal statements, an imperativist strategy can perhaps be useful in discriminating "important" from "unimportant" social processes. This strategy is explicitly advocated by Parsons. Although Merton's paradigm and protocol seem to place less emphasis on this analytical tack, his attempts to apply his protocol reveal the similarity of his theoretical strategy to that of Parsons. The major difference in their respective functional strategies concerns the degree of abstractness each considers appropriate for sociological theorizing at the present time. For Parsons, functional theory is to be a grand system of concepts encompassing as wide a range of phenomena as possible; whereas, for Merton, sociological theorizing should initially be confined to specific and delimited empirical phenomena.

Whether functional theorizing is conducted at the "grand" or "middle range" level, it has inspired considerable criticism, debate, and controversy in sociology. While much of this criticism has been counterproductive, it has resulted in the codification of alternative theoretical perspectives. The suggestiveness of these perspectives would indicate that the excessive critical climate surrounding functionalism has not been totally futile. And so, it is to a discussion of these alternative perspectives that the next three sections of this book are directed.

SELECTED BIBLIOGRAPHY ON FUNCTIONAL THEORIZING

Barber, Bernard. "Structural-Functional Analysis: Some Problems and Misunderstandings." *American Sociological Review* 21 (April 1956): 129–35.

Braithwaite, R. B. *Scientific Explanation.* New York: Harper & Bros., 1953, chaps. 9 and 10.

Bredemeier, Harry C. "The Methodology of Functionalism." *American Sociological Review* 20 (April 1955): 173–80.

Radcliffe-Brown, A. R. "On the Concept of Function in Social Science." *American Anthropologist* 37 (July–September 1935): 392–402.

———. *Structure and Function in Primitive Society.* Glencoe, Ill.: Free Press, 1952.

Buckley, Walter. "Structural-Functional Analysis in Modern Sociology." In *Modern Sociological Theory,* edited by H. Becker and A. Boskoff, pp. 236–59. New York: Holt, Rinehart & Winston, 1966.

Cancian, Francesca. "The Functional Analysis of Change," *American Sociological Review* 25 (December 1960): 818–27.

Cohen, Percy S. *Modern Social Theory.* New York: Basic Books, 1968. Pp. 58–64.

Davis, Kingsley. "The Myth of Functional Analysis as a Special Method in Sociology and Anthropology." *American Sociological Review* 25 (December 1959): 757–72.

Demerath, N. J. "Synecdoche and Structural Functionalism." In *System, Change and Conflict,* edited by N. J. Demerath, III, and R. A. Peterson, pp. 501–20. New York: Free Press, 1967.

Dore, Philip Ronald. "Function and Cause." *American Sociological Review* 26 (December 1961): 843–53.

Durkheim, Emile. *The Division of Labor in Society.* New York: Free Press, 1933.

Erasmus, Charles J. "Obviating the Functions of Functionalism." *Social Forces* 45 (March 1967): 319–28.

Fallding, Harold. "Functional Analysis in Sociology." *American Sociological Review* 28 (February 1963): 5–13.

Gouldner, Alvin W. "Reciprocity and Autonomy in Functional Theory." In *Symposium on Sociological Theory,* edited by L. Gross, pp. 241–70. Evanston, Ill.: Harper & Row, 1959.

Hempel, Carl G. "The Logic of Functional Analysis." In *Symposium on Sociological Theory,* edited by L. Gross, pp. 271–307. New York: Harper & Row, 1959.

Malinowski, Bronislaw. "Anthropology," *Encyclopedia Britannica,* Supp. Vol. 1. London and New York, 1936.

———. *A Scientific Theory of Culture.* Chapel Hill: University of North Carolina, 1944.

———. *Magic, Science and Religion and Other Essays.* Glencoe, Ill.: Free Press, 1948.

Martindale, Don. *The Nature and Types of Sociological Theory.* Boston: Houghton Mifflin Co., 1960. Chaps. 16 and 17.

———. *Functionalism in the Social Sciences.* Philadelphia: American Academy of Political and Social Science, 1965.

Merton, Robert K. "Manifest and Latent Functions." In *Social Theory and Social Structure.* New York: Free Press, 1968.

Mulkay, M. J. *Functionalism, Exchange and Theoretical Strategy.* New York: Schocken Books, 1971. Pp. 1–121.

Nadel, S. F. *Foundations of Social Anthropology.* Glencoe, Ill.: Free Press, 1951. Pp. 373–78.

Nagel, Ernest G. "Teleological Explanation and Teleological Systems." In *Readings in the Philosophy of Science,* edited by H. Feigl and M. Broadbeck, pp. 537–58. New York: Appleton-Century-Crofts, 1953.

Stinchcombe, Arthur L. "Specious Generality and Functional Theory." *American Sociological Review* 26 (December 1961): 929–30.

————. *Constructing Social Theories.* New York: Harcourt, Brace, & World, 1968. Pp. 80–116.

Wallace, Walter. *Sociological Theory.* Chicago: Aldine Publishing Co., 1969. Pp. 24–31, 36–44.

Zetterberg, Hans. *On Theory and Verification in Sociology.* Totowa, N.J.: Bedminister Press, 1965. Pp. 74–79.

Part II

Conflict Theory

5

The Conflict Heritage

During the 1950s, as the essentials of the Parsonian scheme were unfolding, one body of criticism was taking on a clear focus. Functional theory in sociology, especially the Parsonian variety, was seen as underemphasizing the conflictual nature of social reality. Soon, attacks along these lines became ceremonial rituals for sociologists who sought theoretical redemption for past sins and who now held that conflict theory was to carry sociology out of its theoretical morass.

As David Lockwood argued in 1956,[1] Parsons, in continually assuming for analytical purposes a system in equilibrium, had created a fictionalized conception of the social world. From this world of fantasy, as Lockwood phrased the matter, it was inevitable that analysis would emphasize mechanisms that maintained social order rather than those that systematically generated disorder and change. Furthermore, by assuming order and equilibrium, the ubiquitous phenomena of instability, disorder, and conflict too easily became viewed as deviant, abnormal, and pathological. For, in reality, Lockwood insisted, there were "mechanisms" in societies that made conflict inevitable and inexorable. For example, power differentials assured that some groups would exploit others, and constituted a built-in source of tension and conflict in social systems. Additionally, the existence of scarce resources in societies would inevitably generate fights over the distribution of these resources. And finally, the fact that different interest groups in social systems pursued different goals, and hence often had to vie with one another, assured that conflict would erupt. These forces, Lockwood contended, represented "mechanisms" of social disorder that should be as analytically significant to the understanding of social systems as Parsons's mechanisms of socialization and social control.

---
[1] David Lockwood, "Some Remarks on 'The Social System,' " *British Journal of Sociology* 7 (June 1956): 134–46.

As noted in chapter 3, Ralf Dahrendorf crystallized this line of argument toward the end of the decade by comparing functional theory to a utopia.[2] Utopias usually have few historical antecedents—much like Parsons's hypothesized equilibrium; utopias display universal consensus on prevailing values and institutional arrangements—in a vein remarkably similar to Parsons's concept of institutionalization; and utopias always display processes that operate to maintain existing arrangements—much like the "mechanisms" of Parsons's "social system." Hence, utopias and the social world when viewed from a functional perspective do not change very much, since they do not concern themselves with history, dissensus over values, and conflict in institutional arrangements.

Conflict and change were thus rediscovered by the beginning of the last decade, moving some to proclaim the conflict perspective as the "new sociology."[3] But in fact, the conflict perspective is as old as functionalism, finding its inspiration in the works of two German sociologists, Karl Marx and Georg Simmel, who were approximate contemporaries of prominent organicists. And just as contemporary functionalism reflects the legacy of these organicists, so contemporary conflict theory is indebted to the thinking of Marx and Simmel.

KARL MARX AND DIALECTICAL CONFLICT THEORY

In developing a model of revolutionary class conflict and social change, Marx delineated an image of social organization which still influences a major portion of contemporary sociological theory. Marx began with a simple—and in retrospect, simplistic—assumption: Economic organization, especially the ownership of property, determines the organization of the rest of a society. The class structure and institutional arrangements, as well as cultural values, beliefs, religious dogmas, and other idea systems are ultimately a reflection of the economic base of a society. He then added an additional assumption: Inherent in the economic organization of any society—save the ultimate communistic society —are forces inevitably generating revolutionary class conflict. Such revolutionary class conflict is seen as dialectical and conceptualized as occurring in epochs, with successive bases of economic organization sowing the seeds of their own destruction through the polarization of classes and subsequent overthrow of the dominant by the subjugated class. Hence, a third assumption: Conflict is bipolar, with exploited classes under conditions created by the economy becoming aware of their true "interests" and eventually forming a revolutionary political organization that stands against the dominant, property-holding class.

---

[2] Ralf Dahrendorf, "Out of Utopia: Toward a Reorientation of Sociological Analysis," *American Journal of Sociology* 744 (September 1958): 115–27.

[3] For example, see Irving Louis Horowitz, *The New Sociology: Essays in Social Science and Social Theory* (New York: Oxford University Press, 1964).

The criticisms leveled against these assumptions are perhaps self-evident:[4] (1) Societies are more than mere reflections of economic organization and patterns of property ownership; (2) social conflict is rarely bipolarized across an entire society; (3) interests in a society do not always cohere around social class; (4) power relations in a society are not always direct reflections of ownership of property; and (5) conflict does not always cause social change, dialectical or otherwise. In addition to a whole series of incorrect predictions—such as the formation of the modern proletariat into a revolutionary class during the present "capitalistic" epoch, the subsequent overthrow of capitalist economic systems, and the formation of a communist society—the wisdom of following Marx's lead can be questioned.

With abstraction above the specifics of Marx's economic determinism and excessive polemics, however, there emerges a set of assumptions from his work which directly challenge those imputed to functionalism and which serve as the intellectual springboard for the conflict alternative in sociological theorizing:

1. While social relationships display systemic features, these relationships are rife with conflicting interests.
2. This fact reveals that social systems systematically generate conflict.
3. Conflict is therefore an inevitable and pervasive feature of social systems.
4. Such conflict tends to be manifested in the bipolar opposition of interests.
5. Conflict most frequently occurs over the distribution of scarce resources, most notably power.
6. Conflict is the major source of change in social systems.

In addition to this assumptive legacy, the form and substance of Marx's causal imagery appears to have been equally influential on the development of modern conflict theory. This imagery takes the general form of assuming that conflict is an inevitable and inexorable force in social systems and is "activated" under certain specified conditions. Some of these conditions are viewed as allowing for the transformation of latent class interests (lying in a state of "false consciousness") into manifest class interests ("class consciousness"), which, under additional conditions, lead to the polarization of society into two classes joined in revolutionary conflict. Thus, for Marx, there are a series of conditions that are cast into the role of intervening variables, which accelerate or retard the inevitable transformation of class interests into revolutionary class conflict.

In addition to the form of the argument (to be discussed more thoroughly in the next chapter), the substance of the Marxian model is of great importance

---

[4] C. Wright Mills, *The Marxists* (New York: Harcourt, Brace, 1948); Ralf Dahrendorf, *Class and Class Conflict in Industrial Society* (Stanford, Calif.: Stanford University Press, 1959), pp. 36–71.

in understanding modern sociological theory. Again, this substantive contribution can best be seen if the propositions of Marx's theoretical scheme are stated in more abstract form, and thereby divorced from his polemics and rhetoric about social class and revolution. While much of the flavor of Marx's analysis is lost in such an exercise,[5] the indebtedness of modern sociological theory to Marxian propositions can be made more evident. These propositions are delineated in Table 5–1.[6]

In Table 5–1, Marx's assumptions about the nature of the social world and the key causal connections in this world are stated propositionally. For it is in a propositional form that Marx's contribution to modern social theory promises to endure (see following chapters 6, 7, and 8). In Proposition I of Table 5–1, the degree of inequality in the distribution of resources is held by Marx to influence the extent to which segments of a social system will reveal conflicts of interest. Proposition II then documents some of the conditions that would make members of deprived or subordinate segments of a population aware of their conflict of interest with those holding the largest share of scarce resources. For once segments of a population become aware of their true interests, they will begin to question the legitimacy of a system in which they come out on the short end of the distribution of scarce resources. Propositions II-A, B, C, and D deal, respectively, with the disruption in the social situation of deprived populations, the amount of alienation people feel as a result of their situation, the capacity of members of deprived segments to communicate with each other, and their ability to develop a unifying ideology that codifies their true interests. These conditions are seen by Marx as factors that increase and heighten awareness of subordinates' collective interests and, hence, decrease their willingness to accept as legitimate the right of superordinates to command a disproportionate share of resources.

In turn, some of these forces heightening awareness are influenced by such structural conditions as ecological concentration (II-C-1), educational opportunities (II-C-2), the availability of ideological spokesmen (II-D-1), and the control of socialization processes and communication networks by superordinates (II-D-2). In Proposition III, Marx hypothesizes that the increasing awareness by deprived classes of their true interests and the resulting questioning of the legitimacy of the distribution of resources serves to increase the likelihood that

---

[5] See Dahrendorf, *Class and Class Conflict*, pp. 2–35, for a paraphrasing of this substance and flavor.

[6] Curiously, the causal argument is much more explicit in Marx's polemic writings, such as *The Communist Manifesto*. In Marx's more philosophical works, such as *Capital*, his causal imagery is considerably more vague. Furthermore, as should be obvious, these propositions not only represent abstractions from Marx's more specific propositions, but also a simplification of much of their subtlety and complexity. Yet, it is these propositions that have been taken over into modern conflict theory, and therefore are of concern here.

TABLE 5–1

Marx's Key Propositions

   I. The more unequal the distribution of scarce resources in a system, the more conflict of interest between dominant and subordinate segments in a system

  II. The more subordinate segments become aware of their true collective interests, the more likely they are to question the legitimacy of the existing pattern of distribution of scarce resources

      A. The more social changes wrought by dominant segments disrupt existing relations among subordinates, the more likely are the latter to become aware of their true interests

      B. The more practices of dominant segments create alienative dispositions among subordinates, the more likely are the latter to become aware of their true collective interests

      C. The more members of subordinate segments can communicate their grievances to each other, the more likely they are to become aware of their true collective interests

         1. The more ecological concentration of members of subordinate groups, the more likely communication of grievances

         2. The more the educational opportunities of subordinate group members, the more diverse the means of their communication, and the more likely they are to communicate their grievances

      D. The more subordinate segments can develop unifying ideologies, the more likely they are to become aware of their true collective interests

         1. The greater the capacity to recruit or generate ideological spokesmen, the more likely ideological unification

         2. The less the ability of dominant groups to regulate the socialization processes and communication networks in a system, the more likely ideological unification

 III. The more subordinate segments of a system are aware of their collective interests and the greater their questioning of the legitimacy of the distribution of scarce resources, the more likely they are to join overt conflict against dominant segments of a system

      A. The less the ability of dominant groups to make manifest their collective interests, the more likely subordinate groups are to join in conflict

      B. The more the deprivations of subordinates move from an absolute to relative basis, the more likely they are to join in conflict

      C. The greater the ability of subordinate groups to develop a political leadership structure, the more likely they are to join in conflict

 IV. The greater the ideological unification of members of subordinate segments of a system and the more developed their political leadership structure, the more polarized the dominant and subjugated segments of a system

  V. The more polarized the dominant and subjugated, the more violent the conflict will be

 VI. The more violent the conflict, the more structural change of the system and the greater the redistribution of scarce resources

---

the disadvantaged strata will begin to organize collectively their opposition against the dominant segments of a system. This organization is seen as especially likely under several conditions: the more disorganized the dominant segments with respect to understanding their true interests (III-A), the more the subordinates' deprivations escalate as they begin to compare their situation with that of the privileged (III-B), and the more the ease with which the deprived can develop political leadership to carry out the organizational tasks of mobilizing subordinates (III-C). In Proposition IV, Marx emphasizes that once deprived groups possess a unifying ideology and political leadership, their true interests begin to take on clear focus and their opposition to superordinates begins to increase. As polarization increases, the less possibility there is for reconciliation, compromise, or mild conflict, since now the deprived are sufficiently alienated, organized, and unified to press for a complete change in the pattern of resource distribution (V)—thus making violent confrontation the only way to overcome the inevitable resistance of superordinates. Finally (VI), Marx notes that the more violent the conflict, the greater the change in patterns of organization in a system, especially its distribution of scarce resources.

In sum, then, the Marxian legacy consists of a set of conflict-oriented assumptions, a particular form of causal analysis that stresses the importance of intervening conditions for accelerating or retarding inexorable conflict processes, and a series of substantive propositions that in greatly altered form are still conspicuous in the current literature. While this heritage is extensive, Marx is not the only intellectual predecessor of modern conflict theory. Later, at the turn of the century, another German sociologist, Georg Simmel, was developing a somewhat different approach to the analysis of conflict phenomena which was to influence another branch of contemporary conflict theorizing.

GEORG SIMMEL AND CONFLICT FUNCTIONALISM

Georg Simmel was committed to developing a body of theoretical statements that captured the *form of basic social processes,* an approach he labeled formal sociology. Primarily on the basis of his own observations, he attempted to make abstractions of the formal properties of processes and events in a wide variety of social contexts. In doing so, Simmel hoped to develop abstract statements that depicted the most fundamental social processes underlying patterns of social organization. Nowhere is his genius in such activity more evident than in a short essay on conflict,[7] which has come to serve as a major source for contemporary conflict theory in sociology.

Much like Marx, Simmel viewed conflict as ubiquitous and inevitable in society; but, unlike Marx, social structure was seen not so much as composed of domination and subjugation, but of various inseparable associative and dissociative processes, which are separable only in analysis:

> The structure may be *sui generis,* its motivation and form being wholly self-consistent, and only in order to be able to describe and understand it, do we put it together, *post factum,* out of two tendencies, one monistic, the other antagonistic.[8]

---

[7] All subsequent references to this work are taken from Georg Simmel, *Conflict and the Web of Group Affiliation,* trans. Kurt H. Wolff (Glencoe, Ill.: Free Press, 1956).

[8] Ibid., p. 23. However, with his typical caution, Simmel warns: "This fact should not lead us to overlook the numerous cases in which contradictory tendencies really co-exist in separation and can thus be recognized at any moment in the over-all situation" (pp. 23–24).

Part of the reason for this emphasis lies in Simmel's "organismic" view of the social world: In displaying formal properties, social processes evidence a systemic character—a notion apparently derived from the organismic doctrines dominating the sociology of his time. This subtle organicism led Simmel to seek out the consequences of conflict for social continuity rather than change:

> Conflict is thus designed to resolve dualisms; it is a way of *achieving some kind of unity*, even if it be through the annihilation of one of the conflicting parties. This is roughly parallel to the fact that it is the most violent *symptom of a disease* which represents the effort of the *organism* to free itself of disturbances and damages caused by them. [Italics added][9]

In apparent contradiction to the harmony implied by this organicism, Simmel postulated an innate "hostile impulse" or a "need for *hating* and *fighting*" among the units of organic wholes, although this instinct was mixed with others for love and affection and was circumscribed by the force of social relationships. Therefore, Simmel viewed conflict as a reflection of more than just conflicts of interest, but also of those arising from hostile instincts. Such instincts can be exacerbated by conflicts of interest, or mitigated by harmonious relations as well as by instincts for love. But in the end, Simmel still viewed one of the ultimate sources of conflict to lie in the innate biological makeup of human actors.

Perhaps in an effort to reconcile his assumptions about the nature of the social organism with notions of hating and fighting instincts, Simmel devoted considerable effort to analyzing the positive consequences of conflict for the maintenance of social wholes and their subunits. In this way, hostile impulses were seen not so much as a contradiction or cancer to the organic whole, but as one of many processes maintaining the body social. Thus, while Simmel recognizes that an overly cooperative, consensual, and integrated society would show "no life process," his analysis of conflict is still loaded in the direction of how conflict promotes solidarity and unification.

It is this aspect of Simmel's work on conflict which reveals an image of social organization decidedly different from that emphasized by Marx:

1. Social relationships occur within systemic contexts that can only be typified as an organic intermingling of associative and dissociative processes.
2. Such processes are a reflection of both the instinctual impulses of actors and the imperatives dictated by various types of social relationships.
3. Conflict processes are therefore a ubiquitous feature of social systems, but they do not necessarily, in all cases, lead to breakdown of the system and/or to social change.
4. In fact, conflict is one of the principal processes operating to preserve the social whole and/or some of its subparts.

---

[9] Ibid., p. 13.

These assumptions are reflected in a large number of specific propositions,[10] which Simmel apparently developed from direct observations of events occurring around him and from readings of historical accounts of conflict. In these propositions, Simmel views conflict as a *variable* that manifests different states of intensity or violence. The polar ends of a variable continuum appear to be "competition" and the "fight," with competition involving the more regulated and parallel strivings of parties toward a mutually exclusive end and with fight denoting the less regulated and more direct combative activities of parties against each other.[11] While he does not elaborate extensively on the variable properties of conflict, or consistently employ his labels, Simmel's distinctions have inspired a long debate among contemporary sociologists on what is, and what is not, conflict.[12] This debate has often degenerated into terminological quibbling, but at its heart is the important issue of clarifying the concepts to be employed in propositions on conflict processes—a theoretical issue that Simmel clearly recognized as crucial.

Simmel's organicism probably was critical in forcing this conceptualization of conflict as a variable phenomenon. Unlike Marx, who saw conflict as ultimately becoming violent and revolutionary and leading to the structural change of the system, Simmel was quite often led to the analysis of the opposite phenomena— less intense and violent conflicts that promoted the solidarity, integration, and orderly change of the system.[13] Yet, within the apparent constraints of his subtle organicism, Simmel enumerated a number of suggestive propositions on the intensity of conflict, that is, the degree of direct action and violence of parties against each other. As with Marx, the full impact of Simmel's analysis on modern theory can be seen more readily when his propositions are stated more formally and abstractly than in his discursive essay. These propositions are listed in Table 5–2.

In Proposition I of Table 5–2, Simmel addresses the question of emotional involvement of the parties to a conflict, hypothesizing that the greater their emotional involvement, the greater the potential for violence. Propositions

---

[10] Simmel was not concerned with developing scientific theory, but rather, he was interested in inducting social forms from interaction processes. This emphasis on forms makes many of Simmel's analytical statements rather easily converted into propositions. It should be emphasized, however, that transforming Simmel's analytical statements into propositions involves the risk of misinterpretation.

[11] Simmel, *Conflict*, p. 58.

[12] For an excellent summary of this debate, see C. F. Fink, "Some Conceptual Difficulties in the Theory of Social Conflict," *Journal of Conflict Resolution* 12 (December 1968): 412–60.

[13] Pierre van de Berge has argued that a dialectical model of conflict is ultimately one where unification, albeit temporary, emerges out of conflict. But, as will be examined extensively in the next chapter, the ontological differences between Marx and Simmel have inspired vastly different theoretical perspectives in contemporary sociology. See Pierre van de Berghe, "Dialectic and Functionalism: Toward a Theoretical Synthesis," *American Sociological Review* 28 (October 1963): 695–705.

TABLE 5–2

Simmel's Key Propositions on Conflict Intensity

I. The greater the degree of emotional involvement of parties to a conflict, the more intense the conflict*
  A. The greater the degree of previous intimacy among parties to a conflict, the greater the emotional involvement†
  B. The greater the degree of previous hostility between parties to a conflict, the greater the emotional involvement‡
  C. The greater the degree of previous jealousy between parties to a conflict, the greater the emotional involvement§
II. The greater the degree of "ingroupness" of parties involved in a conflict, the more intense the conflict‖
III. The greater the degree of respective solidarity of parties to a conflict, the more intense the conflict#
IV. The greater the degree of previous harmony among parties to a conflict, the more intense the conflict**
V. The less isolation and segregation of conflicting parties is allowed by the broader social structure, the more intense the conflict††
VI. The less conflict is simply a means toward an end, but an end in itself, the more intense the conflict‡‡
VII. The more conflict is perceived by participants to transcend individual aims and interests, the more intense the conflict§§

---

*Georg Simmel, *Conflict and the Web of Group Affiliation*, trans. Kurt H. Wolff (Glencoe, Ill.: Free Press, 1956), pp. 38–39.
  † Ibid., pp. 45–46
  ‡ Ibid., p. 48.
  § Ibid., p. 50.
  ‖ Ibid., p. 33.
  # Ibid., p. 49.
  ** Ibid., p. 43.
  †† Ibid., pp. 66–67.
  ‡‡ Ibid., pp. 27–28.
  §§ Ibid., p. 39.

I-A–I-C appear to concern interpersonal conflicts among individuals, emphasizing that emotional arousals stemming from previous intimacy, hostility, and jealousies will increase the intensity of such conflict. In Propositions II–VII, Simmel shifts analysis to conflict among groups rather than individuals. He proposes that the more distinct and identifiable the conflicting groups (II), the greater will be the groups' internal solidarity (III). Further, the likelihood that conflict will involve violence will be greater, the more conflicting groups previously have had harmonious relations (IV), the less conflict groups can be isolated and segregated (V), the more conflict is defined by each group as an end or goal in itself (VI), and the more a conflict is defined by group members to transcend their individual interests (VII).

As is readily apparent, many of these propositions overlap with Marx's, for, much like Marx, Simmel perceives that the cohesive and unified organization of conflict groups (Propositions II and III) whose members are emotionally involved (I) and whose goals are defined as transcending the individuals (VII) will result in violent conflicts. Unlike Marx, Simmel did not view such intense conflicts as necessarily causing the reorganization of the social system. While both Marx and Simmel appear to ask the theoretical question, What are the consequences of conflict for the social system and its conflicting parties? And while both authors view conflict as uniting into cohesive and polarized units the respective conflict groups, they part company when Simmel emphasizes that conflict integrates the broader social system within which the conflict occurs. This concern with the integrative functions of conflict for *both* the parties to the conflict and the social whole as well was probably inevitable in light of the organismic assumptions underlying Simmel's formulation of specific propositions. In Tables 5–3 and 5–4, respectively, the functions of conflict for the parties joined therein and for the body social are summarized.[14]

In Table 5–3, Propositions I–III point to the consequences of conflict for organization of conflict groups. Back in Table 5–2, the nature of group organization and the broader structural context of the conflict were seen to influence the intensity of conflict. Conversely, as the propositions of Table 5–3 now document, Simmel indicates that the intensity of conflict causes changes in the organization of conflict groups, thus promoting different patterns of organization under different conditions. Seemingly, Simmel visualizes a reciprocal feedback process, in which group organization at one point in time determines the intensity of conflict, the intensity subsequently affects group organization, which, in turn, would affect the intensity of further conflict, and so on, until one of the conflicting parties or some third party is able to bring the conflict to a close. In this cyclical feedback process, a high degree of conflict intensity is seen by Simmel to cause the clear demarcation of group boundaries (Proposition I); despotic leadership (II), especially when the group was initially unintegrated; and internal solidarity (III), particularly when a group is small (III-A), when the group is in a minority position (III-B), and when the group is engaged in self-defense (III-C).

In Table 5–4, Simmel indicates some of the functions of conflict for creating varying patterns of system integration under different conditions. In Proposition I, Simmel hypothesizes that in differentiated social systems based upon functional interdependence of parts, mild conflicts will increase the systems' integration (presumably by keeping intense and disruptive conflicts from emerging). In Proposition II, Simmel clarifies and supplements Proposition I by noting that frequent conflicts of a low degree of intensity will allow for the release of hostilities by giving group members a sense of control over their destiny; and, in so doing, frequent and mild conflicts will strengthen integration by keeping hostilities and frustrations from accumulating. In Proposition III, Simmel further

---

[14] Simmel clearly recognized the phenomena of war and revolution and the disruptive changes these could generate, but the weight of his analysis focuses on less intense forms of conflict and on their consequences for stasis, adaptability, and orderly social change.

TABLE 5-3

The Functions of Social Conflict for Respective Parties to Conflict

I. The more intense intergroup hostilities and the more frequent conflict among groups, the less likely group boundaries are to disappear*

II. The more intense the conflict, and the less integrated the group, the more likely despotic centralization of conflict groups†

III. The more intense the conflict, the greater the internal solidarity of conflict groups‡

    A. The more intense the conflict, and the smaller the conflict groups, the greater their internal solidarity§

        1. The more intense the conflict and the smaller the conflict groups, the less tolerance of deviance and dissent in each group‖

    B. The more intense the conflict and the more a group represents a minority position in a system, the more the internal solidarity of the group #

    C. The more intense the conflict and the more a group is engaged in purely self defense, the more the internal solidarity

---

    * Georg Simmel, *Conflict and the Web of Group Affiliation,* trans. Kurt H. Wolff (Glencoe, Ill.: Free Press, 1956), p. 18.
    † Ibid., pp. 87–88; 92–93.
    ‡ Ibid., p. 92.
    § Ibid., p. 96.
    ‖ Ibid., pp. 93–97.
    # Ibid., p. 96.

TABLE 5-4

The Functions of Conflict for the Social Whole

I. The less intense the conflict,* and the more the social whole is based upon functional interdependence,† the more likely is conflict to have integrative consequences for the social whole‡

II. The more frequent and less intense the conflict, the more members of subordinate groups can release hostilities and have a sense of control over their destiny and thereby maintain the integration of the system§

III. The less intense and more frequent the conflict, the more likely the creation of norms to regulate the conflict‖

IV. The greater the hostile relations between groups in a social hierarchy, but the less frequent the open conflict between them, the greater is their internal solidarity and the more likely they are to maintain social distance and thereby preserve the existing social hierarchy #

V. The more prolonged and less intense the conflict between groups of different degrees of power, the more likely they are to regularize power relations

VI. The more intense and prolonged the conflict, the more likely is the formation of coalitions among previously unrelated groups**

VII. The more prolonged the threat of intense conflict between parties, the more enduring the coalitions of each of the respective conflict parties††

---

    * Georg Simmel, *Conflict and the Web of Group Affiliation,* trans. Kurt H. Wolff (Glencoe, Ill.: Free Press, 1956), pp. 34–37.
    † Ibid., pp. 73–75.
    ‡ Ibid., pp. 17–18.
    § Ibid., p. 19.
    ‖ Ibid., p. 26.
    # Coser's interpretation; see Lewis A. Coser, *The Functions of Conflict* (London: Free Press, 1956), pp. 34–35.
    ** Simmel, *Conflict,* pp. 103, 49.
    †† Ibid., p. 104.

indicates how frequent conflicts of low intensity can promote system integration, by becoming institutionalized and hence normatively regulated. In Proposition IV, he postulates that in hierarchically structured systems, where conflict has infrequently erupted, the internal solidarity of potentially conflicting groups increases, but so does their insulation and segregation from each other—thereby promoting the hierarchical basis of system integration. Proposition V denotes that prolonged and mild conflicts among groups of different degrees of power are likely to become institutionalized and regulated by norms (presumably because those in power find the conflict a nuisance and hence in need of regulation, while those without power would find an "all out" conflict potentially destructive and thus in need of regulation). In Proposition VI intense and prolonged conflicts are seen to create coalitions not only among the various parties involved in a conflict but also among those that could be affected by the conflict; thus, conflict is viewed as providing a basis for integration of previously unrelated groups. Finally, in Proposition VII, the more prolonged and intense the threat of conflict, the more likely to endure are the coalitions among those potentially involved.

Looking back on Simmel's major propositions in Tables 5–2, 5–3, and 5–4, they are obviously many gaps, vague references, and perhaps incorrect conclusions to be found. Furthermore, in Tables 5–3 and 5–4, the propositions would seem to dwell excessively on only the positive functions of conflict. While the inverse of each proposition might indicate some of the conditions under which conflict disrupts the "body social," Simmel did not seem concerned with explicating them–preferring instead to buttress his organicism with one-sided functional statements. Despite these difficulties, however, Simmel's scheme is impressive in its suggestiveness. Not only does the substance of each proposition touch upon crucial social processes that need to be explored further, but the form of his analysis—that is, of abstracting from observations and stating the conditions under which events are likely to occur—represents an appropriate model for contemporary theorizing.

THE EMERGENCE OF CONFLICT THEORY: AN OVERVIEW

While both Marx and Simmel viewed conflict as a pervasive and inevitable feature of social systems, their respective assumptions about the nature of society were vastly different: Marx emphasized the divisiveness of conflict; Simmel, the integrative consequences of conflict. These differences are reflected in the types of propositions they chose to develop, with Marx addressing the conditions under which violent conflict would be accelerated and Simmel asking questions about the conditions under which the intensity of conflict might vary. Furthermore, Marx was vitally concerned with the social structural causes of conflict, whereas Simmel tended to concentrate attention on the form and consequences of conflict once it was initiated, while making only vague references to "fighting instincts."

These differences in analytical emphasis are sufficiently great to suggest that taken together they offer a more complete set of theoretical statements about the causes, intensity, and consequences of conflict in social systems. For Marx, the sources of conflict must be sought within the distribution of resources and the conflicts of interest inhering to unequal distribution. For both Marx and Simmel, the intensity of conflict appears to reflect the relative degree of internal solidarity of groups involved in conflict, with both thinkers specifying additional structural conditions of the more inclusive social system that might also influence the intensity of conflict between opposed parties.

Equally intriguing in comparisons of Marx and Simmel are the contradictory propositions that can be uncovered. For example, Simmel argued that the more clear-cut the goals pursued by conflicting parties, the more likely was conflict to be viewed as merely a means to an end, with the result that both parties to a conflict would be motivated to seek compromises and alternative means in an effort to avoid the high costs of intense or violent conflict. On the other hand, Marx argues just the opposite in holding that once a social class recognizes its true interests (hence, has a clear conception of its goals), then violent conflict is highly probable. The divergence of these propositions probably stems from the different assumptions of their authors, for Marx assumes that intense conflict is an inevitable and inexorable feature of social systems and their change, whereas Simmel merely assumes that conflict is simply one process, varying in intensity and consequences, within a social whole. In this particular instance, Simmel may have been more "correct," in that his proposition would seemingly fit the facts of what really happened in labor-management relations in capitalist economic systems, since compromise became typical once labor was organized to pursue specific goals. On the other hand, violent conflict appears to have occurred when labor did not have a clear conception of goals but only a sense of diffuse frustration. Naturally, this argument is open to debate and is not central to the current discussion, since what is of more importance for present purposes is the recognition that by reducing the Marxian and Simmelian propositions to their most generic form, it is possible to compare the overlaps, gaps, and contradictions among them and thereby gain some insight into possible strategies for effecting reformulation.

To some extent, modern conflict theory has attempted to combine the promising features of the schemes of both Marx and Simmel; but, even when this has been done, contemporary theorists have tended to embrace more enthusiastically the assumptions and propositions of either one or the other of these thinkers. Such selectivity has created two dominant contemporary conflict perspectives in sociological theory, each owing its inspiration to either Marx or Simmel: (1)

dialectical conflict theory and (2) conflict functionalism. These perspectives are the ones most often seen as promising a "new" alternative to functional theory in sociology, and hence a more adequate solution to the Hobbesian problem of order: How and why is society possible?

6

Dialectical Conflict Theory: Ralf Dahrendorf

Ralf Dahrendorf has persistently argued that the Parsonian scheme, and functionalism in general, offers an overly consensual, integrated, and static vision of society. While society is seen as having "two faces"—one of consensus, the other of conflict—Dahrendorf has maintained that it is time to begin analysis of the "ugly face" of society and abandon the utopian image of society created by functionalism. To leave utopia, Dahrendorf offers the following advice:

> Concentrate in the future not only on concrete problems but on such problems as involve explanations in terms of constraint, conflict, and change. This second face of society may aesthetically be rather less pleasing than the social system—but, if all sociology had to offer were an easy escape to Utopian tranquility, it would hardly be worth our efforts."[1]

To escape out of utopia therefore requires that a one-sided conflict model be substituted for the one-sided functional model. While this conflict perspective is not considered by Dahrendorf to be the only face of society,[2] it is a necessary supplement that will make amends for the past inadequacies of functional theory. The model that emerges from this theoretical calling is a dialectical-conflict

---

[1] Ralf Dahrendorf, "Out of Utopia: Toward a Reorientation of Sociological Analysis, "*American Journal of Sociology* 64 (September 1958): 127.

[2] As Dahrendorf emphasizes: "I do not intend to fall victim to the mistake of many structural-functional theorists and advance for the conflict model a claim to comprehensive and exclusive applicability . . . it may well be that in a philosophical sense, society has two faces of equal reality: one of stability, harmony, and consensus and one of change, conflict, and constraint" (ibid.). Such disclaimers are, in reality, justifications for arguing for the primacy of conflict in society. By claiming that functionalists are one-sided, it becomes fair game to be equally one-sided in order to "balance" past one-sidedness.

perspective, which, Dahrendorf claims, has more correspondence to what occurs in the factual world than functionalism and is therefore the only path out of utopia. In his analysis, Dahrendorf is careful to note that processes other than conflict are evident in social systems and that even the conflict phenomena he proposes to examine are not the only kinds of conflict in societies. Having said this, however, Dahrenforf then launches into an analysis that appears to contradict these qualifications, for there is a persistent hint that the conflict model presented represents a more comprehensive "theory" of society, providing a more adequate solution to the Hobbesian problem of order.

DAHRENDORF'S IMAGE OF THE SOCIAL ORDER[3]

For Dahrendorf, institutionalization involves the creation of "imperatively coordinated associations" (hereafter referred to as ICAs), which, in terms of criteria not specified, represent a distinguishable organization of roles. This organization is characterized by power relationships, with some clusters of roles having power to extract conformity from others. While Dahrendorf is somewhat vague on the point, it appears that *any* social unit—from a small group or formal organization to a community or an entire society—can be considered for analytical purposes an ICA if an organization of roles displaying power differentials exists. Furthermore, while power denotes the coercion of some by others, these power relations in ICAs tend to become legitimated and can therefore be viewed as *authority* relations in which some positions have the "accepted" or "normative right" to dominate others.[4] The "social order" is thus conceived by Dahrendorf to be maintained by processes creating authority relations in the various types of ICAs existing throughout all layers of social systems.

At the same time, however, power and authority are the scare resources over which subgroups within a designated ICA compete and fight and are thereby the major sources of conflict and change in these institutionalized patterns. This conflict is ultimately a reflection of where clusters of roles in an ICA stand in relation to authority, since the "objective interests" inhering to any role is a direct function of whether that role possesses authority and power over other roles. However, even though roles in ICAs possess varying degrees of authority, any

---

[3] There are a number of contemporary dialectical conflict models that could be discussed in this chapter. For example, John Rex (*Key Issues in Sociological Theory* [London: Routledge & Kegan Paul, 1961]) has presented a model similar to Dahrendorf's. But since Dahrendorf is the most conspicuous conflict theorist in contemporary sociology, it is considered best to examine his model intensely rather than spread analysis across several dialectical-conflict models.

[4] Ralf Dahrendorf, "Toward a Theory of Social Conflict," *Journal of Conflict Resolution* 2 (June 1958): 170–83; Ralf Dahrendorf, *Class and Class Conflict in Industrial Society* (Stanford, Calif.: Stanford University Press, 1959): 168–69; Ralf Dahrendorf, *Gesellschaft un Freiheit* (Munich: R. Piper, 1961); Ralf Dahrendorf, *Essays in the Theory of Society* (Stanford, Calif.: Stanford University Press, 1967).

particular ICA can be typified in terms of just two basic types of roles, ruling and ruled, with the ruling clusters of roles having an "interest" in preserving the status quo and the ruled clusters having an "interest" in redistributing power, or authority. Under certain specified conditions, awareness of these contradictory interests increases, with the result that ICAs polarize into two conflict groups, each now aware of its objective interests, which then engage in a contest over authority. The "resolution" of this contest or conflict involves the redistribution of authority in the ICA, thus making conflict the source of social change in social systems. In turn, the redistribution of authority represents the institutionalization of a new cluster of ruling and ruled roles, which under certain conditions polarizes into two interest groups that initiate another contest for authority. Social reality is thus typified in terms of this unending cycle of conflict over authority within the various types of ICAs comprising a social system. Sometimes the conflicts within diverse ICAs in a society overlap, leading to major conflicts cutting across large segments of the society, while, at other times and under different conditions, these conflicts are confined to a particular ICA.

As is clearly acknowledged by Dahrendorf, this image of social organization represents a revision of Marx's portrayal of social reality:

1. Social systems are seen by both Dahrendorf and Marx as in a continual state of conflict.
2. Such conflict is presumed by both authors to be generated by the opposed interests that inevitably inhere in the social structure of society.
3. Opposed interests are viewed by both Marx and Dahrendorf as reflections of differences in the distribution of power among dominant and subjugated groups.
4. Interests are seen by both as tending to polarize into two conflict groups.
5. For both, conflict is dialectical, with resolution of one conflict creating a new set of opposed interests, which, under certain conditions, will generate further conflict.
6. Social change is thus seen by both as a ubiquitous feature of social systems and the result of inevitable conflict dialectics within various types of institutionalized patterns.

This image of institutionalization as a cyclical or dialectic process has led Dahrendorf, much like Marx before him, into the analysis of only certain key causal relations. (1) Conflict is assumed to be an inexorable process arising out of opposing forces within social structural arrangements; (2) such conflict is accelerated or retarded by a series of intervening structural conditions or variables; (3) conflict "resolution" at one point in time creates a structural situation, which, under specifiable conditions, inevitably leads to further conflict among opposed forces.

For Marx, the source of conflict ultimately lay beneath cultural values and institutional arrangements, which represented edifices constructed by those with power. In reality, the dynamics of a society are found in society's "substructure," where the differential distribution of property and power inevitably initiates a sequence of events leading, under specifiable conditions, to revolutionary class conflict. While borrowing much of Marx's rhetoric about power and coercion in social systems, Dahrendorf actually ends up positing a much different source of conflict: the institutionalized authority relations of ICAs. Such a position is much different from that of Marx, who viewed such authority relations as simply a "superstructure" erected by the dominant classes, which, in the long run, would be destroyed by the conflict dynamics occurring below institutional arrangements. While Dahrendorf acknowledges that authority relations are imposed by the dominant groups in ICAs, and frequently makes reference to such things as "factual substrates," the source of conflict becomes, upon close examination, the legitimated authority role relations of ICAs. This drift away from Marx's emphasis on the institutional "substructure" forces Dahrendorf's analysis to seek the source of conflict in those very same relations that integrate, albeit temporarily, an ICA. By itself, this shift in emphasis is perhaps desirable, since Dahrendorf clearly recognizes that not all power is a reflection of property ownership—a fact Marx's polemics tended to underemphasize. But as will become evident, to view power as only authority can lead to analytical problems that are easily as severe as those encountered in the polemical extremes of Marx's model.

Although they emphasize different sources of conflict, the models of both Dahrendorf and Marx reveal a similar causal chain of events leading to conflict and reorganization of social structure: Relations of domination and subjugation lead to the "objective" opposition of interests; awareness or consciousness by the subjugated of this inherent opposition of interests occurs under certain specifiable conditions; under other conditions this new-found awareness leads to the political organization and then polarization of subjugated groups, who then join in conflict with the dominant group; the outcome of the conflict will usher in a new pattern of social organization; this new pattern of social organization will have within it relations of domination and subjugation which set off another sequence of events leading to conflict and then change in patterns of social organization.

The intervening conditions affecting these processes are outlined by both Marx and Dahrendorf only with respect to the formation of awareness of opposed interests by the subjugated, the politicization and polarization of the subjugated into a conflict group, and the outcome of the conflict. The intervening conditions under which institutionalized patterns generate dominant and subjugated groups and the conditions under which these can be typified as having opposed interests remain unspecified—apparently because they are in the nature of institutionaliza-tion, or ICAs, and hence do not have to be explained.

In Figure 6–1, an attempt is made to outline the causal imagey of Marx and Dahrendorf. At the top of the figure are Marx's analytical categories, stated in their most abstract form. The other two rows specify the empirical categories of Marx and Dahrendorf, respectively. Separate analytical categories for the Dahrendorf model are not enumerated because they are the same as those in the Marxian model. As is clear, the empirical categories of the Dahrendorf scheme differ greatly from those of Marx. But the form of analysis is much the same, since each considers as nonproblematic and not in need of causal analysis the empirical conditions of social organization, the transformation of this organi-zation into relations of domination and subjugation, and the creation of opposed interests. The causal analysis for both Marx and Dahrendorf begins with an elaboration of the conditions leading to growing class consciousness (Marx) or awareness among quasi groups (Dahrendorf) of their objective interests; then analysis shifts to the creation of a politicized class "for itself" (Marx) or a true "conflict group" (Dahrendorf); and finally, emphasis focuses on the emergence of conflict between polarized and politicized classes (Marx) or conflict groups (Dahrendorf).

CRITICISMS OF THE DIALECTICAL CONFLICT MODEL

Problems in the Causal Analysis

The most conspicuous criticism of Dahrendorf's causal imagery comes from Peter Weingart,[5] who has argued that in deviating from Marx's conception of the "substructure" of opposed interests existing below the cultural and institu-tional edifices of the ruling classes, Dahrendorf forfeits a genuine causal analysis of conflict, and therefore of how patterns of social organization are changed. This criticism asks questions reminiscent of Dahrendorf's portrayal of Parsonian func-tionalism: How is it that conflict emerges from legitimated authority relations among roles in an ICA? How is it that the same structure that generates integra-tion also generates conflict? Although for the Marxian scheme there are empirical problems, the causal analysis does not pose an analytical problem, since the source of conflict—the opposition of economic interests— is clearly distinguished from the institutional and cultural arrangements maintaining a temporary order—the societal superstructure. Dahrendorf, however, has failed to make explicit this distinction and thus falls into the very analytical trap he has imputed to func-

---

    [5] Peter Weingart, "Beyond Parsons? A Critique of Ralf Dahrendorf's Conflict Theory," *Social Forces* 48 (December 1969): 151–65.

Figure 6–1

The Dialectical Causal Imagery

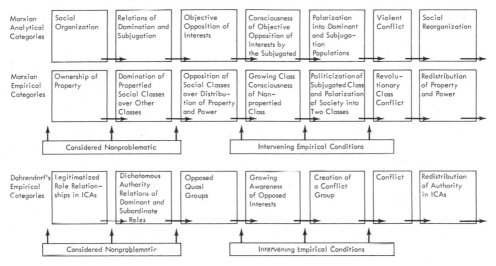

tional theory: Change inducing conflict must mysteriously arise from the legitimated relations of the social system.

In an attempt to escape this analytical trap, the causal analysis often becomes confusing. One tack Dahrendorf employs is to assert that many roles also have a nonintegrative aspect, because they represent fundamentally opposed interests of their incumbents. These opposed interests are reflected in role conflict, which seemingly reduces the issues of role strain and conflict to dilemmas created by objectively opposed interests—surely a dubious assertion that is correct only some of the time. In equating interests and role expectations, Dahrendorf would seemingly have to hypothesize that all institutionalized patterns, or ICAs, display two mutually contradictory sets of role expectations—one to obey, the other to revolt—and that actors must "decide" which set they will follow. Presumably, actors "wish" to realize their "objective interests" and hence revolt against the role expectations imposed upon them by the dominant group. This tack forces the Dahrendorf model to reduce the origins of conflict to the wishes, wills, and sentiments of a person or group[6]—a reductionist imperative that Dahrendorf would reject, but one which his causal imagery would seemingly dictate.

Many of these problems might be overcome if Dahrendorf had provided a series of existence and relational statements that would indicate the conditions under which legitimatized role relationships in ICAs create dichotomous au-

---

[6] Ibid., p. 158.

thority relations of domination and subjugation. To simply assume that this is the case is to avoid the critical causal link in his analytical scheme. These kinds of necessary propositions—or, as Dahrendorf describes them, "intervening empirical conditions"—are a necessary part of the model, for without them it is unclear how the types of authority, coercion, and domination which lead to conflict ever emerge in the first place. Assuming that they just emerge, or are an endemic part of social structure, is to define away the theoretically important question about what types of authority in what types of ICAs lead to what types of domination and subjugation, which, in turn, lead to what types of opposed interests and what types of conflict.[7] These are all phenomena that must be conceptualized as variables and incorporated into the causal chains of the dialectical-conflict model. Referring back to Figure 6–1, this task would involve stating the "intervening empirical conditions" at each juncture of all of Dahrendorf's empirical categories. What is now considered "nonproblematic" would become as problematic as subsequent empirical conditions.

Initiating this task is difficult, but to do so would enable Dahrendorf to avoid some of the more standard criticisms of his causal imagery:[8] (1) Conflict not only causes change of social structure, but changes of structure also cause conflict (under conditions that need to be specified); (2) not all conflict leads to change (under conditions that need to be specified in greater detail than Simmel's initial analysis); and (3) conflict can inhibit change (again, under conditions that need to be specified). Unless these conditions are part of the causal imagery, conflict theory merely states the rather obvious fact that change occurs, without answering the theoretical question of *why, when,* and *where* does such change occur?

Despite the vagueness of Dahrendorf's causal analysis, he has attempted to state systematically the "intervening empirical conditions" that cause "quasi groups" to become "conflict groups," as well as the conditions affecting the intensity (involvement of group members) and violence (degree of regulation) of the conflict and the degree and the rate of structural change caused by conflict. More formally, Dahrendorf outlines three types of intervening empirical conditions: (1) "conditions of organization" which affect the transformation of latent quasi groups into manifest conflict groups; (2) "conditions of conflict" which determine the form and intensity of conflict; and (3) "conditions of structural change" which influence the kind, speed, and the depth of the changes in social structure.[9]

Thus, the explicitly acknowledged variables in the theoretical scheme are the

[7] Alvin Boskoff, *The Mosaic of Sociological Theory* (New York: Thomas Y. Crowell Co., 1972), p. 83.

[8] For a convenient summary of these, see Percy Cohen, *Modern Sociological Theory* (New York: Basic Books, 1968), pp. 183–91.

[9] Dahrendorf, "Toward a Theory of Social Conflict."

(1) degree of conflict-group formation, (2) the degree of intensity of the conflict; (3) the degree of violence of the conflict; (4) the degree of change of social structure; and (5) the rate of such change. It is significant, for criticisms to be delineated later, that concepts such as ICAs, legitimacy, authority, coercion, domination, and subjugation are not *explicitly* characterized as variables requiring statements on the conditions affecting their variability. Rather, these concepts are simply defined and interrelated to each other in terms of definitional overlap or stated as assumptions about the nature of social reality.

For those phenomena that are conceptualized as variables, Dahrendorf's propositions[10] appear to be an elaboration of those developed by Marx (see Table 5–1), as can be seen in Table 6–1.

These propositions follow Marx's substantive and formal legacy and represent, in terms of explicitness, considerable improvement over functional formulations, in which there is a noticeable absence of systematically interrelated propositions. Furthermore, Dahrendorf is to be commended for actually attempting to place the propositions in a reasonably systematic format—a difficult task too infrequently performed by theorists in sociology. However, even though this propositional inventory represents a promising attempt, a number of criticisms have been leveled against the scheme and should be summarized here with an eye toward the improvements they suggest.

One of the most obvious criticisms of the Dahrendorf perspective is the failure to visualize crucial concepts as *variables*. Most conspicuous of these are the concepts of authority, domination-subjugation, and interest. Since it is from legitimated authority relations that conflict ultimately springs, it is somewhat surprising that this concept is not viewed as a variable, varying at a minimum in terms of such properties as intensity, scope, and legitimacy. Rather Dahrendorf has chosen to define away the problem:

> "No attempt will be made in this study to develop a typology of authority. But it is assumed throughout that the existence of domination and subjection is a common feature of all possible types of authority and, indeed, of all possible types of association and organization."[11]

A typology of authority would give some indication of the variable states of authority and related concepts—a fact Dahrendorf appears content to ignore by simply arguing that authority implies domination and subjugation, which in turn gives him the structural dichotomy necessary for his dialectical theory of conflicting interests. He refuses to speculate on *what types* of authority displaying *what*

---

[10] The propositions listed below differ from a list provided by Dahrendorf, *Class and Class Conflict*, pp. 239–40 in two respects: (1) they are phrased consistently as statements of co-variance and (2) they are phrased somewhat more abstractly without reference to "class," which in this particular work was Dahrendorf's primary concern.

[11] Ibid., p. 169.

TABLE 6–1

The Propositions of the Dahrendorf Scheme

I. The more members of quasi groups in ICAs can become aware of their objective interests and form a conflict group, the more likely is conflict to occur

   A. The more the "technical" conditions of organization can be met, the more likely is the formation of a conflict group

      1. The more a leadership cadre among quasi groups can be developed, the more likely are the "technical" conditions of organization to be met

      2. The more a codified idea system, or charter, can be developed, the more likely are the "technical" conditions of organization to be met

   B. The more the "political" conditions of organization can be met, the more likely is the formation of a conflict group

      1. The more the dominant groups permit organization of opposed interests, the more likely are the "political" conditions of organization to be met

   C. The more the "social" conditions of organization can be met, the more likely is the formation of a conflict group

      1. The more opportunity for members of quasi groups to communicate, the more likely are the "social" conditions of organization to be met

      2. The more recruiting is permitted by structural arrangements (such as propinquity), the more likely are the "social" conditions of organization to be met

II. The more the "technical," "political," and "social" conditions of organization are met, the more intense is the conflict

III. The more the distribution of authority and other rewards are associated with each other (superimposed), the more intense is the conflict

IV. The less the mobility between super- and subordinate groups, the more intense is the conflict

V. The less the "technical," "political," and "social" conditions of organization are met, the more violent is the conflict

VI. The more the deprivations of the subjugated in the distribution of rewards shifts from an absolute to relative basis, the more violent is the conflict

VII. The less the ability of conflict groups to develop regulatory agreements, the more violent is the conflict

VIII. The more intense the conflict, the more structural change and reorganization it will generate

IX. The more violent the conflict, the greater is the rate of structural change and reorganization

---

variable states lead to *what types of variations* in domination and subjugation, which in turn cause *what variable types* of opposed interests leading to *what variable types* of conflict groups. Thus, Dahrendorf links only by assumption and definition crucial variables that causally influence each other as well as the more explicit variables of his scheme: the degree of conflict, the degree of intensity of conflict, the degree of violence in conflict, the degree of change, and the rate of change. In fact, it is likely that these unstated variable properties of authority, domination, and interests have as much influence on the explicit variables in the scheme as the "intervening empirical conditions" Dahrendorf chooses to emphasize. Furthermore, as noted earlier, when viewed as variables, the concepts of authority, domination-subjugation, and interests require their own "intervening empirical conditions." These conditions may in turn influence other, subsequent intervening conditions in much the same way as the "conditions of organization" also influence the subsequent intensity and violence of conflict in the scheme.

Inattention to these questions greatly reduces the predictive value of the Dahrendorf model, but it does more: It reduces much of the model to a tautology. Conflict groups would appear to follow from the definition of ICAs as dichotomous authority structures composed of opposed interests. This tautology is made more bearable by Dahrendorf's insertion of the notion of "quasi groups" (members of ICAs not yet aware of the true interests), which, under the "conditions of organization," lead to true conflict-group formation. But this distinction simply delays the question of how opposed quasi groups emerged, to which Dahrendorf should answer: by definition and assumption. Instead, he chooses to answer: "As to the . . . statement, the one with the dichotomy of authority positions in imperatively coordinated associations, it is not, I suggest, either an assumption or an empirical hypothesis, but an analytical statement." Just what an "analytical statement" is in this context is left vague, but it appears to be a way to avoid concluding that a major portion of his propositions about conflict-group formation are little more than rephrasings of his definitions and assumptions about the nature of ICAs and society.

These criticisms suggest an obvious solution: to conceptualize ICAs, legitimacy, authority, domination-subjugation, and interests as variable phenomena and to attempt a statement of the "intervening empirical conditions" influencing their variability. Expanding the propositional inventory in this way would reduce the vagueness of the causal imagery and make less tautologous the specific propositions. Such an alteration would also cut down on the rather protracted set of dialectical assumptions—which are of dubious isomorphism with all of reality—and address a theoretical (rather than philosophical) question: Under what conditions do ICAs create legitimated authority relations that generate clear relations of domination and subjugation leading to strongly opposed interests? Coupled with Dahrendorf's tentative answer to the subsequent question —Under what conditions do conflict groups emerge and cause what kinds of conflict and change?—these additional propositions, and their inverse, would provide a significant theoretical advance in answering the ultimate theoretical question of "how and why society is possible."

Methodological Problems

Dahrendorf is careful to provide formal definitions of major concepts and to suggest operational clues about their application in concrete empirical settings, as is evident in his analysis of class conflict in industrial societies.[12] Furthermore,

---

[12] Ibid., pp. 241–318.

the incorporation of at least *some* concepts into an explicit propositional inventory—albeit an incomplete one—makes the scheme *appear* more testable and amenable to refutation.

However, a number of methodological problems remain, one of which concerns the extremely general definitions given to concepts. While these definitions are stated formally, they are often so general that they can be used in an *ad hoc* and ex post facto fashion to apply to such a wide variety of phenomena that their current utility for the development and testing of theory can be questioned. For example, power, legitimacy, authority, interests, domination, and even conflict are defined so broadly that instances of these concepts can be found in almost any empirical situation that Dahrendorf desires—a strategy that insures confirmation of his assumptions about the nature of social life, but which inhibits empirical investigation of these assumptions. This problem was emphasized in an earlier discussion in which it was noted that Dahrendorf appeared reluctant to view crucial concepts, such as authority and domination, as variables. If these concepts were so conceptualized, it would be easier for investigators to put empirical "handles" on them, since definitional statements about their variable states would specify more precisely the phenomena denoted by the concept. Dahrendorf rarely does this service, preferring to avoid typologies; and even when concepts are defined as variables, Dahrendorf avoids the issue with such statements as the following: "The intensity of class conflict varies on a scale (from 0 to 1)." Coupled with the formal definition of conflict intensity as the "energy expenditure and degree of involvement of conflicting parties," empirical investigators are given few operational guidelines about how such a concept might be measured. Were these definitions supplemented with, at a minimum, a few examples of prominent points along the "0 to 1" scale, then the concepts and propositions of the scheme would be more amenable to empirical investigation. As the definitions stand now, Dahrendorf does the very thing for which he has so resoundingly criticized Parsons: He uses concepts in an *ad hoc* and ex post facto fashion to interpret past events in such a way that they confirm the overall scheme. More attention by Dahrendorf to providing operational definitions would give the concepts as incorporated into propositions a priori predictive power of future events—a more fruitful theoretical enterprise.

Another related methodological problem with the scheme stems from the tautologous character of the entire theoretical perspective. To the extent that the propositions of the scheme are true more by definition than derivation, then the entire theoretical scheme is not refutable—even in principle—and hence is of little use in the development of scientific theory. As long as dichotomous authority relations of domination-subjugation leading to objectively opposed interests are part of the definition of social reality, it is difficult to see how the formation of conflict groups and emergence of open conflict follows other than by definition—despite the scientific appearance of specific propositions about "intervening empirical conditions" that "cause" such conflict to occur. As noted earlier, this danger of tautology can be corrected by conceptualizing as variables such central concepts as legitimacy, authority, domination-subjugation, and interests and by providing a tentative list of "intervening empirical conditions" affecting their variability.

In sum, then, the Dahrendorf scheme presents a number of problems for empirical investigators. Such a statement can be made for almost all theoretical perspectives in sociology and by itself is not a unique indictment. For the Dahrendorf scheme, however, it appears that methodological problems could be minimized with just a little additional work. To the extent that the suggested corrections are made, it is likely that the dialectical-conflict perspective will offer a fruitful strategy for developing sociological theory.

FROM UTOPIA TO WHERE? A CONCLUDING COMMENT

As was emphasized at the beginning of this chapter, Dahrendorf has been one of the most harsh critics of functional forms of theorizing, likening them to an ideological utopia. In order to set sociological theorizing on the road "out of utopia," Dahrendorf has felt compelled to delineate a dialectical-conflict scheme, which presumably mirrors more accurately than Parsonian functionalism the "real character" of the social world. In so doing, Dahrendorf would view his theoretical perspective and strategy as providing a more adequate set of theoretical guidelines for resolving the Hobbesian problem of order: How and why is society possible? And under that conditions are various patterns of organization likely to be created, maintained, and changed?

What is curious about Dahrendorf's "solution" to the "problem of order" is that, upon close examination, it appears quite similar to that he has imputed to Parsonian functionalism.[13] For example, a number of commentators[14] have noted that both Parsons and Dahrendorf view the social world in terms of institutionalized patterns—for Parsons, the "social systems"; for Dahrendorf, "imperatively coordinated associations." Both view societies as composed of subsystems involving the organization of roles in terms of legitimate normative prescriptions. For Dahrendorf, these legitimated normative patterns reflect power differentials in a system; and, despite his rhetoric about the "coercive" nature of these relations, this vision of power is remarkably similar to Parsons's conception of power as the legitimate right of some status roles to regulate the expectations attendant upon other statuses.[15] Furthermore, in Dahrendorf's

---

[13] For the best of these critiques, see Weingart, "Beyond Parsons."

[14] Ibid.; Pierre L. van den Berghe, "Dialectic and Functionalism: Toward a Theoretical Synthesis," *American Sociological Review* 28 (October) 1963): 695–705.

[15] For example, see Talcott Parsons and Edward Shils, eds., *Toward a General Theory of Action* (New York: Harper & Row, 1962), pp. 197–205.

model, deviation from the norms established by them will lead dominant groups to attempt to employ negative sanctions—a position that is very close to Parsons's view that power exists to correct for deviations within a system.[16]

The apparent difference in Dahrendorf's and Parsons's emphasis with respect to the "functions" of power in "social systems" (or ICAs) is that Dahrendorf argues explicitly that power differentials cause *both* integration (through legitimated authority relations) and disintegration (through the persistence of opposed interests). However, to state that conflict emerges out of legitimated authority is nothing more than to state, a priori, that opposed interests exist and cause conflict. The emergence of conflict follows from vague assumptions about such processes as the "inner dialectic of power and authority" and the "historical function of authority,"[17] rather than from carefully documented causal sequences. Thus, the genesis of conflict in Dahrendorf's own model remains as unexplained as it does in his portrayal of the inadequacies of the functional utopia, primarily because its emergence is set against a background of unexplained conceptions of "system" norms and legitimated authority.[18]

Dahrendorf's problem in explaining why and how conflict groups can emerge from a legitimated authority structure is partly a reflection of his hidden assumptions of "functional requisites." In a subtle and yet consistent fashion, he assumes that authority is a functional requisite for system integration and that the conflict that somehow emerges from authority relations is a functional requisite for social change. The "purpose and the consequence," or "the historical function of authority," is to generate conflict, and thereby, presumably, maintain the vitality of social systems. From this notion of the requisite for change, it is all too easy to assert that conflict exists to meet the system's "needs" for change—an illegitimate teleology that transforms Marx's teleological assumption that cycles of dialectical change are necessary to create the "communist" utopia.

More fundamentally, however, Dahrendorf's inability to explain how conflict and change emerge stems from his inability to address the problem of order seriously: How and why is the organization of ICAs possible? To assert that they are organized in terms of power and authority defines away the problem of how, why, and through what processes the institutionalized patterns generating both integration and conflict come to exist. Parsons's analysis does attempt—however inadequately— to account for how institutionalized patterns, or "social systems," become organized: Through actors adjusting their various orientations, normative prescriptions emerge which affect the subsequent organization of action; such organization is maintained by various mechanisms of social control—interper-

---

16 Ibid., p. 230.
17 Weingart, "Beyond Parsons," p. 161.
18 Boskoff, "Mosaic of Sociological Theory," pp. 82–83.

sonal sanctions, ritual activity, safety-valve structures, role segregation, and, on some occasions, power—and mechanisms of socialization—the internalization of relevant values and the acquisition of critical interpersonal skills. Quite naturally, because of his commitment to developing "systems of concepts" instead of formats of propositions, Parsons gives only a vague clue about the variables involved in the process of institutionalization by which the types of opposed interests that lead to the organization of conflict groups and social change are created. However, Parsons at least attempts to conceptualize—albeit inadequately—the variables involved in creating and maintaining the very social order that Dahrendorf glosses over in his formulation of the ICA concept. Yet, it is from the institutionalized relations in ICAs that conflict-ridden cycles of change are supposed to emerge. Asserting one's way out of utopia, as Dahrendorf prefers to do, will not obviate the fundamental theoretical question facing sociological theory: How is society, in all its varied and changing forms, possible?

In sum, then, the critics would contend that Dahrendorf has used the rhetoric of "coercion," "dialectics," "domination and subjugation" and "conflict" to mask a vision of social reality which is close to the utopian image he has imputed to Parsons's work. In Dahrendorf's ICA is Parsons's "social system"; in his concepts of roles and authority is Parsons's concern with social control; in his portrayal of conflict, the origin of conflict is just as unclear as he assumes it to be in Parsons's work; and even in the analysis of social change, conflict is considered, in a way reminiscent of Parsons, to meet the functional need for change. One extreme conclusion to be drawn from these facts is that little progress has been made on the road out of utopia.

7

Conflict Functionalism:
Lewis A. Coser

As the criticisms of functionalism began to look much the same—berating Parsons and others for viewing society as overly institutionalized and equilibrating—the conflict schemes offered as alternatives revealed considerable diversity. The divergence in conflict theory is particularly evident when the conflict functionalism of Lewis Coser is compared with Ralf Dahrendorf's dialectical-conflict perspective. Although Coser has consistently criticized Parsonian functionalism for its failure to address the issue of conflict, he has also been sharply critical of Dahrendorf for underemphasizing the positive functions of conflict for maintaining social systems. This two-pronged indictment has allowed Coser to formulate a theoretical scheme that can supplement both functional and dialectical-conflict forms of theorizing.

In his first major work on conflict,[1] Coser launched what was to become the typical polemic against functionalism: Conflict is not given sufficient attention, with related phenomena such as deviance and dissent too easily viewed as "pathological" for the equilibrium of the social system. In his concern for delineating a system of concepts denoting how the process of institutionalization resolves the "problem of order," Parsons has come to underemphasize conflict in his formal analytical works, seemingly viewing conflict as a "disease" that needs to be "treated" by the "mechanisms" of the "body social."[2] From this interpretation of Parsonian functionalism, it was then a rather simple matter to assert the need for balancing the assumed one-sidedness of Parsonian functionalism with

---

[1] Lewis A. Coser, *The Functions of Social Conflict* (London: Free Press of Glencoe, 1956).
[2] Ibid., pp. 22–23.

another kind of analytical one-sidedness focusing on conflict phenomena. Apparently such analytical compensation was carried out for well over a decade, since after the tenth anniversary of his first polemic Coser was moved to reassert his earlier claim that it was "high time to tilt the scale in the direction of greater attention to social conflict."[3]

While Coser has consistently maintained, much like Dahrendorf, that functional theorizing "has too often neglected the dimensions of power and interest,"[4] he has not followed either Marx's or Dahrendorf's emphasis on the disruptive consequences of violent conflict. On the contrary, he has tended to correct for what he views as Dahrendorf's analytical excesses by emphasizing primarily the integrative and "adaptability" functions of conflict for social systems. Thus, in effect, Coser has been able to justify his efforts through criticism of functionalism for ignoring conflict, and of conflict theory for underemphasizing the functions of conflict. In so doing, Coser has provided a somewhat unique "solution" to the problem of order, for, in a vein similar to Georg Simmel, even open conflict is seen, under certain conditions, as maintaining the vitality and flexibility of institutionalized patterns of social organization.[5]

IMAGES OF SOCIAL ORGANIZATION

To the extent that Émile Durkheim can be considered one of the fathers of functionalism, it is significant that Coser has devoted a critical essay to Durkheim's image of social reality.[6] Most particularly, Durkheim is viewed as taking a conservative orientation to the study of society, an orientation that "prevented him from taking due cognizance of a variety of societal processes, among which social conflict is the most conspicuous." Furthermore, this abiding conservatism forced Durkheim to view crises such as violence and dissent as deviant and pathological to the social equilibrium, rather than as opportunities for construc-

---

[3] Lewis A. Coser, "Some Social Functions of Violence," *Annals of the American Academy of Political and Social Science* 364 (March 1966): 10.

[4] Lewis A. Coser, *Continuities in the Study of Social Conflict* (New York: Free Press, 1967), p. 141.

[5] A listing of some of Coser's prominent works, to be utilized in subsequent analysis reveals the functional flavor of his conflict perspective: Coser, *Functions of Social Conflict;* Coser, "Some Social Functions of Violence"; Lewis A. Coser, "Some Functions of Deviant Behavior and Normative Flexibility," *American Journal of Sociology* 68 (September 1962): 172–81; and "The Functions of Dissent," in *The Dynamics of Dissent* (New York: Grune & Stratton, 1968), pp. 158–70. Other prominent works with less revealing titles, but critical substance, include: "Social Conflict and the Theory of Social Change," *British Journal of Sociology* 8 (September 1957): 197–207; "Violence and the Social Structure" in *Science and Psychoanalysis,* ed. J. Masserman, vol. 7 (New York: Grune & Stratton, 1963), pp. 30–42. These and other essays are collected in Coser's *Continuities in the Study of Social Conflict.*

[6] Lewis Coser, "Durkheim's Conservatism and Its Implications for His Sociological Theory," in *Émile Durkheim, 1858–1917: A Collection of Essays,* ed. K. H. Wolff (Columbus: Ohio State University Press, 1960) (also reprinted in Coser's *Continuities,* pp. 153–80).

tive social changes. While Coser appears intent on rejecting the organicism of Durkheim's sociology, his own work is filled with organismic analogies. For example, in describing the "functions of violence"[7] Coser likens violence to pain in the human body, since both can serve as a danger signal that allows the "body social" to readjust itself. To take another example, in his analysis of the "functions of dissent"[8] Coser rejects the notion that dissent is explainable in terms of individual "sickness" and embraces the assumption that "dissent may more readily be explained as a reaction to what is perceived as a sickness in the body social." This form of analogizing does not necessarily reduce the power of Coser's analysis, but it does reveal that he has not rejected organicism. Apparently, Coser has felt compelled to criticize Durkheim's organicism because it did not allow the analysis of conflict as a process that could promote the further adaptation and integration of the "body social."[9]

In rejecting the analytical constraints of Durkheim's analogizing, Coser was led to embrace Georg Simmel's organicism (see chapter 5). For now, conflict can be viewed as a process that can, under certain conditions, "function" to maintain the "body social" or some of its vital parts. From this vantage point, Coser has developed an image of society that stresses:

1. The social world can be viewed as a system of variously interrelated parts.
2. All social systems reveal imbalances, tensions, and conflicts of interests among variously interrelated parts.
3. Processes within and between the system's constituent parts operate under different conditions to maintain, change, and increase or decrease a system's integration and "adaptability."
4. Many processes, such as violence, dissent, deviance, and conflict, which are typically viewed as disruptive to the system can also be viewed, under specifiable conditions, as strengthening the system's basis of integration as well as its "adaptability" to the environment.

It is from these assumptions that Coser has developed a rather extensive set of propositions about the functions (and to a limited extent the dysfunctions) of conflict for social systems. While Coser does offer some propositions about the conditions under which conflict leads to disruption and malintegration of social systems, the main thrust of his analysis revolves around the sorting out the causal chains involved in how conflict maintains or reestablishes system integra-

---

[7] Coser, "Some Functions of Violence," pp. 12–13.

[8] Coser, "The Functions of Dissent," pp. 159–60.

[9] It is of interest to note that such an emphasis on the "positive functions" of conflict could be construed as the pinnacle of conservative ideology—surpassing that attributed to Parsons. Even conflict promotes integration rather than disruption, malintegration, and change. Such a society, as Dahrendorf would argue, no longer has an ugly face and is as utopian as that of Parsons'. For Coser's reply to this kind of charge, see *Continuities*, pp. 1, 5.

tion and adaptability to changing conditions. This imagery reveals a consistent series of causal nexuses: (1) Imbalances in the integration of constituent parts of a social whole leads to (2) the outbreak of varying types of conflict among constituent parts, which, in turn, causes (3) temporary reintegration of the systemic whole, which, under certain conditions, causes (4) increased flexibility in the system's structure, which, in turn, (5) increases the system's capability to resolve future imbalances through conflict, leading to a system that (6) reveals a high level of adaptability to changing conditions.

This causal imagery presents a number of obvious problems, the most important of which is that, much like the functional imperativism of Parsons, system processes are too frequently viewed as contributing to system integration and adaptation. Such an emphasis on the positive functions of conflict may reveal hidden assumptions of system "needs" that can be met only through the functions of conflict. While Coser is careful to point out that he is simply correcting for analytical inattention to the positive consequences of conflict, the strategy of correcting analytical imbalances is of dubious value, since it leads to the same kind of analytical one-sidedness that the author is trying to correct. It is perhaps a wiser strategy to develop ordered propositions about conflict processes, per se, for this in itself would be a vast improvement over the current attempts by theorists to correct for the imputed skewedness in their errant colleagues' analytical schemes.[10]

Despite these shortcomings, Coser's image of social organization has been translated into a series of suggestive propositions about the functions of conflict in social systems. As such, the scheme takes on considerably more clarity than when stated as a cluster of assumptions and causal images. Equally significant, the scheme becomes more testable and amenable to reformulation on the basis of empirical findings.

PROPOSITIONS ON CONFLICT PROCESSES

Using both the substance and style of Georg Simmel's provocative analysis, Coser has expanded the scope of Simmel's initial insights, incorporating proposi-

---

[10] It is somewhat tragic for theory building in sociology that the early promising lead of Robin M. Williams, Jr., in his *The Reduction of Intergroup Tensions: A Survey of Research on Problems of Ethnic, Social, and Religious Group Relations* (New York: Social Science Research Council, 1947) was not consistently followed. Most of the propositions developed by Dahrendorf and Coser were summarized in this volume ten years prior to their major works. More important, they are phrased more neutrally, without an attempt to reveal society's "ugly face" or correct for inattention to the "functions of conflict." The result of this failure to follow Williams's lead has been a rather low payoff in terms of refining and adding to theoretical statements on conflict processes in social systems. Until sociological theorists get to the task of building theory rather than straw men (to be knocked down), the cumulation of a systematic propositional inventory on social processes will continue to be thwarted.

tions not only from Marx but also from diverse sources in the contemporary literature on conflict. While his scheme reveals a large number of problems, stemming from his primary concern with the functions of conflict, Coser's conflict perspective still remains one of the most comprehensive in the current literature. This comprehensiveness is revealed in the broad range of variable phenomena covered by the propositions: (1) the causes of conflict; (2) the intensity of conflict; (3) the duration of conflict; and (4) the functions of conflict. Under each of these headings a variety of specific variables are incorporated into relational statements among abstract concepts.

One drawback to Coser's propositional inventory is that, unlike Dahrendorf's efforts, it has not been presented in a systematic or ordered format. Rather, the propositions appear in a number of discursive essays on substantive topics and in his analysis of Simmel's essay on conflict. While each discrete proposition is usually stated quite clearly, it is often necessary to interpret—with some danger of misinterpretation—the exact interrelationships among the various propositions. This fact makes the attempt at a systematic presentation of Coser's propositions an *ad hoc* exercise that not only rips propositions from their substantive context, but also runs the danger of misinterpreting the intended significance of certain propositions. Yet, the burden of systematic presentation would seem to be on the theorist; and thus, misinterpretation of certain propositions by commentators who wish to sort out the interrelations among abstract theoretical statements and thereby begin to build true theory, must be accepted by those who would prefer not to do so themselves.[11]

The Causes of Conflict

In Table 7–1, the causes of conflict are viewed by Coser as ultimately residing in the conditions generating the withdrawal of legitimacy from the existing system of distribution and in the intensification of deprivations (Table 7–1, Propositions 1 and 2). In turn, the withdrawal of legitimacy is seen as affected by social structural variables such as the degree of openness to expression of grievances in a social system, the degree of crosscutting loyalties demanded by a social system, and the degree of mobility allowed in a system, while the intensification of deprivations is considered to be affected by the context of socialization and the kinds of structural constraints that can be applied to deprived groups.

This inventory of propositions is clearly indebted to Marx, since the source

---

[11] Again, it should be emphasized that it is dangerous and difficult to pull from diverse sources discrete propositions and attempt to relate them systematically without doing some injustice to the theorist's intent. However, unless this kind of exercise is performed the propositions will contribute little to the development of sociological theory.

TABLE 7-1

The Causes of Conflict

I. The more deprived groups question the legitimacy of the existing distribution of scarce resources, the more likely they are to initiate conflict*

   A. The fewer the channels for addressing grievances over the distribution of scarce resources by deprived groups, the more likely they are to question legitimacy†

      1. The fewer internal organizations there are segmenting the emotional energies of members in deprived groups, the more likely are deprived groups without grievance alternatives to question legitimacy‡

      2. The greater the ego deprivations of members of groups deprived of grievance channels, the more likely they are to question legitimacy§

   B. The more membership in privileged groups is sought by members of deprived groups, and the less mobility allowed, the more likely they are to withdraw legitimacy‖

II. The more a group's deprivations are transformed from absolute to relative, the more likely these groups are to initiate conflict #

   A. The less the degree to which socialization experiences of members of deprived groups generate internal ego constraints, the more likely they are to experience relative deprivation**

   B. The less the external constraints applied to members of deprived groups, the more likely they are to experience relative deprivation††

---

   * Coser defines conflict in this way. it is behavior that involves a struggle with an opponent over scarce resources that involves attempts to neutralize, injure, or eliminate opponents (Lewis A. Coser, *The Functions of Social Conflict* [London: Free Press of Glencoe, 1956], p. 8). This proposition is found in Lewis A. Coser, "Social Conflict and the Theory of Social Change," British Journal of Sociology 8 (September 1957): 197–207; and "Internal Violence as a Mechanism for Conflict Resolution," as well as in *Functions of Social Conflict*, p. 37.

   † While Coser tends to hedge on specifying the conditions leading to the withdrawal of legitimacy—"What factors lead groups to question . . . the legitimacy of a system of distribution of rewards, lies largely outside the scope of present inquiry"—he had done so in numerous articles (quote taken from "Social Conflict and the Theory of Social Change," p. 203; proposition taken from "Internal Violence").

   ‡ Ibid.

   § Ibid.

   ‖ *Functions of Social Conflict*, pp. 37–38.

   # "Social Conflict and the Theory of Social Change"; and Lewis A. Coser "Violence and Social Structure," in *Science and Psychoanalysis*, ed. J. Masserman, vol. 7 (New York: Greene & Stratton, 1963), pp. 30–42.

   ** Ibid.

   †† Ibid.

of conflict is seen to lie in the unequal distribution of rewards and in the dissatisfaction of the deprived with such distribution. There is also an emphasis, presumably borrowed from Marx, on the structural conditions (Propositions I-A, I-A, 1, 2) affecting the mobilization of a deprived group's emotional energies, especially as deprivations move from absolute to relative (Proposition II). At the same time, Coser has emphasized, in common with Dahrendorf, the significance of social mobility between dominant and subordinate groups in decreasing the probability of conflict. Additionally, there appears to be an emphasis on the psychological variables, such as ego deprivations and ego constraints, which are influenced by structural forces, and which, in turn, affect the probability of open conflict.

What is especially clear from Coser's analysis is that the propositions of this inventory are vague and in need of supplementation from other sources. This lack of attention to the causes of conflict is perhaps understandable in light of

TABLE 7–2

The Intensity of Conflict

I. The more the conditions causing the outbreak of conflict are realized, the more intense the conflict*

II. The greater the emotional involvement of members in a conflict, the more intense the conflict†

    A. The more primary the relations among parties to a conflict, the more emotional involvement

        1. The smaller the primary groups where conflict occurs, the more emotional the involvement

        2. The more primary the relations among parties, the less likely the open expression of hostility, but the more intense the expression in a conflict situation

    B. The more secondary relations among parties to a conflict, the more segmental their participation and the less the emotional involvement

        1. The more secondary relations, the more frequent the conflict, but the less the emotional involvement

        2. The larger the secondary group, the more frequent the conflict, but the less the emotional involvement

III. The more rigid the social structure, the less will be the availability of institutionalized means for absorbing conflict and tensions, and the more intense the conflict

    A. The more primary the relations among parties where conflict occurs, the more rigid the structure

        1. The less stable the primary relations, the more rigid the structure of those relations

        2. The more stable the primary relations, the less rigid the structure of those relations

    B. The more secondary (based on functional interdependence) the relations among parties where conflict occurs, the more likely are institutionalized means for absorbing conflict and tensions, and the less intense the conflict

    C. The greater the control mechanism of the system, the more rigid the structure and the more intense the conflict‡

IV. The more groups engage in conflicts over their realistic (objective) interests, the less intense the conflict§

    A. The more groups conflict over realistic interests, the more likely they are to seek compromises over means to realize their interests

        1. The greater the power differentials between groups in conflict, the less likely alternative means are to be sought

        2. The more rigid the system where conflict occurs, the less availability of alternative means

V. The more groups conflict over nonrealistic issues (false interests), the more intense the conflict‖

    A. The more conflict occurs over nonrealistic issues, the greater the emotional involvement of the parties in the conflict and the more intense the conflict

        1. The more intense previous conflict between groups, the greater the emotional involvement in subsequent conflicts #

    B. The more rigid the system where conflict occurs, the more likely is the conflict to be nonrealistic**

    C. The more realistic conflict endures, the more nonrealistic issues emerge††

    D. The more the conflicting groups have emerged for purposes of conflict, the more nonrealistic the subsequent conflicts‡‡

VI. The more conflicts are objectified above and beyond individual self-interest, the more intense the conflict

    A. The more ideologically unified a group, the more conflicts transcend individual self-interest

        1. The more ideologically unified is a group, the more common are the goals of a group, and the more they transcend individual self-interest

        2. The more ideologically unified is a group, the more will conflicts be entered with a clear conscience, and the more they transcend individual self-interest

VII. The more the conflict in a group occurs over core values and issues, the more intense the conflict
  A. The more rigid the structure where conflict occurs, the more likely is conflict to occur over core values and issues
  B. The more emotional involvement in a situation where conflict occurs, the more likely it is to occur over core values and issues

---

* Coser appears to define intensity in two related ways: (1) the degree of direct action of one conflict party against another and (2) the degree of violence in such action. Yet, acknowledging Dahrendorf's distinction between intensity (energy and involvement) and violence (weapons chosen to release energy), Coser notes that "these and other highly valuable distinctions will no doubt have to be incorporated into any future codification of a general theory of social conflict" (Lewis A. Coser, *Continuities in the Study of Social Conflict*, [New York: Free Press, 1967], p. 3). As is evident in Coser's propositions, these variables are incorporated, for emotionl involvement is critical in determining, under additional conditions, the degree of violence of a conflict. It appears that Dahrendorf employs different definitions of intensity, but in reality violence and involvement are seen as separate variables by both authors.

  † Lewis A. Coser, *The Functions of Social Conflict*, (London: Free Press of Glencoe, 1956), p. 59. For following propositions see ibid., pp. 98–100; 98–100; 62–63, 68; 85; 85; 98–99; 85, 68–70; 83–85; 85, respectively.

  ‡ Lewis A. Coser, "Social Conflict and the Theory of Social Change," *British Journal of Sociology* 8 (September 1957): 202.

  § For Coser, realistic conflict involves the pursuit of specific aims against the real sources of hostility, with some estimation of the costs involved in such pursuit. In this & following propositions, see *Functions of Social Conflict*, pp. 49, 50, 45, and 45, respectively.

  ‖ Nonrealistic conflict involves the release of hostilities against objects other than those generating the hostilities, without a clear calculation of the costs involved; for this and following proposition, see ibid., p. 50.

  # Ibid., pp. 98–99; Lewis A. Coser, "Internal Violence as a Mechanism for Conflict Resolution," in *Continuities on the Study of Social Conflict*, edited by L. A. Coser (New York: Free Press, 1967).

  ** Lewis A. Coser, "Social Conflict and the Theory of Social Change," *British Journal of Sociology* 8 (September 1957): 197–207.

  †† Coser, "Internal Violence as a Mechanism for Conflict Resolution"; *Functions of Social Conflict*, pp. 58–59.

  ‡‡ For this and the following propositions, see Coser, *Functions of Social Conflict*, pp. 54, 116, 113, 113, 113, 75, 79, and 76, respectively.

Coser's intellectual debt to Simmel, who had very little to say about this phase of the conflict process. However, it is Coser's debt to Simmel, plus his awareness of Marx, that makes more powerful his analysis of the intensity, duration, and functions of conflict.

The Intensity of Conflict

In the propositions listed in Table 7–2, Coser suggests that the intensity of conflict relations in a system can be accounted for by looking at the interrelationships among variables, such as the emotional involvement of participants, the rigidity of social structure, the degree of realism of the conflict, the extent to which conflict occurs over core values and issues, and the degree to which it can be objectified beyond individual self-interest. While all these variables are deemed important, Coser has tended to stress the primacy of the first two, the rigidity of social structure and emotional involvement, which appear to determine whether conflict is objectified, realistic, and occurs over core values and issues.

Of particular interest are Propositions IV and IV-A because they run directly counter to Marx's emphasis that consciousness of objective interests leads to intense (revolutionary) conflict. Borrowing from Simmel, Coser emphasizes that clear awareness of conflicting interests (realistic conflict) is likely to lead conflict parties to seek compromises and alternative means to open conflict in an effort to avoid the high costs of intense conflict. Furthermore, contrary to Marx, Coser recognizes that in rigid social systems—like the ones Marx tended to describe—there is a high probability of nonrealistic conflict, since realization of true interests is unlikely. However, Marx did correctly perceive that intense conflict in such

TABLE 7–3

The Duration of Conflict

I. The less limited the goals of the opposing parties in a conflict, the more prolonged the conflict*
   A. The less emotional involvement, rigidity of structure, and nonrealistic the character of the conflict, the more likely the goals of parties to a conflict are to be limited†
II. The less consensus over the goals of conflict between conflicting parties, the more prolonged the conflict‡
   A. The less realistic the conflict, the more likely dissensus over the goals of conflict§
III. The less the parties in a conflict can interpret their adversaries' symbolic points of victory and defeat, the more prolonged the conflict
   A. The less the consensus by both parties over symbols, the less the ability of each to interpret their adversaries' symbolic points of victory and defeat
      1. The greater the polarization of conflict parities and the superimposition of conflicts upon one another, the less consensus over symbolic points of victory and defeat
      2. The fewer the extremist factions within each party to a conflict, the more likely is consensus over symbolic points of victory and defeat
IV. The more leaders of conflicting parties can perceive that complete attainment of goals is possible only at costs higher than those required for victory, the less prolonged the conflict
   A. The more equal the power between two conflicting parties, the more likely are leaders to perceive the high costs of complete attainment of goals #
   B. The more clear-cut the indexes of defeat or victory in a conflict, the more likely leaders are to perceive the high costs of complete attainment of goals**
      1. The more consensus over symbols of defeat and victory, the more clear-cut the indexes of defeat or victory
V. The greater the capacity of leaders of each conflict party to persuade followers to terminate conflict, the less prolonged the conflict
   A. The greater leaders' knowledge of their followers' symbols and the more consensus over these symbols, the greater the capacity to persuade followers
   B. The more centralized the conflict parties, the greater the capacity of leaders to persuade followers††
   C. The fewer the internal cleavages of conflict parties, the greater the capacity of leaders to persuade followers
   D. The more leaders can claim that some gains have been made, the greater their capacity to persuade followers§§

---

* Lewis A. Coser, "The Termination of Conflict," in *Continuities in the Study of Social Conflict* (New York: Free Press, 1967), pp. 37–52.
† Lewis A. Coser, *The Functions of Social Conflict* (London: Free Press of Glencoe, 1956), pp. 48–55, 59.
‡ Lewis A. Coser, "The Termination of Conflict."
§ Lewis A. Coser, *The Functions of Social Conflict*, p. 50.
‖ Coser, "The Termination of Conflict," for this and following propositions.
Coser, *Functions of Social Conflict*, p. 20.
** Coser, "The Termination of Conflict," for this and following propositions.
†† Coser, *Functions of Social Conflict*, pp. 128–33.
‡‡ Coser, "The Termination of Conflict."
§§ Ibid.

rigid systems is highly probable, since it is more likely to be nonrealistic (Coser's Proposition V), laden with emotional involvement (II), the result of accumulated grievances III and objectified beyond self-interest (VI).

Thus, Coser appears to have effectively incorporated the insights of Simmel and Marx into a propositional inventory that highlights each thinker's important theoretical contribution and underplays some of their more tenuous theoretical statements. Additionally, it is now clear that, while he consistently used Simmel as his theoretical inspiration, Coser's theoretical scheme is heavily indebted to that developed by Marx, and in many ways provides some tentative guidelines for synthesizing the legacy of Marx and Simmel.

The Duration of Conflict

In the propositions of Table 7–3, Coser has focused attention on a facet of conflict that was virtually ignored by Marx, Simmel, and Dahrendorf. From Coser's perspective, the clarity of the goals of conflict parties, the degree of consensus between conflict parties over points of victory and defeat, and the capacity of leaders to perceive the costs of victory and persuade followers of the desirability of termination are critical in determining the duration of conflict. Each of these variables reveals certain interrelations, which, in turn, are influenced by other variables, such as emotional involvement (I-A), degree of realism of the conflict (II-A), extent of polarization (III-A, 1), respective degrees of power (III-A), clarity of indices of victory (IV-B) and degree of centralization (V-B). While the interrelations among the propositions reveal considerable overlap and lack of logical rigor, they do offer a suggestive lead for refinement of theoretical statements on the duration and termination of conflict in social systems. In sociology, the analysis of time variables, such as duration, has received scant attention; and it is to Coser's credit that he incorporated some of these variables into his analysis of conflict.

Thus, by also analyzing the causes, intensity, and duration of conflict, Coser has avoided at least some of the analytical dangers of focusing on the "functions of social conflict." Yet, as the propositions summarized in the next section reveal, it is evident that he has chosen to concentrate primarily on the positive functions of conflict for maintaining various institutionalized patterns for both entire social systems and its subunits.

The Functions of Conflict

Following Simmel's lead, Coser has indicated in the propositions listed in Table 7–4 some of the consequences for each of the respective parties to a conflict (I–IV) and for the social whole within which the conflict occurs (V–IX). In the

TABLE 7–4

The Functions of Conflict

   I. The more intense the conflict, the more clear-cut the boundaries of each respective conflict party*

  II. The more intense the conflict and the more differentiated the division of labor of each conflict party, the more likely each to centralize its decision-making structure†

     A. The more intense the conflict, the less differentiated the structure; and the less stable the structure and internal solidarity, the more centralization is despotic

 III. The more intense the conflict and the more it is perceived to affect all segments of each group, the more conflict promotes structural and ideological solidarity among members of respective conflict groups

 IV. The more primary the relations among the members of respective conflict groups, and the more intense the conflict, the more conflict leads to suppression of dissent and deviance within each conflict group and to forced conformity to norms and values

     A. The more conflict between groups leads to forced conformity, the more the accumulation of hostilities and the more likely internal group conflict in the long run

   V. The less rigid the social structure where conflict between groups occurs and the more frequent and less intense the conflict, the more likely is conflict to change the system in ways promoting adaptability and integration‡

     A. The less rigid the system, the more likely is conflict to promote innovation and creativity in the system

     B. The less rigid the system, the less likely is conflict to involve displacement of hostilities to alternative objects and the more likely is conflict to confront realistic sources of tension§

         1. The more a system is based upon functional interdependence, the more frequent and less intense the conflict and the more likely it is to release tensions without polarizing the system

         2. The more stable the primary relations in a system and the more frequent and less intense is the conflict, the more likely it is to release tensions without polarizing the system, but not to the extent of a system based upon secondary relations

     C. The less rigid the system, the more likely is conflict to be perceived by those in power as signals of maladjustment that need to be addressed‖

  VI. The more frequently conflict occurs, the less likely it is to reflect dissensus over core values, and the more functional for maintaining equilibrium it is likely to be#

     A. The more a conflict group can appeal to the core values of a system, the less likely the conflict is to create dissensus over these values and the more likely it is to promote integration of the system**

     B. The more a conflict group does not advocate extreme interpretations of core values, the less likely is a counterconflict group to form and the less disruptive the conflict for the system

 VII. The more frequent and less intense are conflicts, the more likely they are to promote normative regulation of conflict

     A. The less rigid a system, the more frequent and less intense the conflict††

         1. The less rigid the system, the more likely conflict to revitalize existent norms‡‡

         2. The less rigid the system, the more likely conflict to generate new norms

     B. The more frequent and less intense conflicts, the more likely groups are to centralize in an effort to promote conformity of each group's membership to norms governing the conflict§§

         1. The more equal the power of conflict groups, the more likely is conflict to generate centralization promoting normative conformity

VIII. The less rigid the system, the more likely it is that conflict can establish balances and hierarchies of power in a system

     A. The less knowledge of the adversary's strength and the fewer the indexes of such strength, the more likely is conflict between two groups vying for power to promote a balance of power relations in a system

IX. The less rigid the system, the more likely is conflict to cause formation of associative coalitions that increase the cohesiveness and integration of the system
  A. The more other parties in a system are threatened by coalitions of other parties, the more likely they are to form associative coalitions
  B. The more a system is based upon functional interdependence, the more likely coalitions are to be instrumental and less enduring
      1. The more a system reveals crosscutting cleavages, the more likely groups in a coalition are to have their own conflicts of interests, and the more likely is the coalition to be instrumental
      2. The more a coalition is formed for purely defensive purposes, the more likely it is to be instrumental.
  C. The more tightly structured and primary the relations in a system, the more likely coalitions are to develop common norms and values and form a more permanent group
      1. The more coalitions are formed of individuals (or more generally, the smaller the units forming a coalition), the more likely they are to develop into a permanent group
      2. The more interaction required among the parties of a coalition, the more likely it is to form a permanent group

---

* Lewis A. Coser, *The Functions of Social Conflict* (London: Free Press of Glencoe, 1956), pp. 37–38.
† For this and following propositions, see ibid., pp. 95; 92; 93; 69–72; and 48, respectively.
‡ Ibid., pp. 45–48, Lewis A. Coser, "Internal Violence as Mechanisms for Conflict Resolution"; Lewis A. Coser, "Social Conflict and the Theory of Social Change," *British Journal of Sociology* 8 (September 1957): 197–207. This proposition is implied in the others that follow and is thus considered crucial in determining whether conflict is functional or dysfunctional for system integration and adaptability.
§ Lewis A. Coser, "Internal Violence as a Mechanism for Conflict Resolution"; Coser, *Functions of Social Conflict*, pp. 45–48; for following two propositions, see ibid, pp. 85; and 83 and 85, respectively.
‖ Lewis A. Coser, "Some Social Functions of Violence," *Annals of the American Academy of Political and Social Science* 364 (March 1966): 10; Coser, "Internal Violence as a Mechanism for Conflict Resolution."
Coser, *Functions of Social Conflict*, p. 73.
** See Lewis A. Coser, "The Functions of Dissent," in Coser, *The Dynamics of Dissent* (New York: Greene & Stratton, 1968), for this and the following proposition.
†† Coser, "Social Conflict and the Theory of Social Change," and *Functions of Social Conflict*, p. 125
‡‡ See ibid, for this and the following proposition.
§§ See ibid., p. 129; for the following propositions, see ibid, pp. 129; 133–38; 136; 140; 148; 142; 143; 149; 142; 146; and 146, respectively.

---

first group of propositions, conflict can cause a shoring up of group boundaries, centralization of decision making, ideological solidarity, and increased social control. As in previous propositions, these events occur only under specified conditions, including the degree of rigidity and differentiation in social structure, the intensity of the conflict, and the extent to which conflict is perceived to affect all factions of the group. Of particular interest is the fact that only in Proposition IV-A is there a clear statement about the potential dysfunctions of conflict for each respective conflict group. Furthermore, in this particular inventory it is not immediately evident that stating the inverse of the propositions would reveal the conditions under which conflict leads to disintegration of conflict groups. For example, taking Proposition III, it would be difficult to maintain that if all group members did not perceive the conflict to affect them, ideological disunity would be forthcoming. Such might be one outcome, but some additional propositions would be necessary to establish the conditions under which this outcome could be expected. Coser is clearly aware of these facts, but in choosing to focus primarily on the *positive functions* of conflict, instead of the more neutral phenomenon of outcomes or consequences,[12] the net effect of the propositions is to connote, in a vein similar to that imputed by critics to Parsonian functionalism, an overly integrated view of the social world, even in the face of open conflict among groups.

This unfortunate connotation is buttressed by Propositions V–IX, in which conflict in loosely structured systems is seen as promoting integration, innovation, creativity, releases of hostilities, and attention of elites to system maladjustments. Furthermore, under conditions of conflict frequency and intensity, conflict can promote varying degrees and types of equilibrium, normative regulation, and associative coalitions. While the inverse of some of these propositions perhaps indicate a few of the conditions promoting disequilibrium, anomie, and antagonisms among subgroups, the propositions still remain overly loaded in the direction of emphasizing system integration and adaptability.

Returning to a simple but important point made earlier: To attempt to "correct" for other theorists' one-sidedness by offering another form of analytical one-sidedness will fail, since such an effort would call forth still another one-sided "corrective" scheme. Had Coser chosen to focus just on the outcomes of conflict for systems and their subparts, his theoretical perspective would have been even more "corrective" to the one-sidedness of earlier theorists. Thus, in effect, Coser has fallen into the same analytical trap that he has imputed to Parsons, for the net impact of his propositions is to portray a world in which conflict promotes only institutionalization and integration. While this portrayal is not quite the same as "Parsons's utopia," it is perhaps no less unrealistic.

Finally, it should be noted that the propositions of Coser's suggestive scheme present a lack of rigor. They overlap; they fail to specify clearly the social units—groups, individuals, organizations, societies, and so forth—to which they apply; they reveal gaps; definitions of concepts are far from adequate; and some border on being tautologies. Many of these inadequacies stem from the fact that a secondary reviewer has constructed the propositional inventory—a dangerous enterprise, for misinterpretation is inevitable. However, without attempts at codification at an abstract level, Coser's scheme would be less powerful, since the propositions would remain isolated, disconnected, and tied to temporally bound events. It is felt that the propositions and the theoretical perspective they imply are far too suggestive and important to remain disjointed and concrete.

---

[12] This proposition, as acknowledged by Coser, was borrowed from Williams's (*Reduction or Intergroup Tension*, p. 58) 1947 discussion of conflict phenomena. But in this latter discussion, the proposition is placed in a context in which outcomes, as opposed to functions, is the theoretical referent. For this reason, the earlier discussion appears much more balanced and less loaded in the direction of emphasizing integration.

In sum, while Coser's scheme lacks the logical rigor of fully developed scientific theory, it is one of the most comprehensive and provocative of the current conflict perspectives in sociology. The incorporation of the scheme into abstract propositions has revealed both its comprehensiveness and inadequacies.

STRATEGIES FOR REFORMULATING COSER'S SCHEME

As has been emphasized, Coser's approach represents an analytical one-sidedness, which, if followed exclusively, would produce a skewed vision of the social world. While Coser begins with statements about the inevitability of force, coercion, constraint, and conflict, his analysis quickly turns to the integrative and adaptive consequences of such processes. This analytical emphasis could rather easily transform the integrative and adaptive "functions" of conflict into functional "needs" and "requisites" that necessitate, or even cause, conflict to occur. Such teleology was inherent in Marx's work, where revolutionary conflict was viewed as necessary to meet the "need" for a communist society. But Coser's teleological inspiration appears to have come more from Simmel's organic model than Marx's dialectical scheme. Once he became committed to documenting how conflict contributes to the systemic whole, or "body social," as he is prone to say, it is sometimes inadvertently implied that the body social causes conflict in order to meet its integrative needs. While conflict is acknowledged to cause change in social systems, it is still viewed primarily as a crucial process in promoting integration or equilibrium—albeit a "moving equilibrium" as Parsons likes to call it.

Dahrendorf has noted with respect to Parsonian functionalism:

> The difference between utopia and a cemetery is that occasionally some things do happen in utopia. But . . . all processes going on in utopian societies follow recurrent patterns and occur within . . . the design of the whole. Not only do they not upset the status quo: they affirm and sustain it, and it is in order to do so that most utopias allow them to happen at all.[13]

Does Coser's model reveal a similar weakness? On the one hand, it is possible to note that Coser has continually emphasized the limitations and "corrective" one-sidedness of his scheme, while, on the other hand, critics can charge that Parsons's scheme, no less than Coser's, also started out with good intentions, but in the end was weakened by implicit organicism.

Looking at the bulk of Coser's work, this assessment is perhaps the most appropriate, since Coser's assumptions, images of causal processes, and abstract propositional statements, all point to a system in which conflict functions in

---

[13] Ralf Dahrendorf, "Out of Utopia: Toward a Reorientation of Sociological Analysis," *American Journal of Sociology* 64 (September 1958): 115–27.

positive ways to either maintain the system or change it in such a way as to increase adaptability.

To correct for this problem, little substantive redirection of Coser's propositions on the causes, intensity, and duration of conflict appears necessary. These propositions address important questions neutrally and do not attempt to "balance" or "correct for" past theoretical one-sidedness with another kind of one-sidedness. In fact, they display an awareness of key aspects of conflict in social systems; and, with obviously needed supplementation and reformulation, they offer an important theoretical lead. The substantive one-sidedness in the scheme comes with his borrowing and then supplementing Simmel's functional propositions; and it is here that drastic changes in the scheme must come. One corrective strategy, which does not smack of another form of one-sidedness, is to ask the more neutral theoretical question: Under what conditions can what kinds of outcomes of conflict for what types of systems and subsystems be expected? While this is not a startling theoretical revelation, it keeps assessments of conflict processes in systems away from what ultimately must be evaluative questions of "functions" and "dysfunctions." If the question of outcomes of conflicts were more rigorously pursued, the resulting propositions would present a more balanced and substantively accurate view of social reality.

Given the long and unfortunate organic connotations of words such as "function" it might be wise to drop their use in sociology, since they all too frequently create logical and substantive problems of interpretation. While Coser appears well aware of these dangers, he has invited misinterpretation by continually juxtaposing notions of "the body social" and the "functions" of various conflict processes and related phenomena such as dissent and violence. Had he not done this, he would have better achieved his goal of correcting for the inadequacies of functional and conflict theorizing in sociology.

In sum, then, it would make little sense to have more "new perspectives" that "correct" for the deficiencies of either dialectical- or functional-conflict theory. Sociological theory has far too long engaged in this kind of activity and it is now a wiser strategy to begin reconciling the propositions in order to: (1) specify more clearly the units of analysis (classes, groups, organizations, societies) to which they apply; (2) close the gaps among the propositions; (3) reconcile the divergent conclusions; and (4) supplement them with the generalization from the research literature. Such a strategy offers a greater payoff for ascertaining the conditions under which different patterns of social organization emerge, persist, change, and break down. For only in this way will sociological theory be capable of providing a scientific solution to the Hobbesian problem of order.

8

Dialectical and Functional Conflict Theories: A Strategy for Synthesis

CURRENT PROBLEMS WITH THEORETICAL SYNTHESIZING

While both dialectical- and functional-conflict theory have their own intellectual roots in the works of Marx and Simmel, each has taken on sharper focus when seen as an alternative to Parsonian functionalism.[1] The sometimes-extreme polemics of conflict theorists against functionalism have created a climate of controversy that has now lasted for two decades.[2] As is now typical with such chronic controversies in sociological theorizing, this debate has become locked into an unfortunate course of events: (1) initial and somewhat mild criticism of a scheme; (2) vicious and polemical criticism of the scheme; (3) the proposal of alternative theoretical schemes; (4) counterattack on the inadequacies of the criticism and the alternative; (5) attempts by "wise sages" at reconciliation between the criticized scheme and proposed alternatives; and (6) questioning about the worth of all this activity for advancing sociological theory. This se-

---

[1] See, for example, Ralf Dahrendorf, "Out of Utopia: Toward a Reorientation of Sociological Analysis," *American Journal of Sociology* 64 (September 1958): 115–27; Lewis A. Coser, *The Functions of Social Conflict* (London: Free Press, 1956), pp. 1–20.

[2] In addition to Dahrendorf's and Coser's polemics, see John Horton, "Order and Conflict Theories of Social Problems as Competing Ideologies," *American Journal of Sociology* 71 (May 1966): 701–13; Irving Louis Horowitz, "Consensus, Conflict and Cooperation: A Sociological Inventory," *Social Forces* 41 (December 1962): 177–88; David Lockwood, "Some Remarks on 'The Social System,'" *British Journal of Sociology* 7 (June 1956): 134–46; Pierre van de Berghe, "Dialectic and Functionalism: Toward a Theoretical Synthesis," *American Sociological Review* 28 (October 1963); 695–705.

quence has occurred again and again among sociological theorists, but nowhere are steps 1–6 more evident than in the conflict theorist-functionalist debate. This situation is therefore of specific interest to the present discussion of conflict theory, as well as to the general concern for an understanding of why sociological theorizing so repeatedly gets bogged down in seemingly endless controversies.

Both the critics and the synthesizers in this chronic controversy have employed a similar tactic of listing what they consider to be the assumptions of functionalism and conflict theory. Such delineation usually takes the form of a side-by-side listing of assumptions, as is revealed by two prominent examples presented in Figure 8–1.[3]

Among the critics of functionalism, the claim is usually made that the conflict alternative is more nearly isomorphic with reality, although there is a qualification usually inserted about how the functionalist tenets do refer to *some* features of the social world. The synthesizers claim that both formulations are too extreme (a fact that they assure by listing them in extreme form) and that taken together in mitigated form the two schemes offer a more accurate picture of reality. The synthesizers then knock the extremes off the two lists and point to areas of "convergence" or "reconciliation" between the less extreme lists.

One of the most influential attempts at synthesis was performed by Pierre van den Berghe in the early years of the 1960s.[4] His strategy was to expand what he termed the "functional-equilibrium model" to take account of conflict and dissension and, at the same time, to "minimize" the "dialectic conflict model" to the point that it revealed only that social change can be endogenous and the product of oppositions inhering in social structures. From this analytical activity, van den Berghe reached a number of conclusions: Systems display interdependence, but the degree of such interdependence can vary; interdependence can imply both mutual adjustment and opposition; conflict can come from various sources; conflict can lead to both change and stasis; and, conversely, consensus can lead to malintegration and conflict. Recognition of these facts, he argued, would lead sociological theory toward a synthesis or reconciliation of the divergent claims of conflict theory and functionalism.

Several problems are raised by this form of theoretical analysis. First, the arguments are couched in metaphysical terms, leading to a situation in which the author is trying to reconcile basic assumptions about the nature of reality. Such activity is akin to reconciling opposed value judgments about what is, or

---

[3] In addition to the two lists appearing in Figure 8–1, see van den Berghe, "Dialectic and Functionalism"; Horowitz, "Consensus, Conflict, and Cooperation"; Horton, "Order and Conflict Theories"; Dahrendorf, "Out of Utopia"; and Robert Cole, "Structural-Functional Theory, the Dialectic and Social Change," *Sociological Quarterly* 7 (Winter 1966): pp. 39–58.

[4] van den Berghe, "Dialectic and Functionalism." For an example of a similar attempt, see Cole, "Structural—Functional Theory."

FIGURE 8-1

Lists of Assumptions in Conflict-Functional Debate

Synthesizer's List*

Model A	Model B
1. Norms and values are the basic elements of social life	1. Interests are the basic elements of social life
2. Social life involves commitments	2. Social life involves inducement and coercion
3. Societies are necessarily cohesive	3. Social life is necessarily divisive
4. Social life depends on solidarity	4. Social life generates opposition, exclusion, and hostility
5. Social life is based on reciprocity and cooperation	5. Social life generates structured conflict
6. Social systems rest on consensus	6. Social life generates sectional interests
7. Society recognizes legitimate authority	7. Social differentiation involves power
8. Social systems are integrated	8. Social systems are malintegrated and beset by "contradictions"
9. Social systems tend to persist	9. Social systems tend to change

Dahrendorf's List†

1. Every society is subjected at every moment to change: social change is ubiquitous	1. Every society is a relatively persisting configuration of elements
2. Every society experiences at every moment social conflict: social conflict is ubiquitous	2. Every society is a well-integrated configuration of elements
3. Every element in a society contributes to its change	3. Every element in a society contributes to its functioning
4. Every society rests upon constraint of some of its members by others	4. Every society rests upon the consensus of its members

º From Percy Cohen, *Modern Social Theory* (New York: Basic Books, 1968), p. 167.
† This excerpt from "Toward a Theory of Social Conflict," by Ralf Dahrendorf is reprinted from the *Journal of Conflict Resolution* Vol. 2, No. 2 (June 1958), pp. 170–183 by permission of the publisher, Sage Publications, Inc.

should be, out there in the "real world"; in the nature of this kind of activity, the reconciliation will be accepted only by those whose judgments or assumptions reflect van den Berghe's. Second, as long as the positions are couched in metaphysical terms, there can be no resolution to such debates and attempts at reconciliation. Each position lends itself to a countermetaphysical assertion, which, in turn, suggests to someone else another assertion; and so on, as articles and rejoinders to rejoinders accumulate in the literature.

Synthesis and reconciliation of assumptions is thus a questionable approach for resolving theoretical controversies. Robin Williams[5] has emphasized that

---

[5] Robin M. Williams, Jr., "Some Further Comments on Chronic Controversies," *American Journal of Sociology* 71 (May 1966): 717–21.

arguments over whether consensus-equilibrium or coercion-change is most typical of social systems are "bootless," for these are in reality empirical issues: Under what conditions does consensus, coercion, constraint, dissent, cooperation, integration, equilibrium, or change typify the social world?

Just as these questions cannot be answered by assumptive assertions, they cannot be synthesized or reconciled at that level. The arguments over conflict and functional theory, as well as attempts at theoretical reconciliation, have thus tended to ignore the theoretically interesting and important question: Under *what empirical conditions* do the propositions inspired by the assumptions of conflict or functional images of social organization hold?

In sum, then, the sociological literature does not need another synthesis or reconciliation of assumptions. These have served their purpose in pointing out some seemingly obvious things, including the recognition that social reality reveals conflict-cooperation, consensus-dissensus, tension-equilibrium, and stasis-change (and much more). As emphasized in the opening pages of this book, the task of sociological theory is to discover the conditions under which any of these states in the social world occur. In all the debate and controversy over conflict-consensus, integration-malintegration, and stasis-change, this task has been delayed. Thus, in this chapter an attempt to outline an alternative strategy for resolving theoretical controversies will be made: What points of divergence and convergence are evident in the *propositions* of prominent theoretical perspectives?

In the context of the dialectical- and functional-conflict perspectives of Dahrendorf and Coser, this strategy would suggest the utility of examining their respective propositional inventories. That is, what do the combined propositional inventories of Dahrendorf and Coser reveal about conflict in social systems? In answering this question, it will be evident that Coser's and Dahrendorf's divergent frames of reference have resulted in somewhat different theoretical statements on conflict processes.

As will also emerge from the discussion to follow, however, the two inventories of propositions complement each other in their divergence. Indeed, some of the deficiencies in one inventory will be shown to be partially corrected by the strengths in the other.

This exercise promises considerably more theoretical payoff than the side-by-side listing of assumptions, as has been amply documented by the futile debate among conflict theorists and functionalists. Furthermore, by examining the combined inventories of propositions of Dahrendorf and Coser, subsequent comparisons with similarly combined inventories of propositions from various schools of functional theorizing could hold the promise of real theoretical reconciliation and synthesis. Although this latter task of reconciling functional and conflict theorizing is beyond the scope of this volume,[6] this chapter seeks to present a strategy for eventually achieving this end by initiating a necessary preliminary task: presenting the points of divergence and convergence in the propositions of two varieties of conflict theory. After many such reconciliations of propositions among the diverse schools of thought within the conflict-[7] and functional-theoretic traditions, then synthesis of these two major theoretical traditions will prove theoretically meaningful—thereby providing a more adequate solution to the problem of order: How and why is society possible?

COMPLIMENTARY SETS OF PROPOSITIONS

From the presentation in chapters 6 and 7, the propositions developed by Dahrendorf and Coser might appear, at first glance, to be similar, in that they can be conveniently analyzed under the general headings: (1) causes of conflict; (2) intensity and violence of conflict; (3) duration of conflict; and (4) outcomes of conflict. Furthermore, some of the explicit variables that each author incorporates into his propositions reveal considerable overlap; and yet, these similarly conceived variables appear at different places in the propositional inventories. Furthermore, for all the similarity in the variables conceptualized, Coser and Dahrendorf address different variable properties of the causes, intensity, duration, and outcomes of conflict, with the result that the propositional inventories are divergent, and yet as will become evident, highly complementary.

Causes of Conflict

In Table 8–1, the propositions[8] developed by Coser and Dahrendorf with respect to the causes of conflict are listed. Those propositions that point to similar

---

[6] It is relatively easy to synthesize assumptions (this is probably why it is so frequently done), but synthesizing complex inventories of propositions of two long-standing theoretical traditions, such as functional and conflict theory, is probably beyond the abilities of any single author, certainly the present one.

[7] For illustrations of such statements in the conflict tradition, see Herbert M. Blalock, Jr., *Toward a Theory of Minority-Group Relations* (New York: John Wiley & Sons, 1967); James Coleman, *Community Conflict* (Glencoe, Ill.: Free Press, 1957); James C. Davies, "Toward a Theory of Revolution," *American Sociological Review* 27 (February 1962): 5 and 19; William A. Gamson, *Power and Discontent* (Homewood, Ill.: Dorsey Press, 1968); Raymond W. Mack and Richard C. Snyder, "The Analysis of Social Conflict—Toward an Overview and Synthesis," *Journal of Conflict Resolution* 1 (June 1957): 212–48; Robin M. Williams, Jr., *The Reduction of Intergroup Relations* (New York: Social Science Research Council, 1947); Robin M. Williams, Jr., "Conflict and Social Order: A Research Strategy for Complex Propositions," *Journal of Social Issues* 28 (February 1972); Robin M. Williams, Jr., "Social Order and Social Conflict," *Proceedings of the American Philosophical Society* 114 (June 1970): 217–25.

[8] The propositions in this and succeeding tables are taken from the discussion of Dahrendorf and Coser presented in chapters 6 and 7. The Dahrendorf propositions are rephrasings (to facilitate comparison with Coser's) of those in his most formal statement of his theory: Ralf Dahrendorf, *Class*

TABLE 8–1

Propositions on the Causes of Conflict

Dahrendorf	Coser
I. The more members of quasi groups in ICAs can become aware of their objective interests and form a conflict group, the more likely is conflict to occur	I. The more deprived groups question the legitimacy of the existing distribution of scarce resources, the more likely they are to initiate conflict (1956, p. 37; 1957)
A. The more the "technical" conditions of organization can be met, the more likely is the formation of a conflict group	A. The fewer the channels for addressing grievances over the distribution of scarce resources by deprived groups, the more likely they are to question legitimacy (1967c)
1. The more a leadership cadre among quasi groups can be developed, the more likely are the "technical" conditions of organization to be met	1. The fewer internal organizations there are segmenting emotional energies of the members of deprived groups, the more likely are deprived groups without grievance alternatives to question legitimacy (1967c)
2. The more a codified idea system, or charter, can be developed, the more likely are the "technical" conditions of organization to be met	2. The greater the ego deprivations of members of groups deprived of grievance channels, the more likely they are to question legitimacy (1967c)
B. The more the "political" conditions of organization can be met, the more likely is the formation of a conflict group	B. The more membership in privileged groups is sought by members of deprived groups, and the less mobility allowed, the more likely they are to withdraw legitimacy (1956, pp. 37–38)
1. The more the dominant groups permit organization of opposed interests, the more likely are the "political" conditions of organization to be met	

C. The more the "social" conditions of organization can be met, the more likely is the formation of a conflict group
   1. The more opportunity for members of quasi groups to communicate, the more likely are the "social" conditions of organization to be met
   2. The more recruiting is permitted by structural arrangements (such as propinquity), the more likely are the "social" conditions of organization to be met

II. The more a group's deprivations are transformed from absolute to relative, the more likely these groups are to initiate conflict (1957; 1967b)
   A. The less the degree to which socialization experiences of members of deprived groups generate internal ego constraints, the more likely they are to experience relative deprivation (1967b)
   B. The less the external constraints applied to members of deprived groups, the more likely they are to experience relative deprivation (1967b)

NOTE: Dates in parentheses refer to bibliography at end of chapter.

variable phenomena are listed side by side, while those that do not appear alone, but in the logical progression intended by the author.

In these two propositional inventories, the first major proposition points to dissatisfaction of deprived groups[9] with the current distribution of scarce resources. For Dahrendorf, the important theoretical question is one of explicating the conditions under which the deprived become first aware of their objective interests and then organized to pursue these interests through conflict. In these propositions, the only acknowledged social psychological variable is "awareness" (Proposition I), with "structural" variables such as leadership (I-A, 1), codification of ideologies (I-A, 2), power relations (I-B, 1), opportunity for communication (I-C, 1), and capacity to recruit (I-C, 2) affecting such "awareness." On the other hand, Coser's propositions place greater reliance upon social psychological variables as they affect the question of "legitimacy" (as opposed to Dahrendorf's "awareness"). The result of this emphasis is for a series of structural variables, such as grievance channels (I-A), social mobility (I-B), socialization II-A) and external control (II-B), to affect psychological variables, such as the degree of emotional energies (I-A, 1), ego deprivations (I-A, 2), mobility aspirations (I-B), and relative deprivation. In turn, these psychological variables affect the degree of questioning of legitimacy (Proposition I) and the likelihood that conflict will be initiated (Proposition II).

The inclination of Coser and Dahrendorf to incorporate social psychological variables into their respective theoretical systems stems, in part at least, from their divergent assumptions. Since for Dahrendorf there is an inherent opposition of interests in all social systems, or "imperatively coordinated associations" (ICAs), which, in the long run, will inevitably generate conflict, the propositions developed from such a perspective would be likely to point to the structural conditions that "activate" awareness or consciousness of inherent oppositions in ICAs and that allow such awareness to become the basis for conflict-group formation.[10] Since conflict is assumed to be ubiquitous and inevitable, theoretical questions about the probability of conflict in different types of ICAs, revealing what types of legitimated authority and what types, if any, of opposed interests are not seriously addressed. Thus, as long as conflict is viewed as smoldering just

and Class Conflict in Industrial Society (Stanford, Calif.: Stanford University Press, 1959), pp. 236–40. Since the propositions of Coser's scheme come from many different sources, a large number of footnote citations would be necessary, as was the case in chapter 7. To avoid this, references are cited in parentheses at the end of each proposition, directing the reader to the bibliography at the end of the chapter.

[9] The concept of "deprived" is never fully defined by either Coser and Dahrendorf. Usually, individuals or groups are viewed as deprived of scarce resources, such as power; but beyond this definition, neither author has a great deal to say.

[10] Dahrendorf consciously rejects the conspicuous incorporation of psychological variables into a sociological theory of conflict-group formation. While he does not directly say so, he appears to do so for the reasons indicated above.

beneath the surface of all structures, propositions will be loaded in a direction that simply documents those processes involved in releasing inherent conflict potential.

In contrast Coser begins with a less extreme set of assumptions and imagery about the inevitability of conflict. This position leads his analysis to address questions of what types of structures revealing what patterns of legitimacy will display a potential for conflict. To do so requires Coser to delineate those social structural conditions as they affect psychological variables that can account for a breakdown in legitimacy and then mobilization of actors' emotional energies to pursue conflict. Thus, when conflict is not assumed to be automatically forthcoming as a result of inherent oppositions, it becomes necessary to develop propositions that incorporate the psychological variables that would be involved in, first, the withdrawal of legitimacy (Propositions I-A, 1, 2 and I-B) and then the willingness to initiate conflict (II, II-A, II-B).

As is attempted in the format of Table 8–1, the gaps in Coser's and Dahrendorf's propositions suggest lines of synthesis that can build a more adequate set of theoretical statements. Such a synthesis would correct for the one-sidedness of each perspective and allow each to meet some of the important criticisms leveled against them. Furthermore, since the synthesis would be at the propositional level, rather than at the assumptive level, it would not throw theory building back into another futile debate over how much consensus, conflict, equilibrium, or change the real world reveals.

As was emphasized in chapter 7, Dahrendorf's scheme can be criticized for not specifying how conflict can emerge from those very legitimated role relations (or, "relations of authority") in ICAs which maintain order.[11] How is it, the critics charge, that legitimated authority relations are at one time the source of order and stability and at another time the source of conflict? Coser's propositions point to at least a few of the conditions under which a legitimated set of relations in an ICA or some other pattern of social organization might be questioned by its incumbents and actually become a source of motivation by them to pursue conflict as an alternative to continued subjugation. Dahrendorf has too easily assumed that consciousness of opposed interests and political organization are the "causes" of conflict. But Coser's propositions point to the fact that such is unlikely to be the entire explanation, since other structural conditions (Propositions I-A, B; II-A, B) are critical in "activating" actors to a degree sufficient for them to be willing to overcome existing social patterns and engage in conflict. Dahrendorf seemingly relegates these psychological states to a proposition on conflict intensity (see below and Table 8–2), but in reality, such propositions must

---

[11] Peter Weingart, "Beyond Parsons? A Critique of Ralf Dahrendorf's Conflict Theory," *Social Forces* 48 (March): 151–65; Jonathan H. Turner, "From Utopia to Where?: A Strategy for Reformulating the Dahrendorf Conflict Model," *Social Forces* (Winter 1974), in press.

be viewed as causes of conflict, since intrasystem conflict involves overcoming the inertia, through the mobilization of emotional energies, of previous social relations. Thus, Coser's analysis provides balance to the Dahrendorf inventory, while, at the same time, attempting an answer to the question of how legitimated role relations can be both a source of order and conflict.

Conversely, Dahrendorf's inventory can balance the one-sidedness and meet some of the deficiencies of Coser's theoretical statements. One of the criticisms of the Coser scheme leveled by Dahrendorf and others[12] is that it cannot account for the conditions under which conflict parties who question existing patterns become sufficiently organized to initiate and perpetuate highly disruptive conflicts that reorganize social systems. Dahrendorf's reinterpretation of the Marxian legacy can provide part of the necessary correction, for in his propositions on "technical," "political," and "social" conditions, Dahrendorf offers some clues about how withdrawal of legitimacy and an escalating sense of deprivation can lead to the organization of groups capable of varying forms of conflict. As they now stand, Coser's propositions offer few insights into the causes of organized and pervasive conflicts. Since Coser develops a series of propositions on the impact of such conflict on group organization in his discussion of the intensity, duration, and outcomes of conflict, the theoretical question of how such organization emerges and takes the form it does needs to be addressed in a discussion of the causes of conflict. Dahrendorf's inventory thus provides some of the necessary statements about how conflict within a previously legitimated social order (ICA) can involve more than spontaneous emotional outbursts among disaffected and deprived segments.[13]

Intensity and Violence of Conflict

Dahrendorf is careful to make a distinction between the variables of intensity and violence. Intensity refers to the degree of emotional involvement and energy expenditure of parties to a conflict, while violence pertains to the degree of combativeness among conflict parties.[14] Coser has also implicitly made this distinction in his work, although he commends Dahrendorf for explicitly separat-

---

[12] See, for example, John Rex, *Key Issues in Sociological Theory* (London: Routledge & Kegan Paul, 1961).

[13] However, despite the suggestiveness of this kind of analysis, it should be evident that Dahrendorf's and Coser's theoretical statements have been couched at a highly abstract level and thus need to be supplemented by statements that bear a closer relationship to the empirical world. Furthermore, it should be clear that these propositions do not consistently indicate the units of analysis (whether groups, classes, collectivities, or individuals) to which they are directed. Thus, a long series of additional propositions would be necessary to clarify the vaguely stated propositions of the respective schemes of Dahrendorf and Coser. Yet, it is only after these authors' arguments are phrased propositionally that oversights become so manifestly evident—thus arguing for the potential utility of the kind of analysis performed in Table 8–1 (and Tables 8–2, 8–3, and 8–4).

[14] Dahrendorf, *Class and Class Conflict*, pp. 211–12.

ing the two variables and notes that "these and other highly valuable analytical distinctions will no doubt have to be incorporated into any future codification of a general theory of social conflict."[15]

In Table 8–2, the propositions developed by Coser and Dahrendorf with respect to these variable features of conflict are juxtaposed as in Table 8–1. As is evident, the propositions denoting intensity and violence are clearly evident in Dahrendorf's inventory, while for the Coser model, distinctions between violence and intensity need to be inferred. While Coser has written a number of essays on "violence,"[16] he tends to follow Simmel's[17] lead and discuss violence and intensity simultaneously, without making Dahrendorf's important distinction.

In Propositions I–III in Table 8–2, Dahrendorf indicates some of the conditions under which conflict is likely to be intense, increasing the involvement and energies of participants. For Dahrendorf, (a) the more the conditions of organization are met (see Table 8–1), (b) the more distribution of scarce resources are correlated with each other, and (c) the less mobility between super- and subordinate groups, the more intense the conflict. Coser similarly recognizes that the more those conditions causing conflict are met, the more intense the conflict. Unlike Dahrendorf, Coser then attempts to indicate some of the other conditions —in addition to Dahrendorf's "conditions of organization"—which will increase the emotional involvement of participants and hence the intensity of conflict (Propositions II-A, B). In Coser's Proposition III can be found Dahrendorf's "technical conditions," especially his Proposition I-A, 2 in Table 8–1 on the causes of conflict. Yet, Dahrendorf also emphasizes that variables denoting ideological unity affect conflict intensity, as is revealed by the recognition in Proposition I of Table 8–2 that the "technical conditions" of organization increase intensity. For Dahrendorf's second proposition on the superimposition of resource distribution, there is no direct parallel in the Coser inventory. However, Coser's propositions on the mitigating impact of secondary relations (II-B, II-B 1, 2) on conflict intensity appear to specify some of the structural conditions under which superimposition of rewards is unlikely and thereby suggest that a series of additional propositions is necessary to increase the utility of Dahrendorf's proposition. Dahrendorf's third proposition on the impact of mobility on conflict intensity is found in Coser's discussion in Table 8–1 on the causes of conflict, for, in his analysis of psychological variables that underlie the willingness to initiate conflict, Coser saw mobility as critical. Dahrendorf similarly views mobil-

---

[15] Lewis A. Coser, *Continuities in the Study of Social Conflict* (New York: Free Press, 1967), p. 3.

[16] Lewis A. Coser, "Violence and the Social Structure," Ibid., pp. 53–72; Lewis A. Coser, "The Social Functions of Violence," *Annals of the American Academy of Political and Social Science* 364 (March 1966): 8–18.

[17] Georg Simmel, "Conflict," trans. Kurt H. Wolff, in *Conflict and the Web of Group Affiliations* (Glencoe, Ill.: Free Press, 1955).

TABLE 8–2
The Intensity and Violence of Conflict

Dahrendorf	Coser
Degree of Intensity	
I. The more the "technical," "political," and "social" conditions of organization are met, the more intense is the conflict	I. The more the conditions causing the outbreak of conflict are realized, the more intense the conflict (1967a)
	II. The greater the emotional involvement of members in a conflict, the more intense the conflict (1956, p. 59)
	A. The more primary the relations among parties to a conflict, the more emotional involvement (1956, pp. 98–100)
	1. The smaller the primary groups where conflict occurs, the more emotional the involvement (1956, p. 100)
	2. The more primary the relations among parties, the less likely the open expression of hostility, but the more intense the expression in a conflict situation (1956, pp. 62–63, 68)
	B. The more secondary relations among parties to a conflict, the more segmental their participation and the less the emotional involvement (1956, p. 85)
	1. The more secondary relations, the more frequent the conflict, but the less the emotional involvement (1956, p. 85)
	2. The larger the secondary group, the more frequent the conflict, but the less the emotional involvement (1956, pp. 98–99)
	III. The more conflicts are objectified above and beyond individual self-interest, the more intense the conflict (1956, p. 116)
	A. The more ideologically unified a group, the more conflicts transcend individual self-interest (1956, p. 113)
	1. The more ideologically unified is a group, the more common are the goals of a group, and the more they transcend individual self-interest (1956, p. 113)
	2. The more ideologically unified is a group, the more will conflicts be entered with a clear conscience, and the more they transcend individual self-interest (1956, p. 113)

II. The more the distribution of authority and other rewards are associated with each other (superimposed), the more intense is the conflict

III. The less the mobility between super- and subordinate groups, the more intense is the conflict

Degree of Violence

IV. The less the "technical," "political," and "social" conditions of organization are met, the more violent is the conflict

IV. The more groups engage in conflicts over their realistic (objective) interests, the less intense the conflict
  A. The more groups conflict over realistic interests, the more likely they are to seek compromises over means to realize their interests (1956, p. 50)
    1. The greater the power differentials between groups in conflict, the less likely alternative means are to be sought (1956, p. 45)
    2. The more rigid the system where conflict occurs, the less availability of alternative means (1956, p. 45)

V. The more groups conflict over nonrealistic issues (false interests), the more intense the conflict (1956, p. 50)
  A. The more conflict occurs over nonrealistic issues, the greater the emotional involvement of the parties in the conflict and the more intense the conflict (1956, p. 50)
    1. The more intense previous conflict between groups, the greater the emotional involvement in subsequent conflicts (1956, pp. 98–99; 1967c)
  B. The more rigid the system where conflict occurs, the more likely is the conflict to be nonrealistic (1957)
  C. The more realistic conflict endures, the more nonrealistic issues emerge (1956, esp. 58:59; 1967c)
  D. The more the conflicting groups have emerged for purposes of conflict, the more nonrealistic the subsequent conflicts (1956, p. 54)

TABLE 8-2 (Continued)

Dahrendorf	Coser

Degree of Violence

Dahrendorf

V. The more the deprivations of the subjugated over the distribution of rewards shifts from an absolute to relative basis of deprivation, the more violent is the conflict

VI. The less the ability of conflict groups to develop regulatory agreements, the more violent the conflict

Coser

VI. The more rigid the social structure, the less will be the availability of institutionalized means for absorbing conflict and tensions, and the more intense the conflict (1956, p. 85)

  A. The more primary the relations among parties where conflict occurs, the more rigid the structure

    1. The less stable the primary relations, the more rigid the structure of those relations (1956, pp. 68–70)

    2. The more stable the primary relations, the less rigid the structure of those relations (1956, pp. 83–85)

  B. The more secondary (based on functional interdependence) the relations among parties where conflict occurs, the more likely are institutionalized means for absorbing conflict and tensions, and the less intense the conflict (1956, p. 85)

  C. The greater the control mechanism of the system, the more rigid the structure and the more intense the conflict (1957)

VII. The more the conflict in a group occurs over core values and issues, the more intense the conflict (1956, p. 75)

  A. The more rigid the structure where conflict occurs, the more likely is conflict to occur over core values and issues (1956, p. 79)

  B. The more emotional involvement in a situation where conflict occurs, the more likely it is to occur over core values and issues (1956, p. 76)

NOTE: Dates in parentheses refer to bibliography at end of chapter.

ity as generating emotional involvement, but strangely he fails to view it as an underlying cause of conflict (see Table 8–1).

Each of Dahrendorf's propositions on intensity, even when complemented by Coser's inventory, poses an analytical problem raised earlier: Why is it that the intensity of emotional involvement and the structural conditions that cause such involvement are not viewed as a cause of conflict? It would seem that there is almost an arbitrary distinction between the "technical," "political," and "social" conditions of organization and the "conditions" creating conflict intensity listed in Propositions I–III in Table 8–2. In fact, it might well be argued, as Coser appears to do, that Dahrendorf's "conditions of organization" will have little impact without the *prior* existence of the conditions generating emotional intensity. What is more, there is likely to be a complex cyclical feedback process between emotional involvement and the conditions of organization: One level of intensity makes actors more amenable to organization into conflict groups, which in turn affects, in ways not specified, subsequent levels of intensity, and so on in a temporal sequence that needs to be clarified. Dahrendorf's model seems to underemphasize this kind of feedback process as his conflict dialectic mechanically and inexorably unfolds, whereas Coser's consistent inclusion of both psychological and structural variables in his analysis at all phases of the conflict process (see Tables 8–1, 8–2, 8–3, 8–4) would indicate more understanding of the cyclical feedback processes as conflict unfolds.

To improve the power of the Dahrendorf scheme, it would therefore appear necessary for his propositions on the superimposition of rewards and mobility (Propositions II and III in Table 8–2) to be woven into Coser's propositions in Table 8–1 on the conditions affecting the questioning by actors of the legitimacy of the existing system of resource distribution (Proposition I in Table 8–1). In this way Dahrendorf's first proposition in his scheme (Proposition I in Table 8–1) on the awareness of inequality can be cast against a background of conditions raising emotions and conditions causing emotionally mobilized actors (Coser's Propositions I and II in Table 8–1) to become organized (Dahrendorf's propositions I-A–I-C in Table 8–1) into conflict groups. Then, Coser's propositions in Table 8–2 on the types of organized groups where emotion is heightened can begin to help account for the degree of ongoing intensity once Dahrendorf's initial "conditions of organization" have been met. By pursuing this strategy, the propositions in a theory of conflict would point to at least a few of the (1) structural conditions that lead to emotional arousal of actors over inequality in resource distribution; (2) the conditions of organization that channel such emotional arousal into conflict groups; and (3) the interaction between group organization and subsequent emotional involvement.[18]

---

[18] Naturally, such propositions would not indicate very precisely the conditions under which conflict would not occur and in which various types of other, nonconflictual processes could be

Such reorganization of the scheme would then generate a more adequate account of the conditions under which conflict is likely to be violent, as is seen in Dahrendorf's Propositions IV, V, and VI in Table 8–2. In Proposition IV, Dahrendorf indicates that the greater the intensity (emotional arousal) and the less the channeling of that emotion into organized groups, the more violent the conflict.[19] Coser's analysis of realistic and nonrealistic [20] conflict in Propositions III and IV of Table 8–2 points to the same phenomenon, but, as with his other propositions, it further specifies some of the conditions where the channeling of emotion into organized groups will prove ineffective and hence increase emotional involvement and presumably the violence of conflict when it eventually erupts. Again, unlike Dahrendorf, Coser appears attuned to the interaction between psychological and structural variables at all stages of conflict processes. Just as structural conditions arouse emotions that could under additional conditions become channeled and organized into conflict groups, which, in turn, under still further conditions could increase or decrease intensity, so a given level of intensity and conflict-group formation interacts with additional conditions to affect the degree of violence in conflict (see Propositions IV-A, 1, 2; V-A, 1, V-B, C, D; VI; VI-A; VI-A, 1, 2; VI-B, C). Since some of these conditions involve the same variables as produced the initial withdrawal of legitimacy, arousal of emotion, organization into conflict groups, and increased emotional involvement, Coser's inventory points to some of the shifting interaction effects of structural and psychological variables at different points or stages in the conflict process.

However, in Dahrendorf's proposition V in Table 8–2, it is he who introduces an important psychological variable that Coser appears to omit: relative deprivation.[21] While Coser introduces this variable under the causes of conflict in Table 8–1, Dahrendorf's incorporation of this variable at this point in the model supplements a gap in Coser's propositions. While relative deprivation is a crucial force in the causes of conflict, it also interacts with various structural conditions (Dahrendorf's Proposition IV and Coser's Propositions IV and V) to affect the level of violence of conflict.

In each author's Proposition VI in Table 8–2, he recognizes that the capacity

---

expected to occur. Furthermore, Marx appears to have understood this interaction between psychological and structural variables better than Dahrendorf, who, in his attempt to modernize Marx, has forfeited some of the suggestiveness of the Marxian model.

[19] This is a very questionable proposition, since it is obvious that armies are highly organized and capable of initiating a high degree of violence, without any great emotional involvement on the part of their members. Thus, if the proposition is to hold, the scope of its applicability needs to be specified.

[20] This analysis, as Coser acknowledges, is heavily indebted to Simmel's essay on "Conflict."

[21] For some authors, relative deprivation is considered a social structural variable, since deprivations are always relative to some social condition. Yet, in the end, relative deprivation involves the perception of events and subsequent emotional arousal by individuals, and hence is considered here a social psychological variable.

of a system to institutionalize conflict will affect the level of violence, but Coser's proposition points to some of the conditions affecting a system's capacity to regularize normatively antagonistic relations. Finally, Coser's propositional inventory recognizes that the values and issues that divide antagonistic parties will affect the level of violence (Proposition VII in Table 8–2), while Dahrendorf seemingly ignores this variable, presumably because conflict reflects a "contest for authority" and other issues simply represent a "superstructure" that mask the real sources of conflict. Yet, even as such, it would seem likely that the type of symbolic superstructure used to mobilize or tranquilize conflict parties would greatly affect the violence of conflict. While Dahrendorf implicitly recognizes this variable in his discussion of how the absence of "technical" conditions of organization increases the probability of violent conflict (Proposition IV in Table 8–2), his incorporation of this variable appears to be tangential to the scheme. Coser's Proposition VII thus provides a needed supplement to the Dahrendorf inventory.

Duration of Conflict

As is immediately evident in Table 8–3, Dahrendorf offers no propositions in his formal inventory on the duration of conflict. Such an omission represents a serious weakness to the inventory, since the duration of conflict will clearly have feedback implications for causitive variables affecting the emergence of subsequent conflicts, as well as for the level of intensity and violence of such conflicts. In contrast to Dahrendorf, Coser provides an interesting list of propositions. For Coser, the clarity of the goals of conflict parties, the degree of consensus between conflict parties over points of victory and defeat, and the capacity of leaders to perceive the costs of victory and persuade followers of the desirability of termination are critical in determining the duration of conflict. Each of these variables is in turn influenced by other variables, such as emotional involvement (I-A), degree of realism to the conflict (II-A), extent of polarization (III-A, 1), respective degrees of power (III-A), clarity of indices of victory (IV-B) and degree of centralization (V-B).

Outcomes of Conflict

In Table 8–4, the propositions on the outcomes of conflict from the two schemes are listed as in earlier tables. For Dahrendorf as for Marx, the only outcome incorporated into the model is social change, with only the amount (Proposition I) and the rate (Proposition II) of such change visualized as variable phenomena. Coser, on the other hand, has conceptualized just the opposite phenomena.

TABLE 8–3
The Duration of Conflict

	Dahrendorf	Coser

Coser

I.   The less limited the goals of the opposing parties in a conflict, the more prolonged the conflict (1967d)
   A.   The less emotional involvement, rigidity of structure, and non-realistic the character of the conflict, the more likely the goals of parties to a conflict are to be limited (1956, 48–55, 59)

II.   The less consensus over the goals of conflict between conflicting parties, the more prolonged the conflict (1967d)
   A.   The less realistic the conflict, the more likely dissensus over the goals of conflict (1956, p. 50)

III.   The less the parties in a conflict can interpret their adversaries' symbolic points of victory and defeat, the more prolonged the conflict (1967d)
   A.   The less the consensus by both parties over symbols, the less the ability of each to interpret its adversaries' symbolic points of victory and defeat (1967d)
      1.   The greater the polarization of conflict parities and the superimposition of conflicts upon one another, the less consensus over symbolic points of victory and defeat (1967d)
      2.   The fewer the extremist factions within each party to a conflict, the more likely is consensus over symbolic points of victory and defeat (1967d)

IV.   The more leaders of conflicting parties can perceive that complete attainment of goals is possible only at costs higher than those required for victory, the less prolonged the conflict (1967d)
   A.   The more equal the power between two conflicting parties, the more likely leaders are to perceive the high costs of complete attainment of goals (1956, p. 20)
   B.   The more clear-cut the indexes of defeat or victory in a conflict, the more likely leaders are to perceive the high costs of complete attainment of goals (1967d)

1. The more consensus over symbols of defeat and victory, the more clear-cut the indexes of defeat or victory (1967*d*)

V. The greater the capacity of leaders of each conflict party to persuade followers to terminate conflict, the less prolonged the conflict (1967*d*)

   A. The greater the leaders' knowledge of their followers' symbols and the more consensus over these symbols, the greater the capacity to persuade followers (1967*d*)

   B. The more centralized the conflict parties, the greater the capacity of leaders to persuade followers (1956, pp. 128–33)

   C. The fewer the internal cleavages of conflict parties, the greater the leader's capacity to persuade followers (1967*d*)

   D. The more leaders can claim that some gains have been made, the greater their capacity to persuade followers (1967*d*)

NOTE: Dates in parentheses refer to bibliography at end of chapter.

TABLE 8-4
The Outcomes of Conflict

Dahrendorf

I. The more intense the conflict, the more structural change and reorganization it will generate

II. The more violent the conflict, the greater the rate of structural change and reorganization

Coser

I. The more intense the conflict, the more clear-cut the boundaries of each respective conflict party (1956, pp. 37–38)

II. The more intense the conflict and the more differentiated the division of labor of each conflict party, the more likely each to centralize its decision-making structure (1956, p. 95)

   A. The more intense the conflict, the less differentiated the structure and the less stable the structure and internal solidarity, the more centralization is despotic (1956, p. 92)

III. The more intense the conflict and the more it is perceived to affect all segments of each group, the more conflict promotes structural and ideological solidarity among members of respective conflict groups (1956, p. 93)

IV. The more primary the relations among the members of respective conflict groups, and the more intense the conflict, the more conflict leads to suppression of dissent and deviance within each conflict group and to forced conformity to norms and values (1956, pp. 69–72)

   A. The more conflict between groups leads to forced conformity, the more the accumulation of hostilities and the more likely internal group conflict in the long run (1956, p. 48)

V. The less rigid the social structure where conflict between groups occurs and the more frequent and less intense the conflict, the more likely conflict to change the system in ways promoting adaptability and integration (1956, pp. 45–48)

   A. The less rigid the system, the more likely is conflict to promote innovation and creativity in the system (1957)

B. The less rigid the system, the less likely is conflict to involve displacement of hostilities to alternative objects and the more likely is conflict to confront realistic sources of tension (1956, pp. 45–48; 1967c)

1. The more a system is based upon functional interdependence, the more frequent and less intense the conflict, and the more likely it is to release tensions without polarizing the system (1956, p. 85)

2. The more stable the primary relations in a system, and the more frequent and less intense is the conflict, the more likely it is to release tensions without polarizing the system, but not to the extent of a system based upon secondary relations (1956, pp. 83, 85)

C. The less rigid the system, the more likely is conflict to be perceived by those in power as signals of maladjustment that need to be addressed (1966; 1967c)

VI. The more frequently conflict occurs, the less likely it is to reflect dissensus over core values and the more functional for maintaining equilibrium it is likely to be (1956, p. 73)

A. The more a conflict group can appeal to the core values of a system, the less likely the conflict to create dissensus over these values and the more likely it is to promote integration of the system (1968)

B. The more a conflict group does not advocate extreme interpretations of core values, the less likely a counterconflict group to form and the less disruptive the conflict for the system (1968)

VII. The more frequent and less intense are conflicts, the more likely they are to promote normative regulation of conflict

A. The less rigid a system, the more frequent and less intense the conflict (1956, p. 125; 1957)

1. The less rigid the system, the more likely conflict to revitalize existent norms (1956, p. 125)

TABLE 8–4 (Continued)

Dahrendorf	Coser

Coser

2. The less rigid the system, the more likely conflict to generate new norms (1956, p. 125)

B. The more frequent and less intense conflicts, the more likely are groups to centralize in an effort to promote conformity of each group's membership to norms governing the conflict (1956, p. 129)

  1. The more equal the power of conflict groups, the more likely is conflict to generate centralization promoting normative conformity (1956, p. 129)

VIII. The less rigid system, the more likely it is that conflict can establish balances and hierarchies of power in a system (1956, pp. 133–38)

A. The less knowledge of the adversary's strength and the fewer the indexes of such strength, the more likely is conflict between two groups vying for power to promote a balance of power relations in a system (1956, p. 136)

IX. The less rigid the system, the more likely is conflict to cause formation of associative coalitions that increase the cohesiveness and integration of the system (1956, p. 140)

A. The more other parties in a system are threatened by coalitions of other parties, the more likely they are to form associative coalitions (1956, p. 148)

B. The more a system is based upon functional interdependence, the more likely coalitions are to be instrumental and less enduring (1956, p. 142)

  1. The more a system reveals crosscutting cleavages, the more likely groups in a coalition are to have their own conflicts of interests, and the more likely is the coalition to be instrumental (1956, p. 142)

  2. The more a coalition is formed for purely defensive purposes, the more likely it is to be instrumental (1956, p. 149)

C. The more tightly structured and primary the relations in a system, the more likely coalitions are to develop common norms and values and form a more permanent group (1956, p. 142)

  1. The more coalitions are formed of individuals (or more generally, the smaller the units forming a coalition), the more likely they are to develop into a permanent group (1956, p. 146)

  2. The more interaction required among the parties of a coalition, the more likely it is to form a permanent group (1956, p. 146)

NOTE: Dates in parentheses refer to bibliography at end of chapter.

Following Simmel's lead, Coser outlines in these propositions the integrative and "adaptability" functions of conflict for each of the parties to a conflict (Propositions I–IV) and for the more inclusive system within which the conflict occurs (Propositions V–IX). In Propositions I–IV conflict can cause a shoring up of group boundaries, centralization of decision making, ideological solidarity, and increased social control. These events occur only under specified conditions, including the degree of rigidity and differentiation in social structure, the intensity of the conflict, and the extent to which conflict is perceived to affect all factions of the group.

In both the Dahrendorf and Coser inventories there are imperativist assumptions: Conflict is functionally necessary for either system adjustment (Coser) or system change (Dahrendorf). Such imperativist connotations are probably inevitable with the excessive one-sidedness of their respective inventories. While the divergence of the two inventories suggest a high degree of complementarity, Dahrendorf's inventory is too incomplete to provide a set of propositions that might "balance" Coser's statements. To provide such balance, Dahrendorf's inventory would have to be expanded to include a series of additional statements: (1) One group of such statements would indicate just how the type of structure in which conflict occurs affects the outcomes of either intense or violent conflict. While Coser's propositions are excessively one-sided, emphasizing primarily the positive functions of conflict, there is an attempt to document how the structure within which the conflict occurs can influence different degrees and types of integration and adaptability. (2) Another group of statements would concern the feedback of the actual outbreak of conflict on conflict-group formation (or disintegration). Dahrendorf appears content to ignore the fact that the actual conflict itself is another "condition or organization," which influences the subsequent course of antagonistic interactions. This insight was, of course, one of Simmel's important contributions and Coser has wisely incorporated it—albeit in a one-sided fashion—into his inventory (Propositions I–IV in Table 8–4).

Thus, Coser's propositions suggest some of the lines along which revision of Dahrendorf's propositions should occur. Conversely, Dahrendorf's concern with social change points rather dramatically to Coser's overly "functional" conception of reality, for even conflict appears to foster only integration and "adaptability." To correct for this skewedness, Coser's inventory of propositions would need some additional statements suggested by the Dahrendorf scheme: The most important set of these statements would indicate the variable impact of intense and/or violent conflict on both the parties to a conflict and the systemic whole within which the conflict occurs. Such propositions would address the question of how varying forms of conflict interact within varying structural contexts to promote, not only integration and adaptability, but also such processes as change, reorganization, and dissolution of the parties to the conflict and the system in which conflict occurs. In fact, the variable of adaptability should be abandoned, since it makes inevitable a value judgment as to what the "proper" state of system must be with respect to its environment. Instead, both the inventories should strip away some of their imperativist assumptions about the functions of conflict (whether for change or stasis) and focus simply on the outcomes of conflict for the systemic whole and its various subparts. In this way, the interaction effects of the many variables involved in generating varying outcomes could be more easily incorporated into a balanced set of theoretical statements.

PROPOSITIONAL SYNTHESIS: A CONCLUDING POINT OF VIEW

This short chapter has performed an exercise that unkind critics might label ad hoc juggling of disparate propositions. An exercise like that performed in Tables 8–1 through 8–4, critics could claim, takes propositions out of their analytical and substantive context and reduces theory building to the art of creating "jigsaw puzzles" of propositions. Such schemes will inevitably lack the continuity of good theory, for how can the propositions of diverse thinkers be ripped from context and fitted together to form a coherent theoretical system that can inspire attempts at empirical investigation? To these critics, who would become easily fatigued by the exercise performed in Tables 8–1 through 8–4, there are several lines of response.

First, sociological theorizing has for some time become bogged down in the construction of conceptual perspectives that often appear to be a mixture of stated and unstated assumptions as well as implicit and explicit propositions. Such perspectives have typically been constructed in either relative isolation from each other or in the spirit of overreaction to the assumptions of some undesirable perspective (typically, functionalism). While each respective scheme that has been constructed in this manner may reveal the desired continuity and coherence of mature theory, the end result has been for the theoretical perspectives in sociology to stand at odds with each other as proponents line up into particular schools of thought. Then, depending upon the psychological propensity of each school's adherents, thinkers either engage in polemics against other perspectives in an effort to expose the virtues of their own; or they elaborate their particular scheme seemingly without much awareness of the contributions that other perspectives might be able to make to it. This situation is what enables a book or theory to divide its subject matter into four general schools or perspectives—such as the functional, conflict, interactionist, and exchange perspectives covered in this volume—and then to discuss the schemes of major thinkers working within the confines of each general perspective.

Second, as was emphasized earlier, when attempts are made to break down these somewhat arbitrary barriers, synthesizers typically attempt to reconcile the *assumptions* (rather than propositions) of two or more perspectives, which, for the synthesizer, reveal more convergence than was heretofore perceived by members of the discipline. Such activity can prove useful if it is followed by a more difficult task: synthesizing the actual theoretical statements that were inspired by the respective assumptions of each of the synthesized perspectives. Without this latter kind of activity, it can be asked: Of what use is reconciliation of assumptions in building theory, for "value judgments" about what is "really real" in the social world can only be confirmed or refuted when stated as testable propositions? In theory building, it is often useful to understand a theorist's assumptions, but what really counts are the testable propositions of each theorist. For indeed, testable propositions are what distinguish science from philosophical treatises on metaphysics. It is unfortunate that much of what passes for theoretical synthesis in sociology resembles a reconciliation of philosophical assumptions about the nature of reality rather than a set of testable statements that would confirm or refute such assumptions.

For all the crudity of the presentation in Tables 8–1 through 8–4 of this chapter, a clear strategy for building theory is advocated: Attempt to abstract the propositions of various thinkers and begin the difficult task of synthesizing these statements with (*a*) each other, (*b*) with other theoretical perspectives, and, most important, (*c*) with whatever empirical evidence is available. This chapter has only performed the first part of this strategy—attempting to reconcile abstract theoretical statements of one theoretical orientation—and would be strengthened by attention to other theoretical perspectives and whatever empirical evidence there is. This latter task of bringing to bear empirical evidence is perhaps more difficult than the exercise performed in Tables 8–1 through 8–4, but it can be carried out more efficiently when the abstract theoretical statements of thinkers are made explicit and organized into a theoretical format—even a crude and tentative one as delineated here. Only in this way can theory inform research, and research force revision of theory.

For those critics who wish to avoid constructing formats of theoretical statements, it can only be concluded that they are more interested in social philosophy than science. For those critics who would point to the efforts of this chapter as an ad hoc exercise, it can only be assumed that they are not concerned with building theoretical formats but with "coherent" perspectives where assumptions and propositions remain implicit—and hence untestable. For those critics who would point to the "paucity" of Coser's and Dahrendorf's thought, as revealed in Tables 8–1 through 8–4, it can only be argued that initial attempts at building theory, as opposed to metaphysical schemes, will be modest. It is to the credit of Coser and Dahrendorf that, in the end, they chose to state their arguments propositionally and thereby open their respective schemes to the kind of examination that promises real *theoretical* payoff in sociology. When viewed in this context, Coser and Dahrendorf have made an important contribution to theory building; in so doing, they have advanced sociology's capacity to find a scientific solution to the Hobbesian problem of order.

SELECTED BIBLIOGRAPHY OF RALF DAHRENDORF'S THEORETICAL WORK

Dahrendorf, Ralf. *Class and Class Conflict in Industrial Society.* Stanford, Calif.: Stanford University Press, 1957.

———. "Toward a Theory of Social Conflict." *Journal of Conflict Resolution* 2 (June 1958): (a)

———. "Out of Utopia: Toward a Reorientation of Sociological Analyses." *American Journal of Sociology* 64 (September 1958): (b)

———. *Gesellschaft und Freiheit.* Munich: R. Piper, 1961.

———. *Essays in the Theory of Society.* Stanford, Calif.: Stanford University Press, 1967.

SELECTED BIBLIOGRAPHY OF LEWIS A. COSER'S THEORETICAL WORK

Coser, Lewis A. *The Functions of Social Conflict.* London: Free Press, 1956.

———. "Social Conflict and the Theory of Social Change." *British Journal of Sociology* 8 (September 1957): 197–207

———. "Some Functions of Deviant Behavior and Normative Flexibility," *American Journal of Sociology* 68 (September 1962):

———. "Social Functions of Violence." *Annals of the American Academy of Political and Social Science* 364 (March 1966): 9–18

———. *Continuities in the Study of Social Conflict.* New York: Free Press, 1967. (a)

———. "Violence and the Social Structure." In *Continuities in the Study of Social Conflict,* edited by L. A. Coser, pp. 53–72. New York: Free Press, 1967. (b)

———. "Internal Violence as a Mechanism for Conflict Resolution." In *Continuities in the Study of Social Conflict,* edited by L. A. Coser, pp. 93–110. New York: Free Press, 1967. (c)

———. "The Termination of Conflict." In *Continuities in the Study of Social Conflict,* edited by L. A. Coser, pp. 37–52. New York: Free Press, 1967. (d)

———. "The Functions of Dissent." *The Dynamics of Dissent.* New York: Grune & Straton, 1968. Pp. 158–70.

———. "The Visibility of Evil." *Journal of Social Issues* 25 (Winter 1969): (a)

———. "Unanticipated Conservative Consequences of Liberal Theorizing." *Social Problems* 16 (Summer 1969): (b)

Part *III*

Interaction Theory

9

The Emergence of
Interactionism

Some of the most intriguing questions of social theory concern the relationships between society and the individual. In what ways does one mirror the other? How does society shape individuals, or how do individuals create, and maintain, and change society? In what ways do society and the personality of individuals represent interrelated and yet separate, emergent phenomena?

It is to these questions that sociological theory turned near the close of the 19th century, as the grand analytical schemes of Marx, Durkheim, Spencer and other Europeans were supplemented by a concern for the specific processes that linked individuals to one another and to society. Instead of focusing on the macro structures and processes, such as evolution, class conflict, and the nature of the "body social," attention shifted to the study of processes of social interaction and their consequences for the individual and society.

George Simmel was perhaps the first European sociologist to begin the serious exploration of interaction, or "sociability" as he called it. In so doing, he elevated the study of interaction from the taken-for-granted.[1] For Simmel, as for the first generation of American sociologists, the macro structures and processes studied by functional and some conflict theories—class, the state, family, religion, evolution—were ultimately reflections of the specific interactions among people. While these interactions had resulted in emergent social phenomena, considerable insight into the latter could be attained by understanding the basic interactive

---

[1] Georg Simmel, "Sociability," in *The Sociology of Georg Simmel*, ed. Kurt H. Wolff (New York: Free Press, 1950), pp. 40–57. For an excellent secondary account of Simmel's significance for interactionism, see Randall Collins and Michael Makowsky, *The Discovery of Society* (New York: Random House, 1972), pp. 138–42.

151

processes that first gave and then sustained their existence. Although Simmel was to achieve many remarkable insights into the forms of interaction, the concepts that were to guide the contemporary interactionist perspective were formulated in America as thinkers grappled with the related issues of how interaction among individuals shaped social structure and how social structures as networks of interaction molded individuals.

MIND, SELF, AND SOCIETY

The names of William James, Charles Horton Cooley, James Mark Baldwin, and John Dewey figure prominently in the development of interactionism. However, as significant as the individual contributions of each of these thinkers were, it was left to George Herbert Mead to bring their related concepts together into a coherent theoretical perspective that linked the emergence of the human mind, the social self, and the structure of society to the process of social interaction.[2]

Mead appears to have begun his synthesis with two basic assumptions: (1) The biological frailty of human organisms forced their cooperation with each other in group contexts in order to survive; and (2) those actions within and among human organisms that facilitated their cooperation, and hence their survival, would be retained. Starting from these assumptions, Mead was able to reorganize the concepts of others so that they denoted how mind, the social self, and society arose and were sustained through interaction.

Mind

For Mead, the unique feature of the human mind is its capacity to (1) use symbols to designate objects in the environment, (2) to rehearse covertly alternative lines of action toward these objects, and (3) to inhibit inappropriate lines of action and select a proper course of overt action. Mead terms this process of using symbols or language covertly "imaginative rehearsal," revealing his conception of mind as a *process* rather than a structure. Further, as will be developed more fully in later pages, the existence and persistence of society, or cooperation in organized groups, is viewed by Mead as dependent upon this capacity of

---

[2] Mead wrote very little, and thus most of his seminal ideas can only be found in the published lecture notes of his students. His most important exposition of interactionism is found in his *Mind, Self, and Society*, ed. Charles W. Morris (Chicago: University of Chicago Press, 1934). Other useful sources include George Herbert Mead, *Selected Writings* (Indianapolis: Bobbs-Merrill Co., 1964); and Anselm Strauss, ed., *George Herbert Mead on Social Psychology* (Chicago: University of Chicago Press, 1964). For excellent secondary sources on the thought of Mead, see Tomatsu Shibutani, *Society and Personality: An Interactionist Approach* (Englewood Cliffs, N.J.: Prentice Hall, Inc., 1962); Anselm Strauss, *Mirrors and Masks: The Search for Identity* (Glencoe, Ill.: Free Press, 1959); and Bernard N. Meltzer, "Mead's Social Psychology," in *The Social Psychology of George Herbert Mead* (Ann Arbor, Mich.: Center for Sociological Research, 1964), pp. 10–31.

humans to "imaginatively rehearse" lines of action toward each other and thereby select those behaviors that could facilitate cooperation and adjustment.

Much of Mead's analysis focuses not so much on the mind of mature organisms, but on how this capacity first evolves in humans. Unless infants develop mind, neither society nor self can exist. For Mead, mind arises out of a selective process in which the initially wide repertoire of random gestures emitted by an infant are narrowed as some gestures bring favorable reactions from those upon whom the infant is dependent for survival. Such selection of gestures facilitating adjustment can occur either through trial and error or through conscious coaching by those with whom the infant must cooperate. Eventually, through either of these processes, gestures come to have "common meanings" for both the infant and those in his environment. With this development, gestures now denote the same objects and carry similar dispositions for all the parties to an interaction. When gestures have such common meanings, Mead denotes them "conventional gestures." These conventional gestures have increased inefficiency for interaction among individuals, because they allow for more precise communication of desires and wants as well as intended courses of action—thereby increasing the capacity of organisms to adjust to one another.

The ability to use and to interpret conventional gestures with common meanings represents a significant step in the development of mind, self, and society. By perceiving and interpreting gestures, humans reveal the capacity to "take the role of the other," since they can now assume the perspective (dispositions, needs, wants, and propensities to act) of those with whom they must cooperate for survival. By reading and then interpreting covertly conventional gestures, individuals are able to imaginatively rehearse alternative lines of action that will facilitate adjustment to others. Thus, by being able to put oneself in another's place, or to "take the role of the other" to use Mead's concept, the covert rehearsal of action can take on a new level of efficiency, since actors can better gauge the consequences of their actions for others and thereby increase the probability of cooperative interaction.

Thus, when an organism develops the capacity (1) to understand conventional gestures, (2) to employ these gestures to take the role of others, and (3) to imaginatively rehearse alternative lines of action, Mead believes such an organism to possess *mind*.

Self

Just as humans can designate symbolically other actors in the environment, so they can symbolically represent themselves as an object. The interpretation of gestures, then, can not only facilitate human cooperation, it can also serve as the basis for self assessment and evaluation. This capacity to derive images of oneself as an object of evaluation in interaction is dependent upon the processes of mind. What Mead sees as significant about this process is that, as organisms mature, the transitory "self-images" derived from specific others in each interactive situation eventually become crystallized into a more or less stabilized "self-conception" of oneself as a certain type of object. With the emergence of these self-conceptions, actions of individuals are seen by Mead to take on consistency, since they are now mediated through a coherent and stable set of attitudes, dispositions, or meanings about oneself as a certain type of person.

Mead chooses to highlight three stages in the development of self, each stage marking not only a change in the kinds of transitory self-images an individual could derive from role taking, but also an increasing crystallization of a more stabilized self-conception. The initial stage of role taking in which self-images could be derived is termed by Mead as "play." In play, infant organisms are capable of assuming the perspective of only a limited number of others, at first only one or two. Later, by virtue of biological maturation and practice at role taking, the maturing organism becomes capable of taking the role of several others engaged in organized activity. Mead terms this stage the "game," because it designates the capacity of individuals to derive multiple self-images from, and to cooperate with, a group of individuals engaged in some coordinated activity. (Mead typically illustrates this stage by giving the example of a baseball game in which all individuals must symbolically assume the role of all others on the team in order to participate effectively.) The final stage in the development of self occurs when an individual can take the role of the "generalized other" or "community of attitudes" evident in a society. At this stage, individuals are visualized by Mead as capable of assuming the overall perspective of a community, or the general beliefs, values, and norms of an individual's various spheres of interaction. This means that humans can both (1) increase the appropriateness of their responses to others with whom they must interact and (2) expand their evaluative self-images from the expectations of specific others to those of the broader community. Thus, it is through this ever-increasing capacity to take roles with an ever-expanding body of "others" which marks the stages in the development of self.

Society

For Mead, *society,* or "institutions" as he often phrases the matter, represents the organized and patterned interactions among diverse individuals. Such organization of interactions is dependent upon mind. Without the capacities of mind to take roles and imaginatively rehearse alternative lines of activity, individuals could not coordinate their activities. Mead emphasizes:

The immediate effect of such rôle-taking lies in the control which the individual is able to exercise over his own response. The control of the action of the individual in a co-operative process can take place in the conduct of the individual himself if he can take the rôle of the other. It is this control of the response of the individual himself through taking the rôle of the other that leads to the value of this type of communication from the point of view of the organization of the conduct in the group.[3]

Society is also dependent upon the capacities of self, especially the process of evaluating oneself from the perspective of the "generalized other." Without the ability to see and evaluate oneself as an object from this "community of attitudes," social control would rest solely on self-evaluations derived from role taking with specific and immediately present others—thus making coordination of diverse activities among larger groups extremely difficult.[4]

While Mead is vitally concerned with how society and its institutions are maintained and perpetuated by the capacities of mind and self, these concepts also allow him to view society as constantly in flux and rife with potential change. The fact that role taking and imaginative rehearsal are ongoing processes among the participants in any interaction situation reveals the potential these processes give individuals for adjusting and readjusting their responses. Furthermore, the insertion of self as an object into the interactive process underscores the fact that the outcome of interaction will be affected by the ways in which self-conceptions alter the initial reading of gestures and the subsequent rehearsal of alternative lines of behavior. Such a perspective thus emphasizes that society and various patterns of social organization are both perpetuated and altered through the adjustive capacities of mind and the mediating impact of self:

> Thus the institutions of society are organized forms of group or social activity— forms so organized that the individual members of society can act adequately and socially by taking the attitudes of others toward these activities. . . . [But] there is no necessary or inevitable reason why social institutions should be oppressive or rigidly conservative, or why they should not rather be, as many are, flexible and progressive, fostering individuality rather than discouraging it.[5]

In this passage is a clue to Mead's abiding distaste for rigid and oppressive patterns of social organization. He views society as a *constructed* phenomenon that arises out of the adjustive interactions among individuals; as such, society can be altered or reconstructed through the processes denoted by the concepts of mind and self. However, Mead frequently appears to have gone one step further to stress that not only is change likely, but also that it is frequently unpredictable, even by those emitting the change-inducing behavior. To account

---

[3] Mead, *Mind, Self, and Society*, p. 254.

[4] Ibid., pp. 256–57.

[5] Ibid., pp. 261–62.

for this indeterminacy of action, Mead develops two additional concepts, the "I" and the "me."[6] For Mead, the "I" points to the impulsive tendencies of individuals, while the "me" represents the self-image of the behavior in question after it has been emitted. With these concepts Mead emphasizes that the "I," or impulsive behavior, cannot be predicted, because the individual can only "know in experience" (the "me") what has actually transpired and what the consequences of the "I" for the interaction are to be.

In sum, then, society for Mead represents those constructed patterns of coordinated activity that are maintained by, and changed through, symbolic interaction among and within actors. Both the maintenance and change of society, therefore, occur through the processes of mind and self. While many of the interactions causing both stability and change in groups are viewed by Mead as predictable, the possibility for spontaneous and unpredictable actions that could alter existing patterns of interaction is always possible.

This conceptual legacy had a profound impact on a generation of American sociologists prior to the posthumous publication in 1934 of Mead's lectures. However, by that time, it was becoming evident that, despite the suggestiveness of Mead's concepts, they failed to address some important theoretical issues.

The most important of these issues concerned the vagueness of his concepts in denoting the nature of social organization or "society" and the precise points of articulation between society and the individual. Mead viewed society as organized activity, regulated by the generalized other, in which individuals made adjustments and cooperated with one another. Such adjustments and the cooperation they insured were then seen as possible by virtue of the capacities of "mind" and "self." While mind and self emerged out of existent patterns of social organization, the maintenance or change of such organization was seen by Mead as a reflection of the processes of mind and self. Although these and related concepts of the Meadian scheme pointed to the mutual interaction of society and the individual, and although the concepts of mind and self denoted crucial processes through which this dependency was maintained, they did not allow for the analysis of variations in patterns of social organization and in the various ways individuals were implicated in these patterns. To note that "society" was coordinated activity and that such activity was maintained and changed through the role-taking and the self-assessment processes of individuals offered only a broad conceptual portrait of the linkages between the individual and society. Indeed, Mead's picture of society did not indicate how variable types of social organization reciprocally interacted with variable properties of self and mind. Thus, in the end, Mead's concepts appeared to emphasize that society shaped mind and

---

[6] These actually represent reformulations of concepts developed much earlier by William James. See, for example, James's *Principles of Psychology*, 2 vols. (New York: Henry Holt, 1890); more accessible is his abridgement of these volumes (Cleveland: World Publishing Co., 1948); see especially pp. 135–76.

self and that mind and self affected society—a simple but profound observation for the times, but one that needed supplementation.

The difficult task of filling in the details of this broad portrait began only four decades ago, as researchers and theorists began to encounter the vague and circular nature of Mead's conceptual perspective. The initial efforts at documenting more precisely and less tautologously the points of articulation between society and the individual led to attempts at formulating a series of concepts that could expose the basic units from which society was constructed. It was felt that in this way the linkages between society and the individual could be more adequately conceptualized.

ROLE, STATUS, SOCIETY, AND THE INDIVIDUAL

Inspired in part by Mead's concept of role taking and by his own studies in Europe, Jacob Moreno was one of the first to develop the concept of role playing. In *Who Shall Survive* [7] and in many publications in the journals he founded in America, Moreno began to view social organization as a network of roles that constrained and channeled behavior. In his early works, Moreno began to distinguish different types of roles: (a) "psychosomatic roles," in which behavior was related to basic biological needs, as conditioned by culture, and in which role enactment was typically unconscious; (b) "psychodramatic roles," in which individuals behaved in accordance with the specific expectations of a particular social context; and (c) "social roles," in which individuals conformed to the more general expectations of various conventional social categories (for example, worker, Christian, mother, father, and so forth).

Despite the suggestiveness of these distinctions, their importance came not so much from their substantive content, but from their intent: to conceptualize social structures as organized networks of expectations that required varying types of role enactments by individuals. In this way, analysis was able to move beyond the vague Meadian conceptualization of society as coordinated activity, regulated by the "generalized other," to a more sophisticated conceptualization of social organization as various *types* of interrelated role enactments regulated by varying *types* of expectations.

Shortly after Moreno's publication of *Who Shall Survive*, the anthropologist Ralph Linton further conceptualized the nature of social organization, and the individual's imbeddedness in it, by distinguishing the concepts of role, status, and individuals from one another:

A status, as distinct from the individual who may occupy it, is simply a collection of rights and duties. . . . A *role* represents the dynamic aspect of status. The

---

[7] Jacob Moreno, *Who Shall Survive*, Nervous and Mental Disease Publication (Washington, D.C., 1934); rev. ed. (New York: Beacon House, 1953).

individual is socially assigned to a status and occupies it with relation to other statuses. When he puts the rights and duties which constitute the status into effect, he is performing a role.[8]

In this passage are a number of important conceptual distinctions. Now social structure is perceived to reveal several distinct analytical elements: (a) a network of positions, (b) a corresponding system of expectations, and (c) patterns of behavior which are enacted with regard to the expectations of particular networks of interrelated positions. While, in retrospect, these distinctions may appear self-evident and trivial, they made possible the subsequent elaboration of many interactionist concepts:

1. Linton's distinctions allowed for the conceptualization of society in terms of clear-cut variables: the nature and kind of interrelations among positions and the types of expectations attending these positions.

2. The variables Mead denoted by the concepts of mind and self could be analytically distinguished from both social structure (positions and expectations) and behavior (role enactment).

3. By conceptually separating the processes of role taking and imaginative rehearsal from both social structure and behavior, the points of articulation between society and the individual could be more clearly marked, since role taking would pertain to covert interpretations of the expectations attending networks of statuses, and role would denote the enactment of these expectations as mediated by self.

Thus, by offering more conceptual insight into the nature of social organization, Moreno and Linton provided a needed supplement to Mead's suggestive concepts. For now it would be possible to understand more precisely the nature of, and the interrelations among, mind, self, and society.

MODERN INTERACTIONISM: A PREVIEW

The Meadian legacy has inspired a theoretical perspective that can best be termed "symbolic interactionism." This perspective—to be discussed in chapter 11—focuses on how the symbolic processes of role taking, imaginative rehearsal, and self-evaluation by individuals attempting to adjust to one another lay the basis for the understanding of how social structure is constructed, maintained, and changed. While accepting the analytical importance of these symbolic processes, a more recent theoretical tradition has placed more conceptual emphasis on the vision of social structure connoted by Moreno's and Linton's concepts. Although not as clearly codified or as unified as the symbolic interactionist position, this theoretical perspective—the subject of chapter 10—can be labeled "role theory,"

---

[8] Ralph Linton, *The Study of Man* (Copyright © 1936 by D. Appleton-Century Company, Inc.).

because it focuses primary analytical attention on the *structure of status networks and attendant expectations* as they circumscribe the internal symbolic processes of individuals and the eventual enactment of roles.

In some respects, the distinction between symbolic interactionism and role theory may initially appear arbitrary, since each perspective relies heavily on the thought of George Herbert Mead and since both are concerned with the relationship between the individual and society. As the following two chapters will reveal, however, the assumptions and images of society connoted by the two perspectives differ to such an extent that each implies a somewhat different strategy for constructing theoretical statements and conducting research.

10

Role Theory: In Search of Conceptual Unity

Role theorists[1] are fond of quoting a famous passage from Shakespeare's *As You Like It* (act 2, scene 7):[2]

> All the world's a stage
> And all the men and women merely players:
> They have their exits and their entrances;
> And one man in his time plays many parts.

The analogy is then drawn between the players on the stage and the actors of society. Just as players have a clearly defined part to play, so actors in society occupy clear positions; just as players must follow a written script, so actors in society must follow norms; just as players must obey the orders of a director, so actors must conform to the dictates of those with power or those of importance; just as players must react to each other's performance on the stage, so members of society must mutually adjust their responses to one another; just as players respond to the audience, so actors take the role of various audiences or "generalized others"; and just as players with varying abilities and capacities bring to each role their own unique interpretation, so actors with varying self-conceptions and role-playing skills have their own styles of interaction.

---

[1] For the first early analytical statements, see Jacob Moreno, *Who Shall Survive*, rev. ed. (New York: Beacon House, 1953) (original ed., 1934); and Ralph Linton, *The Study of Man* (New York: Appleton-Century, 1936).

[2] For an example of this form of analogizing, see Bruce J. Biddle and Edwin Thomas, *Role Theory: Concepts and Research* (New York: John Wiley & Sons, 1966), pp. 3–4. For the best-known "dramaturgical" model, see Irving Goffman, *The Presentation of Self in Everyday Life* (New York: Doubleday & Co., 1959).

Despite its simplicity, the analogy is appropriate, for as this chapter unfolds, it will become evident that the role-theoretic perspective supports the thrust of Shakespeare's passage. However, at the outset it should be noted that, despite its pervasiveness in sociology, role analysis is far from being a well-articulated and unified theoretical perspective. In fact, the very task of reviewing the many diverse substantive and theoretical works on role theory requires a tentative theoretical synthesis.[3]

IMAGES OF SOCIETY AND THE INDIVIDUAL

Shakespeare's passage provides the general outline of what role theorists assume about the social world. In the "stage" are assumptions about the nature of social organization; in the concept of "players" are implicit assumptions about the nature of the individual; and in the vision of men and women as "merely players" who have "their exits and their entrances" are a series of assumptions about the relationship of individuals to patterns of social organization.

The Nature of Social Organization

For role theorists, the social world is viewed as a network of variously inter-related *positions*, or statuses, within which individuals enact roles.[4] For each position, as well as for groups and classes of positions, various kinds of *expectations* about how incumbents are to behave can be discerned.[5] Thus, social organization is ultimately composed of various networks of statuses and expectations.

Statuses are typically analyzed in terms of how they are interrelated to one another to form various types of social units. In terms of variables such as size, degree of differentiation, and complexity of interrelatedness, status networks are classified into forms, ranging from various types of groups to larger forms of collective organization. While there has been some analysis on their formal properties, status networks[6] are rarely analyzed independently of the types of

---

[3] For some recent attempts to bring together role-theoretic concepts, see Biddle and Thomas, *Role Theory*, pp. 1–64; Morton Deutsch and Robert M. Krauss, *Theories in Social Psychology* (New York: Basic Books, 1965), pp. 173–211; and Marvin E. Shaw and Philip R. Costanzo, *Theories of Social Psychology* (New York: McGraw-Hill Book Co., 1970), pp. 326–46.

[4] For an early analysis of this viewpoint, see Kingsley Davis, *Human Society* (New York: Macmillan Co., 1949); Linton, *Study of Man;* Moreno, *Who Shall Survive;* Emile Benoit, "Status, Status Types, and Status Interrelations," *American Sociological Review* 9 (April 1944): 151–61; George P. Murdock, *Social Structure* (New York: Macmillan Co., 1949); and Robert K. Merton, *Social Theory and Social Structure* (New York: Free Press, 1951), pp. 368–79.

[5] Mead's concept of the "other" pointed to the impact of perceived expectations upon the way individuals enacted roles. However, it was not until after World War II that the systematic analysis of types of expectations was undertaken.

[6] See, for example, Jacob L. Moreno, "Contributions of Sociometry to Research Methodology in Sociology," *American Sociological Review* 12 (June 1947): 287–92; and J. L. Moreno, ed., *The*

expectations attendant upon them. Part of the reason for this close relation between form and content is that the types of expectations that typify particular networks of positions represent one of their defining characteristics. It is usually assumed that the behavior emitted by incumbents is not an exclusive function of the structure of positions, per se, but also of the kinds of expectations that inhere in these positions.

The range of expectations denoted by role-theoretic concepts is diverse. Pursuing the dramaturgical analogy to a play, three general classes of expectations appear to typify role theory's vision of the world: (a) expectations from the "script"; (b) expectations from other "players"; and (c) expectations from the "audience."

Expectations from the "Script."   Much of social reality can be considered to read like a script in that for many positions there are *norms* specifying just how an individual ought to behave. The degree to which activity is regulated by norms varies under different conditions; thus, one of the theoretical questions to be resolved by role theory concerns the conditions under which norms vary in terms of such variables as scope, power, efficacy, specificity, clarity, and degree of conflict with each other.[7]

Expectations from Other "Players."   In addition to the normative structuring of behavior and social relations, role theory also focuses on the demands emitted by the "other players" in an interaction situation. Such demands, interpreted through role taking of other's gestures, constitute one of the most important forces shaping human conduct.

Expectations from the "Audience."   A final source of expectations comes from the "audiences" of individuals occupying statuses. These audiences can be real or imagined, constitute an actual group or a social category, involve membership or simply a desire to be a member. It is only necessary that the expectations imputed by individuals to such variously conceived audiences be used to guide conduct. As such, the audiences comprise a frame of reference, or reference group,[8] that circumscribes the behavior of actors in various statuses.

Sociometry Reader (Glencoe, Ill.: Free Press, 1960); Oscar A. Oeser and Frank Harary, "Role Structures: A Description in Terms of Graph Theory," *Human Relations* 15 (May 1962): 89–109; and Darwin Cartwright and Frank Harary, "Structural Balance: A Generalization of Heider's Theory," *Psychological Review* 63 (September 1956): 277–93.

[7] For early analysis of normative phenomena, see Davis, *Human Society;* Samuel Stauffer, "An Analysis of Conflicting Social Norms," *American Sociological Review* 14 (December 1949): 707–17; Robin M. Williams, Jr., *American Society: A Sociological Interpretation,* 2d ed. (New York: Alfred Knopf, 1960), pp. 25–38; and George C. Homans, *The Human Group* (New York: Harcourt, Brace & World, 1950). For a diversity of more recent citations, see Biddle and Thomas, *Role Theory;* pp. 23–63.

[8] Mead's concept of the "generalized other" anticipated this analytical concern with reference groups. For some of the important conceptual distinctions in the "theory" of reference group behavior, see Robert K. Merton, "Continuities in the Theory of Reference Groups and Social

In sum, then, much of the social world is assumed by role theory to be structured in terms of expectations from a variety of sources, whether the script, other players, or various audiences. Just which types of expectations are attendant upon a given status, or network of positions, is one of the important empirical questions that follows from this assumption.

Although role theory implicitly assumes that virtually the entire social spectrum is structured in terms of statuses and expectations, rarely is this whole spectrum studied. In fact, role analysis usually concentrates on restricted status networks, such as groups and small organizations, and the types of expectations evident in these more micro social units. Such an emphasis can be seen as representing a strategy for analytically coping with the incredible complexity of the entire status network and attendant expectations of a society or of some of its larger units. In this delimitation of the field of inquiry, however, there is an implicit assumption that the social order is structured only by certain basic kinds of micro groups and organizations. Larger analytical phenomena, such as social classes or nation-states and relations among them, are less relevant, because there is a presumption that these phenomena can be understood in terms of their constituent groups and organizations.

This emphasis on the micro structures of society is perhaps inevitable in light of the fact that role theory ultimately attempts to account for types of role performances by individuals. While macro patterns of social organization are viewed as providing much of the "order" to these performances, society cannot be conceptualized independently of its individual incumbents and their performances.

The Nature of the Individual

Individuals occupying positions and playing roles are typically conceptualized by role theory as revealing two interrelated attributes: (*a*) self-related characteristics, and (*b*) role-playing skills and capacities. The self-related concepts of role theory are diverse, but they tend to cluster around an analytical concern for the impact of self-conceptions on the interpretation of various types of expectations that guide conduct in a particular status. Role-playing skills denote those capacities of individuals to perceive various types of expectations and then, with varying degrees of competence and with different role-playing styles, to follow a selected

---

Structure," pp. 225–80; Tomatsu Shibutani, "Reference Groups as Perspectives," *American Journal of Sociology* 60 (May 1955): 562–69; Harold H. Kelley, "Two Functions of Reference Groups," in *Readings in Social Psychology*, ed. G. E. Swanson, et al. (New York: Henry Holt Co., 1958); Ralph H. Turner, "Role-taking, Role Standpoint, and Reference Group Behavior," *American Journal of Sociology* 61 (January 1956): 316–28; and Herbert Hyman and Eleanor Singer, eds., *Readings in Reference Group Behavior* (New York: Free Press, 1968).

set of expectations. These two attributes—self and role-playing skills—are perceived to be highly interrelated, since self-conceptions will mediate the perception of expectations and the way roles are enacted, while role-playing skills will determine the kinds of self-images, to use Mead's concept, which are derived from an interaction situation and which go into the construction of a stable self-conception.

This conceptualization of the individual roughly parallels Mead's portrayal of mind and self. For both Mead and contemporary role theorists, it is the capacity to take roles and mediate self-images through a stable self-conception that distinguishes the human organism. Although this conceptualization of self and role-playing capacities offers the potential for visualizing unique interpretations of expectations and for analyzing spontaneous forms of role playing, the opposite set of assumptions are more often connoted in role theory. That is, concern appears to be with the way individuals conform to what is expected of them by virtue of occupying a particular status. The degree and form of conformity are usually seen as the result of a variety of internal processes operating on individuals. Depending upon the interactive situation, these internal processes are conceptualized in terms of variables such as (1) the degree to which expectations have been internalized as a part of individual's need structure,[9] (2) the extent to which negative or positive sanctions are perceived by individuals to accompany a particular set of expectations,[10] (3) the degree to which expectations are used as a yardstick for self-evaluation,[11] and (4) the extent to which expectations represent either interpretations of others' actual responses or merely anticipations of their potential responses.[12] Just which combination of these internal processes operates in a particular interaction situation depends upon the nature of the statuses and attendant expectations. While this complex interactive process has yet to be comprehended with even an incipient inventory of theoretical statements, it remains one of the principal goals of role theory.

From this conceptualization, the individual is assumed to be not so much a creative role entrepreneur who tries to change and alter social structure through varied and unique responses, but rather a pragmatic performer who attempts to cope with and adjust to the variety of expectations inhering to social structure.

---

[9] For example, Talcott Parsons, *The Social System* (New York: Free Press, 1951), pp. 1–94; and William J. Goode, "Norm Commitment and Conformity to Role-Status Obligations," *American Journal of Sociology* 66 (November 1960): 246–58.

[10] For example, B. F. Skinner, *Science and Human Behavior* (New York: Macmillan Co., 1953), pp. 313–55, 403–19; Biddle and Thomas, *Role Theory*, pp. 27–28; Shaw and Costanzo, *Theories of Social Psychology*, pp. 332–33.

[11] Biddle and Thomas, *Role Theory*, p. 27; Kelley, "Two Functions of Reference Groups"; Turner, Role-taking, Role Standpoint"; and Ralph H. Turner, "Self and Other in Moral Judgement," *American Sociological Review* 19 (June 1954): 254–63.

[12] Turner, "Role-taking, Role Standpoint"; Biddle and Thomas, *Role Theory*.

These implicit assumptions about the nature of the individual are consistent with Mead's concern with the adaptation and adjustment of the human organism to society, but they clearly underemphasize the creative consequences of mind and self for the construction and reconstruction of society. Thus, role theory has tended to expand conceptually upon only part of the Meadian legacy. While this tendency assures some degree of assumptive one-sidedness, it is understandable in light of the role theorists' concern for sorting out only certain types of dynamic interrelationships between society and the individual.

The Articulation between the Individual and Society

The point of articulation between society and the individual is denoted by the concept of "role" and involves individuals who are incumbent in statuses employing self and role-playing capacities to adjust to various types of expectations. Despite agreement over these general features of role, current conceptualizations differ.[13] Depending upon which component of role is emphasized, three basic conceptualizations are evident.[14]

Prescribed Roles. When conceptual emphasis is placed upon the expectations of individuals in statuses, then the social world is assumed to be composed of relatively clear-cut prescriptions. The individual's self and role-playing skills are then seen as operating to meet such prescriptions, with the result that analytical emphasis is drawn to the degree of conformity to the demands of a particular status.

Subjective Roles. Since all expectations are mediated through the prism of self, they are subject to interpretations by individuals in statuses. When conceptual emphasis falls upon the perceptions and interpretations of expectations, then the social world is conceived to be structured in terms of individuals' subjective assessments of the interaction situation. Thus, conceptual emphasis is placed upon the interpersonal style of individuals who interpret and then adjust to expectations.

Enacted Role. Ultimately, expectations and the subjective assessment by individuals of these expectations are revealed in behavior. When conceptual priority is given to overt behavior, then the social world is viewed as a network

---

[13] For summaries of the various uses of the concept, see Lionel J. Neiman and James W. Hughes, "The Problem of the Concept of Role—A Re-survey of the Literature," *Social Forces* 30 (December): 141–49; Ragnar Rommetveit, *Social Norms and Roles: Explorations in the Psychology of Enduring Social Pressures* (Minneapolis: University of Minnesota Press, 1955); Biddle and Thomas, *Role Theory;* Shaw and Costanzo, *Theories of Social Psychology,* pp. 334–38; and Deutsch and Krauss, *Theories in Social Psychology,* pp. 173–77.

[14] Deutsch and Krauss, *Theories in Social Psychology,* p. 175; Daniel J. Levinson, "Role, Personality, and Social Structure in the Organizational Setting," *Journal of Abnormal and Social Psychology* 58 (March 1959): 170–80.

of interrelated behaviors. The more conceptual emphasis is placed upon overt role enactment, the less analytical attention to the analysis of either expectations or individual interpretations of them.

Obviously, when viewed separately from each other, these three conceptual notions are inadequate. Indeed, overt human behavior involves a subjective assessment of various types of expectations. In fact, in reviewing the research and theoretical literature on role theory, it is evident that, although the prescriptive, subjective, or enacted component of role may receive particular emphasis, theoretical efforts usually deal with the complex causal relationships among these components.

Perhaps more than any conceptual perspective, role theory portrays images of causality rather than an explicit set of causal linkages. Part of the reason for this vagueness stems from the fact that the label "role theory" embraces a wide number of specific perspectives in a variety of substantive areas. Despite these qualifications, however, role theorists have tended to develop concepts that denote specific interaction processes without revealing the precise ways these concepts are causally interrelated.

To the extent that role theory's causal images can be brought into focus, they appear to emphasize the deterministic consequences of social structure on interaction. However, rarely are larger, more inclusive units of culture and structure included in this causal analysis. Rather, concern tends to be with the impact of specific norms, others, and reference groups associated with particular clusters of status positions on (a) self-interpretations and evaluations, (b) role-playing capacities, or (c) overt role behavior. While considerable variability is evident in the role-theoretic literature, self-interpretations and evaluations are usually viewed as having a deterministic impact on role-playing capacities, with role-playing capacities then circumscribing overt role behavior. Despite the fact that particular concern with prescribed roles, subjective roles, or role enactment will influence which causal nexus is emphasized, the general causal imagery still tends to portray this sequence, as is delineated in the top portion of Figure 10–1.

As the middle section of Figure 10–1 reveals, the specific causal images evident in the literature are more complex than the general portrayal at the top of the figure. While expectations are still viewed as determinative, role theorists have frequently emphasized the reciprocal nature of causal processes. That is, certain stages in the causal sequence are seen as "feeding back" and affecting the subsequent causal relations among the analytical units in the middle section of Figure 10–1. Although there are numerous logical interconnections among these units, role theory has emphasized only a few of these causal linkages, as is designated by the solid arrows in the figure. Furthermore, to the extent that specific units of analysis are conceptualized for expectations, self-variables, role-playing skills, and overt behavior, only some of the causal interconnections among these units are explored, as is revealed at the bottom of Figure 10–1.

FIGURE 10–1
The Causal Imagery of Role Theory

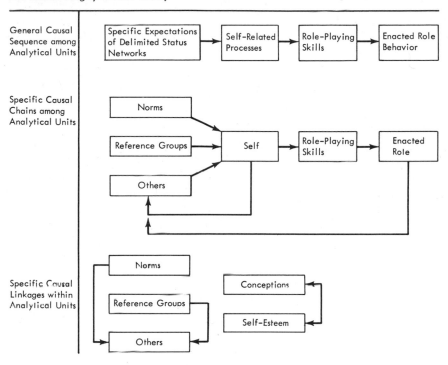

With respect to the interrelations among expectations, self, role-playing skills, and overt behavior, role theory appears to be concerned primarily with conceptualizing how different types of expectations emanating from different sources—norms, others, and reference groups—are mediated by self-interpretations and evaluations and then circumscribed by role-playing skills in a way that a given style of role performance is evident. This style is then typically analyzed in terms of its degree of conformity to expectations.[15] However, at each stage in this sequence, certain "feedback" processes are also emphasized so that the degree of "significance" of norms, others, or reference groups for the maintenance of self-conceptions of individuals is considered critical in influencing which expectations are most likely to receive the most attention. Emphasis in this causal nexus is on the degree of imbeddedness of self in certain groups,[16] the degree of

[15] The study of deviance, socialization, and role playing in complex organizations and small groups has profited from this form of analysis.

[16] For example, see Norman Denzin, "Symbolic Interactionism and Ethnomethodology" in *Understanding Everyday Life: Toward a Reconstruction of Sociological Knowledge*, ed. Jack D. Douglas (Chicago: Aldine Publishing Co., 1970), pp. 259–84. For the most thorough set of such studies in this area, see Sarbin's examinations of the intensity of self-involvement and role-playing

intimacy with specific others,[17] and the degree of commitment to, or internalization of, certain norms.[18] Another prominent feedback process that has received considerable attention is the impact of overt behavior at one point in time on the expectations of others as they shape the individual's self-conception and subsequent role behavior at another point in time. In this context, the childhood and adult socialization of the individual and the emergence of self have been extensively studied,[19] as has the analysis of the emergence of deviant behavior.[20]

With respect to interrelations within the analytical units of the overall causal sequence, the arrows at the bottom of Figure 10–1 portray the current theoretical emphasis of the literature. In regard to the interrelations among types of expectations, analytical attention appears to be on how specific "others" personify group norms or the standards of reference groups. In turn, these "significant" others are often viewed as deterministically linking the self-interpretations and evaluations of an individual to either the norms of a group or the standards of a reference group.[21] With respect to the relations among the components of self, analysis appears to have followed the lead of William James [22] by focusing on the connections between the "self-esteem" and the self-conception of an individual.[23] In turn, the interaction between self-esteem and other components of self is viewed as the result of reactions from various others who affect the self-images of the individual. Finally, all these components interact in complex ways to shape the overt behavior of the individual.

Thus, looking back at Figure 10–1, it is evident that of the many possible causal interrelations, only a few have been extensively conceptualized in the role-theoretic literature. While studies can be found which draw attention to

---

behavior: Theodore R. Sarbin, "Role Theory" in *Handbook of Social Psychology*, G. Lindzey, vol. 1 (Reading, Mass.: Addison-Wesley Publishing Co., (1954), pp. 223–58; Theodore R. Sarbin and Norman L. Farberow, "Contributions to Role-taking Theory: A Clinical Study of Self and Role," *Journal of Abnormal and Social Psychology* 47 (January 1952): 117–25; and Theodore R. Sarbin and Bernard G. Rosenberg, "Contributions to Role-taking Theory," *Journal of Social Psychology* 42 (August 1955): 71–81.

[17] See, for example, Tomatsu Shibutani, *Society and Personality* (Englewood Cliffs, N.J.: Prentice-Hall, Inc., 1961), pp. 367–403.

[18] John Finley Scott, *Internalization of Norms: A Sociological Theory of Moral Commitment* (Englewood Cliffs, N.J.: Prentice-Hall, Inc., 1971), pp. 127–215; William Goode, "Norm Commitment and Conformity"; B. F. Skinner, *Science and Human Behavior.*

[19] For example, see Anselm Strauss, *Mirrors and Masks* (Glencoe, Ill.: Free Press, 1959), pp. 100–118; Shibutani, *Society and Personality*, pp. 471–596; Orville G. Brim and Stanton Wheeler, *Socialization after Childhood* (New York: John Wiley & Sons, 1966).

[20] See Edwin Lemert, *Social Pathology* (New York: McGraw-Hill Book Co., 1951); Thomas Scheff, "The Role of the Mentally Ill and the Dynamics of Mental Disorder: A Research Framework," *Sociometry* 26 (December 1963): 436–53; Howard Becker, *Outsiders: Studies in the Sociology of Deviance* (New York: Free Press, 1963).

[21] Turner, "Role-taking, Role Standpoint"; Shibutani, *Society and Personality*, pp. 249–80.

[22] William James, *Principles of Psychology*, 2 vols. (New York: Henry Holt, 1890).

[23] See Shibutani, *Society and Personality*, pp. 433–46.

each possible causal nexus, little theoretical attention has been paid to the following connections: (a) broader social and cultural structure and specific patterns of interaction, (b) enacted role behaviors and their effect on role-playing capacities, (c) these role-playing capacities and self, and (d) enacted roles and the self assessments that occur *independently* of role taking with specific others or groups.[24] Rather, concern has been on the relations between self and expectations as they affect, and are affected by, enacted roles.

PROBLEMS IN BUILDING ROLE "THEORY"

Constructing Propositions

To this point, role-theoretic concepts provide a means for categorizing and classifying expectations, self, role-playing capacities, role enactment, and relationships among these analytical units. The use of concepts is confined primarily to classification of different phenomena, whether attention is drawn to the forms of status networks,[25] types and sources of expectations,[26] relations of self to expectations,[27] or the enactment of roles.[28] While the concepts of scientific theory must be capable of classifying events, they should also be incorporated into associational and causal statements. As yet, role theory has made little progress in this direction, with the result that it is difficult to discern statements approximating the form: Under $C_1, C_2, C_3, \ldots, C_n$, x causes variation in y.

In the future, as they begin the difficult task of building interrelated invento-

---

[24] There is a large experimental literature on the impact of various types of "contrived" role playing on attitudes and other psychological attributes of individuals; as yet, the findings of these studies have not been incorporated into the role-theoretic framework. For some examples of these studies, see Bert T. King and Irving L. Janis, "Comparison of the Effectiveness of Improvised versus Non-improvised Role-playing in Producing Opinion Changes," *Human Relations* 9 (May 1956): 177–86; Irving C. Janis and Bert T. King, "The Influence of Role Playing on Opinion Change," *Journal of Abnormal and Social Psychology* 49 (April 1954): 211–18; Paul E. Breer and Edwin A. Locke, *Task Experience as a Source of Attitudes* (Homewood, Ill.: Dorsey Press, 1955); Theodore Sarbin and V. L. Allen, "Role Enactment, Audience Feedback, and Attitude Change," *Sociometry* 27 (June 1964): 183–94.

[25] For example, see Davis, *Human Society;* Merton, *Social Theory and Social Structure;* Benoit, "Status, Status Types"; and Biddle and Thomas, *Role Theory*, pp. 23–41.

[26] Davis, *Human Society;* Richard T. Morris, "A Typology of Norms," *American Sociological Review* 21 (October 1956): 610–13; Alan R. Anderson and Omar K. Moore, "The Formal Analysis of Normative Concepts," *American Sociological Review* 22 (February 1957): 9–16; Williams, *American Society.*

[27] Turner, "Role Taking, Role Standpoint"; and Sarbin and Allen, "Role Enactment, Audience Feedback."

[28] Goffman, *Presentation of Self;* Sarbin, "Role Theory"; John H. Mann and Carola H. Mann, "The Effect of Role-playing Experience on Role-playing Ability," *Sociometry* 22 (March 1959): 69–74; and William J. Goode, "A Theory of Role Strain," *American Sociological Review* 25 (August 1960): 483–96.

ries of propositions, role theorists confront several theoretical problems. First, it will be necessary to fill in the gaps in their causal imagery. To continue emphasizing only some causal links at the expense of ignoring others is to invite an incomplete and inaccurate set of theoretical statements. Particularly crucial in this context will be the development of propositions that specify the linkages between concepts denoting more inclusive social and cultural variables, on the one hand, and concepts pointing to specific interaction variables, on the other.

Second, the current "propositions" that do exist in the role-theoretic literature will have to be reformulated so that conditional statements specifying when certain processes are likely to occur will be more explicit. For example, in the "theory" of reference-group behavior, propositions take the form of asserting that the use of a particular group as a frame of reference is likely to occur when: (a) contact with members of a reference group are likely, (b) dissatisfaction with alternative group memberships exists, (c) perception of potential rewards from a group is likely, (d) the perception of that group's standards is possible, and (e) perception of the availability of significant others in the group is possible.[29] Although these propositions are suggestive, they offer few clues as to what forms of contact, what levels of dissatisfaction, what types of rewards and costs, which group standards, and what type of significant others serve as conditions for use as a frame of reference by an individual. Furthermore, many relevant variables are not included in these propositions. For instance, in order to improve the "theory" of reference-group behavior, it would be minimally necessary to incorporate theoretical statements on the intensity of self-involvement, the capacity to assume roles in a group, the nature of group standards and their compatibility with various facets of an individual's self-conception.

These are the problems that a theoretical perspective attempting to link social structural and individual personality variables will inevitably encounter. When psychological variables, such as self-concept, self-esteem, and role-playing capacities, are seen as interacting with cultural and structural variables, such as status, norm, reference group, and "others," the resulting inventory of theoretical statements will become complex. Such an inventory must not only delve into the internal states of individuals, but must also cut across several levels of emergent phenomena—at a minimum, the individual, the immediate interaction situation, and the more inclusive structural and cultural contexts within which the interaction occurs.

Methodological Implications

The potential utility of role theory derives from its concern with the complex interrelations among the expectations derived from social structure, the media-

---

[29] Example drawn from summary in Alvin Boskoff, *The Mosaic of Sociological Theory* (New York: Thomas Y. Crowell Co., 1972), pp. 49–51.

tion of these expectations through self and role-playing capacities of actors in statuses, and the resulting enactment of role behaviors. Measurement of role enactment does not pose a major methodological obstacle, since it is the most observable of the phenomena studied by role theorists. However, to the extent that such overt behavior is considered to reflect the impact of expectations and self-related variables, several methodological problems become evident. The complexity of the interrelations between role behavior, on the one hand, and self and expectations, on the other, as well as the difficulty of finding indicators of these interrelations, poses a series of methodological problems that will continue to make it difficult to construct bodies of theoretical statements on the relation between society and the individual.

Since one of the assumed links between society and the individual revolves around the expectations that confront individuals, it is theoretically crucial that various types of expectations, and the ways they affect individuals, be measurable. To the degree that these concepts cannot be measured, the utility of role-theoretic perspective for building sociological theory can be questioned. One method that has been employed in the measurement of expectations is to infer from observed behavior the kinds of expectations that guided its unfolding. The most obvious and important problem with such a method is that expectations can only be known after the fact of the behavior they are supposed to circumscribe. Therefore, the concept of expectations as inferred from behavior has little theoretical utility, since it cannot be measured independently of behavior. Hence, role behavior cannot be predicted from the content of expectations and their relationship to self. An alternative method involves (a) the accumulation of verbal accounts of individuals[30] prior to a particular interaction sequence, (b) the inference of what types of expectations are guiding conduct, and (c) the prediction of how role behavior will unfold in terms of these expectations. This method has the advantage of making predictions about the impact of expectations, but it suffers from the fact that, much like inferences drawn from role enactment, expectations are not measurable independently of the individual who is to be guided by them.[31] The end result of these methodological dilemmas is for expectations to represent analytical inferences that are difficult to discern independently of the behavior—whether verbal accounts or role enactment—that they are supposed to guide.

A final alternative to this methodological problem is for researchers to become active participants in social settings, and from this participation to derive some

---

[30] There are many ways to accumulate such accounts, ranging from informal observations and unstructured interviews with subjects to highly structured interviews and questionnaires. All of these have been employed by role theorists, whether in natural settings or the small-group laboratory.

[31] This dilemma anticipates the discussion of ethnomethodology to be undertaken in chapter 17, for, as the ethnomethodologist would argue, these verbal accounts are the "reality" that guides conduct. From this perspective, the assumption of a "really real" world, independent of an actor's mental construction of it, is considered to be unfounded.

"intuitive sense" of the kinds of expectations that are operating on actors. From this "intuitive sense" it is then presumed that more formal conceptual representation of different types of expectations, and of their varying impact on selves and behavior, can be made. The principal drawback to such an approach is that one researcher's "intuitive sense" is not another's, with the result that *the* expectation structure observed by different researchers in the same situation might well be a "negotiated" product as researchers attempt to achieve consensus as to exactly what this structure is to be. However, to the extent that such a negotiated conceptualization has predictive value, it would represent an indicator of the expectation structure that is, in part at least, derived independently of the verbal statements and behavior of those whose conduct it is supposed to guide.

In sum, then, studying expectations is a difficult enterprise. Since most bodies of sociological theory assume the existence of an expectation structure, it is crucial that these methodological problems be exposed, because they have profound implications for theory building. The most important of these implications concerns the possibility of building theory with concepts that are not measurable, even in principle. Examining either role behavior or verbal statements and then inferring the existence of expectations tends to make specific propositions tautologous, since variation in behavior is explained by variation in phenomena inferred from such behavior. The use of participant or observational techniques overcomes this problem, but presents the equally perplexing issue of how different researchers are to replicate, and hence potentially refute, each other's findings. If conceptualization of the expectation structure is a "negotiated" product, the subsequent investigation of similar phenomena by different investigators would require "renegotiation." When the nature of phenomena that are incorporated into theoretical statements is not explicitly defined and classified in terms of independently verifiable, clear-cut, and agreed-upon standards, but is rather the product of "negotiation," then the statements are not refutable, even in principle. As products of negotiation they have little utility for building a scientific body of knowledge. Ultimately, the severity of these problems is a matter of subjective assessment, since for some they would appear to be fundamental, while for others they stem from the inadequacies of current research techniques.

Whether problems with conceptualizing expectations are seen as either fundamental or technical, they are compounded by the methodological problems of measuring self-related variables. How is it possible to derive operational indicators of self-conceptions, self-esteem, and intrapsychic assessments of the situation? Both verbal accounts and observational techniques have typically been used to tap these dimensions of interaction; while they are "technically" inadequate in that their accuracy can be questioned, they do not raise the same fundamental questions as do expectations, since they do seem measurable in principle. The problems arise only when attempts are made to link these self-related variables to expectations that are presumed to have an independent existence that guides the creation and subsequent operation of self-related processes. While the independent existence of norms, others, reference groups, and the like is intuitively pleasing, just how these phenomena are to be conceptualized and measured separately from the self-related processes they are assumed to circumscribe remains a central problem of role theory. This problem is unlikely to recede in the near future and will continue to call into question the utility of role theory.

Substantive Implications

The substantive criticisms of the role-theoretic perspective focus on the overly structured and circumscribed vision of human behavior, and presumably of social organization, that it connotes. Although it can be argued that current role theory is too diverse to be vulnerable to this line of criticism, its prominent theoretical schemes, as well as the cumulative impact of its empirical studies, reveal a highly structured conceptualization of social reality.

Ontologically, role theory assumes the social world to be structured in terms of status networks, and corresponding clusterings of expectations, within which individuals with selves and various capacities enact roles. Despite the fact that expectations are viewed as mediated by self and role-playing capacities (subjective role), the main analytical thrust is on how individuals adjust and adapt to the demands of the "script," other "actors," and the "audiences" of the "play." Undoubtedly, much social action is structured in this way, but the connotative impact of the concepts loads analysis in the direction of assuming too much structure and order in the social world.

The conspicuous conceptualization of "role conflicts"[32] (conflicts among expectations), "role strain"[33] (the impossibility of meeting all expectations), and "anomie"[34] (the lack of clear-cut expectations) in role theory would seemingly balance this overly structured conception of reality. Yet frequently, strain, conflict, and anomie are viewed as "deviant" situations that represent "exceptions" to the structure of the "normal" social order. What is critical, then, is that these concepts be elaborated upon and inserted into current theoretical statements. In this way, they can serve to specify the conditions under which the social world is less circumscribed by social structure.

The causal imagery of role theory also contributes to an overly structured

[32] For example, see John W. Getzels and E. C. Guba, "Role, Role Conflict, and Effectiveness," *American Sociological Review* 19 (February 1954): 164–75; Talcott Parsons, *Social System*, pp. 280–93; Merton, *Social Theory and Social Structure*, pp. 369–79; and Robert L. Kahn, et al., *Organizational Stress: Studies in Role Conflict and Ambiguity* (New York: John Wiley & Sons).

[33] Goode, "Theory of Role Strain."

[34] Merton, *Social Theory and Social Structure*, pp. 121–51.

vision of social reality. Figure 10–1 emphasizes that the causal thrust of the role theory is on the way expectations, as mediated by selves and role-playing capacities, circumscribe role enactment. Although attention is drawn to the feedback consequences of role enactment for expectations, this analysis usually concerns how behaviors of individuals alter the reactions of others in such a way that self-conceptions are reinforced or changed.

What is ignored are the determinative consequences of role enactments for changes and alterations in social structure. In focusing primarily on how changes of behavior affect self-conceptions, role theory has underemphasized the fact that behavior can also force changes in the organization of status networks, norms, reference groups, the responses of others, and other features of social structure. Until the causal imagery of role theory stresses the consequences of role enactment, not only for self-related variables but also for social structural variables, it will continue to conceptualize the social world as excessively circumscribed by the expectation structure.

Some of the logical problems of role-theoretic analysis further contribute to this conception of the social world. The vagueness of just how and under what conditions social structure affects self and role enactment leaves much of role analysis with the empty assertion that society shapes individual conduct. If role-theoretic assumptions are to have theoretical significance, it is essential to specify just when, where, how, and through what processes this circumscription of role behavior occurs. In fact, in the absence of theoretical specificity, a subtle form of imperativism is connoted: The needs of social structure and the individual require that behavior be circumscribed. This imperativism is further sustained by the classificatory nature of role-theoretic concepts. In denoting the types of interrelations among society, self, and behavior without indicating the conditions under which these relationships are likely to exist, these concepts appear to denote what processes must occur without indicating when, where, and how they are to occur.[35]

Finally, the methodological problems of measuring expectations separately from the very individual processes that they are supposed to circumscribe makes even more "mysterious" just how and in what ways social structure affects individual conduct. Again, the inability to measure this crucial causal nexus leaves the role theorist with the uninteresting assertion, loaded with imperativist connotations, that society shapes and guides individual conduct.

Many of these substantive problems could be overcome with a slight alteration

---

[35] Although most role theorists would vehemently deny it, they have followed Parsons's strategy for building theory, except on a more micro level. In developing concepts to classify and order role-related phenomena, without also developing clear-cut propositions, they have created a conceptual order without indicating when and how the order denoted by concepts is maintained (or broken down or reconstructed).

in role analysis. Ontologically, the recognition that much behavior is not determined by audiences or the script, but by actors mutually adjusting to one another in the absence of these forces, would lead to a more balanced theoretical question: Under what conditions is human behavior shaped by what, if any, types of expectations? Currently, the mania for classifying the types of reference groups, norms, others, and functional relations among these and the individual has allowed the role theorist to avoid asking, to say nothing of answering, this theoretical question.

With respect to the causal imagery, the multiple causal feedback processes must be given more recognition so that the reciprocity among status networks, expectations, self, role-playing capacities, and role behavior will be reflected in theoretical statements. Coupled with a renewed interest in incorporating classificatory concepts into propositions, many of the logical problems as they contribute to substantive difficulties of role theory would be mitigated, since the hidden imperativism would be replaced by more precise statements on when events are likely, and not likely, to occur. The methodological problems of role theory are not easily surmounted and will continue to plague role analysis. However, with these proposed changes in the assumptions, causal imagery, and format of theoretical statements, the inadequacies of methodology would at least no longer contribute to an overly structured vision of the social world.

REDIRECTING ROLE THEORY: SOME CONCLUDING REMARKS

Since the concept of role represents the point of articulation between the individual and society, its examination is necessary for theoretical understanding of why different patterns of social organization emerge, persist, change, and break down. At present, the main thrust of the role-theoretic strategy has been to focus on how specific social contexts determine variations in individual conduct, and to give comparatively little attention to how such conduct, as mediated by self and role-playing capacities, affects these social contexts as well as more general patterns of social organization. While this strategy has provided considerable insight into individual and group processes, role theory has yet to explore the utility of its concepts for understanding more macro social structures and processes.

Until this analytical effort is undertaken, it is difficult to determine the place of the role perspective in sociological theory. Clearly, it has enormous utility for the study of organizations, groups, and individual conduct, but at what point do its concepts, and their incorporation into theoretical propositions, cease being theoretically useful? Role theorists typically presume that the concepts developed by their perspective have wide theoretical applicability. However, except in the most cursory way, they have not incorporated these concepts into propositions that would account for a variety of patterns of social organization. Rather, role theory has been content to assert that, since complex social patterns are ultimately built from the specific role behaviors of individuals with selves and various role-playing capacities, the concepts of role theory will be critical in the development of sociological theory. To assert that such is the case appears to have done little to stimulate the development of generic propositions that would demonstrate the role theorist's case.

In order to realize the full potential of role theory, a shift in strategy is necessary. First, it is critical that role theory begin developing propositions that incorporate its rapidly multiplying body of classificatory concepts. To continue the proliferation of systems of concepts in lieu of developing systems of propositions will prevent role theory from realizing its full potential for developing sociological theory. Second, these propositions must begin to consider not only the implications of self-related processes and role-playing capacities on behavior, but also the consequences of such circumscribed behavior on a variety of patterns of social organization. Third, the accumulation of these latter types of propositions should begin to reveal the power of role-theoretic concepts in providing both prediction and a sense of understanding of social events for different levels of social organization. Should it become evident that role theory does not have theoretical utility for certain emergent social phenomena, then the limitations of role-theoretic concepts will be more evident than is currently the case. In sum, then, it is to the demonstration of its limitations that role-theoretic strategy should now address itself.

11

Symbolic Interactionism

As role theory borrowed selectively from the rich legacy of George Herbert Mead, it began to supplement this legacy with concepts from other theoretical and research traditions and to drift away from the thrust of Mead's analysis. At the same time this alternative interactionist perspective was evolving, a rather persistent conceptual indebtedness to Mead was being maintained by "symbolic interactionists."[1] While there is considerable overlap in the concepts of role theory and symbolic interactionism, these two perspectives differ in many important respects.

IMAGES OF SOCIETY AND THE INDIVIDUAL

The differences between role theory and symbolic interactionism become clearly evident when human interaction is viewed as varying along a continuum.[2] At one pole of this continuum, individuals are seen as players in the "theater," while, at the other end, players are considered to be participants in a "game." When human action is seen as occurring in a theater, interaction is likely to be viewed as highly structured by the script, directors, other actors, and the audience. When conceptualized as a game, however, interaction is more likely to be

---

[1] The most persistent of these codifiers of the Meadian legacy is Herbert Blumer who has consistently criticized sociological theorizing for failing to incorporate the substantive and methodological implications of Mead's concepts into current research and theory-building activity. This chapter is heavily indebted to Blumer's thought, which has been conveniently brought together in a recent volume, Herbert Blumer, *Symbolic Interactionism: Perspective and Method* (Englewood Cliffs, N.J.: Prentice-Hall, Inc., 1969).

[2] Bernard Farber, "A Research Model: Family Crisis and Games Strategy" in *Kinship and Family Organization,* ed. Bernard Farber (New York: John Wiley & Sons, 1966), pp. 430–34. Walter Wallace (*Sociological Theory* [Chicago: Aldine Publishing Co., 1969], pp. 34–35) has more recently chosen this same analogy to describe symbolic interactionism.

seen as unstructured and as influenced by the wide range of tactics available to participants. Thus, in contrast with the tendency of role theory to visualize human interaction as structured by expectations, symbolic interactionists tend to conceptualize human interaction and society in terms of the strategic adjustments and readjustments of players in a game. While games have rules, symbolic interactionists are likely to focus attention on how players interact in ways that, depending upon the course of the interaction, create, maintain, and change the rules of the game. This strategic view of human interaction has been translated into a number of assumptions about (1) the nature of interaction, (2) the nature of social organization, and (3) the nature of the individual.

The Nature of Interaction

Symbolic interactionism emphasizes the process of role taking in which humans mutually emit and interpret each other's gestures. From the information gained through this interpretation of gestures, actors are able to rehearse covertly various lines of activity and then emit those behaviors that can allow cooperative and organized activity. However, such a portrayal represents only the broad contours of the complex symbolic processes that guide and shape interaction. As currently conceptualized, symbolic interaction involves a number of specific processes:

1. In addition to viewing each other as objects in an interaction situation, actors select out and designate symbolically additional objects in any interaction. (a) One of the most important of these objects is the self. On the one hand, self can represent the transitory images that an actor derives from interpreting the gestures of others; on the other, self can denote the more enduring conceptions of himself as an object that an actor brings to and interjects into the interaction. (b) Another important class of objects are the varying types of expectation structures—for example, norms and values—that may exist to guide interaction. (c) Finally, because of the human organism's capacity to manipulate symbols, almost any other "object"—whether another person, a set of standards, or a dimension of self—may be inserted into the interaction.

2. It is toward the objects in interaction situations that actors have various dispositions to act. Thus, in order to understand the potentials for action among groups of individuals, it is necessary to understand the world of objects that they have symbolically designated.

3. In terms of the particular cluster of objects and of the dispositions to act that they imply, each actor arrives at a definition of the situation. Such a definition serves as a general frame of reference within which the consequences of specific lines of conduct are assessed. This process has been termed mapping.

4. The selection of a particular line of behavior involves complex symbolic processes. At a minimum, actors typically evaluate: (a) the demands of others immediately present; (b) the self-images they derive from role taking, not only with others in the situation, but also with those not actually present; (c) the normative expectations they perceive to exist in the situation; and (d) the dispositions to act toward any additional objects they may inject symbolically into the interaction.

5. Once behavior is emitted, redefinition of the situation and perhaps remapping of action may occur as the reactions of others are interpreted and as new objects are injected into, and old ones discarded from, the interaction.

Thus, by emphasizing the interpreting, evaluating, defining, and mapping processes, symbolic interactionism calls attention to the determinative impact of interaction on both the individual and society. Rather than constituting the mere vehicle through which preexisting psychological, social, and cultural structures inexorably shape behavior, the symbolic nature of interaction assures that social, cultural, and psychological structures will be altered and changed through shifting the definitions and behaviors of humans.

The Nature of Social Organization

The symbolic interactionists' concern with the primacy of the interaction process reveals several assumptions about the nature of social organization:

1. Since behavior is a reflection of the interpretive, evaluational, definitional, and mapping processes of individuals in various interaction contexts, social organization represents an active fitting together of action by those in interaction. Social organization must therefore be viewed as more of a process than a structure.

2. While social structure is an emergent phenomenon that is not reducible to the constitutent actions of individuals, it is difficult to understand patterns of social organization without recognizing that they represent an interlacing of the separate behaviors among individuals.

3. While much interaction is repetitive, and structured by clear-cut expectations and common definitions of the situation, its symbolic nature reveals the potential for new objects to be inserted or old ones altered and abandoned in a situation, with the result that reinterpretation, reevaluation, redefinition, and remapping of behaviors can always occur. Social structure must therefore be viewed as rife with potential for alteration and change.

4. Thus, patterns of social organization represent emergent phenomena that can serve as "objects" that define situations for actors. However, the very symbolic processes that give rise and sustain these patterns can also operate to change and alter them.

The Nature of the Individual

This conception of social organization makes several assumptions about the nature of individuals: (1) Humans have the capacity to view themselves as objects and to insert any object into an interaction situation. (2) Human actors are therefore not pushed and pulled around by social and psychological forces, but are active creators of the world to which they respond. (3) Thus, interaction and emergent patterns of social organization can only be understood by focusing on the capacities of individuals to create symbolically the world of objects to which they respond.

Taken together, these assumptions[3] about the nature of interaction, society, and the individual reveal an image of social organization that focuses on the processes whereby individuals fit together their actions through complex symbolic manipulations. While social organization represents an emergent phenomenon and is therefore one of the "objects" of any interaction situation, the interpretative, evaluational, definitional, and mapping processes of actors reveal not only the dependence of social structure upon the symbolic processes of actors, but also the capacity of individuals to reconstruct such structures. Symbolic interactionism thus places considerable emphasis on the specific processes by which interacting individuals[4] with the capacity to construct symbolic environments create, sustain, and change patterns of social organization.

PROBLEMS IN BUILDING SYMBOLIC INTERACTIONIST "THEORY"

Constructing Causal Statements

For contemporary symbolic interactionists, the Meadian legacy challenges the utility of theoretical perspectives that underemphasize the internal symbolic processes of actors attempting to "fit together" their respective behaviors into

---

[3] Blumer, "The Methodological Position of Symbolic Interactionism," in *Symbolic Interactionism*, pp. 1–21. For earlier statements brought together in *Symbolic Interactionism*, see Herbert Blumer, "Sociological Analysis and the 'Variable,'" *American Sociological Review* 21 (December 1956): 683–90; and Herbert Blumer, "Society as Symbolic Interactionism" in *Human Behavior and Social Process*, ed. Arnold Rose (Boston: Houghton Mifflin Co., 1962), pp. 179–92. For other important references delineating the assumptions of symbolic interactionism, see Sheldon Stryker, "Symbolic Interaction as an Approach to Family Research," *Marriage and Family Living* 21 (May 1951): 111–19; Manford H. Kuhn, "Major Trends in Symbolic Interaction Theory in the Past Twenty-five Years," *Sociological Quarterly* 5 (Winter 1969): 61–84; J. D. Cardwell, *Social Psychology: A Symbolic Interactionist Perspective* (Philadelphia: F. A. Davis Co., 1971): and Charles K. Warriner, *The Emergence of Society* (Homewood, Ill.: Dorsey Press, 1970).

[4] Some authors, such as Blumer, have attempted to argue that "actors" can represent larger social units, but, in point of fact, the symbolic interactionist tradition has focused almost exclusively on the interaction of individual persons in different social contexts. While the use of symbolic interactionist concepts might well have considerable utility in the analysis of interactions among such social units as corporations, groups, and institutions, this form of analysis has yet to be seriously undertaken.

an organized pattern. Rather than being the result of system forces, societal needs, and structural mechanisms, social organization is the result of the mutual interpretations, evaluations, definitions, and mappings of individual actors. Thus, the symbolic processes of individuals cannot be viewed as a neutral medium through which social forces operate, but instead, these processes must be viewed as shaping the ways social patterns are formed, sustained, and changed.[5]

Similarly, symbolic interactionism questions the utility of theoretical perspectives that view behavior as the mere releasing of propensities built into a structured personality. Just as patterns of social organization must be conceptualized as in continual state of potential flux through the processes of interpretation, evaluation, definition, and mapping, so the human personality must also be viewed as a constantly unfolding process rather than a rigid structure from which behavior is mechanically released. By virtue of the fact that humans can make varying and changing symbolic indications to themselves, they are capable of altering and shifting behavior, with the result that behavior is not so much "released" as "constructed" by actors making successive indications to themselves.[6]

Central to the symbolic interactionist causal imagery, then, is an emphasis on how the process of interaction deterministically shapes the way personality, behavior, and society become organized. Whether concern is with the formation of self-conceptions, the internalization of cultural values, the genesis of a deviant personality, the process of social control, the formation of a group, a social movement, a pattern of collective behavior, or any of a host of substantive concerns, the process of symbolic interaction is seen as determinative. Thus, the structure of personality, the occurrence of particular behaviors, or the existence of certain patterns of social organization are considered to reflect, in large part, ongoing processes of symbolic interaction among individuals.

However, the relationship between symbolic interaction, on the one hand, and personality, behavioral, and social variables, on the other, is typically viewed as reciprocal. Social structures and the expectations they embody are seen as "objects," which must be interpreted and then used to define a situation and map out the prospective behaviors that ultimately go to make up social structures. Typically, overt behavior at one point in time is considered to result in "self-images" that serve as objects to be used by individuals in symbolically mapping subsequent actions at another point in time, while existing personality traits, such as self-conceptions, self-esteem, and internalized needs, are viewed as mediating each successive phase of interpretation of gestures, evaluation of self-images, definition of the situation, and mapping of diverse behaviors.

---

[5] Blumer, "Society as Symbolic Interaction."

[6] Blumer, "Sociological Implications of the Thought of George Herbert Mead," in *Symbolic Interactionism.*

By viewing symbolic interaction among individuals as both shaping and shaped by personality, behavior, and social organization, the causal imagery becomes incredibly complex, for now it is difficult to sort out which variable—symbolic interaction, personality, behavior, or social structure—is causing variation in the other. It is one thing to note that variables appear to reciprocally influence each other,[7] but quite another to make explicit the conditions under which one variable is causing variation in the other, and vice versa. Currently, a great deal of literature simply denotes the reciprocal feedback processes among symbolic interaction, personality, behavior, and social structural variables without specifying the precise nature of the reciprocity. Whether one is examining the interactions of deviants and others,[8] socializing agents and the young, various groups and their members, or collective behavior and individual participants, the causal imagery of symbolic interactionist analysis points to the reciprocal, feedback processes without also indicating the precise ways and conditions under which the products of symbolic interaction feed back and affect the subsequent course of interaction. Until this kind of specification occurs, the insight of symbolic interactionism into the reciprocal nature of causality between interaction and its personality, behavioral, and social structural products will remain, at best, suggestive, but will continue to frustrate attempts at constructing causal statements.

In sum, then, it is this vagueness that prevents symbolic interactionism from offering much insight into the conditions under which patterns of social organization emerge, persist, change, and break down. Simply asserting that "society is symbolic interaction," as some have done,[9] will not resolve these problems. Nor will assertions about the importance of the processes of interpretation, self-evaluation, definition, and mapping specify the conditions under which social organization is causally linked to these symbolic processes.

Some Methodological Implications

The assumptions and causal imagery of symbolic interactionism have dictated a consistent methodology for conducting sociological research. Since social life

---

[7] For example, see Walter Buckley, *Sociology and Modern Systems Theory* (Englewood Cliffs, N.J.: Prentice-Hall, Inc., 1967), pp. 78–80.

[8] For example, even in the best-developed literature on the genesis of deviant behavior, the various forms of "labeling theory" simply denote a spiraling reciprocal feedback process between the labeling by others and the internalization of a deviant self-concept, without specifying the precise ways and conditions under which the reactions of others cause internalization of a deviant self-concept and, in turn, when such internalization is most likely to alter labeling by others. See Edwin Lemert, *Social Pathology* (New York: McGraw-Hill Book Co., 1951); and Thomas Scheff, "The Role of the Mentally Ill and the Dynamics of Mental Disorder: A Research Framework," *Sociometry* 26 (December 1963): 436–53.

[9] See Blumer, *Symbolic Interactionism.*

is ultimately a product of the interpretive, evaluational, definitional, and mapping activities of individuals attempting to fit together their behaviors, the study of such life must attempt to understand the symbolic processes of individual actors. From this methodological premise, interactionists such as Blumer[10] have mounted a consistent and persistent line of attack on sociological theory and research. This criticism questions the utility of current research procedures for unearthing the symbolic processes from which social structures and personality are built and sustained. Rather than letting the nature of the empirical world dictate the kinds of research strategies used in its study, Blumer and others have argued that present practices allow research strategies to determine what is to be studied:

> Instead of going to the empirical social world in the first and last instances, resort is made instead to a priori theoretical schemes, to sets of unverified concepts, and to canonized protocols of research procedure. These come to be the governing agents in dealing with the empirical social world, forcing research to serve their character and bending the empirical world to their premises.[11]

Too often, then, the fads of research protocol serve to blind investigators and theorists to the "real character" of the social world. Such research and theoretical protocols force analysis away from the direct examination of the empirical world in favor of preconceived notions of what is "true" and how these "truths" should be studied. In contrast, the processes of symbolic interaction dictate that research methodologies should respect the character of empirical reality and adopt methodological procedures that encourage its direct and unbiased examination.[12]

To achieve this end, the research act itself must be viewed as a process of symbolic interaction in which researchers "take the role" of those individuals whom they are studying. To do such "role taking" effectively, researchers must come to the study of interaction with a set of concepts that, rather than prematurely structuring the social world for investigators, "sensitize" them to interactive processes. This approach would enable investigators to maintain the distinction between the concepts of science and those of the interacting individuals under study. In this way, the interpretive and definitional processes of actors adjusting to one another in concrete situations would guide the refinement and eventual incorporation of the concepts of science into theoretical statements on the interactive processes that go to make up society.

---

[10] Blumer has been the most persistent advocate of the methodological position of symbolic interactionism; therefore, the following discussion is heavily indebted to his work. In particular, see Blumer, "Methodological Position," pp. 1–60.

[11] Ibid., p. 33.

[12] For an interesting discussion of the contrasts between these research strategies, see Llewellyn Gross, "Theory Construction in Sociology: A Methodological Inquiry," in *Symposium on Sociological Theory*, ed. L. Gross (New York: Harper & Row, 1959), pp. 531–63.

Blumer[13] has advocated a twofold process of research, involving, first of all, "exploration" in which researchers approach concrete situations prepared to observe and then revise their observations as new impressions of the situation arise. Second, Blumer emphasizes that exploration must be followed by a process of "inspection," whereby researchers use their observations to dictate how scientific concepts are to be refined and incorporated into more abstract and generic statements of relationships among concepts. In this dual research process, investigators must understand each actor's definition of the situation, the relationship of this definition to the objects perceived by actors in this situation, and the relationship of objects to specific others, groups, and expectations in both the actor's immediate and remote social worlds.[14] In this way, the research used to build the abstract concepts and propositions of sociological theory would be connected to the empirical world of actors interpreting, evaluating, defining, and mapping the behaviors that create, maintain, or change patterns of social organization.

This methodological position has generated a number of controversies in the theoretical literature. First, there is a question about the *exclusive* use of this methodological approach in building a body of sociological theory. Rarely is it argued by advocates of any theoretical perspective that the interpretive and definitional processes of actors are irrelevant to the understanding of social processes; on the contrary, understanding at the "level of meaning" is almost always considered essential. The controversy over the symbolic interactionist position comes with the frequent denial that other methodological strategies are also important to the understanding of the processes and structure of society. If indeed social phenomena do emerge out of the basic processes of symbolic interaction, is it possible to study these groups, organizations, and various forms of collective organizations solely through "taking the role" of their constituent members? Or, do additional and emergent social forces exist which must be studied with different, less intuitive research methods? While the analysis of these emergent phenomena may be greatly enlightened by the "exploration-inspection" methodology, it seems unlikely that understanding at the "level of meaning" will provide complete explanation or understanding of emergent social phenomena. Thus, until the exclusive use of the methodological strategy advocated by Blumer and others demonstrates its usefulness for macro forms of collective organization, critics will have ample reason for skepticism with respect to the singular use of any one methodology.

---

[13] Blumer, "Methodological Position."

[14] Norman K. Denzin, *The Research Act: A Theoretical Introduction to Sociological Methods* (Chicago: Aldine Publishing Co., 1970), pp. 185–218; and Norman K. Denzin, "Symbolic Interactionism and Ethnomethodology," in *Understanding Everyday Life: Toward a Reconstruction of Sociological Knowledge,* ed. Jack D. Douglas (Chicago: Aldine Publishing Co., 1970), pp. 259–84.

A second area of controversy over the methodological position advocated by Blumer concerns the issue of operationalization of concepts. How is it possible to operationalize concepts, such as self and definition of the situation, so that different investigators at different times and in different contexts can study the same phenomena? Blumer[15] has typically chosen to define away the problem of how the interpretative, evaluational, definitional, and mapping processes are to be studied in terms of clear-cut operational definitions, for such questions "show a profound misunderstanding of both scientific inquiry and symbolic interactionism." For Blumer, the concepts and propositions of symbolic interactionism allow for the direct examination of the empirical world; therefore, "their value and their validity are to be determined in that examination and not in seeing how they fare when subjected to the alien criteria of an irrelevant methodology." According to Blumer, these "alien criteria" embrace a false set of assumptions about just how concepts should be attached to events in the empirical world. In general, these "false" assumptions posit that for each abstract concept a set of operational definitions should guide researchers, who then examine the empirical cases denoted by the operational definition. In this manner, concrete instances of abstract concepts, and relations among them, can be isolated and used to guide the construction of sociological theory (see chapter 1). To ignore this process of operationalization invites a situation wherein theory remains unconnected to the empirical events to which it is supposedly addressed.

Blumer has consistently emphasized current deficiencies in the attachment of sociological concepts to actual events in the empirical world:

> This ambiguous nature of concepts is the basic deficiency in social theory. It hinders us in coming to close grips with our empirical world, for we are not sure of what to grip. Our uncertainty as to what we are referring obstructs us from asking pertinent questions and setting relevant problems for research.[16]

In answer to his critics, Blumer argues that it is only through the methodological processes of exploration and inspection that concepts can be attached to the empirical. Rather than seeking a false sense of scientific security through rigid operational definitions, sociological theory must accept the fact that the attachment of abstract concepts to the empirical world must be an *ongoing process* of investigators exploring and inspecting events in the empirical world.

In sum, then, Blumer's presentation of the methodological position of symbolic interactionism questions the current research protocols and advocates as an alternate (*a*) the more frequent use of the exploration-inspection process, whereby researchers seek to understand the symbolic processes that shape interac-

---

[15] Blumer, "Methodological Position," p. 49.

[16] Herbert Blumer, "What Is Wrong with Social Theory?" *American Sociological Review* 19 (August 1954): 146–58.

tion; and (*b*) the recognition that only through these research activities can concepts remain attached to the fluid interaction processes of the empirical world. In turn, this methodological position has profound implications for the construction of theory in sociology.

Theory-building Implications

Blumer's assumptions, image of causal processes, and methodological position have all come to dictate a particular conception of sociological theory. The recognition that sociological concepts do not come to grips with the empirical world is seen by Blumer as the result not only of inattention to actual events in the empirical world, but also of the kind of world it is. While the use of more "definitive concepts" referring to classes of precisely defined events is perhaps desirable in theory building, it may be impossible, given the nature of the empirical world. Since this world is composed of constantly shifting processes of symbolic interaction among actors in various contextual situations, the use of concepts that rip from this context only some of the actual ongoing events will fail to capture the contextual nature of the social world. More important, the fact that social reality is ultimately "constructed" from the symbolic processes among individuals assures that the actual instances denoted by concepts will shift and vary and thereby defy easy classification through rigid operational definitions.

These facts, Blumer argues, require the use of "sensitizing concepts," which, while lacking the precise specification of attributes and events of definitive concepts, do provide clues and suggestions about where to look for certain classes of phenomena. As such, sensitizing concepts offer a general sense of what is relevant and thereby allow investigators to approach flexibly a shifting empirical world and "feel out" and "pick one's way in an unknown terrain." The use of this kind of concept does not necessarily reflect a lack of rigor in sociological theory, but rather a recognition that if "our empirical world presents itself in the form of distinctive and unique happenings or situations and if we seek through the direct study of this world to establish classes of objects and relations between classes, we are . . . forced to work with sensitizing concepts."

While the nature of the empirical world may preclude the development of definitive concepts, sensitizing concepts can be improved and refined. By approaching flexibly empirical situations denoted by sensitizing concepts and then by assessing how actual events stack up against the concepts, it is possible to refine and revise concepts. Although the lack of fixed bench marks and definitions makes this task more difficult for sensitizing concepts than for definitive ones, the progressive refinement of sensitizing concepts is possible through "careful and imaginative study of the stubborn world to which such concepts are addressed."[17] Furthermore, sensitizing concepts formulated in this way can be communicated and used to build sociological theory: and although formal definitions and rigid classifications are not appropriate, sensitizing concepts can be explicitly communicated through descriptions and illustrations of the events to which they pertain.

In sum, the ongoing refinement, formulation, and communication of sensitizing concepts must inevitably be the building blocks of sociological theory. With careful formulation, they can be incorporated into provisional theoretical statements that specify the conditions under which various types of interaction are likely to occur. In this way, the concepts of theory will recognize the shifting nature of the social world and thereby provide a more accurate set of statements about the conditions under which patterns of social organization emerge, persist, change, and break down.

The nature of the social world and the type of theory it dictates have profound implications for just how such theoretical statements are to be constructed and organized into theoretical formats. Blumer's emphasis on the constructed nature of reality and the types of concepts this fact necessitates has led him to emphasize inductive theory construction. In inductive theory, generic propositions are abstracted from observations of concrete interaction situations. This emphasis on induction is considered desirable, since current attempts at deductive theorizing in sociology usually do not involve rigorous derivations of propositions from each other, nor a scrupulous search for the negative empirical cases that would refute propositions.[18] These failings, Blumer contends, assure that deductive sociological theory will remain unconnected to the events of the empirical world and, hence, unable to correct for errors in its theoretical statements. Coupled with the tendency for fads of research protocol to dictate research problems, and methods used to investigate them, it appears unlikely that deductive theory and the research it inspires can unearth those processes that would confirm or refute its generic statements. In the wake of this theoretical impasse, then, it is crucial that sociological theorizing refamiliarize itself with the actual events of the empirical world: "no theorizing, however ingenious, and no observance of scientific protocol, however meticulous, are substitutes for developing familiarity with what is actually going on in the sphere of life under study."[19] Without such inductive familiarity, sociological theory will remain a self-fulfilling set of theoretical prophecies bearing little relationship to the phenomena it is supposed to explain.

---

[17] Ibid., p. 150.
[18] Blumer, "Methodological Position."
[19] Ibid., p. 39.

While Blumer appears to argue that the inductive approach is the best strategy for developing sociological theory, his perspective challenges deductive theory on other grounds. From Blumer's assumptions about the nature of the empirical world, an incompatibility between the logic of deductive reasoning and these assumptions becomes evident. This challenge is far more fundamental than that typically leveled by Blumer, since the very possibility, as opposed to the desirability and efficiency, of deductive theory is being questioned.

The general profile of this argument against deductive theory can be delineated as follows:

1. Deductive theory relies upon logical derivations of propositions from each other. This fact necessitates that the concepts of each proposition have clear-cut operational definitions, such that the phenomena denoted by the concepts of logically interrelated propositions are *literally* described.

2. Literal description involves the specification of the features of phenomena in order that they can be seen as unambiguously belonging to a clearly designated class of phenomena. This process of classification must involve the use of well-established and agreed-upon standards that enable a community of scientists, independent of each other, to recognize phenomena as belonging to one class or another.

3. To the extent that social reality is assumed to be the result of the interpretive process of symbolic interaction, scientists' descriptions of these symbolic processes of actors must also represent interpretations, arrived at through role taking and other inferential techniques.

4. "If the only way an observer can identify what actions have occurred is through documentary interpretation, then descriptions are not intersubjectively verifiable in any strong sense—since the interpretations of different individuals will necessarily agree only when they are able to *negotiate a common social reality*" (italics added).[20]

5. Therefore, when descriptions of phenomena must be continually negotiated by a community of scientists, the descriptions of social phenomena cannot be *literal*—because they cannot be unambiguously classified by the scientists of this community—in terms of clear-cut criteria, *independent of each other.*

6. Interpretive and documentary descriptions, then, cannot be organized into a deductive system of theoretical statements.

This argument appears inevitable as long as it is assumed that the social world is constructed from interpretive processes that are amenable *only* to description by sensitizing, as opposed to definitive, concepts. Since deductive theory must assume that its concepts are definitive, and hence capable of logical interrelated-

---

[20] Thomas P. Wilson, "Conceptions of Interaction and Forms of Sociological Explanation," *American Sociological Review* 35 (August 1970): 204.

ness, Blumer's assertion that the nature of reality forces the use of only sensitizing concepts would therefore logically preclude the utilization of deductive theory. Thus, from the symbolic interactionist perspective advocated by Blumer, the inductive construction of theory is not only a better, but also a logically necessary, strategy.

The assumptions, causal imagery, and methodology of symbolic interaction not only have implications for the way sociological theory is constructed, but also for the types of statements such theory can contain. Even though the symbolic interaction perspective of Blumer and others notes that much interaction is patterned and repetitious,[21] the assumptions and causal imagery underscore the fact that there is always a potential for reinterpretation, reevaluation, redefinition, and remapping. Perhaps, following Mead's sense of indeterminacy in the concepts of "I" and "me," modern symbolic interactionists appear to reveal a similar concern with the "creative" and "spontaneous" products of symbolic interaction. To the extent that symbolic interaction generates these creative and spontaneous readjustments of interaction, theoretical statements must be *probabilistic*, offering a set of probabilities about the likelihood of various patterns of interaction continuing or changing. While most theoretical statements in sociology are probabilistic, it can be assumed that this fact is the result of imperfection in their formulation and in the data made available to test them. On the other hand, the symbolic interactionist vision of reality would make inevitable probabilistic, as opposed to deterministic, theoretical statements, since the symbolic capacities of actors make possible the introduction of unique elements into a situation that can change the course of interaction.

Some Substantive Implications

The assumptions, causal imagery, and even the research and theory-building strategies of Blumer and others point to the fact that the basic social process from which personality and social structures are constructed is symbolic interaction. Whether attention is drawn to the structure of personality or society, symbolic interaction among actors is the formative process that creates, sustains, and changes these emergent structures. Although the patterned aspects of personality or of social structure can enter into the course of interaction as "objects" of the situation which shape the interpretative, evaluational, definitional, and mapping processes of actors, symbolic interaction appears to be concerned primarily with the *process of interaction,* per se. The products of such interaction—personality and social structure—have received varying degrees of substantive concern in the literature, where the structuring of different types of

---

[21] Blumer, "Sociological Implications."

personality [22] has been given more substantive attention than the structuring of various patterns of social organization.

The substantive concern with the process of interaction offers a number of advantages over other theoretical perspectives. First, it would appear to correct for the imputed inattention of perspectives such as functionalism and conflict theory to the symbolic processes that underlie the construction and maintenance of patterns of social organization. Second, the concepts of symbolic interaction "theory" are probably more generic than the specific types of interaction advocated by other perspectives, with the result that concepts—such as exchange, communication, and information—can be subsumed by the concepts of symbolic interaction. Third, symbolic interactionist concepts can be used to embrace the full range of human relationships—such as conflict, cooperation, and domination—so that, in principle at least, symbolic interactionism would make unnecessary the construction of separate "theories" of each type of human relationship.

However, as promising as these facts would make the symbolic interactionist perspective appear, several substantive deficiencies remain. Much of symbolic interaction consists of gallant assertions that "society is symbolic interaction," without indicating what types of emergent structures are created, sustained, and changed by what types of interaction in what types of contexts. Much like the critics' allegations about Parsons's "social system" or Dahrendorf's "imperatively coordinated associations," social structural phenomena emerge somewhat mysteriously and are then sustained or changed by vague references to interactive processes. The vagueness of the links between the interaction process and its social structural products[23] leaves symbolic interactionism with a legacy of assertions, but little in the way of carefully documented statements about how, when, where, and with what probability interaction processes operate to create, sustain, and change varying patterns of social organization.

Accordingly, symbolic interactionism represents a vision of the social world which underemphasizes social structures, except as "objects" of actors' orientations or as "things" that somehow just emerge from interaction. Without linking, except by assertion, social processes and social structure, symbolic interaction offers a picture of a constantly flowing and fluctuating world, with actors symbolically interpreting, evaluating, defining, and mapping respective lines of action.

---

[22] The long tradition of speculation and research on the process of socialization in the symbolic interactionist literature documents this contention. The comparatively sparse concern with how groups, organizations, and other forms of collective organization emerge and are sustained should document the lack of concern with patterns of social organization. However, in the area of collective behavior—crowds, mobs, riots, and so forth—symbolic interactionists have made a number of important contributions. And yet, this literature on such transitory collective phenomena makes the lack of attention on more stable patterns of social organization even more evident.

[23] With respect to the structuring of personality, symbolic interactionism has done a much better job of indicating how and in what ways symbolic interaction leads to the emergence of certain types of personality.

While this vision certainly captures crucial social features, it would appear to do so at the expense of ignoring the structures that channel the symbolic processes of actors.

Another related problem with the symbolic interactionist perspective is its current inability to provide a useful set of concepts that can describe the interaction among collective organizations. While Blumer has been insistent that the same processes of interpretation, evaluation, definition, and mapping which characterize the interactions among individuals also pertain to interactions among collective units, he and other interactionists have yet to document just how this is so. At a very general level, it is quite likely that emergent social units do "size up" a situation and "then map" a line of action; however, it can be questioned whether this says very much about the way collective units interact and articulate with one another to form complex patterns of social organization. It seems likely that it will be necessary to develop additional concepts to account for these more complex linkages among larger social units; to the extent that this is necessary, then the concepts of symbolic interaction may be applicable to only those levels of analysis where individuals are the interacting units. If such is the case, the current inability of symbolic interaction to document just how interaction creates, sustains, and changes social structures may be due, in part at least, to the fact that its concepts denote only a limited range of micro phenomena.

Until these problems are resolved by other than confident assertions about the nature of reality and of the causal processes such reality reveals, symbolic interactionism will leave unanswered the important substantive question: Social reality is constructed through a process called symbolic interaction, but just how does such interaction create, maintain, and change different features of social reality?

SYMBOLIC INTERACTIONISM: SOME CONCLUDING REMARKS

Symbolic interactionism advocates a clear-cut strategy for building sociological theory. The emphasis on the interpretive, evaluative, definitional, and mapping processes of actors has come to dictate that it is only through induction from these processes that sociological theory can be built. Further, the ever-shifting nature of these symbolic processes necessitates that the concepts of sociological theory be "sensitizing" rather than "definitive," with the result that deductive theorizing should be replaced by an inductive approach. Thus, whether as a preferred strategy or as a logical "necessity," the symbolic interactionist strategy is to induce generic statements, employing sensitizing concepts, from the ongoing symbolic processes of individuals in concrete interaction situations.

Such a strategy is likely to keep theorizing attuned to the processual nature of the social world. Currently, however, this approach has not been able to link conceptually the processes of symbolic interaction to the formation of different patterns of social organization. Furthermore, the utility of induction from the symbolic exchanges among individuals for the analysis of interaction among more macro, collective social units has yet to be demonstrated. Unless these problems can be resolved, it does not seem wise to follow exclusively the strategy of Blumer and others of his persuasion. Until symbolic interactionists demonstrate in a more compelling manner than is currently the case that the inductive approach, utilizing sensitizing concepts, can account for more complex forms of social organization, pursuit of its strategy will preclude theorizing about much of the social world.

Symbolic interactionism does call attention to some important substantive and theoretical issues that are often ignored. First, it is necessary that sociological theorizing be more willing to undertake the difficult task of linking conceptually structural categories to classes of social processes that underlie these categories. To this task, symbolic interactionism has provided a wealth of suggestive concepts. Second, macro sociological theorizing has traditionally remained detached from the processes of the social world it attempts to describe. Much of the detachment stems from a failure to define concepts clearly and provide operational clues about what processes in the empirical world they denote. To the extent that symbolic interactionist concepts can supplement such theorizing, they will potentially provide a bridge to actual empirical processes and thereby help attach sociological theory to the events it purports to explain.

As should be obvious, it is one thing to note that symbolic interactionism has great potential for correcting the past inadequacies of sociological theory and another thing to demonstrate exactly *how* this corrective influence is to be exerted. It may be well advised for symbolic interactionists to cease defining away the bulk of sociological theory and begin the difficult task of demonstrating in specific theoretical context (other than in socialization and personality theory) the utility of their perspective for supplementing (or replacing) other theoretical perspectives. In particular, symbolic interactionism needs to demonstrate with empirical evidence the utility of its tenets, especially in predicting variation in macro structural phenomena.

12

Functional and Interactionist Theories: Points of Convergence and Divergence

Just as much of conflict theory in sociology has been formulated as a reaction to alleged deficiencies in Parsonian functionalism,[1] so some features of symbolic interactionism have taken on greater focus in the spirit of reaction to Parsonian action theory. While conflict theorists were berating Parsons in the late 1950s and 1960s for failing to conceptualize conflict, change, dissent, and coercion in social systems, a few interactionists were mounting a second line of attack. For these interactionists, most notably Herbert Blumer,[2] Parsons's vision of human action underemphasized the interpretative, evaluative, and choice-making capacities of humans and placed too much emphasis on the imperatives and mechanisms of the personality, social, and cultural systems.

---

[1] See chapters 6 and 7.

[2] For example, Herbert Blumer's polemic in "What Is Wrong with Social Theory?" *American Sociological Review* 19 (August 1954): 143–51; Herbert Blumer, "Society as Symbolic Interaction," in *Human Behavior and Social Processes*, ed. Arnold Rose (Boston: Houghton-Mifflin Co., 1962), pp. 179–92; Herbert Blumer, "Sociological Implications of the Thought of George Herbert Mead," *American Journal of Sociology* 71 (March 1966): 535–44; and Herbert Blumer, "The Methodological Position of Symbolic Interactionism," in his *Symbolic Interactionism: Perspective and Method* (Englewood Cliffs, N.J.: Prentice-Hall, Inc., 1969), pp. 1–60. While Blumer has rarely addressed Parsonian theory explicitly, the implication is clear that functionalism in general, and Parsonian action theory in particular, are under his critical review.

These polemics have been beneficial because they have forced critical examination of questionable features in the functionalist perspective. At the same time, they have brought into greater clarity Blumer's and other interactionist's interpretation of the Meadian legacy. However, these same polemics have also erected of more unified sociological theorizing. By focusing on presumed differences in substantive visions of the social world, critics of functionalism like Blumer have compartmentalized sociological theorizing to the extent that the research findings of one perspective are often not considered relevant to another since the perspectives in sociological theory are thought to hold such divergent conceptions about the nature of social reality.

This partitioning of sociological theorizing and research activity rings especially true for conflict theorists like Ralf Dahrendorf and symbolic interactionists of Blumer's persuasion, for at times their messages have been spread at the cost of grossly misinterpreting Parsonian functionalism and constructing misleading barriers between their respective schemes and Parsons's action scheme. Just as the polemical thrust of Dahrendorf's formulations served to mask many similarities between action theory and his dialectical-conflict perspective, so the polemical arguments of Herbert Blumer have obscured significant points of convergence, with the result that the real differences between action and interactionist forms of theorizing remain obscured.

In this short chapter, it will be argued that, in contrast to Blumer's suppositions, the substantive visions of social organization held by symbolic interactionism and action theory are quite similar, and that the divergence between the two perspectives represents more of a strategic disagreement over how sociological theory should be constructed than a disagreement over the nature of the social world. When such presumed divergence is reduced to a question of strategy rather than to metaphysics or ontology, then theoretical controversies have a better chance for resolution. If the true areas of divergence between Parsons and Blumer are shown to be questions of strategy, the theoretical disagreement between interactionism and action theory can be resolved as research findings by either strategy are compared with the theoretical formulations of each perspective. However, as long as theoretical disputes and arguments are couched polemically, disagreements will too often be viewed as representing divergence in assumptions about the nature of the social world rather than questions of theory building and research strategies. When viewed in this way, theoretical controversies will be perceived to be far more fundamental and unresolvable than they really are.[3]

---

[3] For examples of attempts at perpetuating the interactionist-action-theory controversy, see Blumer's "Society as Symbolic Interaction"; and Dennis Wrong's, "The Over-Socialized Conception of Man in Modern Sociology," *American Sociological Review* 26 (August 1961): 183–93.

CONVERGING VISIONS OF SOCIAL ORGANIZATION

Actors, Situations, and Orientation

Both Blumer's portrayal of symbolic interactionism and Parsons's theory of action begin with the same analytical frame of reference: *Actors oriented* to *objects* in given *situations*. For symbolic interactionists, actors can be both individuals or collective units.[4] These actors are then seen as symbolically defining situations as composed of objects (other people, groups, reference groups, and physical features) toward which they have "meanings" (dispositions to act). Hence, to understand society it is necessary to comprehend the world of objects that actors have created and toward which they are disposed to act. Behavior is therefore goal directed, but the nature of the goals and the "meanings" ascribed to them arise from symbolic and definitional processes among actors.

Parsons began his intellectual career with a similar frame of reference in his "voluntaristic theory of action."[5] In these initial stages, Parsons posited that sociology must always focus on "unit acts" that involve *actors oriented* to *goals* seeking *means* to realize these goals. As Parsons was careful to point out, the processes of orientation, of choosing goals, and of selecting means for their attainment is both definitional (mediated by symbolic processes) and situational (constrained by the physical parameters of situations as interpreted symbolically by actors).

The similarity of these two frameworks is far greater than their dissimilarity: Actors are symbol-using creatures; they interpret and define situations in terms of symbols; such definitional processes create worlds of "objects" or "goals" toward which actors are disposed to behave; and actors choose and select among alternative lines of behavior those considered most appropriate for variously designated objects. This particular similarity between action and interaction theory has frequently been noted; but such commentaries then proceed to reiterate what is now a piece of sociological folklore: Parsons abandoned this promising lead and began to ignore these definitional processes of actors in favor of a concern with the imperatives and mechanisms of the social system.[6] However, in reviewing Parsons's work, it is evident that, contrary to his critics, Parsons has

---

[4] Blumer, "Society as Symbolic Interaction."

[5] Talcott Parsons, *The Structure of Social Action* (New York: McGraw-Hill Book Co., 1937).

[6] For examples of how the folklore has been perpetuated, see John Finley Scott, "Changing Foundations of the Parsonian Action Scheme," *American Sociological Review* 28 (October 1963): 716–35; Edward Tiryakian, "Existential Phenomenology and the Sociological Tradition," *American Sociological Review* 30 (October 1965): 674–88; Pitirim A. Sorokin, *Sociological Theories of Today* (New York: Harper & Row, 1966), pp. 403–5; Walter L. Wallace, ed., *Sociological Theory* (Chicago: Aldine Publishing Co., 1969), p. 39. For an attempt to refute this folklore, see Jonathan H. Turner and Leonard Beeghley, "Current Folklore in the Interpretation of Parsonian Action Theory," *Sociological Inquiry* (Winter 1974), in press.

consistently retained and expanded upon the actor-situation-orientation frame of reference. For example, as was noted in chapter 3, Parsons's first "structural-functional" work, *The Social System*,[7] began with an outline of how actors are oriented to objects: "The situation is defined [by actors] as consisting of objects of orientation, so that the orientation of a given actor is differentiated relative to the different objects and classes of them of which a situation is composed."[8] This position has been consistently maintained in a number of essays[9] and in his more recent analytical works.[10]

The major difference between the interactionist's and the action theorist's actor-situation-orientation frames of reference is that Parsons has been more concerned with analytically classifying the *variable* states of an actor's orientation to situations, whereas those following the Blumer tradition have appeared reluctant to do so. This has led one prominent commentator to note that interactionists have failed "to make appropriate conceptualization of the varieties of functional relations that regularly occur between self and other."[11] Parsons, on the other hand, has devoted considerable effort to conceptualizing the abstract properties of these varieties of "functional relations" between self and other. Ignoring for present purposes the adequacy of this conceptualizing (which indeed is suspect), Parsons has addressed the very theoretical question that interactionism must begin to answer if its conceptual potential is to be realized. For example, in *The Social System*[12] Parsons devotes the opening 100 pages to outlining the abstract properties of relations between actors and various kinds of objects: "Social objects" can be various types of specific others or collectivities; "physical objects" are the empirical constraints on interaction as interpreted by actors; and "cultural objects" are elements of tradition, ideas, beliefs, expressive symbols, and other symbolic elements. While the respective vocabularies differ, it is hardly stretching the argument to compare role-theoretic and symbolic interactionist concepts of "other," "significant other," "generalized other," and "reference group" to Parsons's attempt to categorize situational objects. But Parsons does

---

[7] Talcott Parsons, *The Social System* (Glencoe, Ill.: Free Press, 1951), pp. 3–6.

[8] Ibid., p. 4.

[9] See, for example, Talcott Parsons, "The Point of View of the Author," in *The Social Theories of Talcott Parsons*, ed. Max Black (Englewood Cliffs, N.J.: Prentice-Hall, Inc., 1961), pp. 311–63; Talcott Parsons, "An Approach to the Sociology of Knowledge," in *Sociological Theory and Modern Society*, ed. Talcott Parsons (New York: Free Press, 1967), pp. 134–65; Talcott Parsons, "Evaluation and Objectivity in Social Science: An Interpretation of Max Weber's Contribution," in ibid., pp. 79–101; Talcott Parsons, "The Political Aspect of Structure and Process," in *Politics and Social Structure*, ed. Talcott Parsons (New York: Free Press, 1969), pp. 317–51; and Talcott Parsons, "On Building Social System Theory: A Personal History," *Daedalus* 99 (Fall): 826–81.

[10] For example, see Talcott Parsons, *Societies: Evolutionary and Comparative Perspectives* (Englewood Cliffs, N.J.: Prentice-Hall, Inc., 1966).

[11] Manford H. Kuhn, "Major Trends in Symbolic Interaction Theory in the Past Twenty-five Years," *Sociological Quarterly* 5 (Winter 1964): 61–84.

[12] Parsons, *Social System*, pp. 1–96.

more than simply categorize the objects of the environment; he also attempts to conceptualize *as variables* the kinds of "functional relations" or types of orientations of actors to these objects.

The "pattern variables" represent an incipient, and hence crude, attempt to conceptualize as variable phenomena the "choices" (or if one prefers, the "meanings" or "orientations") of actors toward various types of objects in the environment.[13] Furthermore, for all their inadequacies, the "pattern variables" point to the choice *making* (the interactionist's definitional-interpretive process) of actors. These variables denote, as Parsons points out, "decisions" that actors actually make in interaction with each other and other objects in the environment. While some of these choices are prescribed by cultural objects (value orientations and norms), and circumscribed by physical objects, the pattern variables represent a *voluntaristic* representation of the orientation process, since actors for Parsons make symbolic representations to themselves of objects in the environment and choose for themselves the lines of action they intend to take.[14] The pattern variables thus represent one of the few attempts in literature to develop *generic* variables that account for relations between actors and the symbolic objects of their environment—a strategy that the interactionist frame of reference would seemingly dictate as a necessary first step for its conversion into scientific theory.

Society, Joint Action, and Institutionalization

At the heart of the symbolic interactionist's almost unanimous rejection of action theory are the perceived differences between their image of social organization and that of Parsons. For Blumer, society is built from "joint action" (Mead's concept of "society").[15] As was emphasized in chapter 11, the essence of social organization for Blumer is the ongoing *process* of actors interpreting, defining, mapping, and then fitting together respective lines of action. While concepts such as status point to the respective position of actors engaged in joint acts, and

---

[13] Contrary to Parson's critics, these abstract variables have excited a considerable amount of research. For example, see Peter M. Blau, "Operationalizing a Conceptual Scheme: The Universalism-Particularism Pattern Variable," *American Sociological Review* 27 (April 1962): 159–69; Lois R. Dean, "The Pattern Variables: Some Empirical Operations," *American Sociological Review* 26 (February 1961): 80–90; Peter Park, "Measurement of the Pattern Variables," *American Sociological Review* 30 (June 1965): 187–98; and Harry A. Scan, "Measurement of Particularism," *Sociometry* 27 (December 1964): 413–32.

[14] This is not to deny Parsons's emphasis on the fact that decisions are typically circumscribed. It is perhaps this emphasis on the constraints of the situation that has disturbed interactionists, but, in reality, the interactionist literature points to the same processes whereby "definitions of the situation" are structured by environmental objects.

[15] Blumer, *Symbolic Interactionism*, pp. 16–17.

while concepts such as norms give indication of *some* of the expectations on actors, human action is always an adjustment process among actors and hence is not perfectly structured. While a great deal of joint action reflects "common meanings" and hence reveals stability and repetitiousness, viewing structure as an ongoing process of interpretation and definition points to the "changeability" of structure as people (or collectivities) reinterpret, redefine, and thereby realign their joint actions.

In contrast with this position is the presumed cultural and structural determinism of the Parsonian frame of reference. If critics such as Blumer were correct, Parsons would view structures as pushing and pulling people around, with the interpretive processes of actors representing simply a vehicle or medium through which cultural and structural forces, and the imperatives and requisites imputed to them, operate.[16] While it is hard to deny that prominent in Parsons's scheme are notions of system imperatives, Blumer and other interactionists have sometimes misinterpreted their place in the Parsonian scheme. They have assumed that these concepts represent a metaphysical view of the social world; in reality, and this point will be developed in greater detail later, notions of system imperatives represent more of a methodological *strategy* for conducting research and a set of *procedural guidelines* for constructing theory than a metaphysical vision of society.

When these facts are recognized, the images of society contained in the Parsonian frame of reference are virtually identical to those revealed in the interactionist's framework. At the core of Parsons's framework is the concept of institutionalization, which was first given extensive treatment in *The Social System*[17] and which, all critics would agree, has remained central to his scheme in its subsequent elaboration. What has commonly been ignored by the critics is that for Parsons institutionalization is a *process* out of which structure and culture are built. Furthermore, once stabilized interaction patterns have been constructed, they do not then exist independently of the voluntaristic decision-making process of actors, but rather, in a vein similar to Blumer's analysis,[18] they enter into the symbolic decision-making process as environmental objects toward which actors can have a wide variety of orientations. Some of these orientations perpetuate existing patterns, others do not; but in no sense is structure a static, *ex cathedra* entity that pushes and pulls passive actors around.

This view of the *process* of institutionalization is explicitly stated in the first three chapters of *The Social System*, for, as was emphasized in the discussion of Parsons's scheme in chapter 3, institutionalization involves these interrelated

---

[16] Ibid., pp. 1–64.

[17] Parsons, *Social System*.

[18] See, for example, Blumer, "Society as Symbolic Interaction."

processes: (1) Actors (ego) and others (alter) enter into interaction with a definitional and interpretive legacy from past interactions. (2) Through additional interpretive processes of each other as social objects, as well as renewed interpretation of cultural and physical objects, a readjustment (if necessary) of an ego's and alter's orientation occurs so as to realign action to these newly encountered objects. (3) Out of this realignment of actions, new expectations (norms) arise, or old ones are confirmed, that will serve as the *starting point* for the next encounter between ego and alter. (4) At the time of the next encounter, the above three stages will be initiated again. (5) Those interactive patterns among a plurality of actors that display some stability of expectations are then denoted by the concept of the "social system."

There appears to be little difference in this portrayal of institutionalization and Mead's interpretation of "society" and "institutions"[19] or Blumer's conception of "joint action." They are virtually the same; and, should critics doubt that Parsons was hedging on the importance of the interpretive and decision-*making* processes of actors in his conceptualization of institutionalization, it should be noted that it is just at this point in his presentation that he introduces the pattern variables to denote both actors' decision-making "dilemmas" in each new interaction situation, as well as those more stabilized cultural and normative patterns that have emerged and persisted out of past interactions.

Again, in line with Parsons's commitment to conceptualizing social phenomena as variables, he chose to use the pattern variables to develop a typology of patterns of institutionalization. Unfortunately, it is this kind of "typologizing" that is used to indict Parsons as an overly structural theorist who ignores the symbolic processes that give rise to social and cultural structures. On the contrary, however, Parsons has consistently attempted to delineate generic concepts that depict the variable forms of institutionalization, or "joint action." Quite correctly, Parsons perceived that it is not enough to assert that "society is symbolic interaction" without attempting to conceptualize the generic properties of such interaction. Nevertheless, a great deal of the current interactionist literature consists of gallant assertions about "society as symbolic interaction," with little attention to developing generic concepts that denote the range of variation in the definitional-interpretative process and "joint acts" that emerge from such interaction.[20] Without attempts at this kind of conceptualization, symbolic interactionism will remain only an intuitively pleasing and suggestive framework, which will continue to fail in realizing its full potential.

---

[19] George Herbert Mead, *Mind, Self, and Society* (Chicago: University of Chicago Press, 1934), pp. 260–73.

[20] Some of the most promising and early analytical leads along these lines have seemingly been abandoned; see, for example, the early classic, Hans Gerth and C. Wright Mill, *Character and Social Structure* (New York: Harcourt, Brace, & World, Inc., 1953).

The Social Self and the Personality System

One of the profound contributions of William James[21] and George Herbert Mead[22] was their recognition that human action is reflective, with actors capable of viewing themselves as objects in the environment toward which "meanings" were symbolically constructed. In particular, Mead and his contemporary Charles Horton Cooley[23] saw the significance of this fact for understanding patterns of interaction among human actors ("society" for Mead and "social organization" for Cooley). Just as an actor defines and interprets "others" in his environment, so he sees himself and so he must adjust his actions in accordance with his "self" as well as with other objects of meaning and orientation. Human society is thus understandable only in light of the fact that actors' perceptions of themselves enter into their attempts at "joint action" and hence continually influence either the persistence or realignment of patterns of interaction.

As Blumer[24] has consistently emphasized, just as social organization cannot be explained by social and cultural imperatives, so it cannot be explained by a fixed personality structure that overly regulates actors in interaction situations. Rather, sociological theory must recognize that the "self" as an object can have changing meanings in different interaction context, since the "meanings" one has toward oneself as an object are an outgrowth of assessment from the point of view of the "other" (or Cooley's well-known "looking-glass self"). Hence, personality is not a closed, self-maintaining structure, but, according to Blumer, a *process* of defining, redefining, and then acting in various interaction situations. Thus, the participant in social interaction is an active creator of his action, not a passive robot that has been "programmed" by prior socialization and a presumably emergent personality structure.

As was noted in chapter 9, Mead's concept of the "I" perhaps anticipated much of the current recognition about potential indeterminacy in social action, for, as Mead was prone to emphasize, the "I" can only be known in experience through the retrospective self-images that human organisms derive from their past behaviors. Despite his recognition of the high degree of spontaneity in human action, Mead also appeared to understand that there were emergent or more stable "meanings" toward the "self" (self-conceptions), which arose out of interaction and which affected the subsequent style of interaction of mature human organisms—a point Blumer often appears to underemphasize. Thus, for Mead, the notion of "self" points to a process of role taking, deriving self-images,

---

21 William James, *Principles of Psychology* (New York: Henry Holt, 1890).

22 Mead, *Mind, Self, and Society.*

23 Charles Horton Cooley, *Social Organization* (New York: Scribner's & Son, 1909).

24 Blumer, "Sociological Implications."

and thereby interpreting, defining, and acting toward oneself as an object; but it also denotes the more stable, consistent, and structured "meanings" or "conceptions" that human organisms have of themselves as objects.

While Parsons appears to derive little inspiration from Mead's conception of self, his conceptualization of the "personality system" attempts to capture *both* the processual and structural nature of the actor's personality.[25] In his conceptualization of personality, Parsons begins with a set of assumptions similar to those of Mead or Blumer: The nature of actor as a symbol-using organism forces the conclusion that the actor's internal symbolic manipulations affect, and are affected by, social interaction. To phrase it differently, how does the symbolic repertoire of an actor intervene between the organism and society? While Parsons is more willing than Mead to conceptualize biological impulses and needs, Mead might reconsider his position in an era that has tempered the naïve behavioralism and various "instinct" theories of his time. Aside from this difference, and it is of course a large one, interactionists and action theorists are grappling with the same problem of accounting for the way internal symbolic processes mediate between the individual and society.

While Blumer and others are fond of portraying Parsons's personality system as overly socialized and overly circumscribed by internalized values and norms, they have focused on only part of the Parsonian conceptualization. Furthermore, it would appear that Mead's conceptualization of "generalized others" or more recent role-theoretic notions of "reference groups" point to similar processes of internalization and circumscription by organized groups and their cultural patterns. Equally important, however, is Parsons's concern with the role playing of actors in interaction. Clearly, Parsons's conceptualization of institutionalizations (see above) does not assume that role-playing actors are completely programmed to maintain existing patterns. Rather, actors tend to be both "programmed" and forced to realign behavior in accordance with interpretative and definitional processes (Parsons's voluntarism). While it is hard to deny that Parsons does perhaps devote too much attention to analyzing processes of "programming" or structuring of personality in early works such as *Social System*, the conceptual model of personality also reflects his concern with actors as role players who must frequently readjust their orientations and behaviors. For example, Parsons[26] has devoted considerable attention to discussing the mediating "functions" of ego among the actor's basic biological and social needs, the prescriptions of the current interaction situation, and the actor's immediate perceptions of himself and others as objects.

---

[25] For Parsons's most complete statement on the "personality system," see his "An Approach to Psychological Theory in Terms of the Theory of Action," in *Psychology: A Study of a Science*, ed. Sigmund Koch, vol. 3 (New York: McGraw-Hill Book Co., 1958), pp. 612–711.

[26] Ibid.

It is clear that, while Parsons is concerned with the same problems as interactionists and has moved toward an emphasis on interactive adjustments of the personality system in interaction, there remains a divergence in emphasis between action theory and interactionism in their respective conceptualizations of "self" and "personality." The divergence points to the one-sidedness of both frames of reference; just as Parsons may underemphasize personality as a process, Blumer's interactionism often underemphasizes personality as a structure that shapes processes of symbolic interaction. Since both frameworks are concerned with how role playing influences, and is influenced by, the actor's internal symbolic repertoire, it would appear that the real dispute revolves around the degree of structure or patterning such symbols reveal and the degree of influence they have on the actor's behavior. Translated into these terms, the issue becomes an empirical one that can only be resolved by research: Under what conditions do the structured aspects of personality shape the course of interaction, and vice versa?

In looking back on the action and symbolic interaction theoretic frameworks, it would appear that both hold much the same image of social organization. For each perspective, the actor-situation-orientation is viewed as the most elementary unit of analysis; although the respective terms used by interactionists and action theorists differ, it is clear that the terms define concepts that point to the same phenomenon: the process of symbolically designating the objects toward which action is directed and of covertly rehearsing alternative lines of behavior toward such objects. Similarly, the conceptualization of how such "acts" or "behaviors" become patterned is essentially the same for action and symbolic interaction theory. Actors, in mutually defining each other as objects in a situation, adjust and align their behavior, which, over time, can become regulated by common "expectations" (norms and values) or definitions of how each actor should behave. Such alignment, however, reveals a constant potential for realignment in light of the capacity of humans to interject new objects into the interaction. Finally, while interaction and action theory have drawn upon different intellectual traditions and have given a somewhat varying emphasis on the degree of process or structure in personality, both schemes address the same fundamental question: In what ways does the symbol-using capacities of humans intervene between society and the organism? Thus, in their substantive images of the social world, there is far more convergence between interaction and action theory than would be evident by reading the polemics of Blumer and others of his persuasion. Despite Blumer's often eloquent and always forceful codification of the legacy of George Herbert Mead, what distinguishes interactionism from Parsonian functionalism is not the substantive frame of reference, but rather, the strategy for developing theoretical statements about a similarly conceived world.

DIVERGING THEORETICAL AND RESEARCH STRATEGIES

Herbert Blumer[27] has been perceptive and persistent in his recognition of the divergent strategies for doing research and building theory that interactionism and action theory imply. At the same time, Blumer has been too quick to assume that differences in strategies reflect incompatible frames of reference. While the methods for conducting research and building theory affect the "conceptual image" derived from the "real world," it is important to separate the substantive vision of social organization implied by a frame of reference from the research and theory-building strategy advocated by its various proponents.

If the similarities in frames of reference and the image of "social reality" are recognized, the presumed differences between the perspectives should now excite not so much a metaphysical debate but one involving more answerable questions, including: Which strategy will yield the best predictions about events in a similarly conceived world? Phrased this way, the debate can, in principle, be resolved; phrased in metaphysical terms, the debate will continue without resolution as proponents of what are perceived to be conflicting perspectives assert the "truth" of their "vision" and the "falsity" of others' assumptions about the nature of reality.

The fact that neither the action-theoretic nor the interactionist perspective has been overly fecund in developing ordered formats of clear theoretical statements and a cumulative body of verified research findings is, in part, attributable to the failure to recognize that convergent frames of reference can imply divergent strategies for conducting research and building theory. This failure has created the current situation, where the research findings of one theoretical perspective are often not seen as "relevant" to another, since the "other" perspective holds a different (and bad) vision of social reality. If the similarities of the basic visions of reality are recognized, it is likely that research findings, albeit derived from different methods and directed toward different theory-building strategies, can serve *both* perspectives, whether in making more definitive their similar concepts or in increasing the predictive power of their propositions. Thus, the indiscriminate merging of metaphysical and strategic issues by Blumer and by so many critics of Parsonian action theory has served to compartmentalize theory building and research activities into different "theoretical camps." To continue to hold steadfastly to the illusion that action theory and interactionism embody radically different concepts denoting two entirely different social worlds is to encourage increased encampment of proponents of theoretical perspectives—thereby assuring the slow and discontinuous development of mature sociological theory.

---

[27] Blumer, "Methodological Position."

Among interactionists and action theorists, then, it should be recognized that, while they are committed to building theory about a similarly conceived world, Blumer and Parsons part company over *how* to do so.

Divergent Theory-Building Strategies

From his first statements in *The Structure of Social Action*,[28] Parsons has followed a consistent strategy for building sociological theory. As was outlined in chapter 3, he chose to call this strategy "analytical realism," involving a number of specific tactics: (1) the development of a limited number of generic and abstract concepts that "adequately 'grasp' aspects of the objective external world."[29] (2) the priority over propositional inventories of a "generalized system of concepts," (3) the use of these systems of concepts (rather than propositions) to classify and categorize social phenomena, and (4) then, only after this system of concepts begins to reveal some systemic coherence, the development of systems of propositions. It is this emphasis on the priority of developing systems of concepts that has opened Parsons to a number of attacks by those who would prefer to see all concepts initially incorporated into logico-deductive systems of abstract theoretical statements.[30]

Curiously, Blumer's position as outlined in chapter 11 is remarkably similar to Parsons's, for he places heavy emphasis on first developing a cluster of "sensitizing concepts" that capture the "real character" of the social world.[31] But the "proper" procedure for developing such concepts is markedly different from that suggested by action theory, since Parsons has consistently advocated a form of deductive reasoning as a proper strategy for ultimately developing generic theoretical propositions. Blumer, on the other hand, has been suspect of elaborate conceptual schemes from which systematic deductions to the empirical world are supposed to occur, since "the conventional protocol of scientific analysis still forces . . . data into an artificial framework that seriously limits and impairs genuine empirical analysis."[32]

Both Blumer and Parsons, then, have been particularly concerned with the prior development of adequate concepts in lieu of premature propositional inventories. Parsons's strategy calls for erecting abstract systems of concepts from which more specific concepts can be deduced, whereas Blumer's strategy advocates a close inductive connection between sensitizing concepts and empirical

---

[28] Parsons, *Structure of Social Action.*

[29] Ibid., p. 730.

[30] Enno Schwanenberg, "The Two Problems of Order in Parsons' Theory: An Analysis from Within," *Social Forces* 49 (June 1971): 569–81.

[31] Blumer, "What Is Wrong with Social Theory?"

[32] Blumer, "Methodological Position."

events. These differences over *how* a theory of action or symbolic interaction should be developed point to widely divergent methodological strategies. Indeed, it is these latter differences, as they follow from their respective protocols for developing theory, that have been at the core of interactionists' criticisms of action theory.

Divergent Methodological Strategies

The frames of reference for both action theory and symbolic interaction point to the complexity of social processes as a wide variety of actors orient themselves to situations of varying degrees of stability and align their respective actions. The methodological problems posed by this image of reality, especially as they bear on building theory, revolve around the question of how to capture with generic and abstract concepts, and eventually propositions, the complex process of "joint action" or "institutionalization." To this question, which lies at the core of building a credible body of theory in sociology, Blumer and Parsons have provided widely divergent answers.

Blumer's answer has been emphatic and has constituted a rather persistent line of attack on sociological theory for several decades. For Blumer,[33] the problem with social theory is the lack of connection of concepts to the empirical world. This lack of conceptual connection, as well as self-correction, is the result of the emphasis in sociological theory on the development of concepts that denote variables, such as culture and structure, which ignore the actual *process* of symbolic interaction. Since society is symbolic interaction, involving potentially shifting definitional and interpretive processes, the concepts of social theory must "sensitize" the theorist and researcher to these ever-changing interaction processes.

Parsons, on the other hand, has opted for the strategy of focusing on emergent structures and the various patterns of interaction among them. In this way, it is assumed that it will be possible to understand the complexity of a "real world" composed of individual actors orienting themselves to a wide variety of situations. Not at issue *is* the phenomenon of emergent properties, for both Blumer and Parsons are philosophical realists.[34] What is at issue is *which kind* of phenomena will yield the greatest theoretical payoff in terms of increasing understanding and prediction of events in the social world. For Blumer, the most understanding comes with the study of interpretive and definitional processes of individual

---

[33] Blumer, "What Is Wrong with Social Theory?"

[34] Parsons's realism is well entrenched in the sociological folklore. Blumer also advocates a philosophic realism, for he states: "The recognition that the empirical world has an obdurate character . . . gives full justification to the realist's insistence that the empirical world has a 'real' character" (Blumer, "The Methodological Position," p. 23).

actors, while, for Parsons, the best strategy is to focus on the interaction among emergent patterns of "joint action," to employ Blumer's label.

In this divergence of strategy, Blumer is arguing that causal theoretical statements cannot ignore the interpretive processes of actors defining and redefining situations, since so much of what goes on is accounted for by the fact that actors shift their meanings toward themselves as objects, as well as toward other objects in a particular situation. In light of this fact, it is evident that emergent patterns of joint action, and linkages between these emergent phenomena, are subject to change from the very processes of symbolic interaction from which they emerged. While Parsons accepts the premise that emergent phenomena arise out of, and are altered by, voluntaristic processes of individual actors, he is suggesting that it is not always the best strategy to focus exclusively on voluntaristic processes. To do so creates an analytical situation in which it is impossible to see the "forest through the trees." Hence, while some variance in social systems will always remain unexplained in giving analytical priority to the "forest," or emergent phenomena, Parsons is stressing that a great deal of this "variance" in social life can be accounted for by addressing the causal relations among emergent phenomena *without* focusing on the myriad of voluntaristic unit acts from which the phenomena emerged. Not at issue between Parsons and Blumer is the fact that social life is structured. Even Blumer points out:[35] "Usually, most of the situations encountered by people in a given society are defined or 'structured' by them in the same way. Through previous interaction they develop and acquire common understandings or definitions of how to act in this or that situation." What is at issue, however, is the amount of variation in social life which can be accounted for by emergent, stabilized patterns of interaction. For Blumer, only a little can be so explained, whereas for Parsons much of social life can be understood in this manner. Thus, it is this difference in strategy, rather than in basic visions of "reality," that accounts for the differences in the selection of variables for study by action theorists and symbolic interactionists.

The differences in the variables selected for study dictate different approaches to collecting data. For Blumer, data collection involves the investigator's concern with "taking the role" of the subject under study so as to understand the actor's definition of the situation. To do this, the investigator must suspend his analytical biases and focus on what actors think, perceive, and interpret, since only in this way can the incredible complexity of social processes be understood. For Parsons, this complexity poses the analytical and methodological problem of what to look for in all the complex processes of social life. Without some analytical criteria for assessing which processes are important, investigators will be lost in a maze of "unit acts" of individual actors. It is in this context that Parsons's concern

---

[35] Blumer, "Society as Symbolic Interaction."

for "system imperatives" must be understood. These imperatives are assumed to denote for investigators and theorists those processes that are likely to yield the most theoretical payoff. Too often, they are assumed by critics to be metaphysical entities, whereas a more accurate interpretation is that the imperatives represent criteria for sorting out the "crucial" from "not crucial" processes for investigators. Thus, at issue between Blumer and Parsons is not a separate image of social reality, but the question of whether analytical criteria will enhance investigators' perceptions of social processes, or blind investigators to crucial social processes. Again, regardless of who is more "correct," the issue is one of strategy for conducting research that can build a more adequate body of sociological theory.

CONCLUSION

This chapter has asked that students of sociological theory reexamine some of their comfortable antagonisms, with the hope that real progress can be made in breaking down the barriers that currently separate bodies of theory and research findings. It should be comforting rather than disquieting to social theorists and investigators that Parsons's and Blumer's respective frames of reference are similar and point to a similarly conceived social world. These similarities suggest that sociologists are indeed addressing the same empirical world with similar concepts and that what are perceived as metaphysical disagreements are, in point of fact, arguments over the best strategies for building theory and conducting research. Naturally, the strategy that one employs necessarily has ontological implications; this is in the nature of humans making symbolic representations of the "real world." Even in light of this fact, the perceived nature of the world among interactionists and action theorists is not so different as has frequently been contended.

Once presumed metaphysical and ontological differences are reduced to questions of strategy, it becomes obvious that it is fruitless to argue at the assumptive level, since disagreements over strategy suggest a solution: By following one or the other strategy, just who is more "correct" theoretically should become evident as propositions are tested against research findings. Currently, it appears that a great deal of intellectual effort is wasted in arguing in a research and theoretical vacuum about who is more "correct"; perhaps it is for this reason that neither Blumer's nor Parsons's strategy has done much to develop a format of ordered theoretical statements, or body of cumulative research findings, that can provide a solution to the Hobbesian problem of order: How is society possible?

Part IV

Exchange Theory

13

The Intellectual Roots of Exchange Theory

The intellectual heritage culminating in modern exchange theory is diverse, drawing from sources in economics, anthropology, and psychology. What typifies this heritage as much as its diversity are the frequently vague connections between contemporary exchange theorists and their predecessors. Indeed, current exchange theories appear to be a curious and unspecified mixture of utilitarian economics, functional anthropology, and behavioral psychology. When this mixture is coupled with each contemporary author's attempts to provide an exchange-theoretic alternative to Parsonian functionalism, the development over the last two decades of sociological exchange theories presents a complex picture of selective borrowing of long standing concepts and principles from other disciplines and reaction to imputed inadequacies of functional forms of theorizing. In this chapter, then, a tentative overview of the traditions toward which sociologists turned in seeking the exchange alternative to functionalism is provided.

UTILITARIANISM: THE LEGACY OF "CLASSICAL" ECONOMICS

The names of Adam Smith, David Ricardo, John Stuart Mill, and Jeremy Bentham loom large in the history of economic theorizing between 1750–1850. While each made a somewhat unique contribution to both economic and social thought, certain core assumptions about the nature of man and his relation with others, especially in the economic marketplace, enabled their thought to be labeled "utilitarianism." Although the extreme formulations of utilitarianism have long since been rejected, several key ideas still continue to inform theorizing

211

in the social sciences. For example, as was noted in the discussion of Talcott Parsons's voluntaristic theory of action, there is a clearly acknowledged intellectual debt to utilitarian thought. And so it is with modern exchange theorists, although their intellectual debt is not so thoroughly documented or clearly understood as was the case with Parsons.

Underlying all contemporary exchange theories are reformulations of certain basic utilitarian assumptions and concepts. For classical economists, men were viewed as rationally seeking to maximize their material benefits, or "utility," from transactions or exchanges with others in a free and competitive marketplace. As rational units in a free marketplace, men would have access to all necessary information, could consider all available alternatives, and, on the basis of this consideration, rationally select the course of activity which would maximize material benefits. Entering into these rational considerations were calculations of the "costs" involved in pursuing various alternatives. Such costs must be weighted against material benefits in an effort to determine which alternative would yield the maximum payoff or profit (benefits less costs).[1]

With the emergence of sociology as a self-conscious discipline, there was considerable borrowing, revision, and reaction to this conception of man and his transactions with others. In fact, the debate between the intellectual descendants of utilitarianism and those reacting to this perspective has raged since sociology's inception. For example, the formulations of Comte and Durkheim were in large part an attempt to devise an alternative to the utilitarian thought in the various works of Herbert Spencer. More recently, as was noted in the discussion of Parsonian functionalism, Parsons has attempted to reformulate utilitarian principles and weld them to other theoretical traditions in an effort to correct for Spencer's oversights. Similarly, modern exchange theorists have attempted to reformulate utilitarian principles into various theories of social exchange.

This reformulation has involved the recognition that: (a) rarely do men attempt to maximize profits; (b) men are not always rational; (c) their transactions with each other, whether in an economic marketplace or elsewhere, are not free from external regulation and constraint; and (d) men do not have perfect information on all available alternatives. Recognition of these facts has led to a series of alternative utilitarian assumptions: (1) While men do not seek to maximize profits, they always seek to make some profit in their social transactions with others. (2) While men are not perfectly rational, they engage in calculations of costs and benefits in social transactions. (3) While men do not have perfect information on all available alternatives, they are usually aware of at least some alternatives, which form the basis for assessments of costs and benefits. (4) While

---

[1] For interesting discussions of utilitarian thought as it bears on the present discussion, see Elie Halévy, *The Growth of Philosophical Radicalism* (London: Farber & Farber, 1928); John Plamenatz, *Man and Society* (New York: McGraw-Hill, Book Co., 1963).

there are always constraints on human activity, men compete with each other in seeking to make a profit in their transactions. In addition to these alterations of utilitarian assumptions, exchange theory removes human interaction from the limitations of material transactions in an economic marketplace: (5) While economic transactions in a clearly defined marketplace occur in all societies, they are only a special case of more general exchange relations occurring among individuals in virtually all social contexts. (6) While material goals typify exchanges in an economic marketplace, men also exchange other, nonmaterial commodities, such as sentiments and services of various kinds.

Aside from the substantive legacy of utilitarianism, some forms of modern exchange theory have also adopted the *strategy* of the utilitarians for constructing social theory. In assuming humans to be rational, utilitarians argued that exchanges among men could also be studied by a rational science, one in which the "laws of human nature" would stand at the top of a deductive system of explanation. Thus, utilitarians borrowed the early physical science conception of theory as a logico-deductive system of axioms or laws and various layers of lower-order propositions that could be "rationally" deduced from the laws of economic man. As will be emphasized at the close of this chapter, utilitarianism inspired the development of psychological behaviorism, which not only adjusted the concepts and assumptions of classical economic theory to its purposes, but also adopted the commitment to axiomatic forms of theorizing. This commitment, as inherited directly and indirectly through behaviorism, has persisted to the present day and dominates much of the exchange-theoretic literature.

However, in reviewing the tenets of utilitarianism, only part of the historical legacy of exchange theory is exposed. In addition to influencing behaviorists, who in turn were to influence modern exchange theory, utilitarianism excited considerable debate and controversy in early anthropology. In fact, much of the influence of utilitarianism on current exchange theory appears to have been indirect, passing simultaneously through behaviorism and social anthropology around the turn of this century. Thus, while the exchange theories of sociology may now exert the most influence on social theory, sociological exchange theories have been built upon the pioneering efforts of social anthropologists.

EXCHANGE THEORY IN ANTHROPOLOGY[2]

Sir James Frazer

In 1919 Sir James George Frazer, in the second volume of his *Folklore in the Old Testament,* conducted what was probably the first explicitly exchange-theo-

---

[2] This section is heavily indebted to Peter P. Ekeh's manuscript, "Social Exchange Theory and the Two Sociological Traditions," (Soon to be published by Harvard University Press).

retic analysis of social institutions.[3] In examining a wide variety of kinship and marriage practices among primitive societies, Frazer was struck by the clear preference of Australian aboriginals for cross-cousin over parallel-cousin marriages: "Why is the marriage of cross-cousins so often favored? Why is the marriage of ortho-cousins [i.e., parallel cousins] so uniformly prohibited?"[4]

While the substantive details of Frazer's descriptions of the aboriginals' practices are fascinating in themselves (if only for their inaccuracy), it is the *form* of his explanation that marks his theoretical contribution. In a manner clearly indebted to utilitarian economics, Frazer launched an economic interpretation of the predominance of cross-cousin marriage patterns. In this explanation, Frazer invoked the "law" of "economic motives," since, in having "no equivalent in property to give for a wife, an Australian aboriginal is generally obliged to get her in exchange for a female relative, usually a sister or daughter."[5] Thus, the material or economic motives of individuals in society (lack of property and desire for a wife) explain various social patterns (cross-cousin marriages). What is more, Frazer went on to postulate that once a particular pattern, emanating from economic motives, becomes established in a culture, it circumscribes and constrains other social patterns that can potentially emerge.

For Frazer, then, the institutionalized patterns that come to typify a particular culture are a reflection of economic motives in men who, in exchanging commodities, attempt to satisfy their basic economic needs. While Frazer's specific explanation was to be found sadly wanting by subsequent generations of anthropologists, especially Malinowski and Lévi-Strauss, much modern exchange theory in sociology invokes a similar conception of social organization:

1. Exchange processes are the result of motives among men to realize their needs.

2. When yielding payoffs for those involved, exchange processes lead to the institutionalization or patterning of interaction.

3. Such institutionalized networks of interaction not only serve the needs of men, but they also constrain the kinds of social structures that can subsequently emerge in a social system.

In addition to anticipating the general profile of modern explanations on how elementary-exchange processes create more complex institutional patterns in a society, Frazer's analysis also foreshadowed another concern of contemporary

---

[3] Sir James George Frazer, *Folklore in the Old Testament*, vol. 2 (New York: Macmillan Co., 1919); see also his *Totemism and Exogamy: A Treatise on Certain Early Forms of Superstition and Society* (London: Dawsons of Pall Mall, 1968) (original publication 1910); and his Preface to *Argonauts of the Western Pacific*, by Bronislaw Malinowski (London: Routledge & Kegan Paul, 1922), pp. vii–xiv.

[4] Quote taken from Ekeh's ("Social Exchange Theory," pp. 41–42) discussion of Frazer (original quote in Frazer, *Folklore*, p. 199).

[5] Ibid., p. 195.

exchange theory: the differentiation of social systems in terms of privilege and power. Exchange systems, Frazer noted, allow those who possessed commodities of high economic value to "exploit" those who had few such commodities, thereby enabling the former to possess high privilege and presumably power over the latter. Hence, the exchange of women among the aboriginals was observed by Frazer to lead to the differentiation of power and privilege in at least two separate ways:[6] First, "Since among the Australian aboriginals women had a high economic and commercial value, a man who had many sisters or daughters was rich and a man who had none was poor and might be unable to procure a wife at all."[7] Second, "the old men availed themselves of the system of exchange in order to procure a number of wives for themselves from among the young women, while the young men having no women to give in exchange, were often obliged to remain single or to put up with the cast-off wives of their elders."[8] Thus, at least implicitly, Frazer anticipated a fourth principle of social organization which was to be elaborated upon by contemporary exchange theory:

(4) Exchange processes operate to differentiate groups in terms of their relative access to valued commodities, resulting in differences in power, prestige, and privilege.

As provocative and seemingly seminal as Frazer's analysis appears, it has had little direct impact on modern exchange theory. Rather, it is to those in anthropology who reacted to, and attempted to improve upon, Frazer's brand of utilitarianism that contemporary theory in sociology remains indebted.

Bronislaw Malinowski and Exchange Psychologism

Despite Malinowski's close ties with Frazer, he was to develop an exchange perspective that radically altered the utilitarian slant of Frazer's analysis of cross-cousin marriage. Indeed, Frazer himself in his preface to Malinowski's *Argonauts of the Western Pacific* recognized the importance of Malinowski's contribution to the analysis of exchange relations.[9] In his now-famous ethnography of the Trobriand Islanders—a group of South Seas Island cultures—Malinowski observed an exchange system termed the "Kula Ring," a closed circle of exchange relations among individuals in communities inhabiting a wide ring of islands.[10] What was distinctive in this closed circle, Malinowski observed, was the predominance of exchange of two articles—armlets and necklaces—which constantly

---

[6] This insight comes from Ekeh's provocative manuscript, "Social Exchange Theory," p. 44.

[7] Frazer, *Folklore*, p. 198.

[8] Ibid., pp. 200–201.

[9] Frazer, Preface to *Argonauts*.

[10] Bronislaw Malinowski, *Argonauts of the Western Pacific* (London: Routledge & Kegan Paul, 1922), p. 81.

traveled in opposite directions. In one direction around the Kula Ring, armlets traveled and were exchanged by individuals for necklaces moving in the opposite direction around the ring. In any particular exchange between individuals, then, an armshell would always be exchanged for a necklace.

In interpreting this unique exchange network, Malinowski was led to distinguish material, or economic, from nonmaterial, or symbolic, exchanges. In contrast with the utilitarians and Frazer, who were unable to conceptualize nonmaterial exchange relations, Malinowski recognized that the Kula was not an economic, or material, exchange network, but rather a symbolic exchange, cementing a web of social relationships: "One transaction does not finish the Kula relationship, the rule being 'once in the Kula, always in the Kula,' and a partnership between two men is a permanent and lifelong affair."[11] While purely economic transactions could occur within the rules of the Kula, the ceremonial exchange of armlets and necklaces was observed by Malinowski to be the principle "function" of the Kula.

The natives themselves, Malinowski emphasized, recognized the distinction between purely economic commodities and the symbolic significance of armlets and necklaces. However, to distinquish economic from symbolic commodities should not be interpreted to mean that the Trobriand Islanders did not assign graded values to the symbolic commodities; indeed, they did make such gradations and used them to express and confirm the nature of the relationships among exchange partners as equals, superordinates, or subordinates. But, as Malinowski noted, "in all forms of [Kula] exchange in the Trobriands, there is not even a trace of gain, nor is there any reason for looking at it from the purely utilitarian and economic standpoint, since there is no enhancement of mutual utility through the exchange."[12] Rather, the motives behind the Kula were social psychological, for the exchanges in the Kula Ring were viewed by Malinowski to have implications for the "needs" of both individuals and society. From Malinowski's typical functionalist framework (see chapter 2), he interpreted the Kula to meet "the fundamental impulse to display, to share, to bestow [and] the deep tendency to create social ties."[13] For Malinowski, then, an enduring social pattern such as the Kula Ring is considered to have positively functional consequences for satisfying *individual* psychological needs and *societal* needs for social integration and solidarity.

As Robert Merton and others were to emphasize (see chapter 4), this form of functional analysis presents many logical difficulties. Despite the difficulties, however, Malinowski's analysis made several enduring contributions to modern exchange theory:

---

11 Ibid., pp. 82–83.

12 Ibid., p. 175.

13 Ibid., p. 175.

1. In Malinowski's words, "the meaning of the Kula will consist in being instrumental to dispel [the] conception of a rational being who wants nothing but to satisfy his simplest needs and does it according to the economic principle of least effort."[14]

2. Psychological rather than economic needs are thus the force that initiate and sustain exchange relations and are therefore critical in the explanation of social behavior.

3. Exchange relations can also have implications beyond two parties, for, as the Kula demonstrates, complex patterns of indirect exchange can operate to maintain extended and protracted social networks.

4. Symbolic exchange relations are the basic social process underlying both differentiation of ranks in a society and the integration of society into a cohesive and solidary whole.

Malinowski thus freed exchange theory from the limiting confines of utilitarianism by introducing the importance of symbolic exchanges for both individual psychological processes and patterns of social integration and solidarity. In so doing, he provided the conceptual base for two basic types of exchange perspectives, one emphasizing the importance of psychological processes, and the other stressing the significance of emergent cultural and structural forces on exchange relations. As subsequent chapters will document, modern sociological exchange theories appear to have diverged around these two nodes of emphasis in Malinowski's work.

Marcel Mauss and the Emergence of Exchange Structuralism

Reacting to what he perceived as Malinowski's tendency to overemphasize psychological over social needs, Marcel Mauss was led to reinterpret Malinowski's analysis of the Kula.[15] In this effort, he was to formulate the broad outlines of a "collectivistic," or structural exchange, perspective.[16] For Mauss, the critical question in examining an exchange network as complex as that of the Kula was:

---

[14] Ibid., p. 516.

[15] Marcel Mauss, *The Gift*, trans. Ian Cunnison (New York: Free Press, 1954) (originally published as *Essai sur le don en sociologie et anthropologie* [Paris: Presses universitaires de France, 1925]). It should be noted that Mauss rather consistently misinterpreted Malinowski's ethnography, but it is through such misinterpretation that he came to visualize a "structural" alternative to "psychological" exchange theories.

[16] In Peter Ekeh's excellent discussion of Mauss and Lévi-Strauss ("Social Exchange Theory," pp. 55–122), the term "collectivist" is used in preference to "structural" and is posited as the alternative to "individualistic" or "psychological" exchange perspectives. I prefer the terms "structural" and "psychological"; thus, while I am indebted to Ekeh's discussion, these terms will be used to make essentially the same distinction. My preference for these terms will become more evident in subsequent chapters, since, in contrast with Ekeh's analysis, I consider Peter M. Blau and George C. Homans to have developed, respectively, structural and psychological theories. Ekeh considers the theories of both Blau and Homans to be "individualistic," or psychological.

"In primitive or archaic types of societies what is the principle whereby the gift received has to be repaid? What force is there in the thing which compels the recipient to make a return?" [17]

The "force" compelling reciprocity was, for Mauss, society or the group, since "it is groups, and not individuals, which carry on exchange, make contracts, and are bound by obligations." [18] The individuals actually engaged in an exchange are "persons" who represent the moral codes of the group. Exchange transactions among individuals are conducted in accordance with the rules of the group, while, at the same time, reinforcing these rules and codes. Thus, for Mauss, the individual self-interest of utilitarians and the needs of Malinowski's psychologisms are replaced by a conception of individuals as mere representatives of social groups; in the end, exchange relations create, reinforce, and serve a group morality that is an entity *sui generis,* to borrow a famous phrase from Mauss's colleague, Émile Durkheim. Furthermore, in a vein similar to that of Frazer, once such a morality emerges and is reinforced by exchange activities, it comes to regulate other activities in the social life of a group, above and beyond particular exchange transactions.

While Mauss's work has received but scant attention from sociologists, he was the first to forge a reconciliation between the exchange principles of utilitarianism and the structural, or collectivistic, thought of Durkheim. In recognizing that exchange transactions give rise to and, at the same time, reinforce the normative structure of society, Mauss anticipated the structural position of some contemporary exchange theories, such as that advocated by Blau (see chapter 15). Mauss's influence on modern theory, however, was indirect, for it is only through Lévi-Strauss's structuralism that the French collectivist tradition of Durkheim has had a major impact on both the psychological and structural exchange perspectives of contemporary sociological theorizing.

Claude Lévi-Strauss and Structuralism

In 1949, Claude Lévi-Strauss launched an analysis of cross-cousin marriage in his classic work, *The Elementary Structures of Kinship.* [19] In restating Durkheim's objections to utilitarians such as Spencer, Lévi-Strauss took exception to Frazer's utilitarian interpretation of cross-cousin marriage patterns. And in a

---

[17] Mauss, *The Gift,* p. 1 (italics in original).

[18] Ibid., p. 3.

[19] Claude Lévi-Strauss, *The Elementary Structures of Kinship* (Boston: Beacon Press, 1969). This is a translation of Lévi-Strauss's 1967 revision of the original *Les structures élémentaires de la parenté* (Paris: Presses universitaires de France, 1949). The full impact of this work was probably never felt in sociology, since until 1969 it was not available in English. Yet, as will be noted in chapter 14 on Homans, it did have a profound impact on Homans's thinking, primarily because Homans felt compelled to reject Lévi-Strauss's analysis.

manner similar to Mauss's opposition to Malinowski's emphasis on psychological needs, Lévi-Strauss developed the most sophisticated of the structural exchange perspectives to predate modern sociological theory's concern with exchange processes.[20]

In reacting to Frazer's interpretation of cross-cousin marriage, Lévi-Strauss first rejects the substance of Frazer's utilitarian conceptualization, for Frazer "depicts the poor Australian aborigine wondering how he is going to obtain a wife since he has no material goods with which to purchase her, and discovering exchange as the solution to this apparently insoluble problem: 'men exchange their sisters in marriage because that was the cheapest way of getting a wife'."[21] In contrast, Lévi-Strauss emphasizes that "it is the exchange which counts and not the things exchanged," since, as will be documented shortly, exchange for Lévi-Strauss must be viewed in terms of its functions for integrating the larger social structure. Lévi-Strauss then attacks Frazer's and the utilitarian's assumption that the first principles of social behavior are economic. Such an assumption flies in the face of the fact that social structure is an emergent phenomenon that operates in terms of its own irreducible laws and principles.

Lévi-Strauss also rejects psychological interpretations of exchange processes, especially the position advocated by behaviorists (see later section). In contrast with psychological behaviorists, who see little real difference between the laws of behavior among animals and humans, Lévi-Strauss emphasizes that humans possess a cultural heritage of norms and values which separates their behavior and organization into society apart from the behavior and organization of animal species. Human behavior is thus qualitatively different from animal behavior, especially with respect to social exchange, for animals are not guided by values and rules that specify when, where, and how they are to carry out social transactions. Unlike animals, humans carry with them into any exchange situation learned and institutionalized definitions of how they are to behave—thus assuring the principles of human exchange will be distinctive.

Furthermore, exchange is more than the result of psychological needs, even those that have been acquired through socialization. Exchange cannot be understood solely in terms of individual motives, because exchange relations are a reflection of patterns of social organization which exist as an entity, *sui generis*, to the psychological dispositions of individuals. Exchange behavior is thus regulated from without by norms and values, with the result that exchange processes can only be analyzed in terms of their "consequences," or "functions," for these norms and values.

In arguing this point of view, Lévi-Strauss posits several fundamental exchange

---

[20] The present discussion of Lévi-Strauss is heavily indebted to Ekeh's discussion ("Social Exchange Theory," pp. 68–94).

[21] Lévi-Strauss, *Elementary Structures of Kinship*, p. 138.

principles: First, all exchange relations involve costs for individuals, but, in contrast with economic or psychological explanations of exchange, such costs are attributed to society—to its customs, rules, laws, and values. These features of society require behaviors that incur costs; thus, the individual does not assess the costs to himself, but to the "social order" requiring that costly behavior be emitted. Second, for all those scarce and valued resources in society—whether material objects, such as wives, or symbolic resources like esteem and prestige—their distribution is regulated by norms and values. As long as resources are in abundant supply or not highly valued in a society, their distribution goes unregulated, but once they become scarce and highly valued, their distribution is soon institutionalized. Third, all exchange relations are regulated by a norm of reciprocity, requiring those receiving valued resources to bestow on their benefactors other valued resources. What is critical in Lévi-Strauss's conception of reciprocity is that there are various patterns of reciprocity specified by norms and values. In some situations, following norms of reciprocity requires "mutual" and direct rewarding of one's benefactor, whereas in other situations the reciprocity can be "univocal" involving diverse patterns of indirect exchange in which actors do not reciprocate directly but only through various third (fourth, fifth, and so forth) parties. Within these two general types of exchange reciprocity—mutual and univocal—numerous subtypes of exchange networks can be normatively regulated.

Lévi-Strauss's enumeration of these three principles offered for him a more useful set of concepts to describe cross-cousin marriage patterns. Now these patterns can be viewed in terms of their functions for the larger social structure. Particular marriage patterns and other features of kinship organization no longer need be interpreted merely as direct exchanges among individuals, but can be conceptualized as univocal exchanges between individuals and society. In freeing exchange from concepts forcing the analysis of only direct and mutual exchanges, Lévi-Strauss goes on to offer a tentative theory of societal integration and solidarity. His explanation represents an attempt to extend Durkheim's provocative analysis and involves an effort to indicate how various subtypes of direct and univocal exchange both reflect and reinforce different patterns of societal integration and organization.

This theory of integration is, in itself, of theoretical importance, but more significant for present purposes is Lévi-Strauss's impact on current sociological exchange perspectives. As will become evident in subsequent chapters, two of his concepts appear to have had a strong influence on modern sociological theory:

1. Various forms of social structure rather than individual motives are the critical variables in the analysis of exchange relations.

2. Exchange relations in social systems are frequently not restricted to direct interaction among individuals, but protracted into complex networks of indirect

exchange. On the one hand, these exchange processes are caused by patterns of social integration and organization; on the other hand, they promote diverse forms of such organization.

In looking back on the anthropological heritage, Lévi-Strauss's work can be seen to represent the culmination of reaction to economic utilitarianism as it was originally incorporated into anthropology by Frazer. Malinowski recognized the limitations of Frazer's analysis of only material or economic motives in direct exchange transactions. As the Kula Ring demonstrated, exchange could be generalized into protracted networks involving noneconomic motives which had implications for societal integration. Mauss drew explicit attention to the significance of social structure in regulating exchange processes and to the consequences of such processes for maintaining social structure. Finally, in this intellectual chain of events in anthropology, Lévi-Strauss began to indicate how different types of direct and indirect exchange were linked to different patterns of social organization. While this intellectual heritage has influenced both the substance and strategy of exchange theory in sociology, it has done so only after considerable modification by assumptions and concepts borrowed from a particular strain of psychology: behaviorism.

PSYCHOLOGICAL BEHAVIORISM AND EXCHANGE THEORY

Psychological behaviorism as a theoretical perspective has historically drawn its principles from the observation of subhuman, animal behavior. From the first insights of Pavlov into the responses of dogs to a light that had previously been associated with food to the experimental manipulations of pigeons and mice in the famous Skinner box, it has been assumed by many behaviorists that the elementary principles describing animal behavior will form the core of a deductive system of propositions explaining human behavior. Of critical importance in understanding the position of some behavioralists is the presumption that it is unnecessary to delve into the "black box" of human thought and cognition, since it is quite possible and desirable to study only *overt* behavior as a response to *observable* stimuli in the environment. Although this extreme position is not accepted by all behaviorists, it has been the guiding assumption behind the work of the scholars, such as B. F. Skinner,[22] who have had the most influence on sociological exchange theory.

In many ways, behaviorism is an extreme variant of utilitarianism, since it operates on the principle that animals and humans are both reward-seeking organisms that pursue alternatives that will yield the most reward and least

---

[22] See, for example, B. F. Skinner, *The Behavior of Organisms* (New York: Appleton-Century-Crofts, 1938); and B. F. Skinner, *Science and Human Behavior* (New York: Macmillan, 1953).

punishment. Rewards are simply a way of rephrasing the economist's concept of "utility," while "punishment" is a somewhat revised notion of "cost." For the behaviorist, reward is any behavior that reinforces or meets the needs of the organism, whereas punishment is behavior of the organism itself or of others in the environment which inhibits the organism from meeting its needs—most typically, the need to avoid pain.

Modern exchange theories have borrowed from behaviorists the notion of reward and used it to reinterpret the utilitarian exchange heritage. In place of utility, the concept of reward has been inserted, primarily because it allows exchange theorists to view behavior as motivated by psychological needs. However, the utilitarian concept of cost appears to have been retained in preference to the behaviorist's vague formulation of "punishment," since the notion of "cost" allows exchange theorists to visualize more completely the alternative rewards that organisms forgo in seeking to achieve a particular reward. Seemingly, "punishment" is too closely associated with the concept of "pain," which does not necessarily allow for the conceptualization of humans as choice-making organisms who not only seek to avoid pain, but who also can choose among several rewarding alternatives in most situations.

Despite these modifications of the basic concepts of behaviorism, several of its key theoretical generalizations have been incorporated, with relatively little change, into some forms of sociological exchange theory:

1. In any given situation, organisms will emit those behaviors that will yield the most reward and least punishment.
2. Organisms will repeat those behaviors which have proved rewarding in the past.
3. Organisms will repeat behaviors in situations that are similar to those in the past in which behaviors were rewarded.
4. Present stimuli that on past occasions have been associated with rewards will evoke behaviors similar to those emitted in the past.
5. Repetition of behaviors will occur only as long as they continue to yield rewards.
6. An organism will display emotion if a behavior that has previously been rewarded in the same, or similar, situation suddenly goes unrewarded.
7. The more an organism receives rewards from a particular behavior, the less rewarding that behavior becomes (due to satiation) and the more likely the organism to emit alternative behaviors in search of other rewards.

Since these principles were discovered in laboratory situations where experimenters typically manipulated the environment of the organism, it is difficult to visualize the experimental situation as *interaction,* for the tight control of the situation by the experimenter precludes the possibility that the animal will affect significantly the responses of the experimenter. This fact has forced modern exchange theories using behaviorist principles to incorporate the utilitarian's concern with "transaction," or "exchanges," since in this way humans can be seen as mutually affecting each other's opportunities for rewards. In contrast with animals in a Skinner box or some similar laboratory situation, humans exchange rewards, with the result that each person represents a potentially rewarding stimulus situation for the other.

As sociological exchange theorists have attempted to apply behaviorist principles to the study of human behavior, they have inevitably confronted the problem of "the black box": Humans differ from laboratory animals in their greater ability to engage in a wide variety of complex cognitive processes. Indeed, as the utilitarians were the first to emphasize, what is distinctly human is the capacity to abstract, to calculate, to project outcomes, to weigh alternatives, and to perform a wide number of other covert cognitive manipulations. Furthermore, in borrowing behaviorist's concepts, contemporary exchange theorists have also had to introduce the concepts of an introspective psychology and structural sociology, for humans not only think in complex ways, their thinking is emotional and circumscribed by many social and cultural forces (first incorporated into the exchange theories of Mauss and Lévi-Strauss). Once it is recognized that behaviorist principles must incorporate concepts denoting both internal psychological processes and constraints of social structure and culture, it is also necessary to visualize exchange as frequently transcending the mutually rewarding activities of individuals in direct interaction. The organization of behavior by social structure and culture, coupled with man's complex cognitive abilities, allows protracted and indirect exchange networks to exist.

In looking back upon the impact of behaviorism on some forms of contemporary exchange theory, a curious marriage of concepts and principles appears to have occurred. While the vocabulary and general principles of behaviorism are clearly evident, the concepts have been redefined and the principles altered to incorporate the insights of the early utilitarians as well as the anthropological reaction to utilitarianism. The end result has been for proponents of an exchange perspective employing behaviorist concepts and principles to abandon much of what made behaviorism a unique perspective as they have dealt with the complexities introduced by human cognitive capacities and their organization into sociocultural groupings.

14

Exchange Behaviorism:
George C. Homans

One of the most eloquent contemporary spokesmen for the exchange perspective is George C. Homans. In a long career devoted to theoretical explanation, Homans has increasingly advocated a particular strategy for building sociological theory which increasingly has become predicated upon exchange principles. Much of Homans's advocacy is directed toward providing an alternative to Talcott Parsons's theoretical strategy and conceptual edifice. Yet curiously, in light of the widespread acceptance of criticisms against Parsonian functionalism, Homans's exchange scheme has been subjected to a barrage of criticism usually reserved only for functional theorizing. Interestingly, this criticism comes not just from "functional" theorists, but from all theoretical camps. Thus, the task of this chapter is, first of all, to trace the development of Homans's exchange perspective and then to explicate and analyze the reasons behind the widespread criticisms of the perspective.

HOMANS ON THEORY BUILDING IN SOCIOLOGY

The Early Inductive Strategy

By 1950, with the publication of *The Human Group*,[1] Homans's work revealed a clear commitment to an inductive strategy for building sociological theory. In studies ranging from the analysis of a work group in a factory and a

---

[1] From *The Human Group* by George C. Homans, copyright, 1950, by Harcourt Brace Jovanovich, Inc., and reprinted with their permission.

street gang to the kinship system of a primitive society and the structure of an entire New England community, he stressed the importance of observing people's actual behaviors and activities in various types of groups. By observing what people actually do, it would be possible to develop concepts that are "attached" to the ongoing processes of social systems. Such concepts were termed by Homans "first-order abstractions," since they merely represent "names" that observers use to signify a "single class of observations" in a group. Homans chose the words "first-order abstractions" carefully, because he wanted to emphasize their difference from the "second-order abstractions" commonly employed by sociologists. As distinct from the abstractions he prefers, second-order abstractions refer to several classes of observations and are thereby somewhat detached from ongoing events in actual groups. For example, "status" and "role" are favorite concepts used by sociologists to denote processes in groups, but upon careful reflection, it is evident that one does not observe directly a "status" or "role"; rather, they are highly abstract names, which subsume numerous types and classes of events occurring in groups.

The typical practice of jumping to second-order abstractions in building theory is viewed by Homans as premature:

> [Sociologists should initially] attempt to climb down from the big words of social science, at least as far as common sense observation. Then, if we wish, we can start climbing up again, but this time with a ladder we can depend on.[2]

In constructing a firm "bottom rung" to the abstraction ladder, Homans introduced three first-order abstractions that provided labels or names to the actual events occurring in groups: activities, interaction, and sentiments. Activities pertain to "what men do" in a given situation; interaction denotes the process in which one unit of activity stimulates a unit of activity in another person; and sentiments refer to the internal psychological states of men engaged in activities and interaction.

The three first-order abstractions, or "elements," as Homans was fond of calling them, were seen as existing within an "external system," which for Homans was the environment parameters of a particular group under study. As he was to later label this analytical approach, the external system represented the "givens" of a particular situation, which, for the purposes at hand, are not examined extensively. Of more interest, however, was the "internal system," which operated within the constraints imposed by the external system and which was composed of the interrelated activities, interactions, and sentiments of group members. The fact that activities, interactions, and sentiments were interrelated was of great analytical significance, since, for Homans, changes in one element led to changes in the other elements within the internal system.

---

[2] Ibid., p. 13.

Of critical importance in the analysis of internal systems is the process of "elaboration" in which new patterns of organization among activities, interaction, and sentiments are constantly emerging by virtue of their interrelatedness with each other and with the external system. A group thus "elaborates itself, complicates itself, beyond the demands of the original situation"; in so doing, it brings about new types of activities, forms of interaction, and types of sentiments.

In *The Human Group*, Homans's strategy was to present a descriptive summary of five case studies on diverse groups. From each summary, Homans attempted to incorporate the "elements" of the internal system into propositions that described the empirical regularities he "observed"[3] in the case study. As he proceeded in his summaries of the case studies, Homans attempted to substantiate the generalizations from one study in the next, while at the same time using each successive study as a source for additional generalizations. With this strategy, it was hoped that a body of interrelated generalizations describing the various ways different types of groups elaborated their internal systems of activities, interactions, and sentiments would emerge. In this way, the first rungs of the abstraction ladder used in sociological theorizing would be "dependable," providing a firm base for subsequent theorizing at a more abstract level.

For example, in Homans's summary of the now-famous Bank Wiring Room in the Hawthorne Western Electric Plant, Homans observed these regularities:[4] (1) If the frequency of interaction between two or more persons increases, the degree of their liking for one another will increase, and vice versa.[5] (2) Persons whose sentiments of liking for one another increase will express these sentiments in increased activity, and vice versa.[6] (3) The more frequently persons interact with one another, the more alike their activities and their sentiments tend to become, and vice versa.[7] (4) The higher the rank of a person within a group, the more nearly his activities conform to the norms of the group, and vice versa.[8] (5) The higher the person's social rank, the wider will be the range of his interactions.[9]

---

[3] In Homans's work, he rarely makes direct observations himself. Rather, he has tended to rely upon the observations of others, making from their reports inferences about events. As would be expected, Homans has often been criticized for accepting too readily the imprecise, and perhaps inaccurate, observations of others as an inductive base for theorizing.

[4] This extended example is adapted from Mulkay's discussion of Homans's propositions in M. J. Mulkay, *Functionalism and Exchange and Theoretical Strategy* (New York: Schocken Books, 1971), pp. 135–41. As was done by Mulkay, some of Homans's propositions are reworded in an effort at simplification.

[5] Homans, *Human Group*, p. 112.

[6] Ibid., p. 118.

[7] Ibid., p. 120.

[8] Ibid., p. 141.

[9] Ibid., p. 145.

These propositions describe some of the group-elaboration processes that Homans "observed" in the Bank Wiring Room. Propositions 1 and 2 summarize Homans's observation that the more the workers in the Bank Wiring Room interacted, the more they appeared to like one another, which, in turn, seemed to cause further interactions above and beyond the work requirements of the external system. Such elaboration of interactions, sentiments, and activities was also seen as resulting in the differentiation of subgroups, which revealed their own levels of output, topics of conversation, and patterns of work assistance. This tendency is denoted by Proposition 3. Another pattern of differentiation in the Bank Wiring Room is described by Proposition 4, whereby the ranking of individuals and subgroups was viewed to occur when group members compared their activities with those of other members and the output norms of the group. Proposition 5 describes the tendency in the Bank Wiring Room of high-ranking members to interact more frequently with all members of the group, offering more on-the-job assistance.

Having tentatively established these, and other, empirical regularities in the Bank Wiring Room, Homans then analyzed the equally famous Norton Street Gang, described in William Whyte's *Street Corner Society.* In this second case study, Homans followed his strategy of confirming his earlier propositions, while inducing further generalizations: (6) The higher a man's social rank, the larger will be the number of persons that originate interaction for him, either directly or through intermediaries.[10] (7) The higher a man's social rank, the larger will be the number of persons for whom he originates interaction, either directly or through intermediaries.[11] (8) The more nearly equal in social rank a number of men are, the more frequently they will interact with one another.[12]

Propositions 6 and 7 are simply corollaries of Proposition 5, since it follows, almost by definition, that those with a wide range of interactions will receive and initiate more interaction. However, Propositions 6 and 7 were induced separately from Homans's "observation" that Doc, the leader of the Norton Street Gang, was in the center of a complex network of communication. Such a pattern of communication was not observable in the Bank Wiring Room because stable leadership ranks had not emerged. Proposition 8 describes another process Homans observed in groups with clear leadership: The internal system tended to differentiate into super- and subordinate subgroups, whose members appeared to interact more with each other than those of higher or lower rank.

After using the group-elaboration processes in the Norton Street Gang to confirm and supplement the propositions induced from the Bank Wiring Room,

----

[10] Ibid., p. 182.

[11] Ibid.

[12] Ibid., p. 184.

Homans then examined the Tikopia family, as described in Raymond Firth's famous ethnography. As with the Norton Street Gang, the Tikopia family system was used by Homans to confirm earlier propositions and as a field from which to induce further propositions: (9) The more frequently persons interact with one another, when no one of them originates interaction with much greater frequency than the others, the greater is their liking for one another and their feeling of ease in one another's presence.[13] (10) When two persons interact with one another, the more frequently one of the two originates interaction for the other, the stronger will be the latter's sentiment of respect (or hostility) toward him, and the more nearly will the frequency of interaction be kept to a minimum.[14]

These propositions reveal another facet of Homans's inductive strategy, because they establish some conditions under which proposition 1 will hold. In proposition 1, Homans noted that increased interaction between two persons increases their liking, but in the Tikopia family system Homans "discovered" that this generalization holds true only under conditions where authority of one person over another is low. In the Tikopia family system, brothers revealed sentiments of liking as a result of their frequent interactions, primarily because they did not have authority over one another. However, frequent interaction with their father, who did have authority, was tense, since the father initiated the interaction and since it usually involved the exercise of his authority.

Perhaps less critical than the substance of Propositions 9 and 10 is the strategy they reveal. Homans had used an inductive technique to develop a large number of propositions that described empirical regularities. By continually "testing" them in different types of groups, he was able to "confirm" them, or, as is the case with Propositions 9 and 10, qualify these earlier propositions. By following this strategy, Homans argued that it was possible to develop a large body of empirical statements that reveal the form: y varies with x, under C_1, C_2, C_3, . . . ,C_n. Stated in this form and with a clear connection to actual events in human groupings, such propositions would encourage the development of more abstract concepts and theoretical statements. In addition, Homans hoped, these statements would be induced from a firm empirical footing—a footing that would allow the abstract statements of sociology to be tested against the facts of ongoing group life.

In recent decades, Homans appears to have abandoned this strategy and, in its place, advocated a deductive approach. Ostensibly, Homans has become concerned with explanations of empirical regularities, such as those described in *The Human Group* and in the research literature that has accumulated since 1950. As will be examined in some detail shortly, explanation, for Homans,

---

[13] Ibid., p. 243.
[14] Ibid., p. 247.

involves the construction of deductive systems of propositions; and it is this fact that will help account for Homans's concern with *deducing to,* as opposed to *inducing from,* empirical findings. However, the critics of Homans's recent theoretical strategy, and the exchange perspective it has inspired, contend that Homans's switch in strategy stems from basic problems contained in his inductive efforts. Discussion of these problems might ordinarily be omitted, since primary concern in this chapter is with Homans's exchange perspective, regardless of why he abandoned the strategy advocated in *The Human Group.* But, as the critics argue, Homans repeats many of the same conceptual mistakes of his inductive strategy in his deductive approach to theory building.

An inductive strategy to theory building requires two important tasks to be continually performed: (*a*) Generalizations induced from one body of data should be tested against other data so that propositions abstracted from one study can be confirmed, altered, expanded, and refined in another (much as Homans did in his five case studies in *The Human Group*). (*b*) The first-order abstractions of inductive theory should continually be refined so that the propositions of such theorizing may offer precise indicators of actual events in the empirical world and thereby provide higher-order concepts and statements with a firm empirical base. After *The Human Group,* Homans makes few attempts to perform either of these tasks, with the result that the generalizations of *The Human Group* provide a poor set of generalizations for either an inductive or a deductive strategy.

The difficulties in *The Human Group* stem primarily from the imprecision of the critical variables of his propositions: activity, interaction, and sentiments. Homans's attempt to climb down from the "big words" and abstractions of social science is not complete. In fact, his first-order abstractions are more complex and abstract than he admits. For example, the term "sentiment" is used to encompass "affection," "sympathy," "rage," "thirst," "hunger," "nostalgia," "scorn," or any "internal state of the human body."[15] The diversity of phenomena subsumed under the concept of "sentiment" would seemingly make it highly abstract and thus in need of refinement, such that various types of sentiments would refer to, in Homans's words, "a single class of observable data." From the logic of an inductive strategy, then, Homans should have begun the difficult task of developing true first-order abstractions, with clear empirical referents, to be incorporated into a more precise body of empirical propositions. Instead, Homans chose to bypass this task and began to "explain" in the vocabulary of deductive theory a body of empirical generalizations that were in need of considerable refinement.[16]

---

[15] Ibid., pp. 36–40.

[16] Mulkay, *Functionalism and Exchange,* pp. 161–63 and Pitirim Sorokin, *Sociological Theories of Today* (New York: Harper & Row, 1966), pp. 34–36, are particularly unkind to Homans in this regard.

Similar problems exist for Homans's concepts of activity and interaction. Since activities are behaviors and interaction is activity that stimulates further activities in others, interaction must be a type of activity—one where mutual stimulation is involved. Hence, activity cannot be a first-order abstraction, because, according to Homans, first-order abstractions "refer not to several classes of fact at the same time but to one and one only."[17] This imprecision of Homans's first-order abstractions and the failure to distinguish between critical concepts like activities and interactions makes propositions incorporating these variables highly vague and suspect. Furthermore, the likelihood of tautologous propositions is increased, especially when activity is seen as co-varying with the concept of interaction, which is defined as a certain type of the very thing with which it varies, activity. This problem is compounded when the empirical referents of these concepts are not clearly and precisely stated in terms of clear-cut criteria, for without unambiguous empirical referents that distinguish the type of interaction from the type of activity to be described in a proposition, the proposition becomes circular. For example, the proposition "Persons who interact with one another frequently are more like one another in their activities than they are like other persons with whom they interact less frequently"[18] can be interpreted as a tautology, since it is difficult to establish that the variable of "similar activities" is really different from the variable of "interaction frequency." While the social context from which the proposition was induced can offer some clues about how the variables can be distinguished, the stated generalization reveals very little about events in the real world and thus is not very useful for either inductive or deductive theorizing. Had Homans spent more time refining the concepts of interaction and activity into true first-order abstractions describing various *types* of interaction and activity, then noninteractive types of activity could be legitimately related to various types of interaction without the current vagueness or dangers of tautology. Again, without this precision, the utility of linking inductive propositions to higher-order theoretical statements is negligible, since the vagueness of the empirical generalization would make refutation of the higher-order generalization difficult. If theoretical statements are not refutable by empirical statements, they cannot be a part of a scientific theory.

Despite its deficiencies, *The Human Group* provided a very provocative and promising beginning to inductive theorizing. What is curious is that Homans failed to follow the next steps dictated by his strategy and began to refine his first-order concepts and propositions. Apparently, the need to "explain" these imprecise generalizations became consuming as he began to develop the abstract principles of his exchange theory. Ironically, however, the very vagueness of the

---

[17] Homans, *Human Group*, pp. 109–10.
[18] Ibid., p. 135.

empirical generalizations developed in *The Human Group* and employed in Homans's recent deductive strategy makes impossible the true scientific explanations he has so eloquently championed, since these vague and potentially tautologous generalizations cannot, in principle, refute his abstract exchange principles.

The Recent Deductive Strategy

The logic of Homans's inductive strategy would have dictated that, after reasonable attempts at improving the precision of his first-order concepts and propositions, he make an effort to induce more abstract and general propositions from a survey of his own (and others') empirical generalizations. Whether due to the inadequacy of his empirical generalizations or a new-found excitement with abstract exchange principles, Homans adopts a much simpler strategy for developing sociological theorizing, that is, borrowing from economics and psychology some basic principles that could become the axioms of a deductive system of theoretical statements. In an effort to maintain the illusion of continuity between the strategy of *The Human Group* and that now advocated, Homans has chosen to call the development of abstract exchange principles "induction":

> The process of borrowing or inventing the more general propositions I call *induction*, whether or not it is the induction of the philosophers; the process of deriving the empirical propositions from the more general ones I call explanation, and this is the *explanation* of the philosophers.[19]

Assuredly, Homans's notion of induction is not that of the philosophers, nor that of *The Human Group*. But his portrayal of explanation is that of some philosophers—especially those advocating a natural science interpretation of scientific explanation. Since it is this somewhat distorted notion of induction and more accurate conception of explanation that has guided the development of Homans's exchange perspective, it is wise to discern just what Homans now considers explanation in the social sciences to be.[20]

Since the publication of *The Human Group*, Homans has mounted an increasingly pointed criticism of sociological theorizing, with the hope that "we bring what we say about theory into line with what we actually do, and so put an end to our intellectual hypocrisy." First on the road out of "intellectual hypocrisy" is a rejection of the Parsonian strategy of developing systems of concepts and categorical schemes:

> Some students get so much intellectual security out of such a scheme, because it allows them to give names to, and to pigeonhole, almost any social phenomenon,

---

[19] From *Social Behavior; Its Elementary Forms* by George C. Homans, © 1961, by Harcourt Brace Jovanovich, Inc., and reprinted with their permission.

[20] Ibid.

that they are hesitant to embark on the dangerous waters of actually saying something about the relations between the phenomena—because they must actually take the risk of being found wrong.[21]

For Homans, a more proper strategy—one that allows theories to be proven wrong—is the construction of deductive systems of propositions. At the top of the deductive system are the general axioms, from which lower-order propositions are logically deduced. The lowest-order propositions in the scheme are those composed of first-order abstractions that describe actual events in the empirical world. Because these empirical generalizations are logically related to a hierarchy of increasingly abstract propositions, culminating in logical articulation with the axioms, the empirical generalizations are assumed to be explained by the axioms (see chap. 1, appendix for a discussion of axiomatic formats). Thus, for Homans, to have deduced logically an empirical regularity from a set of more general propositions and axioms is to have *explained* the regularity.[22]

THE EXCHANGE MODEL

Sources of Homans's Psychological Exchange Perspective

Homans's exchange scheme first surfaced as a polemical reaction to Lévi-Strauss's structural analysis of cross-cousin marriage patterns. In collaboration with David Schneider, Homans in 1955 previewed what were to become the persistent themes in his recent writings:[23] (1) a skeptical view of any form of functional theorizing, (2) an emphasis on psychological principles as the axioms of social theory, and (3) a preoccupation with exchange-theoretic concepts.

In their assessment of Lévi-Strauss's exchange functionalism, Homans and Schneider took exception to virtually all that made Lévi-Strauss's theory an

---

[21] George C. Homans, *The Nature of Social Science* (New York: Harcourt, Brace, & World, 1967), p. 13. Parsons has replied that such systems of concepts can be theory: "I emphatically dispute this [deductive theory] is all that can legitimately be called theory. In biology, for example, I should certainly regard the basic classificatory schemes of taxonomy, for example in particular the comparative anatomy of vertebrates, to be theoretical. Moreover very important things are, with a few additional facts, explained on such levels such as the inability of organisms with lungs and no gills to live for long periods under water" (Talcott Parsons, "Levels of Organization and the Mediation of Social Interaction," *Sociological Inquiry* 34 [Spring 1964]: 219–20).

[22] Homans has championed this conception of theory in a large number of works; see, for example, Homans, *Social Behavior;* Homans, *Nature of Social Science;* George C. Homans, "Fundamental Social Processes," in *Sociology,* ed. N. J. Smelser (New York: John Wiley & Sons, 1967), pp. 27–78; George C. Homans, "Contemporary Theory in Sociology," in *Handbook of Modern Sociology,* ed. R. E. L. Faris (Chicago: Rand-McNally, 1964), pp. 251–77; and George C. Homans, "Bringing Men Back In," *American Sociological Review* 29 (December 1964): 809–18. For an early statement of his position, see George C. Homans "Social Behavior as Exchange," *American Journal of Sociology* 63 (August): 597–606.

[23] George C. Homans and David M. Schneider, *Marriage, Authority, and Final Causes: A Study of Unilateral Cross-Cousin Marriage* (New York: Free Press, 1955).

important contribution to social theory. First, the conceptualization of different forms of indirect, generalized exchange was rejected, for in so conceptualizing exchange Lévi-Strauss was viewed to have "thinned the meaning out of it." Second, the Lévi-Straussian position that different forms of exchange symbolically reaffirmed and integrated different patterns of social organization was questioned, for an "institution is what it is because it results from the drives, or meets the immediate needs, of individuals or subgroups within a society."[24] The end result of this rejection of Lévi-Strauss's thought was for Homans and Schneider to argue that exchange theory must initially emphasize face-to-face interaction, focus primarily on limited and direct exchanges among individuals, and recognize the psychological (as opposed to social structural) impetus to exchange relations.

With this extreme polemic against the anthropological tradition that had flourished as a reaction to utilitarianism, Homans resurrected the utilitarian's concern with individual self-interest in the conceptual trappings of psychological behaviorism. For indeed, as Homans and Schneider emphasized: "We may call this an individual self-interest theory, if we remember that interests may be other than economic."[25] As was to become evident by the early 1960s, this self-interest theory was to be cast in the behaviorist language of B. F. Skinner. Given Homans's commitment to axiomatic theorizing and his concern with face-to-face interaction among individuals, it was perhaps inevitable that he would look toward Skinner and borrow concepts and principles from his colleague's controlled laboratory experiments with animals.[26] Stripped of its subtlety, as Homans prefers, Skinnerian behaviorism states, as its basic principle, that if an animal has a need it will perform activities that in the past have satisfied that need. A first corollary to this principle is that organisms will attempt to avoid unpleasant experiences, but will endure limited amounts of such experiences as a cost in emitting the behaviors that satisfy an overriding need. A second corollary is that organisms will continue emitting certain behaviors only as long as they continue to produce desired and expected effects. A third corollary of Skinnerian psychology emphasizes that as needs are satisfied by a particular behavior, animals are less likely to emit the behavior. A fourth corollary states that if in the recent past a behavior has brought rewards and if these rewards suddenly stop, the organism will appear angry and gradually cease emitting the behavior that for-

---

[24] Ibid., p. 15.

[25] Ibid.

[26] Homans, *Social Behavior*, pp. 1–83. For an excellent summary of the Skinnerian principles incorporated into Homans's scheme, see Richard L. Simpson, "Theories of Social Exchange" (Morristown, N.Y.: General Learning Press, 1972), pp. 3–4. As an interesting aside, Peter P. Ekeh, "Social Exchange Theory and the Two Sociological Traditions" (Soon to be published by Harvard University Press) has argued that had Homans not felt so compelled to reject Lévi-Strauss, he would not have embraced Skinnerian principles. Ekeh goes so far as to offer a hypothetical list of axioms that Homans would have postulated, had he not cast his scheme into the terminology of behaviorism.

merly satisfied its needs. A final corollary holds that if an event has consistently occurred at the same time as a behavior that was rewarded or punished, the event becomes a stimulus and is likely to produce the behavior or its avoidance.

These principles were derived from behavioral psychologists' highly controlled observations of animals, whose needs could be inferred from deprivations imposed by the investigators. Although human needs are much more difficult to ascertain than those of laboratory pigeons and mice and despite the fact that humans interact in groupings that defy experimental controls, Homans perceived that the principles of operant psychology could be applied to the explanation of human behavior in both simple and complex groupings. One of the most important adjustments of Skinnerian principles to fit the facts of human social organization involves the recognition that needs are satisfied by other people and that people reward and punish each other. In contrast with Skinner's animals, which only indirectly interact with Skinner through the apparatus of the laboratory and which have little ability to reward Skinner (except perhaps to confirm his principles), humans constantly give and take, or exchange, rewards and punishments.

The conceptualization of human behavior as exchanges of rewards (and punishments) among interacting individuals led Homans to incorporate, in altered form, the first principle of elementary economics: Humans rationally calculate the long-range consequences of their actions in a marketplace and attempt to maximize their material profits in their market transactions. However, as Homans emphasized, this simple economic principle needed reformulation:

> Indeed we are out to rehabilitate the economic man. The trouble with him was not that he was economic, that he used resources to some advantage, but that he was antisocial and materialistic, interested only in money and material goods and ready to sacrifice even his old mother to get them.[27]

Thus, to be an appropriate explanation of human behavior, this basic economic assumption needed to be altered in four ways: (a) People do not always attempt to maximize profits; they seek only to make some profit in exchange relations. (b) Humans do not usually make either long-run or rational calculations in exchanges, for, in everyday life, "the theory of Games is good advice for human behavior but a poor description of it." (c) The things exchanged involve more than money, but other commodities, including approval, esteem, compliance, love, affection, and other less materialistic goods. (d) The "marketplace" is not

---

27 Homans, *Social Behavior*, p. 79. Kenneth Boulding ("An Economist's View of 'Social Behavior: Its Elementary Forms,'" *American Journal of Sociology* 67 [January 1962]: 458) has noted that in Homans's work "economic man is crossed with the psychological pigeon to produce what the unkind might call the Economic Pigeon theory of human interaction." For a more detailed and serious analysis of Homans's meshing of elementary economics and psychology, see Ekeh, "Social Exchange Theory," pp. 162–71.

a separate domain in human exchanges, for all interaction situations involve individuals exchanging rewards (and punishments) and seeking to derive profits.

The Basic Concepts of Homans's Exchange Perspective[28]

In borrowing from the assumptions and principles of behaviorism, Homans introduces new behavioral concepts, while redefining behavioristically old concepts that he had outlined earlier in *The Human Group*. In appearing to be concerned with whether behaviors are externally observable, Homans broadens the scope of the concept "activity" and uses it in his definitions of key exchange concepts:

> *Activity*—behaviors aimed at deriving rewards.
>
> *Rewards*—anything a person receives, or any activity directed toward him, that is defined by the person as valuable
>
> *Value*—the degree of reinforcement or capacity to meet needs of an activity for an individual—whether his own activity or activity directed toward him
>
> *Sentiment*—activities in which individuals communicate their "internal dispositions," such as liking-dislike or approval-disapproval, of each other
>
> *Interaction*—behaviors in which people direct their activities in order to derive rewards, and avoid punishments, from each other
>
> *Norms*—verbal statements—a type of activity—in which people communicate the kinds of activities that should, or should not occur, in a situation
>
> *Quantity*—the number of units of an activity (whether rewarding or punishing) emitted and/or received over a particular period of time.

While Homans's debt to Skinnerian psychology is extensively documented, the remaining concepts of his theory appear inspired more by elementary economics than by operant psychology:

> *Cost*—an activity that is punishing, or an alternative reward that is forgone in order to get another reward
>
> *Investments*—a person's relevant past activities (such as skill, education, and expertise) and social characteristics (such as sex, age, and race) which are brought to a situation and evaluated by both the person and those with whom he is interacting

---

[28] Homans, *Social Behavior*, pp. 52–82.

Profit—rewards, minus the costs and investments, for engaging in a certain activity

Distributive justice—activities involving the calculation of whether costs and investments have led to a "fair" profit by individuals in an exchange.

The Explanatory Principles of Social Organization

With these concepts providing their theoretical underpinnings, Homans then enumerates the five basic axioms, or higher-order propositions, which will be used to explain patterns of social organization:[29]

1. If in the past a particular stimulus situation has been the occasion on which an individual's activity was rewarded, then the more similar the present stimulus situation is to the past one, the more likely he is to emit the activity, or similar activity, now.

2. The more often within a given period of time an individual's activity rewards that of another, the more often the other will emit the activity.

3. The more valuable to an individual a unit of the activity another gives him, the more often he will emit activity rewarded by that of the other.

4. The more often an individual has in the recent past received a rewarding activity from another, the less valuable any further unit of that activity becomes to him.

5. The more to an individual's disadvantage the rule of distributive justice fails of realization, the more likely he is to display the emotional behavior we call anger.

In Propositions 1–3, the principles of Skinnerian psychology are restated in greatly simplified form. The more valuable an activity (3), the more frequently such activity is rewarded (2), and the more a situation approximates one in which activity has been rewarded in the past (1), then the more likely a particular activity will be emitted. Proposition 4 indicates the condition under which the first three fall into temporary abeyance, for, in accordance with the reinforcement principle of satiation or the economic law of marginal utility, humans eventually define as less valuable rewarded activities and begin to emit other activities in search of different rewards (again, however, in accordance with the principles enumerated in Propositions 1–3). Proposition 5 introduces a more complicated set of conditions which qualifies Propositions 1–4. From Skinner's observation that pigeons reveal "anger" and "frustration" when they do not receive an expected reward, Homans reasons that humans will probably reveal basically the

---

[29] Ibid., pp. 53, 54, 55, 75, respectively.

same behavior. However, humans are more intellectually sophisticated than either pigeons or mice and engage in a series of implicit calculations before they emit the pigeon's type of anger. The most important of these are calculations of "distributive justice," whereby, in accordance with an implicit formula, humans assess whether the rewards received from a situation are proportional to the costs incurred in it and the investments brought to it. Distributive justice is thus an expected ratio of investments and costs to rewards; when this expectation is not realized, humans, much like their simpler animal counterparts in the Skinner box, get angry.

These basic principles or "laws" of human behavior are intended to explain, in the sense of deductive explanation, patterns of human organization. As is obvious, they are psychological in nature.[30] What is more, these psychological axioms constitute the only general sociological propositions, since "there are no general sociological propositions that hold good of all societies or social groups as such."[31]

However, the fact that psychological propositions are the most general does not make any less relevant or important sociological propositions stating the relationships among group properties or between group properties and those of individuals. On the contrary, these are the very propositions that are to be deduced from the psychological axioms. Thus, sociological propositions will be conspicuous in the deductive system emanating from the psychological principles. Homans stresses that sociology will finally bring what it says about theory into what it actually does when it arranges both abstract sociological statements and specific empirical generalizations in a deductive system with the psychological axioms at its top. For, as he continually emphasizes, to deduce propositions from one another is to explain them.

Constructing Deductive Systems, Homans Style

The fact that the basic axioms to be used in sociological explanation seem to be "obvious truisms" should not be a cause for dismay. Too often, Homans insists, social scientists assume that the basic laws of social organization will be more esoteric—and certainly less familiar—since for them the game of science involves the startling discovery of new, unfamiliar, and, presumably, profound principles. In reference to these social scientists, Homans writes:

> All this familiarity has bred contempt, a contempt that has got in the way of the development of social science. Its fundamental propositions seem so obvious as to be boring, and an intellectual, by definition a wit and a man of the world, will go to great lengths to avoid the obvious.[32]

---

[30] Ibid.

[31] Homans, "Bringing Men Back In."

[32] Homans, *Nature of Social Science*, p. 73.

However, if the first principles of sociology are obvious, despite the best efforts of "scientists" to the contrary, Homans suggests that sociology cease its vain search for the esoteric and begin constructing deductive systems that recognize the fact that the most general propositions are not only psychological but familiar. In fact, if sociologists crave complexity, this task should certainly be satisfying, since the deductive systems emanating from these "simple" principles to observed empirical regularities will be incredibly complex.

The theoretical task of social science, then, is the construction of true theory, which, at this point, involves filling in the void between the rapidly accumulating body of empirical propositions of sociology's research literature and the general psychology principles. According to Homans, adherence to this strategy offers more theoretical payoff than the various alternatives, whether the elaboration of taxonomies of concepts as in Parsonian "theory" or the search for sociology's own first principles. In a wide number of works, Homans has attempted to construct deductive systems that conform to his avowed strategy; while it is not possible to summarize them all, several examples are offered as illustrative of Homans's efforts to fill in the gaps between observed empirical events and the psychological axioms.

Early Deductive Efforts: Status and Conformity. In *The Human Group*, one of Homans's most conspicuous propositions was that "the higher the rank of a person within a group, the more nearly his activities conform to the norms of the group, and vice versa." This proposition was induced from Homans's discussion of the Bank Wiring Room, especially from his discussion of that group's incipient leader, a fellow named Taylor who conformed strictly to the output norms of the group. In addition to his high rank, Taylor also was able to initiate and receive frequent interactions from others who all seemed to like him. In trying to explain why Taylor conformed, Homans anticipated the exchange perspective to be developed a decade later: "so far as he [Taylor] *enjoyed* his rank, his associations, and his influence, a change in his output rate would have *hurt* him."[33] In other words, the costs of deviation from the output norms were high, whereas the rewards to be derived from conformity were great. Thus, only conformity could be expected.

However, Homans's subsequent reflection on this early hypotheses reveals just the opposite occurrence: Leaders are perhaps the most likely to deviate from group norms. Therefore, in his major work on explanation,[34] Homans sought to clarify the apparent contradiction between his observations in *The Human Group* and in his review of additional literature. In summarizing other field studies and a series of experimental studies on group rank and conformity, Homans was led

---

[33] Homans, *Human Group*, p. 296 (italics added).
[34] Homans, *Social Behavior*, chap. 16.

to this empirical regularity: "High-ranking" and "low-ranking" members of groups are the least likely to conform in groups, while "middle-ranking" members are the most likely to conform. As with Taylor in the Bank Wiring Room, Homans invokes exchange principles to explain this regularity; this time, however, the exchange principles have been more explicitly formulated and thus should allow for a more adequate explanation than that provided for Taylor's behavior.

To explain the regularity, Homans first sets the stage by defining the variables involved in the exchange and the limits of his explanation. Homans takes as a "given" the fact that the groups have an existent ranking—high, middle, and low—which has been experimentally introduced or which is endemic to an ongoing group. This strategy of taking as a given the group structure should be familiar, for in fact the givens are another label for the "external system" employed in *The Human Group.*

By defining away certain variables and therefore taking them as givens, Homans can then analyze more adequately the particular variables that are, for the purposes at hand, of interest to him. This approach leads Homans to enumerate the kinds of rewards to be derived from conformity, or nonconformity (the "activity" of interest), in the experimental results he summarizes. One reward is obviously the esteem associated with high rank in a group; people find esteem and the rank associated with it rewarding, much like Taylor in the Bank Wiring Room. Conformity can also be rewarding, for, in accordance with Homans's first axiom, conformity has in the past been rewarded for most people. Another reward appears to be "acceptance by the group" of an individual as a member, for it is assumed that people value group membership and acceptance. The final reward enumerated by Homans requires more explanation, since it derives in part from the kinds of experimental manipulations performed in the studies from which he discerned the empirical regularity that he is attempting to explain. With some simplification of Homans's presentation, the findings he reports deal primarily with experimental situations in which group members could either conform or not conform to a group decision that would later be "exposed" as correct or incorrect. Thus, to conform to a group's decision that he felt was wrong meant that a member would have to sacrifice the "self-respect" that comes with being correct, a sentiment that in the past has been rewarding for most people. Self-respect then becomes the last variable type of reward inserted into Homans's explanation.

While Homans is not quite this explicit in his enumeration of variables, these four variables—conformity (nonconformity), esteem or rank, acceptance by group members, and self-respect—are inserted into the explanation of the empirical regularity, and thus, appear to be the key variables in his deductions. However, the deductive steps in Homans's discussion are not unambiguous and therefore must be inferred. Hence, while Homans does not explicitly say so, the explanation of the relationship between rank and conformity appears to be derived from Axioms 1, 3, and 4, of his general exchange scheme.

AXIOM 1.   High rank, acceptance by groups, conformity to group opinions, and self-respect have in the past been occasions for rewards; thus any behavior in pursuit of these rewards is possible.

AXIOM 3.   The more a person finds rewarding, or valuable, conformity, self-respect, group membership, and high rank, the more likely he is to emit activity that allows the receipt of any of these rewards from others.

To explain the regularity, Homans must introduce a corollary, or, if one prefers, a deduction, from these two axioms:

DERIVATION 1.   "When the ratio between the values of two rewards is greater than the ratio between the probabilities of attaining them, it is wiser to go for the greater value than the greater probability."[35]

To translate: If some activities are more valuable than others, but the chances of deriving rewards from any one of them are about the same, then one can get the most reward by engaging in the activity that promises the greatest reward. But what determines whether conformity or nonconformity will be the most valuable or rewarding? Presumably, the value of group membership, the esteem that comes from rank, or the self-respect that sticking to one's convictions allows will determine the value of conforming or nonconforming activities. In turn, the value of these activities is a function of the principles enumerated in Axiom 4:

AXIOM 4.   The more satiated with esteem and rank, self-respect, and group membership, the less likely are group members to engage in the activities, such as conformity, which bring about these rewards.

But satiation is not the only exchange principle that influences the ratio of values between conformity and nonconformity (Derivation 1). In addition, Homans would have to make explicit an assumption underlying Axiom 3, for the degree of value of an activity is a reflection of the costs less rewards, or profit, incurred in emitting that activity.

DERIVATION 2.   The value of an activity is a function of the profits that an individual perceives he can derive from emitting that activity.

With this somewhat awkward conceptual edifice, Homans can now "derive" the findings he reports on rank and conformity, and thereby provide for their "explanation." To do so, it is necessary to use "derivations" from Axiom 3, plus

---

[35] Ibid., p. 350.

Axiom 4, to determine the "ratio" between the values of various potential activities—in this case, conformity and nonconformity. Then, with derivation 1 from Axiom 3, plus the assumption provided by Axiom 4, it is possible to "explain" why high-, middle-, and low-ranking group members show different degrees of conformity. Homans does this manipulation in a somewhat discursive way by assessing the potential profits to be derived by variously ranked group members who agree or disagree with the group opinion:[36]

High status: If the group is right, and he is wrong, he will not have lost much esteem or rank, since he had a surplus of this and will probably have enough left to play with. And he will have at least maintained what is perhaps a more valuable reward in the face of satiated esteem: self-respect. If he is right, and the group is wrong, then he will have increased his esteem as a possessor of rare insight. If he follows his convictions and both he and the group are wrong (or right), he gains self-respect with no real loss in esteem or acceptance in group.

Thus, in accordance with Derivations 1 and 2 from Axiom 3 plus Axioms 1 and 4, the greatest potential profit comes with sticking to one's convictions. Since leaders are the most likely to be satiated with esteem and a sense of acceptance by the group and thus do not have to worry about being wrong, they can derive the greater profit by maintaining their convictions, which, should the group be wrong and they correct, can be converted into increased esteem.

Middle status: If the group is right, and he is wrong, he has hurt himself in status, for he is not that far from low-status members and a single mishap can propel him downward. If he is right, and the group wrong, he gains status, but not enough on this one occasion to propel him to high status. If he is wrong and the group is wrong, then it is just another "boob" along with the others. If both he and the group are correct, then he confirms his status as a member of the group.

Thus, in accordance with Derivations 1 and 2, the middle-ranking individual's greatest reward comes in conforming, since not to conform and be correct in one instance does not lead to a great increase in esteem or a sense of belonging to the group, whereas not to conform and be wrong would lead to a potentially great loss in esteem and acceptance as a full-fledged group member. Hence, for those middle-status members whose esteem and group membership are somewhat precarious, to run the risk of being wrong is a high cost for the relatively small rewards that come with being right. Therefore, these members are likely to conform in order to maintain their precarious rank and sense of belonging to the group as full-fledged members.

Low Status: If the group is right, and he is wrong, he has not lost much esteem,

---

[36] See, for a somewhat different presentation of this example, James Davis, "A Sociologists View of Homans' Social Behavior: Its Elementary Forms," *American Journal of Sociology* 67 (January 1962): pp. 454–58.

since he had none to lose; but he has increased his self-respect by sticking to his convictions. If he and the group agree, this one instance of conformity will do little to increase either his esteem or acceptance as a full-fledged group member. But conformity will involve the cost of sacrificing self-respect.

Thus, in accordance with Derivations 1 and 2 from Axiom 3, nonconformity is most likely, since it means maintaining self-respect—the only real reward that low-status individuals can derive from a group in which they are held in low esteem.

What emerges from this prolonged example is the implicit nature of Homans's "derivations," since he applies the concepts of his theory in only a very discursive way to empirical findings. The awkwardness of the "deductive system" in this example stems from the fact that it is necessary to construct the "derivations" from Homans's provocative, but none the less vague, prose. In addition to the lack of what he has promised—a deductive system—Homans does not even employ his concepts consistently. For example, self-respect as a cost for conformity is discussed for high-and low-status people, but not for those in the middle ranks. Furthermore, the satiation principle, Axiom 4, is invoked for high status, but the deprivation obverse is never applied to low-ranking individuals. One conclusion to be drawn from these facts is that no real theoretical deductions have been performed by Homans in his major theoretical work, leading James Davis[37] to proclaim that "the relationship between status and conformity cannot be deduced from the theory, but follows from a number of implicit *ad hoc* principles." However, before the adequacy of Homans's deductions can be fairly assessed, it is perhaps prudent to examine a more recent example of his deductive strategy, for indeed Homans's early deductive efforts may have suffered from the fact that they represented a radical departure from his earlier inductive strategy.

A Recent Deductive Effort: Subsuming Golden's Law. The psychological nature of Homans's exchange concepts, and their incorporation into axioms, has drawn considerable criticism. The presumption that all sociological propositions are reducible to these axioms has been a point of considerable contention (see later discussion), for sociologists have questioned the adequacy of deductive explanations that have psychological axioms as their highest-order propositions. Homans's response to this questioning has been to challenge sociologists to delineate a sociological law that is more general than, and which cannot be derived from, psychological principles.[38]

Taking the challenge, Robert Blain[39] proposed that "Golden's law" was not only as general, but also not reducible to any of Homans's psychological axioms

[37] Ibid., p. 457.

[38] George C. Homans, "Commentary," *Sociological Inquiry* 34 (Spring 1964): 229.

[39] Robert R. Blain, "On Homans' Psychological Reductionism," *Sociological Inquiry* 41 (Winter 1971): 3–25.

and thus could be considered a general explanatory proposition—thus refuting Homans's claim that all sociological propositions were reducible to psychological principles. In brief, Golden's law states: The degree of literacy in a society will always be positively linked to a society's level of industrialization. In Hilda Golden's studies, she found that the two variables—literacy and industrialization—were always highly correlated, presumably making the correlation a true sociological, as opposed to psychological, law. Blain then challenged Homans to reduce this proposition to psychological principles.

To wit, Homans constructed the following "deductive" system:[40]

1.   Men are more likely to perform an activity, the more valuable they perceive the reward of that activity to be.
2.   Men are more likely to perform an activity, the more successful they perceive the activity to be in getting that reward.
3.   Compared with agricultural societies, a higher proportion of men in industrial societies are prepared to reward activities that involve literacy. (Industrialists want to hire book-keepers, clerks, persons who can make and read blueprints, manuals, etc.
4.   Therefore, a higher proportion of men in industrial societies will perceive the acquisition of literacy as rewarding.
5.   And (by (1)) a higher proportion will attempt to acquire literacy.
6.   The provision of schooling costs money, directly or indirectly.
7.   Compared with agricultural societies, a higher proportion of men in industrial societies is, by some standard, wealthy.
8.   Therefore a higher proportion is able to provide schooling (through government or private charity), and a higher proportion to pay for their own schooling without charity.
9.   And a higher proportion will perceive the effort to acquire literacy as apt to be successful.
10. And (by (2) as by (1)) a higher proportion will attempt to acquire literacy.
11. Since their perceptions are, in general, accurate, a higher proportion of men in industrial societies will in fact acquire literacy. That is, the literacy rate is apt to be higher in an industrial than in an agricultural society.

This deductive system is typical of the more recent attempts by Homans to explain sociological generalizations with psychological principles.[41] In this system, several features in Homans's deductive strategy stand out: (a) The highest-order Propositions (1 and 2) represent derivations from his axioms. But, as was the case in his earlier work on rank, status, and conformity, the logical steps in

---

[40] George C. Homans, "Reply to Blain," *Sociological Inquiry* 41 (Winter 1971): 23.

[41] For additional examples, see Homans, "Contemporary Theory in Sociology," and "Bringing Men Back In."

the derivations are not made explicit. It can only be inferred, therefore, that these two propositions represent derivations from Axioms 1 and 3. (*b*) Propositions 3 and 7 are taken as "givens," for no explanation as to why, when, and under what conditions men will reward literacy is offered, nor is an attempt to explain why wealth increases undertaken. (*c*) These propositions taken as givens are then followed by important logical inferences, signaled by the use of the word "therefore" as a preface to Propositions 4 and 8.

These characteristics of the deductive system—the failure to provide clear derivations from the axioms and the willingness to take as "givens" the interesting sociological questions and then follow them with important logical inferences—suggest that Homans's more recent and seemingly explicit deductive strategy resembles his earlier efforts. Much like the "deductive system" for rank and conformity, the logical calculus of the system appears to be implicit. These two examples of Homans's deductive strategy reveal that perhaps Homans has used the rhetoric of axiomatic, deductive theorizing, while failing to execute very successfully the logical requirements of such theorizing (see chapter 1, appendix). At the very least, some questions about the logical adequacies of Homans's deductive strategy have been raised, questions that must be explored further to determine the utility of Homans's strategy.

THE LOGICAL IMPLICATIONS OF HOMANS'S EXCHANGE PERSPECTIVE

Homans's Exchange Concepts: Ad hoc and Tautologous?

In borrowing the rhetoric of behaviorism, with its concern for *only observable* behavior as the subject matter of science, Homans has elevated the concept of "activity" to prominence. All other concepts are defined as "activity," but in reality Homans uses the concept of "activity" to denote the phenomena of an introspective psychology—love, hate, esteem, prestige, and other "sentiments." Such inclusion of interal states of the human organism would be abhorrent to many strict behaviorists, who, in the rigor of their experiments, have attempted to avoid the "black box" of internal psychological functioning. Homans's recognition that to avoid the "black box" is to ignore everything that is uniquely human is, of course, to be applauded. However, in attempting to account for these internal psychological processes in terms of the concepts of behaviorism, Homans has borrowed concepts that would seem unsuited to the task, since they were not developed to denote the psychological processes of most concern to Homans.

In lieu of delving into the "black box" of human cognition, behaviorists have attempted to conduct their experiments with as many controls as is possible on

environmental factors. Furthermore, they have been able to infer the degree of
reinforcement of various activities by depriving animals of basic necessities, such
as food and water, for precise periods of time—thus enabling the concept of
"deprivation" to serve as an operational indicator of the "reward value" of
activities. In contrast, Homans's concept of value—or the degree of reinforcement of an activity—refers to *any* activity that a person defines, perceives, or
believes to be rewarding. By defining the concept "value," and by implication
"reward" (valuable activity), in such a general way, Homans confronts the problem of how one knows what is valuable or rewarding to a person? Since he cannot
operationally define value as the length of forced deprivation of some known
necessity like food and water, value can only be inferred from the quantity of
activities that a person will expend to get certain rewards. Such a conceptualization can result in tautologous propositions, since it will be difficult to measure
"value" independently of the very "activity" it is supposed to explain.[42] Homans
attempts to avoid this logical problem by emphasizing that a person's values must
be determined on the basis on his personal history, or his past activities; in this
way, he assumes the concepts of value and activity can be incorporated into
nontautologous propositions.[43] But measuring present value by the quantity of
activity expended in the past does not obviate the tautology, for it is still necessary
to insure that the evidence for values is measurable independent of the activities
to be explained by these values.[44]

Similar problems exist with respect to Homans's borrowing of economic concepts, such as cost and profit. In elementary economics, these concepts refer to
phenomena in market transactions, employing, for the most part, the explicitly
defined and *measurable* concept of "money." As soon as these concepts are
applied to introspective psychology, where there is no easily defined or measura-

---

[42] For enlightening discussions of this problem, see Morton Deutsch, "Homans in the Skinner
Box," in H. Turk and R. L. Simpson, eds., *Institutions & Social Exchange: The Sociologies of Talcott
Parsons & George C. Homans* (Indianapolis: Bobbs-Merrill, 1971), pp. 81–92; Bengt Abrahamsson,
"Homans on Exchange: Hedonism Revived," *American Journal of Sociology* 76 (September 1970):
273–85; Pitirim Sorokin, *Sociological Theories of Today* (New York: Harper & Row, 1966), especially
chap. 15, "Pseudo-Behavioral and Empirical Sociologies;" and M. J. Mulkay, *Functionalism and
Exchange, pp. 166–69.*

[43] Parsons ("Levels of Organization," p. 219) notes: "History thus seems to become for Homans
the ultimate residual category, recourse to which can solve any embarrassment which arises from
inadequacy of the more specific parts of the conceptual scheme. The very extent to which he has
narrowed his conceptualization of the variables, in particular adopting the atomistic conception of
value, . . . increases the burden thrown upon history and with it the confession of ignorance
embodied in the statement, 'things are as they are because of ways in which they have come to be
that way.' "

[44] Mulkay, *Functionalism and Exchange*, p. 168. For Homans's most sophisticated discussion of
the problem, see *Nature of Social Science*, pp. 96–103. For some of the further complications
introduced by incorporation of interactionist concepts, see Peter Singelmann, "Exchange as Symbolic
Interaction: Convergences between Two Theoretical Perspectives," *American Sociological Review*
37 (August 1972): 414–24.

ble currency such as "money," they become vague. Cost is reward forgone and profit is reward less cost; but how are these to be assessed independently of the activities they are supposed to explain? While at some times it may be possible to assess the objective costs of an activity independently of the activities to be explained, such is not always the case, for "cost" and "profit" refer ultimately to the "internal calculations" of "value" by each individual actor in an exchange transaction and can therefore only be known after the activities they are to explain have been emitted.

Aside from the risk of generating tautologous propositions, Homans's critical concepts—activity, value, reward, cost, profit—are so generally defined that they can be used for virtually any *ad hoc* purpose. Homans has typically chosen to use these concepts to provide ex post facto interpretations of empirical studies (such as his interpretation of the rank and conformity studies discussed earlier). With each interpretation, the concepts of activity, value, reward, cost, profit (and sometimes investment) are defined to "fit the facts" of the cases under investigation. This strategy has led Bengt Abrahamson to call these after-the-fact "explanations" a game that is played, much like the experimental studies Homans cites in proving his principles, in the following way:

> The player who initiates the game—let us call him Person—invites some friends (for instance, Other and Third Man) to enumerate as many studies of social behavior as they can recall (Other and Third Man should be well read in social psychology to ensure maximum excitement). Other and Third Man stake one dollar each for every study cited, on the condition that Person pays each one of them ten dollars for every study that Person is *in*capable of interpreting in terms of rewards and costs. Person then starts explaining; and, provided that he follows the rules laid down by Homans (i.e., defining "reward" and "cost" in such a way as to include all possible cases) the upper limit of Person's profit will be determined only by the amount of studies that Other and Third Man are able to recite. His own risk of losing money is zero, as long as his colleagues are generous (or naive) enough to allow him to continue using Homans' extremely broad definitions.[45]

Homans's Explanations: Pseudodeductions?

The charge that Homans's concepts are so vague as to result in tautologous and *ad hoc* explanations is indeed serious, for the thrust of Homans's work has been to provide scientific explanations of social phenomena. Before accepting prematurely this serious charge, then, it is wise to examine in more detail whether Homans meets the challenges of his critics in his actual deductions.

---

[45] Abrahamsson, "Homans on Exchange," p. 280. Homans had defended his use of highly general and imprecise concepts. Because it is impossible to enumerate all possible circumstances that affect the "value" of a reward, Homans explains: "It is convenient in the exposition of a theory to use a single term, value, to stand for them all. Then, in explaining particular actions, the relevant circumstances are substituted for the general term value" (Homans, "Commentary," p. 365).

To begin, it is necessary to ask: Are Homans's axioms tautologies? Examining the first four basic propositions in the Homans's scheme, activity and reward are seen as co-varying under other variable conditions: Proposition 1: A present *stimulus situation* which resembles those in the past where activity has been rewarded will result in similar activity in the present. Proposition 2: The *more often* an activity is rewarded in a *given time period,* the more of the activity will be emitted. Proposition 3: The *more valuable* an activity, the more the activity will be emitted. Each of these propositions holds reward as the key causal variable, for variations in activity are to be accounted for by the likelihood of rewards in a situation, the quantity of rewards in that situation, and the value of the rewards. Proposition 4 qualifies these axioms by introducing the principle of satiation and marginal utility: The more often (quantity) activity has been rewarded in the recent past, the less valuable the activity; and hence, in accordance with Proposition 3, the less likely the activity to be emitted in the future. Thus, while somewhat more complicated than Propositions 1–3, Proposition 4 simply specifies another condition—satiation and marginal utility—under which reward causes variation in activity. Proposition 5 is even more complex, for the concept of "distributive justice" is introduced and seen as co-varying with emotional behavior or anger. However, since emotional behavior is an "activity" and distributive justice concerns the internal calculations of Persons as to the "fairness" of rewards in relation to costs and investments, Proposition 5 still views activity as a function of rewards. Thus, despite its apparent complexity, Proposition 5 is much like the previous four propositions, because distributive justice is nothing more than another condition—the degree of justice involved—under which rewards cause variations in activity.

The key question, then, in determining whether these axioms are tautologies is whether it is possible to define reward and activity independently of each other. The other variables in the propositions—stimulus situation, quantity, value, satiation, and justice—specify important conditions that affect the reward-activity causal nexus, but they do not obviate the potential tautology. Only clearly separate definitions for reward and activity can do this. Unfortunately, Homans's definitions do not dispel the charges of his critics, since he is somewhat vague in the definition of these key concepts. Activity is initially defined as a unit of overt behavior,[46] but, in his subsequent discussion, activity is used to refer to behaviors aimed at getting rewards. Rewards are then defined as anything a person receives which is perceived to be valuable. In turn, value is defined as the degree of reinforcement of an activity.[47] Hence, activity appears to be behavior that is seeking rewards (although Homans is somewhat vague here); and rewards

---

[46] Homans, *Social Behavior,* p. 32.

[47] Ibid., p. 46.

are reinforced activities. Thus, there appears to be a circularity in these definitions; while Homans may not have intended this to be the case, his eloquent prose fails to clarify just what he actually intended. Since activity and reward are *the* key variables of the exchange scheme, it is unfortunate that they often appear to be defined in terms of each other; for, in not clearly defining these concepts independently of each other, Homans has left himself open to the indictment that his axioms are in fact circular definitions, or tautologies.

To dispel this kind of indictment, Homans's deductive systems would have to develop derivations from the axioms in which *classes* and *types* of activities are seen as co-varying with independently defined *classes* and *types* of rewards. Then, in the examination of empirical regularities, empirical instances of an activity can be viewed as an indicator of a certain class of activity which brings about a certain type of independently defined and operationalized reward. In this way, the types of activities to be explained by these axioms could be distinguished from the types of rewards used to explain them. Thus, the tautological nature of highly abstract axioms in a deductive system can be obviated when precise and clear derivations from the axioms are performed, since, in this process, independent definitions and indicators of key concepts can be provided. However, if these deductive steps are left out and vague axioms are simply reconciled in an *ad hoc* fashion to empirical events, explanation will tend to be tautological. Unfortunately, Homans does not provide the necessary derivations from his Axioms, since upon close examination his deductive systems typically represent attempts at reconciling his axioms with various empirical generalizations.[48]

For example, in his deductive system "explaining" Golden's law, the two exchange propositions at the top of the deductive system are not clearly derived from the axioms. They are simply introduced in an ad hoc fashion: (1) Individuals are more likely to perform an activity, the more valuable they perceive the reward of that activity to be (presumably this is a corollary of Axiom 3). (2) Individuals are more likely to perform an activity the more successful they perceive the activity to be in getting that reward (another important corollary to Axiom 3 and the above proposition). In these two higher-order propositions, several important variables are introduced, but not systematically related to the exchange

---

[48] Ronald Maris ("The Logical Adequacy of Homans' Social Theory," *American Sociological Review* 35 [December 1970]: 1069–81) came to a somewhat different conclusion about the logical adequacy of Homans's theoretical manipulations. With the aid of symbolic logic, and the addition of some assumptions, "Homans' theory of elementary social behavior has not been proven inadequate." But the criticisms of Maris's logical manipulation are sufficient to suggest that his analysis is not the definitive answer to the logical adequacy of Homans's deductions. For examples of these criticisms, see Don Gray, "Some Comments concerning Maris on 'Logical Adequacy' "; Stephen Turner, "The Logical Adequacy of 'The Logical Adequacy of Homans' Social Theory' "; and Robert Price, "On Maris and the Logic of Time"; all in *American Sociological Review* 36 (August 1971): 706–13. Maris's "Second Thoughts: Uses of Logic in Theory Construction" can also be found in this issue. For a more adequate construction of a logically sophisticated exchange perspective, see B. F. Meeker, "Decisions and Exchange," *American Sociological Review* 36 (June 1971): 485–95.

axioms. The "perception of reward" is the central variable in Proposition 1 above, but nowhere is it systematically defined or explicitly related to the axioms. Rather, it is introduced in an *ad hoc* fashion to account for the empirical regularity described by Golden's law. In Proposition 2 above, another key concept, "perception of success," is introduced in a similar ad hoc fashion to account for why people seek to become literate. These two concepts—perception of reward and perception of success—both need to be more clearly and precisely derived from the axioms, for without demonstrating how they are derived from the axioms, it appears that Homans has just introduced them to explain a particular set of findings. Furthermore, it is not clear whether "perception of reward" and "perception of success" are rewards or activities. On the one hand, perception would seemingly be an activity, or one *class* or *type* of activity that needs to be derived as a corollary from the axioms. On the other hand, perception of "success" and "reward" can perhaps be a type of reward—say a "preliminary reward"—that keeps activity by Persons in the pursuit of literacy, and the long-range rewards to be derived (money? prestige? or what?) from this activity, going. Thus, without precise and logical derivations of corollaries from the axioms and clear definitions of the concepts contained in them, the corollaries resemble the axioms in that activities and rewards cannot be easily distinguished from each other—thereby making the derivations appear as tautologous as the axioms.

Subsequent deductive steps in Homans's "explanation" of Golden's law illustrate additional *ad hoc* procedures as Homans attempts to deduce down to empirical events. Propositions 3–5 will be sufficient to explicate the Homansian technique: (3) Compared with agricultural societies, a higher proportion of men in industrial societies are prepared to reward activities that involve literacy. (Industrialists want to hire book-keepers; clerks, persons who can make and read blueprints, manuals, etc.). (4) Therefore a higher proportion of men in industrial societies will perceive the acquisition of literacy as rewarding. (5) And (by (1)) a higher proportion will attempt to acquire literacy.

In Proposition 3 of the deductive system, the sociologically interesting question is left unanswered and simply taken as a given. The complex institutional processes whereby the emergence of industry generates demands for expanded educational institutions is bypassed with the statement that men "are prepared to reward activities that involve literacy" and with a short parenthetical phrase about industrialists' needs for clerks and bookkeepers. Homans has consistently defended this kind of maneuver by emphasizing that "any deductive system must take certain propositions as given: they are often called the givens or boundary conditions to which the general propositions, in the present case . . . are to be applied."[49] While the logic of the argument that "no theory explains everything"

---

[49] Homans, "Reply to Blain," p. 23. Homans has emphasized this point in response to his critics. For example, see George C. Homans, "Reply to Razak," *American Sociological Review* 31 (August 1966): 543–44.

cannot be refuted, Homans's deductive systems typically define away the complex interaction effects of social variables, giving his systems the appearance of continuity. But to define away important classes of social variables contributes to the impression that Homans has not really provided a useful deductive system, but rather, an *ad hoc* reconciliation of vaguely stated axioms, or equally vague corollaries, to a set of empirical generalizations.

The "therefore" that prefaces Proposition 4 in the scheme underscores how Homans bypasses an interesting set of sociological questions: Why do men perceive the acquisition of literacy as rewarding? What level of industrialization would make this so? What level of educational development? What feedback consequences does desire for literacy have for educational development? Proposition 5 similarly ignores interesting sociological questions, for one is prone to ask: How is perception of the rewards ensuing from literacy translated into the actual attempt to acquire literacy? What forces circumscribe and/or mediate this process? Does not the forced acquisition of literacy sometimes precede the perception of the benefits of literacy (especially among children who are forced into schools by government and family)?

Similar questions arise for the rest of the deductive steps in the system (see entire system as it was presented in an earlier section). From this brief but by no means atypical example, it is possible to see how Homans has afforded himself the luxury of (*a*) introducing new concepts as needed (perception, reward, and success), (*b*) interjecting without rigorous derivations new corollaries to his axioms (Propositions 1 and 2), and (*c*) defining away complex sociological processes so that the simple vocabulary of his exchange behaviorism ("reward" and "activity") can be substituted.[50]

Coupled with the tautologous nature of Homans's axioms, and his attempts at deriving corollaries, it could be concluded that Homans has provided only pseudodeductions. However, even if Homans is given the benefit of the doubt on the issue tautology, it can be questioned if his deductive systems are very useful when they define away as givens or gloss over with the simple words of his exchange behaviorism the complex processes that are of interest to most sociologists. Homans has typically argued that when we talk only in terms of sociological variables and propositions, without deducing them from psychological propositions, we are "too easily satisfied"[51] with what we call explanations. But when these same sociological variables and propositions are defined away as givens or when complex processes are translated into a few simple words in order to deduce

---

[50] For examples of similar criticisms of one of Homans's earlier "deductive systems," see W. Nevell Razak, "Communication on Homans," *American Sociological Review* 31 (August 1966): 542–43; and Berthold Brenner, "On Bringing Men Back In," *American Sociological Review* 30 (December 1965): 945.

[51] For example, see Homans, "Reply to Blain."

complex sociological propositions from vaguely stated psychological axioms, it perhaps becomes less clear to Homans's critics who is "too easily satisfied" with what is termed explanation.

This assessment of Homans's deductive systems is far from a cavalier judgment by the critics, since the utility of deductive systems, when so much is taken as a given and when concepts are so vaguely defined, is being called into question. Logically, there is little wrong with Homans's deductive strategy; and perhaps he is to be commended for attempting to order theoretical statements into a quasi-axiomatic format. Yet, it can be argued that his particular technique has not been so useful as he contends in achieving the goals of science. Have his concepts provided an interesting and enlightening way to order and classify phenomena into typologies? Have his concepts—activity, reward, satiation, frequency, and justice—dramatically increased social scientists' sense of understanding of complex sociocultural processes? And have his deductive systems allowed for accurate a priori predictions? While Homans's exchange perspective is suggestive, it has failed to provide typologies, primarily because the vaguely defined concepts in the scheme fail to specify types or classes of events in the empirical world. Instead, concepts are bent to serve the purposes of a particular ex post facto "explanation." Although Homans's concepts do provide a sense of understanding in the analysis of concrete events, especially in micro social processes, the full utility of his concepts in providing such understanding has not been realized. Furthermore, it seems unlikely that this potential will be realized until Homans takes the next steps in a deductive strategy: (a) defining more precisely his basic concepts so that they denote, a priori, types and classes of activities and rewards; and (b) deriving in a more rigorous fashion from the axioms corollaries that incorporate these more precisely defined concepts. Yet, even if these steps are taken, axiomatic formats always pose a problem in generating a sense of understanding, since actual causal chains are sometimes obscured by the need to arrange propositions in a deductive system (see chapter 1, appendix).[52] However, axiomatic formats should, when constructed properly, yield extremely accurate predictions about future events, for statements in the deductive hierarchy logically flow from the axioms to specific propositions about what should occur in a particular empirical situation.

While Homans's axioms, and the deductive systems they have inspired, do present some obvious problems, perhaps some of these can be compensated for by the fact that they can yield predictions of future events. Although Homans has preferred to construct explanations after the fact, he has attempted to use

---

[52] Also see Paul Davidson Reynolds, *A Primer in Theory Construction* (Indianapolis: Bobbs-Merrill Co., 1971), pp. 107–14. Homans is very clear on this point when he notes: "Causal chains are not explanations in my sense of the word, despite the utility of such things. Causal explanation is not what I mean by explanation" (Homans, "Reply to Blain," p. 21).

his exchange perspective to make predictions before the assessment of actual data. Homans is to be admired for undertaking this task, for in making predictions he does leave himself open to being proved wrong, an opening that few sociological theorists have allowed.[53]

In one study, Homans and several colleagues went to an American factory, collected information on the nature of the work from the factory's personnel department, and, coupled with their own knowledge about American industry, made some predictions based on exchange principles about the relationship between a worker's status in the outside community and esteem bestowed upon him in his work group. The consultation with the factory's personnel department was only to establish the "givens" of the explanation, for Homans and the other investigators were careful not to collect data on the actual behavior in work groups. Since this study was conducted before Homans' axioms had been made explicit, his hypothesis was not deduced formally from the axioms. Yet, given the somewhat contrived character of Homans's current deductions from his axioms, the proposition he developed in this study could be similarly reconciled with the axioms and hence arranged in one of Homans's typical deductive systems. What is important is that Homans clearly had his exchange principles in mind when he formulated the propositions, and he seemingly "deduced" the propositions intuitively from these principles (this is not much different from what he does when he makes the "derivations" explicit). The basic proposition was: High outside status in the community would be associated with high esteem in the work group. This generalization was felt to hold true, because high outside status is associated with experiences that enable high-status individuals to reward others in the work group, thus allowing them to extract esteem from those whom they reward. To test this proposition, Homans and his colleagues first ranked four subsections of a large department in the factory in terms of their external status: rank 1, high-paid machinists; rank 2, high-paid assemblers; rank 3, low-paid machinists; and rank 4, low-paid assemblers. The investigators felt this rank ordering appropriate for two reasons: (*a*) Pay is the most important measure of status. (b) Skilled work requires more training than unskilled work and thus machinists should rank higher than assemblers, as long as there are no large differences in pay. Then, in accordance with the predictions contained in the proposition, this rank ordering should also be the esteem ranking in the work groups. But the subsequent research revealed this esteem ranking: rank 1, high-paid machinists; rank 2, high-paid assemblers; rank 3, low-paid assemblers (there

[53] See Homans's discussion of this predictive attempt in his *Social Behavior*, pp. 221–25. For a more thorough reporting of the study in question, see A. Zalenick, C. R. Christensen, and F. J. Roethlisberger, *The Motivation, Productivity and Satisfaction of Workers* (Cambridge, Mass.: Harvard University Press, 1958).

were no real differences between ranks 2 and 3); and rank 4 low-paid machinists.

Homans felt that, despite the reversal of ranks 3 and 4 and ambiguity for ranks 2 and 3, he had predicted correctly at the very top. The reversal is interpreted in terms of a new variable—status inconsistency—which was not incorporated into the investigator's earlier predictions. Homans then reanalyzes the findings in terms of this variable, but, unfortunately, further predictions and tests of the predictions are not made. Thus, much like his other explanations, an ad hoc interpretation is made to explain the occurrence of events. This is perfectly legitimate as long as such reinterpretations yield new propositions, systematically linked to higher-order propositions, which can serve as the basis for further predictions. Homans however, lets the matter drop with the ad hoc interpretation, apparently feeling that being proved partly right and then "explaining" why he was partly wrong is sufficient. In sum, then, it is not clear how Homans's exchange scheme has offered predictions that can compensate for some of its other logical deficiencies.

The Issue of Reductionism

Periodically old philosophical issues are resurrected and debated fervently. Homans's exchange perspective has rekindled one such debate: the issue of reductionism. Homans's statements on the issue are sometimes tempered and at other times polemic, but the thrust of his argument has been made amply clear. He writes:

> The institutions, organizations, and societies that sociologists study can always be analyzed, without residue, into the behavior of individual men. They must therefore be explained by propositions about the behavior of individual men.[54]

This position has been particularly disturbing to some sociologists, since it appears to pose a problem: If it is accepted that sociological propositions are reducible to those about men, then those about men are reducible to physiological propositions, which, in turn, are reducible to biochemical propositions, and so on in a reductionist sequence ending in the basic laws of physical matter. Homans has not been very helpful in alleviating sociologists' concern with whether he is advocating this kind of reductionism, since, in fact, he is advocating the position that while the psychological axioms "cannot be derived from physiological propositions, . . . this condition is unlikely to last forever."[55]

However, Homans fortunately avoids a related, and equally old, philosophical debate: the realist-nominalist issue. Homans is clearly not a nominalist, for he

---

[54] Homans, "Commentary," p. 231.
[55] Ibid., p. 373.

is not asserting that, to put the matter simply, society and its various collective forms (groups, institutions, organizations, and so forth) are mere names sociologists arbitrarily assign to the only "really real" phenomenon, the individual:

> I, for one, am not going to back into the position of denying the reality of social institutions. . . . The question is not whether the individual is the ultimate reality or whether social behavior involves something more than the behavior of individuals. The question is, always, *how social phenomena are to be explained.* [Italics added][56]

It is the thrust of the last phrase above which has seemingly been underemphasized in the criticisms of Homans's reductionism, for critics have too often implied that his reductionism forces him to embrace a particular variety of nominalism. Yet, for Homans, the issue has always been one of how to explain with deductive—or axiomatic—systems the groups and institutions studied by sociologists.

Homans and the Fallacy of "Misplaced Concreteness." The most persistent criticism of Homans's reductionist strategy has revolved around the assertion that he has fallen into the fallacy of "misplaced concreteness."[57] As originally conceived by the philosopher Alfred North Whitehead,[58] scientists had at one time fallen into the trap of thinking that they could analyze the universe into its constituent parts and thereby eventually discover the basic elements or building blocks of all matter. Once *the* basic building block had been found, it would only then be necessary to comprehend the laws of its operation for an understanding of everything else in the universe. In the eyes of Whitehead and others, these scientists had erroneously assumed that the basic parts of the universe were the only reality of phenomena. In so doing, they had "misplaced" the concreteness of phenomena, for in reality, the *relationships* among parts forming a whole is just as "real" as the constituent parts. The organization of parts is not the "sum of the parts," but rather, the constitution of a new kind of reality.

Has Homans fallen into this fallacy? Numerous critics think that he has when he implies that the behavior of persons or "men" are the basic units, whose laws need only be understood to explain more complex sociocultural arrangements. These critics appear to be overreacting to Homans's reductionism, perhaps confusing his reductionist strategy with the mistaken assumption that Homans is a nominalist in disguise. In reality, Homans has never denied the importance of sociological laws describing complex sociocultural processes; on the contrary, they are critical propositions in any deductive systems that attempts to *explain* these processes. All that Homans has asserted is: These sociological laws are not

---

[56] Homans, *Nature of Social Science*, pp. 61–62.

[57] For examples of this line of criticism, see Parsons, "Levels of Organization"; and Blain, "On Homans' Psychological Reductionism."

[58] Alfred North Whitehead, *Science and The Modern World* (New York: Macmillan Co., 1925).

the most general; they are subsumable under more general psychological laws (his axioms), which eventually, with more knowledge and sophisticated intellectual techniques, will be subsumable under a still more general set of laws. At no point in this reductionist philosophy is Homans asserting that the propositions subsumed by a more general set of laws are irrelevant or unimportant. Thus, Homans has not "misplaced the concreteness" of reality, for he has not denied the metaphysical existence of emergent properties such as groups, organizations, and institutions, nor the theoretical significance of the laws describing these emergent phenomena. Homans is not a nominalist in disguise, but a sociological realist, who is advocating a particular *strategy for understanding sociocultural phenomena.*

The Utility of Homans's Reductionist Strategy.   Once it becomes evident that Homans's reductionism is a theoretical strategy that does not deny the metaphysical or ontological existence of emergent phenomena, the next question in need of an answer becomes: Is this strategy useful in explaining phenomena? Some critics[59] have emphasized that a reductionist strategy will affect the kinds of theoretical and research questions sociologists will ask. If one is concerned primarily with psychological laws as explanatory principles, it is likely that research questions and theoretical generalizations will begin to revolve around psychological and social psychological phenomena, because these phenomena are the most readily derived from psychological axioms. Thus, despite a recognition that complex sociological phenomena are real, the adoption of a reductionist strategy for building theory will inadvertently result in the avoidance of the macro patterns of social organization studied by many sociologists. To the extent that such one-sided research and theory building is the result of a reductionist strategy, then this strategy is undesirable and can be questioned on these grounds alone. However, there are more fundamental grounds on which to reject Homans's strategy: Adherence to his strategy at the present time will lead to logically imprecise and empirical empty theoretical formulations.

This indictment is, of course, severe and needs to be documented. Homans may be correct in holding that logically a deductive axiomatic strategy necessitates reductionism, for the goal of such a strategy is to subsume under ever more general axioms what we previously considered the most general axioms. Such a process of subsumption may indeed lead first to the subsumption of sociological axioms under psychological axioms, and then to the subsequent subsumption of these latter axioms under physiological, biochemical, and physical laws. Just as many of the laws of chemistry can be subsumed under the laws of physics, so sociological laws may be subsumed by the laws of psychology. However, deduc-

---

[59] For example, see Blain, "On Homans' Psychological Reductionism"; Buckley, *Sociology and Modern Systems Theory* (Englewood Cliffs, N.J.: Prentice-Hall, Inc., 1967), pp. 109–11.

tion of sociological laws from psychological axioms should occur in a two-step process: (1) First, a series of well-established sociological laws, from which it is possible to deduce a wide variety of sociological propositions that have received consistent empirical support, must be developed. Then, *and only then*, (2) a clear body of psychological axioms, which are amenable to similar reductions and which have received consistent empirical support, can be used to explain the sociological laws. Step 1 must occur prior to step 2, as it typically has in the physical sciences. Homans has recognized the fact that the social sciences have not achieved step 1 when he notes that the "issue for the social sciences is not whether we should be reductionists, but rather, if we were reductionists, whether we could find any propositions to reduce."[60]

Homans has failed, however, to realize the full implications of his statement. Without well-established sociological laws to subsume, the critics can correctly ask: What is the utility of attempting to subsume what does not exist? Would it not be far wiser to expend our efforts in developing sociological laws and let the issue of reductionism take care of itself when these laws are established? To attempt prematurely to develop psychological axioms and then deduce sociological propositions from them in the absence of well-established sociological laws is likely to generate tautologous axioms and logically imprecise deductions, as has been demonstrated earlier. What Homans typically does in his "deductions" is to (*a*) state in an *ad hoc* manner some general psychological propositions that are not logically derived from his axioms, and (*b*) take as givens all the interesting sociological questions, answers to which would lead to the development of the sociological laws needed to fill out properly his deductive system. The end result of Homans's pseudodeductions is that an empirical generalization—say Golden's law—may be "explained" without any of the logically necessary components of a deductive system—clear sociological laws and psychological axioms.

Such deductive systems will not only be logically useless, but empirically muddled, for they will ultimately boil down to statements like the following: Things are as they are because they are rewarding. What this does is to repeat the empirical generalization to be "explained" in the words of behavioral psychology, without *logically* reducing the generalization to *clear* psychological axioms. Rather, the generalization has been "muddled" with the words and phrases of a behavioral psychology.[61]

---

[60] Homans, *Nature of Social Science*, p. 86.

[61] The concepts of behavioral psychology do not have to muddle empirical generalizations, so long as one does not prematurely try to deduce sociological propositions to crude psychological propositions. In fact, operant principles can be used quite fruitfully to *build* (note: not reduce) more complex exchange principles that pertain to sociological processes (note: not psychological). For an impressive attempt at employing operant principles as a starting point, and then changing them to fit the facts of emergent properties, see Richard M. Emmerson's various works, especially "Power-Dependence Relations," *American Sociological Review* 27 (February 1962): 31–41; "Power-Depend-

In sum, then, the long-range utility of Homans's reductionist strategy may be hard to deny (time will tell). In the short run, the use of Homans's deductive strategy will enable sociologists to define away as givens those sociological problems that need to be studied if true sociological laws are to be developed. Without these laws in the deductive systems advocated by Homans, such systems are logically inadequate and empirically confusing. A far wiser deductive strategy is to attempt to develop the "laws of sociology" that, at some distant point in the future, can be subsumed logically by a more general set of principles—perhaps ones similar to these advocated by Homans. To continue to pursue Homans's platitudinous recommendations for building sociological theory is to assure that such theory will not be developed.

HOMANS'S IMAGE OF SOCIETY

Homans's eloquent advocacy of his theoretical strategy has failed to convert many sociologists, primarily because his exchange scheme is filled with many conceptual and logical problems. Coupled with the methodological difficulties of operationalizing concepts such as value, reward, cost, profit, and distributive justice independently of activities, it is not surprising that Homans's exchange perspective has received considerable criticism. Yet, Homans is probably correct in his assertion that at the elementary level of interaction the processes that his concepts denote do indeed occur, as only a small degree of introspection will reveal.

It is the latter fact that perhaps marks the appeal of Homans's theoretical efforts. For all their logical difficulties, and attendant methodological problems, Homans offers an image of society and social processes that is, if only intuitively, pleasing. The theoretical scheme, per se, is crude and even platitudinous, but the substantive vision of the social world first communicated in *The Human Group* and expanded upon in the later exchange works is provocative and likely to be the most enduring feature of Homans's theoretical perspective.

In *The Human Group*, Homans's numerous empirical generalizations described the processes of group elaboration and disintegration. Groups were observed to differentiate into subgroups, to form leadership ranks, to codify norms, to establish temporary equilibriums, and then, in his last case study of a dying New England town, to reveal the converse of these processes. In the later exchange works, the concepts of "activities," "interactions," and "sentiments,"

---

ent Relations: Two Experiments," *Sociometry* 27 (September 1964): 282–98; "Operant Psychology and Exchange Theory," in *Behavior Sociology: The Experimental Analysis of Social Process,* ed. R. L. Burgess and D. Bushell, Jr. (New York: Columbia University Press, 1969), pp. 379–405; and "Exchange Theory, Part I: A Psychological Basis for Social Exchange" and "Exchange Theory, Part II: Exchange Relations and Network Structures," in *Sociological Theories in Progress,* ed. J. Berger, M. Zelditch, Jr., and B. Anderson (New York: Houghton Mifflin Co., 1972), pp. 38–87.

which were incorporated into the propositions describing such group elaboration, were redefined in order to enable Homans the opportunity to explain why these processes should occur. Human activity became viewed as behavior directed toward the attainment of rewards and avoidance of punishments. Interaction became social behavior where the mutual activities of individuals have cost and reward implications for the parties to the interaction. Men were now seen as emitting those activities that would increase the likelihood of profits—rewards less costs—measured against some standard of distributive justice. Such rewarding and costly exchanges of activities were not viewed as necessarily involving the exchange of material rewards and punishments, but more frequently "psychic profits," or activities called "sentiments."

Just as he did in *The Human Group*, in his recent works Homans enumerates concepts that enable him to denote processes of group elaboration. In *Social Behavior*, the particular *ad hoc* explanations are of less interest than Homans's descriptions (as opposed to "explanations") of how vital group processes—interaction, influence, conformity, competition, bestowal of esteem, justice, ranking, and innovation—ebb and flow as actors seek psychic profits in their exchanges of rewards and punishments. In these descriptions, considerable intuitive insight into the basic processes of human interaction is evident. It was these insights that made *The Human Group* appealing, and it is this same feature of *Social Behavior* that makes it an important work.

Despite the suggestiveness of his descriptions of basic processes, however, the most theoretically interesting section of *Social Behavior* is the closing chapter on "The Institutional and the Subinstitutional." Introduced apologetically as a last-gasp "orgy," Homans nevertheless returns to an issue first raised in *The Human Group:* the relationship of processes in groups to the structures of larger societies, or "civilizations," as he phrased the issue at the time. As he emphasized in the last paragraph of *The Human Group*, the development of civilizations ultimately is carried out by persons in groups:

> At the level of the small group, society has always been able to cohere. We infer, therefore, that if civilization is to stand, it must maintain, in the relation between the groups that make up society and the central direction of society, some of the features of the small group itself.[62]

In *Social Behavior*, Homans has a more sophisticated answer to why it appears that society coheres around the small group: Society is like a group in that it is elaborated and structured from fundamentally the same exchange processes that structure and cause the elaboration of the small group. All social structures are thus built up from basically the same exchange processes; in the explication of why this should be so, Homans provides an interesting image of how patterns

---

[62] Homans, *Human Group*, p. 468.

of social organization are created, maintained, changed, and broken down. This image is not developed into what can be considered adequate theory—as has already been shown. But it does provide a vision of the social world which can perhaps initiate a more useful exchange-theoretic perspective on the processes underlying various patterns of social organization.

To explicate the relationship between elementary exchange processes and more complex patterns of social organization, Homans—much like Parsons a decade earlier—provides a sketch of the process of institutionalization:[63] At points in history, some men have the "capital" to reinforce or provide rewards for others, whether it comes from their possessing a surplus of food, money, a moral code, or valued leadership qualities. With such capital, "institutional elaboration" can occur, since some man or men can "invest" their capital in the form of trying to induce other men (through rewards or threats of punishments) to engage in novel activities. These new activities can involve an "intermeshing of the behavior of a large number of persons in a more complicated or roundabout way than has hitherto been the custom." Whether this "investment" involves conquering territory and organizing a kingdom or creating a new form of business organization, those making the investment must have the resources—whether an army to threaten punishment, a charismatic personality to morally persuade followers, or the ability to provide for peoples' subsistence needs—to keep those so organized in a situation where they derive some profit. At some point in this process, such organization can become more efficient and hence rewarding to all when the rewards are clearly specified in terms of generalized reinforcers, such as money, and when the activities expended to get their rewards are more clearly specified, such as is the case when explicit norms and rules emerge. In turn, this increased efficiency allows for greater organization of activities, thus increasing the likelihood that generalized reinforcers and explicit norms will be used to regulate exchange relations and hence increase the profits of those involved. Eventually, the exchange networks involving generalized reinforcers and an increasingly complex body of rules require differentation or subunits—such as a legal and banking system—that can maintain the stability of the generalized reinforcers and the integrity of the norms.

Out of this kind of exchange process, then, social organization—whether at a societal, group, organizational, or institutional level—is constructed. The emergence of most patterns of organization is frequently buried in the recesses of history, but such emergence is typified by these accelerating processes: (1) Men

---

[63] Homans, *Social Behavior*, chap. 18. The reader should find interesting a comparison of this model of institutionalization and that provided by Parsons, since Homans implicitly sees this model as an alternative to that presented by functionalists such as Parsons. But a careful reading of Talcott Parsons, *The Social System* (New York: Free Press, 1951), pp. 1–91, and his more recent work on evolution would reveal a remarkable similarity between his conceptualization of this basic process and that of Homans.

with "capital" (reward capacity) "invest" in creating more complex social relations that increase their rewards and allow those whose activities are organized to realize a "profit." (2) With increased rewards, these men can invest in more complex patterns of organization. (3) Increasingly complex patterns of organization require, first of all, the use of generalized reinforcers, and then, the codification of norms to regulate activity. (4) With this organizational base, it then becomes possible to elaborate further the pattern organization, creating the necessity for differentiation of subunits that assure the stability of the generalized reinforcers and the integrity of norms. (5) With this differentiation, it is possible to expand even further the networks of interaction, since these are standardized means for rewarding activities and codifying new norms as well as enforcing old rules.

However, these complex patterns of social organization employing formal rules and "secondary" or "generalized" reinforcers can never cease to meet the more "primary"[64] needs of individuals. Institutions first emerged to meet these needs; and no matter how complex institutional arrangements become and how many norms and formal rules are elaborated, these extended interaction networks must ultimately reinforce man's more primary needs. When these arrangements cease meeting the primary needs from which they ultimately sprang, an institution is vulnerable and apt to collapse if alternative activities, which can provide primary rewards, present themselves as a possibility. In this situation, low- or high-status persons, or someone who has little to lose by nonconformity to existing prescriptions, will break from established ways to expose to others a more rewarding alternative; while institutions may continue to extract conformity for a period, they will cease to do so when they lose the capacity to provide primary rewards. Thus, complex institutional arrangements must ultimately be satisfying to individuals, not simply because of the weight of culture or norms, but because they are constructed to serve "men as men":

> Institutions do not keep going just because they are enshrined in norms, and it seems extraordinary that anyone should ever talk as if they did. They keep going because they have pay-offs, ultimately pay-offs for individuals. Nor is society a perpetual-motion machine, supplying its own fuel. It cannot keep itself going by planting in the young a desire for these goods and only those goods that it happens to be in shape to provide. It must provide goods that men find rewarding not simply because they are sharers in a particular culture but because they are men.[65]

The fact that institutions of society must also meet "primary" needs sets the stage for a continual conflict between institutional elaboration and the primary needs of men. As one form of institutional elaboration meets one set of needs,

---

64 Homans, *Social Behavior;* unfortunately, just what a "primary reward" in this context means is not specified.

65 Ibid., p. 390.

it may deprive men of other important rewards—opening the way for deviation and innovation by those presenting the alternative rewards that have been suppressed by dominant institutional arrangements. In turn, the new institutional elaborations that may ensue from innovators who have the capital to reward others will suppress other needs, which, through processes similar to its inception, will set off another process of institutional elaboration.

In sum, this sketch of how social organization is linked to elementary processes of exchange represents an interesting perspective for analyzing how patterns of social organization are built up, maintained, altered, and broken down. While there are obvious conceptual problems—say, for example, the difficulty of distinguishing "primary rewards" of "men as men" from "other types" of rewards provided by institutions—the *image of society* presented by Homans is provocative. It can perhaps lead Homans to a fruitful strategy for developing a theory of exchange relations.

STRATEGIES FOR REDIRECTING HOMANS'S EXCHANGE PERSPECTIVE

The abandonment of Homans's platitudes about the "proper" form of theory is perhaps the first step in reformulating his exchange perspective. Naturally, efforts at deductive theorizing should not be discontinued, but the attempt to derive sociological generalizations from psychological axioms is, even if one accepts a reductionist strategy, premature. Homans could more fruitfully return to the strategy of *The Human Group,* where the formulation of generalizations about human groups or other forms of social organization could serve as an inductive base for more abstract theoretical statements.

By examining social phenomena in his usual insightful way, Homans could begin to use his exchange perspective to develop sociological propositions that attempt to answer some of the sociological questions Homans takes as "givens" in his current reductionist strategy. In tying his more abstract generalizations to *sociological* processes, Homans would be forced to specify the classes and types of value, reward, cost, investment, and justice that would pertain to specific processes in various types of social units, whether groups, organizations, institutions, or some other pattern of collective organization. For example, Homans could begin to specify the classes of rewards and costs appropriate to differentiation of status hierarchies in small groups—say, for example, esteem, self-respect, and sense of group membership—and then formulate generalizations about how these variables operate in the formation, maintenance, and change of such hierarchies. As is evident, Homans begins this task in *Social Behavior,* but it is done in a logically inconsistent manner, primarily because Homans appears more concerned with supporting psychological principles than in developing a logically interrelated set of generalizations, which, in the distant future, could be perhaps derived from psychological (psysiological?, biochemical? and so forth) axioms. The failure to specify classes and types of his main variables becomes even more evident as Homans attempts to reduce prematurely sociological generalizations, such as Golden's law, to his psychological axioms. For the present, a more meaningful explanation of Golden's law would involve an explication in terms of more clearly defined exchange concepts of how the processes of institutionalization in the economic, political, educational, legal, familial, and other spheres makes the "perception of literary as rewarding" by men as men. Homans poses a provocative conception of institutionalization; should he devote his efforts to specifying the classes and types of rewards involved in various forms of institutionalization and then to explicating the relations among these more clearly defined concepts, he would have some interesting sociological generalization to derive from his axioms.[66] To take these processes of institutionalization as givens will consistently make logically incomplete and empirically muddled Homans's deductions (see earlier discussion of these problems).

While constructing these deductive systems makes for good polemics against other forms of theorizing, especially Homans's favorite target, functional theory, they provide a poor alternative to the types of theorizing that Homans finds inadequate. Furthermore, even the logic dictated by a deductive-reductionist strategy would require Homans to concentrate his efforts on the development of the sociological laws, which, if he still finds this task satisfying, he could later derive from psychological axioms.

Homans has often said that if sociologists had some sociological laws of their own, they would be less concerned about whether they were reducible to more general psychological propositions.[67] Homans is correct in this statement, but one suspects that if Homans and others had spent their efforts developing them instead of arguing over whether they were ultimately reducible to psychological laws, deriving these sociological laws from psychological axioms would seem a less compelling task, even for Homans.

SELECTED BIBLIOGRAPHY ON GEORGE C. HOMANS

George C. Homans. *The Human Group.* New York: Harcourt, Brace & World, 1950.
————. *Social Behavior: Its Elementary Forms.* New York: Harcourt, Brace & World, 1961.

---

[66] Homans clearly possesses both the descriptive skills and power of abstraction to perform these activities, as is revealed in his early descriptive work, George C. Homans, *English Villagers of the 13th Century* (New York: Russell & Russell, 1941), and in his numerous abstract formulations in *Human Group* and *Social Behavior.* Unfortunately, however, Homans has become sidetracked from the strategy he advocated in *Human Group,* resulting in poor deductive theorizing from an equally poor inductive base.

[67] For example, Homans, *Nature of Social Science,* p. 86.

————. *Sentiments and Activities.* New York: Free Press, 1962.

————. "Bringing Men Back In." *American Sociological Review* 29 (December 1964): 809–18.

————. "Commentary." *Sociological Inquiry* 34 (Spring 1964): 223–40.

————. "Contemporary Theory in Sociology." In *Handbook of Modern Sociology*, edited by E. L. Faris, pp. 251–77. Chicago: Rand-McNally & Co., 1964.

————. *The Nature of Social Science.* New York: Harcourt, Brace & World, 1967.

————. "Fundamental Social Processes." In *Sociology,* edited by N. J. Smelser, pp. 27–78. New York: John Wiley & Sons, 1967.

————. "Reply to Blain." *Sociological Inquiry* 41 (Winter 1971): 23–30.

15

Exchange Structuralism:
Peter M. Blau

Major theoretical developments in sociology seemingly occur in a spirit of reaction and overreaction to functional forms of theorizing. As preceding chapters have attempted to document, dialectical and functional conflict theories, symbolic interactionism, and the exchange psychologism of George C. Homans have been viewed by their proponents as more desirable alternatives to functional theory, especially that of Talcott Parsons. Yet, as has been argued at various points, Parsonian functionalism and the proposed alternatives have more in common than the framers of conflict theories, interactionism, and some forms of exchange theory have admitted. In only one of the theoretical perspectives to be discussed in this volume is this latent commonality utilized to build an alternative to functionalism which incorporates the "useful" concepts not only from Parsonian functionalism but also from conflict, interactionist, and exchange theory.

This perspective has been advanced by Peter M. Blau. Although his theoretical scheme is an exchange model, it seeks to incorporate many of the assumptions and concepts of functional, conflict, and interactionist theory. In this way, Blau's exchange perspective attempts to bridge the gap between the micro processes of interaction, conflict, and exchange among individuals and the emergent structural units—such as groups, communities, organizations and institutions—at the macro level of analysis. While there are numerous substantive and logical problems in the scheme, it does represent a valuable synthesis of sociological concepts, addressing the theoretical questions of how and why various patterns of social organization emerge, persist, change, and break down.

BLAU'S THEORETICAL STRATEGY

In contrast with Homans's concern with developing deductive explanations, Blau offers what he terms a theoretical "prolegomenon"—or, in other words, a conceptual sketch—which can serve as a preliminary to more mature forms of theorizing.[1] In many ways, Blau's strategy resembles Parsons's, for he appears less concerned with developing a rigorous system of propositions than with enumerating concepts that can capture in loosely phrased and related propositions the fundamental processes occurring at diverse levels of social organization. While there is less categorization than in Parsons's conceptual efforts, Blau is concerned with developing an initial "bundle" of concepts and propositions that can provide insight into the operation of a wide range of sociological processes, from the behavior of individuals in small-group contexts to the operation of whole societies.

To execute this strategy, Blau's major theoretical work undertakes two fundamental tasks: (1) to conceptualize some of the simple and direct exchange processes occurring in relatively small interaction networks, and (2) then expand the conceptual edifice to include some of the complexities inherent in less direct exchange processes in larger social systems. In a vein similar to Homans's analysis, Blau first examines "elementary" forms of social exchange with an eye to how they help in the analysis of "subinstitutional" behavior. Where Homans terminates his analysis by simply presenting a conceptual "orgy" in the last chapter of *Social Behavior*,[2] Blau begins to supplement the exchange concepts describing elementary processes in an effort to understand more completely the complex processes of institutionalization.

Thus, in manner reminiscent of Parsons's analysis of the process of institutionalization in *The Social System*[3] (see chapter 3), Blau begins with a conceptualization of basic interactive processes; then, utilizing and supplementing the concepts developed in this analysis, he shifts to the conceptualization of how more elaborate institutional complexes are created, maintained, changed, and broken down.

---

[1] Peter M. Blau's major exchange work is *Exchange and Power in Social Life* (New York: John Wiley & Sons, 1964). This formal and expanded statement on his exchange perspective was anticipated in earlier works. For example, see Peter M. Blau, "A Theory of Social Integration," *American Journal of Sociology* 65 (May 1960): 545–56; and Peter M. Blau, *The Dynamics of Bureaucracy*, 1st and 2d eds. (Chicago: University of Chicago Press, 1955 and 1963). It is of interest to note that George C. Homans in *Social Behavior: Its Elementary Forms* (New York: Harcourt, Brace & World, 1961) makes frequent reference to the data summarized in this latter work. For a more recent statement of Blau's position see Peter M. Blau, "Interaction: Social Exchange," in *International Encyclopaedia of the Social Sciences*, vol. 7 (New York: Macmillian Co. 1968), pp. 452–58.

[2] Homans, "The Institutional and the Subinstitutional," *Social Behavior*, chap. 18.

[3] Talcott Parsons, *The Social System* (New York: Free Press, 1951), especially pp. 1–200.

BASIC EXCHANGE PRINCIPLES

Blau does not define as explicitly as Homans the variables in his exchange scheme. Rather, considerably more attention is devoted to defining exchange as a particular type of association, involving "actions that are contingent on rewarding reactions from others and that cease when these expected reactions are not forthcoming."[4] For Blau, exchange occurs only among those relationships in which rewards are *expected and received from designated others.* Much like Parsons's conception of voluntarism, Blau conceptualizes as exchange "activities" only those behaviors that are oriented to specified goals, or *rewards,* and that involve actors selecting from various potential alternatives, or *costs,* a particular line of action which will yield an expected reward. In pursuing rewards and selecting alternative lines of behaviors, actors are conceptualized as seeking a *profit* (rewards less costs) from their relations with others. Thus, Blau employs the basic concepts of all exchange theories—reward, cost, and profit—but he limits their application to relations with *others* from whom rewards are *expected* and *received.* This definition of exchange is considerably more limited than Homans's definition, which encompasses *all* activity as exchange, regardless of whether rewards are expected or received.

In common with Homans, however, Blau recognizes that in focusing on associations involving "an exchange of activity, tangible or intangible, and more or less rewarding and costly, between two persons,"[5] an elementary economic model is being employed. Indeed, social life is conceived to be a "marketplace" in which actors negotiate with each other in an effort to make a profit. However, Blau shares the skepticism that led Homans to reject the "theory of games" as "good advice" but a "poor description" of human behavior and that induced Parsons's earlier in *The Structure of Social Action*[6] to discard the extremes of utilitarianism. Blau recognizes that, unlike the simple "economic man" of classical economics (and of more recent rationalistic models of human behavior), humans (1) rarely pursue one specific goal to the exclusion of all others, (2) are infrequently consistent in their preferences, (3) virtually never have complete information of alternatives, and (4) are never free from social commitments limiting the available alternatives. Furthermore, in contrast with a purely economic model of human transactions, social associations involve the exchange of rewards whose value varies from one transaction to another without a fixed market value, and whose value cannot be expressed precisely in terms of a single, accepted medium of exchange (such as money). In fact, the vagueness of the

---

[4] Blau, *Exchange and Power,* p. 6.

[5] Ibid., p. 88.

[6] Talcott Parsons, *The Structure of Social Action* (New York: McGraw-Hill Book Co., 1937).

values exchanged in social life is a "substantive fact, not simply a methodological problem,"[7] for, as Blau emphasizes, the values people hold are inherently diffuse and ill defined.[8]

Unlike Homans, Blau does not state a formal set of exchange principles, primarily because he is not concerned with developing the higher order axioms of a deductive theoretic system. In a less explicit manner, Blau does employ a series of exchange principles. Since these principles are not always enumerated, it is often unclear whether they represent assumptions or statements of co-variance among the variables of his exchange system. Despite the vagueness with which they are stated, Blau's theoretical perspective is not comprehensible without an understanding of the "principles" or "laws" he views as guiding the dynamics of the exchange process. For convenience, these principles will be phrased as statements of co-variance among exchange variables, despite the fact that Blau may have preferred to state them as assumptions.

PRINCIPLE 1.   The more profit a person expects from another in emitting a particular activity, the more likely he is to emit that activity.

This principle combines Homans's Axioms 1, 2, and 3, where rewarding stimulus situations (1), the frequency of rewards (2), and the value of rewards (3) were seen as increasing the likelihood that activities would be emitted. Actually, in Homans's own deductive systems—for example, the one he constructed to "explain" Golden's law—Homans usually collapses his first three axioms and simply states: "Men are more likely to perform an activity the more valuable they perceive the reward of that activity to be."[9] This proposition is then typically followed by a corollary: "Men are more likely to perform an activity the more successful they perceive the activity to be in getting that reward." Thus, in practice, Homans and Blau utilize the same basic principle, for Blau's use of the concept "reward expectation" would encompass the same phenomena denoted by Homans's use of the concepts "perception of reward" and perception of "success in getting a reward."

PRINCIPLE 2.   The more a person has exchanged rewards with another, the more likely are reciprocal obligations to emerge and guide subsequent exchanges among those persons.

---

[7] Blau, *Exchange and Power,* p. 95.

[8] As was noted for Homans's schemes, this "fact" creates both methodological and logical problems. If value cannot be precisely measured, how is it possible to discern just how value influences behavior? If value cannot be measured independently of the behavior it is supposed to regulate, then propositions will be tautologous and of little use in building sociological theory.

[9] George C. Homans, "Reply to Blain," *Sociological Inquiry* 41 (Winter 1971): 23–30.

Drawing from Malinowski's and Lévi-Strauss's initial discussion as reinterpreted by Alvin Gouldner,[10] Blau postulates that "the need to reciprocate for benefits received in order to continue receiving them serves as a 'starting mechanism' of social interaction."[11] Equally important, once exchanges have occurred, a "fundamental and ubiquitous norm of reciprocity" emerges to regulate subsequent exchanges. Thus, inherent in the exchange process, per se, is a principle of reciprocity, which, over time and as the conditions of Principle 1 are met, becomes codified into a social *norm* of reciprocity, whose violation brings about social disapproval and other negative sanctions. Since violations of the norm of reciprocity become significant in Blau's subsequent analysis of opposition and conflict, it is wise to formulate explicitly a corollary of Principle 2, stated here as a separate principle.

PRINCIPLE 3.   The more the reciprocal obligations of an exchange relationship are violated, the more are deprived parties disposed to sanction negatively those violating the norm of reciprocity.

Following economists' analysis of transactions in the marketplace, Blau introduces in his fourth Principle the economic "law" of "marginal utility." The more a person has received a reward, the more satiated he is with that reward, and the less valuable further increments of the reward (Principle 4 is the equivalent to Homans's Axiom 4). Actors will therefore seek alternative rewards until their level of satiation declines.

PRINCIPLE 4.   The more expected rewards have been forthcoming from the emission of a particular activity, the less valuable the activity, and the less likely its emission.[12]

Blau has criticized Homans for tacitly assuming that the principle of "distributive justice" can operate independently of group norms.[13] In implying that distributive justice is a "natural sentiment," Blau charges Homans with underemphasizing the fact that what is considered a "fair" ratio of costs and investments to rewards for the parties to an exchange is an emergent property of social structure. As Blau notes, "while all men undoubtedly have some sense of justice, the system of values and norms that prevails in a society is what gives their notion of justice its specific content and meaning."[14] Thus, it is necessary to rephrase

---

[10] Alvin W. Gouldner, "The Norm of Reciprocity," *American Sociological Review* 25 (April 1960): 161–78.

[11] Blau, *Power and Exchange*, p. 92.

[12] Ibid., p. 90.

[13] See Peter M. Blau, "Justice in Social Exchange," in *Institutions and Social Exchange: The Sociologies of Talcott Parsons and George C. Homans*, ed. H. Turk and R. L. Simpson (New York: Bobbs-Merrill Co. 1971), pp. 56–68; see also: Blau, *Power and Exchange*, pp. 156–57.

[14] Blau, "Justice in Social Exchange," p. 68.

Homans's fifth Axiom on distributive justice in order to make explicit the recognition that constraining all exchanges are norms of "fair exchange," which specify for actors the proper proportion of rewards to costs and investments. Such norms thus set up minimal "expectations" as to what parties in an exchange should receive in various types of exchange relationships. Hence, Blau introduces a fifth Principle:

PRINCIPLE 5. The more exchange relations have been established, the more likely they are to be governed by norms of "fair exchange."

A corollary to this principle modifies Homans's assertion that "anger" is forthcoming when "justice" is not realized. For convenience, this corollary can be stated as a separate principle.

PRINCIPLE 6. The less norms of fairness are realized in an exchange, the more are deprived parties disposed to sanction negatively those violating the norms.

Since Blau's exchange model is vitally concerned with the conditions under which conflict and change occur in social systems, Principle 6 becomes a crucial generalization. In his subsequent analysis, the deprivations arising from violating the norms of fair exchange are viewed as translated, under specified conditions, into retaliation against violators. This concern with enumerating exchange principles that can account for conflict in social relations is underscored by Blau's final exchange principle:[15]

PRINCIPLE 7. The more stabilized and balanced some exchange relations among social units, the more likely other exchange relations are to become imbalanced and unstable.

All established exchange relations involve "costs" or alternative rewards forgone. Since most actors *must* engage in more than one exchange relation, the balance and stabilization of one exchange relation (in accordance with Principles 1, 2, and 4) is likely to create imbalance and strain in other necessary exchange relations. For Blau, social life is thus filled with "dilemmas" in which men must successively trade off stability and balance in one exchange relation for strain in others as they attempt to cope with the variety of relations they must maintain. In his last chapter on institutionalization, Homans hinted at this principle when he emphasized that, in satisfying some needs of men, institutional arrangements denied others and thereby set into motion a perpetual dialectic between dominant institutions and change-oriented acts of innovation and deviance.[16] It is

---

[15] Blau, *Exchange and Power,* p. 14.
[16] Homans, *Social Behavior,* pp. 390–98.

from this concluding insight of Homans into the dialectical nature of relationships between established social patterns and forces of opposition that Blau is to begin his analysis of exchange in social life.

In the formulation of exchange concepts and their incorporation into these seven basic principles, Blau sets the stage for the analysis of social processes that combines elements from functional, conflict, interactionist, and other forms of exchange theory. His basic assumption resembles Parsons's early formulation of the "unit act," in that exchange behavior involves goal-oriented behavior, involving the selection of alternatives, in the pursuit of expected rewards. Furthermore, his concern in Principle 2 with documenting how exchange acts become institutionalized into systems of reciprocity anticipates the concern with the issues first grappled with by functional analysis in anthropology and sociology. In conceptualizing the pursuit of rewards, Blau will also emphasize the importance of the related processes of "role taking" and "presentation of self" in exchange situations as actors align and realign their behaviors in exchange networks. While he does not develop an explicitly interactionist perspective, he recognizes that since each exchange situation constitutes a series of "expectations," exchange involves mutual attempts by actors to realize such "definitions of the situation." Much of social life is to be understood only when the definitions and redefinitions of exchange situations by actors are conceptualized. Blau's emphasis on how exchange processes inevitably generate imbalances and hence deprivations through the violation of the norms of reciprocity and fair exchange previews his concern with conceptualizing the sources of dialectical conflict processes and change in a social system. Yet, Blau's analytical concern with the problem of order and how institutionalized patterns are established from these conflict dialectics will enable him to conceptualize, in a way reminiscent of Simmel and Coser, the positive "functions" served by conflict.

These comments anticipate Blau's conceptualization of social processes and structure, and therefore represent only an introduction to a story yet to be told. But they should be kept in mind as Blau's exchange model unfolds, since Blau has explicitly attempted to synthesize the analytical thrust of sociology's dominant conceptual perspectives.

BASIC EXCHANGE PROCESSES IN SOCIAL LIFE

Elementary Systems of Exchange

Blau initiates his discussion of elementary exchange processes with the assumption that people enter into social exchange because they perceive the possibility of deriving rewards (Principle 1). Blau labels this perception *social attraction* and postulates that unless relationships involve such attraction, they are not relationships of exchange. In entering an exchange relationship, each actor assumes the perspective of another, and thereby derives some perception of the other's needs. Each actor then manipulates the presentation of self so as to convince the other that he has the valued qualities the other appears to desire. In adjusting role behaviors in an effort to impress others with the resources they have to offer, people operate under the principle of reciprocity, for, by indicating that one possesses valued qualities, each person is attempting to establish a claim on others for the receipt of rewards from them. All exchange operates under the presumption that people who bestow rewards will receive rewards in turn as payment for value received.

Actors attempt to impress each other through *competition* in which each actor reveals the rewards he has to offer in an effort to force others, in accordance with the norm of reciprocity, to reciprocate with an even more valuable reward. Social life is thus rife with people's competitive efforts to impress each other and thereby extract valuable rewards. But as interaction proceeds, it inevitably becomes evident to the parties to an exchange that some people have more valued resources to offer than others, putting them in a unique position to extract rewards from all others who value the resources they have to offer.

It is at this point in exchange relations that groups of individuals become *differentiated* in terms of the resources they possess and the kinds of reciprocal demands they can make on others. Blau then asks an analytical question that Homans typically ignored: What generic types or classes of rewards can those with resources extract in return for bestowing their valued resources upon others? Blau conceptualizes four general classes of such rewards: money, social approval, esteem or respect, and compliance. While Homans discussed extensively each of these rewards, he failed to conceptualize them as an exhaustive categorization of types of rewards that could be incorporated into abstract theoretical statements. It is to this end that Blau devotes considerable attention; although he does not make full use of his categorization of classes of rewards, he offers some suggestive clues about how these abstract theoretical statements can be formulated.

Blau first ranks these generalized reinforcers in terms of their value to those in a position to extract rewards from others in exchange for services rendered. In most social relations, money is an inappropriate reward and hence is the least valuable reward. Social approval is an appropriate reward, but for most humans it is not very valuable, thus forcing those who derive valued services to offer with great frequency the more valuable reward of esteem or respect to those providing valued services. In many situations, the services offered can command no more than respect and esteem from those receiving the benefit of services. At times, the services offered are sufficiently valuable to require those receiving them to offer, in accordance with the principles of reciprocity and fair exchange, the most valuable class of rewards—compliance with one's requests.

When a person can extract compliance in an exchange relationship, he is conceived by Blau to have "power," since he has the capacity to withhold rewarding services and thereby punish or inflict heavy costs on those who might withhold compliance. To conceptualize the degree of power possessed by individuals, Blau formulates four general propositions that determine the capacity of powerful individuals to extract compliance:[17]

1. The more services people can supply in return for the receipt of particularly valued services, the less those providing these particularly valued services can extract compliance.
2. The more alternative sources of rewards people have, the less those providing valuable services can extract compliance.
3. The more those receiving valuable services from particular individuals can employ physical force and coercion, the less those providing the services can extract compliance.
4. The more those receiving the valuable services can do without them, the less those providing the services can extract compliance.

These four propositions list the conditions leading to differentiation of members in social groups in terms of power. To the extent that group members can supply some services in return, seek alternative rewards, potentially use physical force, or do without certain valuable services, individuals who can provide valuable services will be able to extract only esteem and approval from group members; thus, groups will be differentiated in terms of prestige rankings but not power. Naturally, as Blau emphasizes, most social groups reveal complex patterns of differentiation of power, prestige, and patterns of approval; but, of particular interest to him, are the dynamics involved in generating power, authority, and opposition.

In focusing almost exclusively on the questions of power, authority, and opposition, Blau fails to complete his analysis of how different types of social structures are influenced by the exchange of different classes of rewards. The logic of Blau's argument would require additional propositions that would indicate how various types of rewards lead to the differentiation of groups, not only in terms of power and authority, but also with respect to esteem and prestige rankings and networks of social approval. Interesting theoretical questions left unanswered include: What are the "conditions" for the emergence of different types of prestige rankings? What are the "conditions" for the creation of various types of approval networks? Presumably, answers to these questions are left to others

---

[17] Blau, *Exchange and Power*, pp. 118–19.

to provide, since Blau focuses primarily on the problem of how power is converted into authority and how, in accordance with his seven basic exchange principles, various patterns of integration and opposition become evident in human groupings.

For Blau, power differentials in groups create two contradictory forces: (1) strains toward *integration* and (2) strains toward *opposition* and conflict.

Strains toward Integration. Differences in power inevitably create the potential for conflict. However, such potential is frequently suspended by a series of forces promoting the conversion of power into authority, in which subordinates accept as legitimate the demands of leaders for compliance. Principles 2 and 5 denote two processes fostering such group integration: Exchange relations always operate under the presumption of reciprocity, forcing those deriving valued services to provide other rewards in payment (Principle 2). In providing these rewards, subordinates are guided by norms of fair exchange, in which the costs they incur in offering compliance are to be "proportional" to the value of the services they receive from leaders (Principle 5). Thus, to the extent that actors engage in exchanges with leaders, and to the degree that the services provided by leaders are considered highly valuable, subordination must be accepted as legitimate in accordance with the norms of reciprocity and fairness which emerge in all exchanges. Under these conditions, groups "elaborate" additional norms specifying just how exchanges with leaders are to be conducted in order to regularize the requirements for reciprocity and to maintain fair rates of exchange. Leaders who conform to these emergent norms can usually assure themselves that their leadership will be considered legitimate. In fact, Blau emphasizes, if leaders abide by the norms regulating exchange of their services for compliance, norms carrying negative sanctions typically emerge among subordinates stressing the need for compliance to leaders' requests. Through this process, subordinates exercise considerable social control over each others' actions and thereby promote the integration of super- and subordinate segments of groupings.

Authority, therefore, "rests on the common norms in a collectivity of subordinates that constrain its individual members to conform to the orders of a superior."[18] In many patterns of social organization these norms simply emerge out of the competitive exchanges among collective groups of actors. Frequently, however, in order for such "normative agreements" to be struck, participants to an exchange must be socialized into a common set of values which define not only what constitutes "fair exchange" in a given situation, but also the way such exchange should be institutionalized into norms for both leaders and superiors. Although it is quite possible for actors to arrive at normative consensus in the course of the exchange process itself, an initial set of common values facilitates

---

[18] Ibid., p. 208.

the legitimation of power. Actors can now enter into exchanges with a common "definition of the situation," which can provide a general framework for the normative regulation of emerging power differentials. Without common values, the competition for power is likely to be severe. In the absence of guidelines about what should constitute "reciprocity" and "fair exchange," considerable strain and tension will persist as definitions of reciprocity and fair exchange are worked out. For Blau, then, legitimation "entails not merely tolerant approval but active confirmation and promotion of social patterns by common values, either pre-existing ones or those that emerge in a collectivity in the course of social interaction."[19]

With the legitimation of power through the normative regulation of interaction, as "confirmed" by common values, the structure of collective organization is altered. One of the most evident changes is the decline in interpersonal competition, for now actors' presentations of self shift from a concern with impressing others with their valuable qualities to an emphasis on confirming their statuses as loyal group members. Subordinates come to accept their statuses and manipulate their role behaviors in an effort to assure that they receive social approval from their peers as a reward for conformity to group norms. Leaders can typically assume a lower profile, since it is no longer necessary to demonstrate in each and every encounter with subordinates their superior qualities—especially since norms now define *when* and *how* they should extract conformity and esteem for providing their valued services. Thus, with the legitimation of power as authority, the interactive processes, involving the way group members define the situation and present themselves to others, undergoes a dramatic change, reducing the degree of competition and thereby fostering group integration.

With these events, the amount of direct interaction between leaders and subordinates usually declines, since power and ranking no longer must be constantly negotiated. This decline in direct interaction marks the formation of distinct subgroupings as members seek to interact with those of their own social rank, avoiding the costs of interacting with either their inferiors or superiors.[20] In interacting primarily among themselves, subordinates avoid the high costs of interacting with leaders; while social approval from their peers is not a particularly valuable reward, it can be extracted with comparatively few costs—thus allowing for a sufficient profit. Conversely, leaders can avoid the high costs (in terms and time and energy) of constantly competing and negotiating with inferiors over when and how compliance and esteem are to be bestowed upon them. Instead, by having relatively limited and well-defined contact with subordinates, they can derive the high rewards that come from compliance and esteem without incurring

---

[19] Ibid., p. 221.

[20] As will be recalled from chapter 14, these processes were insightfully described by George C. Homans in *The Human Group* (New York: Harcourt, Brace & World, 1950).

excessive costs in interacting with subordinates—thereby allowing for a profit.

Strains toward Opposition. Thus far, Blau's exchange perspective is decidedly functional, in that social exchange processes—attraction, competition, differentiation, and integration—have been viewed in terms of how they contribute to creating a legitimated set of normatively regulated relations. In a manner similar to Parsons's discussion of institutionalization, Blau has also emphasized the importance of common values as a significant force in creating patterns of social organization. However, Blau is keenly aware that social organization is always rife with conflict and opposition, creating an inevitable dialectic between integration and opposition in social structures. Recognition of this fact has led Blau to assert:[21]

> The functional approach reinforces the overemphasis on integrative social forces . . . whereas the dialectical perspective counteracts it by requiring explicit concern with disruptive tendencies in social structures. The pursuit of systematic analysis and the adoption of a dialectical perspective create a dilemma for the sociologist, who must rivet his attention on consistent social patterns for the sake of the former and on inconsistencies in accordance with the latter. This dilemma, like others, is likely to give rise to alternating developments, making him veer in one direction at one time and in the opposite at another.

What is important about Blau's perspective is that, unlike Dahrendorf (see chapter 6), in adopting dialectical assumptions he does not reject polemically the useful tenets of a functionalism only to let them back in as was the case with Dahrendorf's conflict perspective (see chapter 8). Blau recognizes that patterns of social organization are created and maintained *as well as* changed and broken down, leading him to seek the principles that can explain this spectrum of events. Thus, unlike Dahrendorf's conflict model, in which the organization of authority relations in "imperatively coordinated associations" (ICAs) and the opposition of "quasi groups" were merely taken *as givens*, Blau has sought to address the question of how, and through what processes, authority structures such as ICAs are created. In so doing, Blau is in a much better analytical position than Dahrendorf to document how the creation of social structure can also, under specifiable conditions, set in motion forces for conflict and change. As was emphasized in the earlier discussion of conflict theory, to *assert* that conflict is endemic to authority relations in social structure, and then to analyze how such conflict changes such structure, is to define away the interesting theoretical question: Under *what* conditions, in *what* types of structures, revealing *what* types of authority which have arisen through *what* processes, is *what* type of conflict

---

[21] Peter M. Blau, "Dialectical Sociology: Comments," *Sociological Inquiry* 42 (Spring 1972): 185. This article was written in reply to an attempt to document Blau's shift from a functional to dialectical perspective; see Michael A. Weinstein and Deena Weinstein, "Blau's Dialectical Sociology," Ibid., pp. 173–82.

likely to emerge? Blau's discussion of "strains for integration" represents an attempt to answer this question and provide a more balanced theoretical framework for discussing opposition and conflict in social systems.

Much as Parsons's emphasis in *The Social System*[22] on the "mechanisms" of socialization and social control implied that a failure in these mechanisms would generate deviance, conflict, and change, so Blau's emphasis on the failure to enter exchange with, or develop through the exchange process, a common set of values and regulative norms reveals how those processes that create patterns of social organization can also operate to create opposition, conflict, and change in social systems. Unlike Parsons, Blau has formulated abstract theoretical statements that help conceptualize more precisely the events that operate to cause a failure in those processes maintaining institutionalized patterns. The first of these abstract theoretical statements can be found in Principles 3, 6, and 7. As Principle 3 documents, the failure to receive "expected" rewards in return for various activities leads actors to attempt to apply negative sanctions, which, when ineffective, can drive people to violent "retaliation" against those who have denied them an expected reward. Such retaliation is intensified by Principle 5 on "fair exchange," since when they violate such norms, those in power inflict excessive costs on subordinates, creating a situation, which, at a minimum, leads to attempts to sanction negatively and, at most, to retaliation. Finally, principle 6 on the inevitable imbalances emerging from multiple exchange relations emphasizes that to balance relations in one exchange context by meeting reciprocal obligations and conforming to norms of fairness is to put into imbalance other relations. Thus, the imbalances potentially encourage a cyclical process in which actors seek to balance previously unbalanced relations and thereby throw into imbalance currently balanced exchanges. In turn, exchange relations that are thrown into imbalance violate the norms of reciprocity and fair exchange, thus causing attempts at negative sanctioning, and, under some conditions, retaliation. For Blau, then, built into *all* exchange relationships are sources of imbalance, which, when severely violating norms of reciprocity and fair exchange, can lead to open conflict among individuals in group contexts.

At this level of generality, however, these suggestive principles simply state what *can* occur, without specifying the conditions under which the forces they denote will actually be set into motion. Unfortunately, despite this promising analytical lead, Blau provides few specific propositions that delineate when the propensities for opposition are activated. It is perhaps at this point that propositions similar to those developed by Dahrendorf could prove useful, since they specify some of the conditions under which those exchange processes leading to patterns of social organization also cause conflict. It is no coincidence, then, that

---

[22] Parsons, *Social System*, pp. 201–325.

when Blau does undertake a limited discussion of the conditions leading to increasingly intense forms of opposition, his analysis resembles Dahrendorf's discussion of the technical, political, and social conditions of conflict group organization:[23]

1. The more exchange relations between super and subordinates become imbalanced, the greater the probability of opposition to those with power.
    a. The more norms of reciprocity are violated by the superordinates, the greater the imbalance.
    b. The more norms of fair exchange are violated by superordinates, the greater the imbalance.
2. The more individuals experience *collectively* relations of imbalance with superordinates, the greater their sense of deprivation, and the greater the probability of opposition to those with power.
    a. The less the spatial dispersion of subordinates, the more likely they are to experience collectively relations of imbalance with superordinates.
    b. The more subordinates can communicate with each other, the more likely they are to experience collectively relations of imbalance with superordinates.
3. The more subordinates can experience collectively deprivations in exchange relations with superordinates, the more likely they are to codify ideologically their deprivations and the greater their opposition to those with power.
4. The more deprivations of subordinates are ideologically codified, the greater the sense of solidarity among subordinates, and the greater the probability of opposition.
5. The greater the sense of solidarity among subordinates, the more they can define their opposition as a noble and worthy cause, and the greater the probability of their opposition to those with power.
6. The greater the sense of ideological solidarity, the more likely are subordinates to view opposition as an end in itself, and the greater the probability of opposition to those with power.

In these few propositions, it is clear that Blau fails to specify separate propositions for different phases in the conflict process. For example, the analysis of Dahrendorf's and Coser's propositional inventories revealed the utility of analyzing, at a minimum, the causes, the degree of intensity and violence, as well as the duration and outcomes of conflict. At best, what emerges from Blau's propositions and the somewhat discursive context in which they are imbedded[24] is a general sense of how he conceptualizes opposition to emerge. Blau seemingly

---

[23] Blau, *Exchange and Power*, pp. 224–52.
[24] Ibid.

hypothesizes that the more imbalanced exchange relations are experienced collectively, the greater the experience of deprivation and the greater is the potential opposition. While he does not explicitly state the case, he appears to hold that increasing ideological codification of deprivations, the formation of group solidarity, and the emergence of conflict as a way of life will increase the intensity of the opposition—that is, members' emotional involvement in and commitment to opposition to those with power.

The vagueness of Blau's model on the various *types* and *classes* of opposition that can emerge from imbalanced exchange relations offers little more than a suggestive lead for conceptualizing inherent processes of opposition in exchange relations. Unlike Dahrendorf's dialectical model, Blau's scheme does offer some important theoretical insights into how the creation of relations of authority can also cause opposition. Beyond the analytical clues provided by Principles 3, 6, and 7 of his general exchange perspective, however, the variables specifying the subsequent course of the opposition—for example, its intensity, violence, duration, and outcomes—remain unspecified.

Blau's conceptualization of the processes of institutionalization *and* conflict in terms of the same abstract exchange principles does represent a significant improvement over Parsons's portrayal of institutionalization, which lacked an explicit formulation of principles governing conflict and change. It also goes beyond Dahrendorf's model, which failed to specify either how institutionalized patterns or latent conflicts first emerged in authority systems. Further, Blau's presentation represents an improvement over Homans's analysis of institutionalization and of the inherent conflict between the institutional and subinstitutional, since in Blau's scheme there is a more adequate conceptualization of the process of institutionalization of the power relations from which opposition, innovation, and deviance ultimately spring. Thus, despite the weakness of his discussion of the dialectical forces of opposition, Blau's efforts do suggest ways the model can be improved: (*a*) by more precise formulation of the conditions under which exchange imbalances are likely for various types of social units; and then (*b*) by specification of the conditions leading to various levels of intensity, violence, and duration in relations of opposition among various types of social units.

In looking back on Blau's discussion of micro exchange processes, it is clear that he visualizes a series of basic exchange processes in human groupings: attraction, competition, differentiation, integration, and opposition. Of particular interest are the processes of differentiation in terms of power and how this pattern of differentiation creates strains for both integration and opposition— thus giving social reality a dialectical character. Also noteworthy in the perspective is the attempt to utilize concepts developed in the analysis of elementary exchange processes in order to examine more complex exchange processes among the macro social units of social systems. Of great significance is the fact that Blau recognizes the necessity for reformulating and supplementing elementary exchange concepts when analyzing more complex social processes. As will become evident, he also realizes that the basic social processes of attraction, competition, differentiation, integration, and opposition still typify exchanges even among macro social units—thus giving social life a degree of continuity.

Complex Exchange Systems

While the general processes of attraction, competition, differentiation, integration, and opposition are evident in the exchanges among macro structures, there are several fundamental differences between these exchanges and those among micro structures:[25]

1. In complex exchanges among macro structures, the significance of "shared values" increases, for it is through such values that indirect exchanges among macro structures are mediated.

2. Exchange networks among macro structures are typically institutionalized. While spontaneous exchange is a ubiquitous feature of social life, there are usually well-established historical arrangements that circumscribe the operation of the basic exchange processes of attraction, competition, differentiation, integration, and even opposition.

3. Since macro structures are themselves the product of more elementary exchange processes, the analysis of macro structures requires the analysis of more than one level of social organization.

Mediating Values. For Blau, the "interpersonal attraction" of elementary exchange is replaced by "shared values" at the macro level. These values can be conceptualized as "media of social transactions," in that they provide a common set of standards for conducting the complex chains of indirect exchanges among social structures and their individual members. Such values are viewed by Blau as providing effective mediation of complex exchanges by virtue of the fact that the individual members of social structures have usually been socialized into a set of common values, leading them to accept them as "appropriate." Furthermore, when coupled with codification into laws and enforcement procedures by those groups and organizations with power, shared values provide a means for mediating the complex and indirect exchanges among the macro structures of large-scale systems. In mediating indirect exchanges among groups and organizations, shared values provide standards for the calculation of: (*a*) expected rewards (Principle 1), (*b*) reciprocity (Principle 2), and (*c*) fair exchange (Principle 5).

Thus, since "men as men," to borrow Homans's phrase, are not the units of complex exchanges, Blau emphasizes that, in order for complex patterns of social

---

[25] Ibid., pp. 253–311.

organization to emerge and persist, it is necessary for a "functional equivalent" of direct interpersonal attraction to exist. This "functional equivalent" assures that exchange can proceed in accordance with Principles 1, 2, and 5. And even when complex exchanges do involve "men," their interactions are frequently so protracted and indirect that one individual's rewards are contingent on others who are far removed, requiring that common values guide and regulate the exchanges.

There is considerable similarity between Blau's concern with "mediating values" and Parsons's recent interest in "generalized media of exchange."[26] While the respective conceptualizations of the general classes and types of media differ, each is concerned with how social relationships utilize in varying contexts distinctive "symbols," not only to establish the respective "values" of actions among exchange units, but also to specify just how the exchange should be conducted. The similarity of their strategies is particularly evident by the fact that Blau employs Parsons's pattern variable, universalism-particularism, in attempting to conceptualize the most generic types of "mediating values" for the processes of attraction, competition, and differentiation. For Blau, "particularistic values" are the media of "integration" and "solidarity" in complex exchange systems. By providing the parties to complex exchange relations with a set of unique standards for judging and evaluating themselves as distinct from other groupings, particularistic values "unite members of a collectivity in common solidarity and extend the scope of integrative bonds far beyond the limits of personal feelings of attraction."[27] Particularistic values thus represent a set of symbols for identifying a group from other collectivities, thereby providing a "medium through which its members are bound together into a cohesive community."[28] So, once accepted and shared by group members, particularistic values serve as "functional substitutes for sentiments of personal attraction that integrate the members of a face-to-face group into a cohesive unit."[29] "Universalistic values" are media of "exchange and differentiation" in complex exchange systems.[30] One of the fundamental problems facing indirect exchange relationships revolves around how to standardize the "value" of various types of activity. Universalistic values perform this "function" of standardizing and making comparable the value of activities across extended networks of exchange relations. Much as money in

[26] See discussion in chapter 3, as well as Talcott Parsons, "On the Concept of Political Power," *Proceedings of the American Philosophical Society* 107 (June 1963): 232–62; Talcott Parsons, "On the Concept of Influence," *Public Opinion Quarterly* 27 (Spring 1963): 37–67; and Talcott Parsons, "Some Problems of General Theory," in *Theoretical Sociology: Perspectives and Developments*, ed. J. C. McKinney and E. A. Tiryakian (New York: Appleton-Century-Crofts, 1970), pp. 28–68. See also T. S. Turner, "Parsons' Concept of Generalized Media of Social Interaction and Its Relevance for Social Anthropology," *Sociological Inquiry* 38 (Spring 1968): 121–34.

[27] Blau, *Exchange and Power*, p. 267.

[28] Ibid.

[29] Ibid.

[30] Ibid., pp. 268–70.

economic transactions represents a measure of value for widely diverse and extended exchanges, so universalistic values provide common standards for measuring people's "contributions" to group activity and the kinds and amounts of variously valued rewards they should receive. In doing so, universalistic values allow for the unequal, but "fair," distribution of rewards and privileges across extended exchange networks. Without such values, social competition and differentiation of super- and subordinates beyond immediate face-to-face relations could not occur, since there would be no way to assess either the value of the services provided by superordinates in large social groupings or the rewards they should receive in return for providing these services. Universalistic values therefore allow ranking and stratification to occur in macro systems, where most exchange relations are indirect.

Thus, the Parsonian concept, universalism-particularism, provides Blau with a way to classify the values necessary for the basic processes of attraction, competition, and differentiation to occur in complex exchange systems. Particularistic values "attract" members of collectivities toward each other, facilitating the expectation of rewards. Universalistic values establish standards for assessing the "winners" and "losers" in competition, while specifying the rate of exchange between services and rewards among subordinates and superordinates in larger collectivities.

In discussing the other two basic social processes—integration and opposition—Blau does not find a convenient parallel in Parsons's pattern variables and thus posits two additional types of mediating values: "legitimating values" and "opposition values." Values legitimating authority are "media of organization, which extend the scope of organized social control."[31] In direct interpersonal exchanges, the exercise of power (demands for compliance in exchange for valuable services) is mediated by norms enforced directly by the participants to the exchange. Values legitimating authority remove regulation of power from the individuals in the exchange by bestowing on various "positions" and "offices," rather than on individuals, the right to demand compliance in some situations. By removing power from the realm of "personal influence," and vesting it in the rights of offices and positions, the range and scope of power is expanded. It now becomes possible to have authority that organizes, for example, an entire nation, as is the case when a government or body of administrative offices is legitimated and given the right to extract compliance in exchange for providing certain services.

"Opposition values" are the media of social change and reorganization in a complex exchange system.[32] Such values allow for the organization of opposition beyond the limits of individual influence and proselytizing by providing a set of

---

[31] Ibid., p. 270.
[32] Ibid., p. 271.

common symbols that can potentially codify the grievances of large and diverse segments of collectivities into a "countervailing force against entrenched powers and existing institutions in the society."[33] These symbols unite those who have suffered deprivations in existing exchange relations and make them willing, under various conditions, to sacrifice their present material welfare in pursuit of change and reorganization of the current exchange system.

In sum, then, complex exchange systems are dependent upon "shared values," which "mediate" exchange relations between individuals and macro structures as well as between various types of macro structures. Without shared values, exchange is tied to the direct interpersonal interactions of individual men. Since virtually all known social systems involve indirect exchange relations among various types of social units—from individuals and groups to organizations and communities—it is necessary to conceptualize just how this can occur. For Blau, mediating values are a critical condition for complex exchange systems to emerge, persist, and break down. Without them, social organization beyond face-to-face interaction would not be possible.

Institutionalization.   While values facilitate processes of indirect exchange among diverse types of social units, institutionalization denotes those processes that regularize and stabilize complex exchange processes.[34] As people and various forms of collective organization become dependent upon particular networks of indirect exchange for expected rewards, pressures for formalizing exchange networks through explicit norms increase. This formalization and regularization of complex exchange systems can be effective under three minimal conditions: (*a*) The formalized exchange networks must have profitable payoffs for most parties to the exchange. (*b*) Most individuals organized into collective units must have internalized through prior socialization the mediating values used to build exchange networks. And (*c*) those units with power in the exchange system must receive a level of rewards that moves them to seek actively the formalization of rules governing exchange relations.

Institutions are historical products, whose norms and underlying mediating values are handed down from one generation to another, thereby limiting and circumscribing the kinds of indirect exchange networks that can emerge. Institutions exert a kind of "external constraint" on individuals and various types of collective units, bending exchange processes to fit their prescriptions and proscriptions. Institutions thus represent a set of relatively stable and general norms regularizing different patterns of indirect and complex exchange relations among diverse social units.

This conception of institutionalization is similar to the somewhat divergent

---

[33] Ibid.
[34] Ibid., pp. 273–80.

formulations of both Parsons and Homans. While institutions represent for both thinkers the regularization through norms of interaction patterns, Parsons visualizes institutions as normative structures, infused with values, which allow for the patterning of interaction among diversely oriented and goal-seeking actors, while Homans considers institutions as the formalization through norms and generalized reinforcers of exchange relations that ultimately have payoffs for each individual person involved. Despite their respective points of emphasis, however, both are concerned with the basic process through which norms emerge to facilitate the attainment of "goals" and "rewards" by social units. The formalization of such institutional norms is viewed by both to allow for expanded networks of "interaction" or "exchange" among various social units: for Homans, the "Person"; and for Parsons, the "Actor." Blau's conceptualization draws from both these perspectives by emphasizing, in a vein similar to Homans, that institutionalized patterns of interaction must have payoffs for the reward-seeking individuals involved and, in a way reminiscent of Parsons, that shared values must exist prior to effective institutionalization of indirect exchange relations. In this way, Blau apparently has sought to weld exchange theoretical principles to the functionalist's concern with how values and norms account for the emergence and persistence of complex social systems.

In doing so, Blau apparently recognizes Homans's failure to develop concepts that describe the various types and classes of institutionalized exchange systems. In an effort to correct for this oversight, Blau develops a typology of institutions embracing both the substance and style of the Parsonian formulation. Just as Parsons employed the pattern variables to describe the values guiding institutionalized patterns, Blau attempts to classify institutions in terms of the values they appear to embody in their normative structure. He posits three generic types of institutions: (a) *integrative institutions* "perpetuate particularistic values, maintain social solidarity, and preserve the distinctive character and identity of the social structure";[35] (b) *distributive institutions* embody universalistic values and operate to "preserve the social arrangements that have been developed for the production and distribution of needed social facilities, contributions, and rewards of various kinds";[36] and (c) *organizational institutions* utilize values legitimating authority and serve "to perpetuate the authority and organization necessary to mobilize resources and coordinate collective effort in the pursuit of social objectives."[37]

---

[35] Ibid., p. 278.

[36] Ibid.

[37] Ibid., p. 279. It is of interest to note that Blau implicitly defines institutions in terms of their functions for the social whole. While these functions are not made explicit, they are similar to Parsons's requisites. For example, "integrative institutions" appear to meet "needs" for "latency"; "distributive institutions," for "adaptation"; and "organizational institutions," for "integration" and "goal attainment."

However, Blau also recognizes that in this form of typologizing the potential is great for connoting an image of society as static and equilibrium maintaining. Thus, drawing from Homans's recognition that institutions are accepted only as long as they have payoffs for men's "primary needs" and from Dahrendorf's concern with the inherent sources of conflict and change in all relations of authority, Blau stresses that all institutionalized exchange systems reveal a *counterinstitutional component,* "consisting of those basic values and ideals that have not been realized and have not found expression in explicit institutional forms, and which are the ultimate source of social change."[38] To the extent that these values remain unrealized in institutionalized exchange relations, individuals who have internalized them will derive little payoff from existing institutional arrangements and will therefore feel deprived, seeking alternatives to dominant institutions. These unrealized values, even when codified into an opposition ideology advocating open revolution, usually contain at least some of the ideals and ultimate objectives legitimated by the prevailing culture, indicating that institutional arrangements "contain the seeds of their potential destruction" by failing to meet all of the expectations of reward raised by institutionalized values.

While Blau does not enumerate extensively the conditions leading to the mobilization of individuals into conflict groups, his scheme explicitly denotes the source of conflict and change: counterinstitutional values whose failure of realization by dominant institutional arrangements create deprivations that, under unspecified conditions, can lead to conflict and change in social systems. In this way, Blau attempts to avoid the predictable charges leveled against almost any form of functional analysis for failing to account for the sources of conflict, deviance, and change in social systems. Unlike the Dahrendorf model of dialectical conflict, however, Blau's scheme does not just assert the pervasiveness of conflict and change in social systems, but attempts to document how opposition forces, culminating in conflict and change, are created by the very processes that lead to the institutionalization of power in complex exchange systems.

Such tendencies for complex exchange systems to generate opposition are explicable in terms of the basic principles of exchange.[39] When certain mediating values are not institutionalized in a social system, exchange relations will not be viewed as "reciprocated" by those who have internalized these values. Thus, in accordance with Blau's Principle 3 on "reciprocity," the more likely are these segments of a collectivity to feel deprived and seek ways of retaliating against the dominant institutional arrangements, which, from the perspective dictated by their values, have failed to reciprocate. For those who have internalized values that are not institutionalized, it is also likely that perceptions of fair exchange have been violated, leading them, in accordance with Principle 6, to attempt to

---

[38] Ibid., p. 279.

[39] Ibid., see chap. 12, "Dialectical Forces," pp. 312–38.

sanction negatively those arrangements that violate alternative norms of fair exchange. Finally, the operation of Principles 3 and 6 in complex exchange systems is assured by the fact that, in accordance with Principle 7, in institutionalized exchange networks the balancing of exchange relations with some segments of a collectivity inevitably umbalances relations with other segments, thereby violating norms of reciprocity and fairness and setting into motion forces of opposition.

Unlike direct interpersonal exchanges, however, opposition in complex exchange systems is between large collective units of organization, which in their internal dynamics reveal their own propensities for integration and opposition. This fact requires that the analysis of integration and opposition in complex exchange networks be attuned to various levels of social organization. Such analysis needs to show, in particular, how exchange process among macro structures, whether for integration or opposition, are partly influenced by the exchange processes occurring among their constituent substructures.

Levels of Social Organization. To a great extent, the "dynamics of macro structures rests on the manifold interdependence between the social forces within and among their substructures."[40] The patterns of interdependence among the substructures of distinguishable macro structures are various, including: (*a*) joint membership by some members of macro structures in constituent substructures; (*b*) mobility of members between various substructures of macro structures; and (*c*) direct exchange relations among the substructures of different macro structures.

To discern these dynamics of substructures and how they influence exchanges among macro structures, Blau first raises the question of what generic types of substructures exist, resulting in the isolation of four classes of substructures: categories, communities, organized collectivities, and social systems. *Categories* refer to an attribute, such as race, sex, and age, that "actually governs the relations among people and their orientations to each other."[41] *Communities* are "collectivities organized in given territories, which typically have their own government and geographical boundaries that preclude their being overlapping, though every community includes smaller and is part of larger territorial organizations."[42] *Organized collectivities* are "associations of people with a distinctive social organization, which may range from a small informal friendship clique to a large bureaucratized formal organization."[43] *Social systems* "consist not of the social relations in specific collectivities but of analytical principles of organization, such as the economy of a society or its political institutions."[44]

---

[40] Ibid., p. 284.
[41] Ibid., p. 285.
[42] Ibid.
[43] Ibid.
[44] Ibid.

Values mediate the processes within these various types of substructures. "Particularistic values" allow for each substructure to create segregating boundaries; "universalistic values" allow for differentiation of units with substructures; "legitimating values" stabilize relations of authority; and "opposition values" give substructures their own internal sources of dialectical change. Discerning the complex relationships between the mediating values of substructures and those of macro structures poses one of the most difficult problems of analysis. On the one hand, some values must cut across the substructures of a macro structure if the latter is to remain minimally integrated; on the other hand, values of various substructures not only can segregate substructures from each other, but also generate conflict among them. Further, the relations among substructures involve the same basic exchange processes of attraction, competition, and differentiation in terms of the services they can provide for each other. It thus becomes evident that the analysis of exchange networks among macro structures forces examination of the exchange processes of their substructures. Additionally, the relations among these substructures are complicated by the fact that they often have overlapping memberships or mobility of members between them, making the analysis of attraction, competition, differentiation, integration, and opposition increasingly difficult.

Blau simplifies the complex analytical task of examining the dynamics of substructures by positing that organized collectivities, especially formal organizations, are the most important substructures in the analysis of macro structures. As explicitly goal (reward) seeking structures that frequently cut across social categories and communities and that form the substructures of analytical social systems, they are mainly responsible for the dynamics of macro structures. Thus, the theoretical analysis of complex exchange systems among macro structures requires that primary attention be drawn to the relations of attraction, competition, differentiation, integration, and opposition among various types of complex organizations. In emphasizing the pivotal significance of complex organizations, Blau posits a particular image of society that should guide the ultimate construction of sociological theory.

BLAU'S IMAGE OF SOCIETY

Organizations in a society must typically derive rewards from each other, thus creating a situation in which they are both "attracted" to, and in competition with, each other. Out of this competition, hierarchical differentiation between successful and less successful organizations operating in the same sphere emerges. Such differentiation usually creates strains toward specialization in different fields among less successful organizations as they seek to provide particular goods and services for dominant organizations and each other. If such differentiation and specialization among organizations is to provide effective means for integration, separate political organizations must also emerge to regulate their exchanges. Such political organizations possess power and are viewed as legitimate only as long as they are considered by individuals and organizations to follow the dictates of shared cultural values. Typically political organizations are charged with several objectives: (a) regulating complex networks of indirect exchange by the enactment of laws; (b) controlling through law competition among dominant organizations, thereby assuring the latter of scarce resources; (c) protecting existing exchange networks among organizations, especially those with power, from encroachment on these rewards by organizations opposing the current distribution of resources.

For Blau, then, it is out of the competition among organizations in a society that differentiation and specialization occurs among macro structures. While mediating values allow differentiation and specialization among organizations to occur, it is also necessary for separate political organizations to exist and regularize, through laws and the use of force, existent patterns of exchange among organizations. Such political organizations will be viewed as legitimate as long as they normatively regulate exchanges that reflect the tenets of mediating values and protect the payoffs for most organizations, especially the most powerful. However, the existence of political authority inevitably encourages opposition movements, for now opposition groups have a clear target—the political organizations—against which to address their grievances. As long as political authority remains diffuse, opposition organizations can only compete unsuccessfully against various dominant organizations. With the legitimation of clear-cut political organizations charged with preserving current patterns of organization, opposition movements can concentrate their energies against one organization, the political system.

In addition to providing deprived groups with a target for their aggressions, political organizations inevitably must aggravate the deprivations of various segments of a population, because political control involves exerting constrains and distributing resources unequally. Those segments of the population that must bear the brunt of such constraint and unequal distribution usually experience an escalated sense of deprivation in terms of the principles of reciprocity and fair exchange, which, under various conditions, causes their *organization* into a movement against the existing political authorities. To the extent that this organized opposition forces redistribution of rewards, other segments of the population are likely to feel constrained and deprived, leading them to organize into an opposition movement. These facts indicate that the organization of political authority assures that, in accordance with Principle 7, attempts to balance one set of exchange relations among organizations throws into imbalance other exchange relations, causing the formation of opposition organizations. Thus, built into the structure of political authority in a society are inherent forces of opposition, giving society a dialectical and dynamic character.

Echoing the assumptions of Dahrendorf and Coser, Blau conceptualizes opposition as representing "a regenerative force that interjects new vitality into a social structure and becomes the basis of social reorganization."[45] However, the extent to which opposition can result in dramatic social change is limited by several counterforces inhering in patterns of organization in complex exchange systems among organizations:[46] (a) The interdependence of the majority of organizations upon each other for rewards gives each a vested interest in the status quo, thus providing strong resistance to opposition organizations. (b) Dominant organizations that have considerable power to bestow rewards on other organizations independently of political organizations have a particularly strong vested interest in existing arrangements, thereby assuring their resistence to change-oriented organizations. (c) By virtue of controlling the distribution of valued resources, both dominant and political organizations are in a strategic position to make necessary concessions to opposition groups, thereby diffusing their effective organization. (d) Opposition movements must overcome the internalization of values by the majority; and without control of the means of socialization, their ideological call for organization is likely to fall on unsympathetic ears. (e) Societies composed of exchange networks among complex organizations typically reveal high levels of social mobility up the organizational hierarchy, thus increasing the difficulties involved in organizing a stable constituency.[47]

In reviewing Blau's analysis of exchanges among organizations in a society, it is evident that he has attempted to cast many of the assumptions and propositions of Parsons, Dahrendorf, and Coser into an exchange perspective that extends Homans's insights beyond the analysis of "men as men." In discussing the development of exchange systems among organizations, and the emergence of political authority, Blau focuses on the institutionalization of relations among what Parsons termed "social systems." The fact that such institutionalization rests upon the internalization of shared values and that institutional patterns can be typologized in terms of the dominance of various clusters of values further underscores Blau's analytical debt to Parsons. In contrast with Parsons's less explicit analysis, Blau's analysis is concerned with "mechanisms" of social change. Embracing Marx's and Dahrendorf's assumptions of the dialectical forces of opposition inherent in all micro and macro relations of power and authority, Blau visualizes the source of conflict as lying in the unbalanced exchange relations,

---

[45] Ibid., p. 301. Such a position is inevitable in light of Blau's explicitly stated belief that "our society is in need of fundamental reforms" (Blau, "Dialectical Sociology," p. 184).

[46] Blau, "Dialectical Sociology," p. 187; Blau, Exchange and Power, pp. 301–9.

[47] However, Blau recognizes that high rates of mobility in a society can also increase the sense of relative deprivation of those who are denied opportunities for advancement—thereby making them likely constituents of an opposition organization.

violating norms of reciprocity and fairness, which are inevitable concomitants of some organizations having a disproportionate hold upon valued resources.

Blau does not enumerate as explicitly as did either Marx or Dahrendorf the conditions leading to the organization of opposition ("conflict groups" for Dahrendorf and "class" for Marx). But his debt to Marx's insightful analysis (see chapter 5) is evident in his analysis on how levels of deprivation are influenced by (a) the degree of ecological concentration and the capacity to communicate among the deprived, (b) the capacity to codify an opposition ideology, (c) the degree of social solidarity among the deprived, and (d) the degree to which opposition organization is political and directed against the political organizations. Furthermore, Blau's incorporation of Dahrendorf's key propositions is shown in his recognition that the capacity of the deprived segments of a population to organize opposition is affected by such variables as the rate of social mobility, the capacity of dominant groups to make strategic concessions, and the number of cross-cutting conflicts resulting from multigroup affiliations. Finally, although Blau does not develop his argument extensively, he clearly has followed Simmel's and Coser's lead in emphasizing that conflict and opposition are a regenerative force in societies, which "constitute countervailing forces against . . . institutional rigidities, rooted in vested powers as well as traditional values, and . . . [which] are essential for speeding social change."[48]

In sum, then, Blau has offered perhaps the most varied "image of society" to be found among current theoretical perspectives in sociology. By incorporating —albeit in an unsystematic manner—the fruitful leads of sociology's other dominant conceptual perspectives, Blau has indeed offered a suggestive theoretical "prolegomenon" that can serve as a guide to more explicit theoretical formulations. Despite its suggestiveness, the scheme presents analytical problems that must eventually be resolved. While Blau's solutions are certainly more elegant than Homans's formative efforts, several serious problems with the scheme remain.

CRITICISMS OF BLAU'S EXCHANGE PERSPECTIVE

Blau's theoretical scheme has been subjected to relatively few criticisms, especially when compared with the controversy generated by Homans's exchange perspective. Part of the reason for this dearth of critical review[49] stems from the fact that, in synthesizing into an exchange perspective previously diverse theoreti-

---

[48] Blau, *Exchange and Power,* p. 302.

[49] For examples of the few criticisms of Blau's work, see M. J. Mulkay, "A Conceptual Elaboration of Exchange Theory: Blau," in his *Functionalism, Exchange, Theoretical Strategy* (New York: Schocken Books, 1971), especially pp. 206–12; Percy S. Cohen, *Modern Sociological Theory* (New York: Basic Books, 1968), pp. 123–27; and Anthony Heath, "Economic Theory and Sociology: A Critique of P. M. Blau's 'Exchange and Power in Social Life,'" *Sociology* 2 (September 1968): 273–92.

cal traditions, Blau offers "something for everyone." For the functionalist, Blau offers the concept of mediating values, types of institutions, and the counterpart of mechanisms of socialization and control that operate to maintain macro social wholes; for the conflict theorist, Blau presents a dialectical-conflict perspective emphasizing the inevitable forces of opposition in relations of power and authority; for the interactionist, Blau's analysis of elementary exchange processes places considerable emphases on role taking, role playing, and manipulation of self as actors compete for rewards; and, for the critic of Homans's reductionism, Blau provides an insightful portrayal of exchanges among emergent social structures which leave the "integrity" of sociological theorizing intact.

In offering a theoretical resting place for the major perspectives in sociology, Blau has perhaps provided a clue about how sociological theorizing should proceed: Rather than becoming bogged down in controversies and debates among proponents of various schools, it is much wiser to incorporate the useful concepts and assumptions of diverse perspectives into one theoretical "prolegomenon" describing how and why patterns of social organization emerge, persist, change, and break down. However, in offering this alternative to continued debate, Blau has left a number of theoretical issues unresolved. These issues are obscured by the insightfulness of his synthesis, and yet their resolution constitutes a critical "next step" in his theoretical strategy.

A System of Concepts or Propositions? Blau's analysis is a mixture of conceptual taxonomies and implicit theoretical generalizations. As was emphasized in the earlier enumeration of the seven exchange principles, these abstract principles are not made explicit. Why should this be so, especially in light of the fact that they so obviously guide his analysis? Perhaps Blau has shied away from statements of sociological laws or axioms, for fear of arousing the avalanche of criticism that accompanied Homans's efforts at stating sociology's first principles. But his failure to make explicit these principles probably has a more deep seated cause: To enumerate sociological laws requires that other concepts be incorporated into the propositions which are to be logically articulated to the laws.

Blau was clearly not prepared to perform this exacting task, preferring instead to delineate, much like Parsons, "bundles of concepts." Such "bundles of concepts" allow Blau considerable analytical leeway, for concepts like mediating values; integrative, distributive, and organizational institutions; counterinstitutional forces; social categories; communities; organized collectivities; and analytical social systems, all appear to overlap conceptually without denoting very precisely the phenomena to which they refer. As such, they can be bent and redefined in an ad hoc fashion to fit whatever the "facts may dictate." Thus, just as Parsons's system of concepts is not tightly interconnected into a logical system, thereby allowing enormous latitude in their use, so Blau's prolegomenon offers the same luxury of applying loosely articulated concepts to empirical phenomena without much possibility of their refutation.

Blau has a ready defense for such criticisms: His goal is not to develop a mature theory, but a scheme that can serve as a "preliminary" to the construction of such theory. The suggestiveness of Blau's perspective gives this defense some credibility; but, unfortunately, few have undertaken the task of making the scheme more theoretically mature. Just why this has been so, especially now that the scheme is 10 years old, is difficult to determine, but part of the reason may lie in Blau's failure to grapple successfully with several additional issues.

The Issue of Tautology. At the very outset of his presentation, Blau suggests that in limiting his definition of exchange to relations in which rewards are expected and forthcoming, his perspective can avoid charges of tautology. Furthermore, if a theoretical perspective allows for the formulation of testable hypotheses, it is not tautologous, for ultimately "the question of whether the theoretical principles are tautologous depends upon the possibility of *inferring* empirically testable hypotheses from them, and some operational hypotheses will be *inferred* to *illustrate* that this possibility exists" (italics added).[50] However, Blau's consistent lack of logical rigor in making empirical "inferences" from more abstract exchange principles does not obviate the potential for tautology, for without clear-cut use of *logical rules of inference*,[51] empirical hypotheses cannot be considered to have been derived from a theory. Thus, the theory has not necessarily been vindicated against charges of tautology, since the empirical hypotheses illustrating instances of nontautology do not bear the necessary logical connections to the theory.

Blau's disclaimers aside, the issue of tautology in exchange theory hinges on the question of whether the value of rewards are conceptualized and measurable independently of the "activities" value is supposed to regulate. As was emphasized in the last chapter, Homans failed to provide such independently defined concepts and empirical indicators of these concepts. However, Blau's scheme reveals a more elegant solution to the problem, for he attempts to define generic types of rewards—money, approval, esteem, and compliance[52]—in terms of their value for participants to an exchange. By analytically distinguishing classes of rewards, it is more likely that reward will be defined independently of the activi-

---

[50] *Exchange and Power*, p. 6.

[51] For an interesting discussion of logical rules of influence, see Karl Popper, "Why Are the Calculi of Logic and Arithmetic Applicable to Reality," in his *Conjectures and Refutations: The Growth of Scientific Knowledge* (Routledge & Kegan Paul, 1963), pp. 201–14.

[52] Homans makes these distinctions in his discussion of empirical phenomena. For example, chapter 16 on "Status, Conformity, and Innovation," in *Social Behavior*, employs a similar set of distinctions. Unlike Blau's scheme, such distinctions are made *after* analysis of data and are not considered to constitute generic types of rewards that can be incorporated into abstract corollaries to his axioms.

ties to be influenced by rewards. In Blau's scheme, such is especially likely to be the case, since Blau attempts to define generic types of institutional activities —integrative, distributive, and organizational—in various generic types of social units—categories, communities, organized collectivities, and social systems. While he does not develop the abstract theoretical statements describing what type of rewards in what type of social units will influence what type of institutional activities, the potential for performing this difficult, but critical, theoretical task remains. In fact, instead of "illustrating" with examples his implicit exchange principles as they apply to various types of institutionalized relations in various social contexts, Blau could have more profitably devoted his effort to linking explicitly his exchange principles to abstract theoretical statements on the relationship among different types of rewards for various types of activities in diverse types of social settings. Only when this difficult analytical task is performed will exchange theory begin to obviate the problem of tautology. It is perhaps the difficulty of this task that has kept sociological theorists from embracing more enthusiastically Blau's suggestive lead on the road "out of tautology."

Bridging the Micro-Macro Gap.   One of the most important analytical problems facing sociological theorizing revolves around the questions: To what extent are structures and processes at micro *and* macro levels of social organization subject to analysis by the same concepts and to description by the same sociological laws? At what levels of sociological organization do emergent properties require use of additional concepts and description in terms of their own unique social laws? In what ways are groups, organizations, communities, or social systems similar and different? These questions are extremely troublesome for sociological theorizing and constitute one of its most enduring problems. Blau has attempted to resolve this problem in several ways: (*a*) by assuming that the basic exchange processes of attraction, competition, differentiation, integration, and opposition occur at all levels of social organization; (*b*) by explicating general exchange principles, incorporating abstract exchange concepts, that can account for the unfolding of these processes at all levels of organization; (*c*) by enumerating additional concepts, such as mediating values and institutionalization, to account for emergent phenomena at increasingly macro levels of social organization; and (*d*) by classifying the generic types of organization—categories, communities, organized collectivities, and social systems—which denote different levels of organization, requiring somewhat different concepts for explication of their operation.

Such an effort constitutes a useful beginning to bridging the micro-macro analytical gap that exists in sociological theorizing. However, a number of problems remain; and it is to their resolution that efforts to improve upon Blau's scheme should be directed. First, Blau defines "organized collectivities" so broadly that they include phenomena ranging from small groups to complex organizations. It is likely that the concepts and theoretical generalizations appropriate to the small primary group, the secondary group, a crowd, a social movement, a small organization, and a large corporate bureaucracy will be somewhat different. Surely there are emergent properties of social organization in a spectrum ranging from a small group to a complex organization. In fact, aside from the study of community, most subfields in sociology fall within Blau's category of "organized collectivity." Thus, Blau has not resolved the problem of emergent properties; rather it has been defined away with an excessively broad category that subsumes most of the emergent properties of interest to sociologists.

Second, the delineation of additional concepts to account for differences in level of organizations only highlights the micro-macro gap without providing a sense of what concepts are needed to understand increasingly macro levels of social organization. What Blau does is to assert that there are certainly elementary exchange processes which occur at macro levels of organization and which require the addition of the concept "mediating values" if these emergent levels of organization are to be understood. But such an analysis begs the key question: When and at what levels of organization do such concepts become critical? Among dyads? triads? primary groups? secondary groups? small organizations? large organizations? To phrase the issue differently, at what point do what kinds of values, operating in accordance with what laws, become analytically significant? Blau simply says that at some point mediating values become critical, and he thereby avoids answering the theoretically interesting question.

Third, as has already been emphasized, Blau's presentation of exchange concepts and their incorporation into exchange principles is vague. Much of the analysis in this chapter has attempted to make more explicit the implicit exchange principles employed in his analysis. Without explicit statements of the exchange laws that cut across levels of organization, Blau fails to address an issue that he claims to be of great significance in the opening pages of his major work.

> The problem *is to derive* the social processes that govern the complex structures of communities and societies from the simpler processes that pervade the daily intercourse among individuals and their interpersonal relations. [Italics added][53]

To make such "derivations," it is necessary to formulate explicitly the laws from which derivations from simpler to more complex structures are to be made. Too often, Blau hides behind the fact that, to use his words, his "intent is not to present a systematic theory of social structure; it is more modest than that."[54] While any "theory," in light of the current state of the discipline, will inevitably appear modest, one of the first steps Blau should take is the clear enumeration of the concepts and propositions that cut across all levels of organization and

---

[53] Blau, *Exchange and Power*, p. 2.
[54] Ibid.

affect the operation of the basic processes of attraction, competition, differentiation, integration, and opposition. This oversight is especially evident when cast against the background of Blau's fairly detailed discussion of other concepts in the scheme. Thus, while Blau's basic exchange principles can be made more explicit by secondary commentators, it would be more desirable that their framer and advocate do so. Once made explicit, derivations can be stated as generic propositions applicable to certain clearly defined generic levels of organization. In trying to link systematically clearly stated abstract exchange principles to propositions describing processes in various social units—whether a type of group, organization, or community—it will become more evident when the derivations from the abstract exchange principles denote emergent social phenomena that require a unique set of abstract statements. As long as the exchange principles are left implicit, it will prove difficult to bridge the micro-macro "gap" with a common set of principles from which the unique laws describing various levels of social organization can be derived.

In sum, then, Blau has not explicitly stated either the general principles that cut across levels of organization or the laws appropriate to any one level of organization. In failing to do so, Blau has not capitalized on what appears to be a most promising beginning in resolving this persistent problem facing sociological theorizing. At a minimum, advocates of the exchange perspective should begin to formulate their basic principles more clearly, while those working in substantive areas, such as small groups, collective behavior, complex organizations, and communities, should begin to ask how the most abstract theoretical statements of each substantive area can be articulated with exchange principles. Out of this activity, considerable insight into how exchange principles help explain different patterns or levels of social organization will emerge. To continue to ignore this task will assure that suggestive "prolegomenons" will continue to accumulate without resolving the important theoretical issues facing sociological theorizing.

Part V

Unresolved Issues in Sociological Theory

16

Rephrasing the Problem of Order

For Thomas Hobbes the "problem of order" concerned how a viable social order was possible. For contemporary sociological theorizing, this central theoretical question has been transformed into a concern with the conditions under which different patterns of social organization are created, maintained, changed or broken down. In providing an "answer" to this theoretical question, each of the major conceptual perspectives discussed thus far provides a series of concepts denoting the fundamental processes of institutionalization and de-institutionalization. While these perspectives point to somewhat different features of institutionalization, their combined conceptual legacy can be viewed as a tentative beginning to resolving the problem of order. Despite the suggestiveness of this beginning, however, it will also be evident that social theory has failed to address some of its most critical questions.

CONCEPTUALIZING THE PROCESS OF INSTITUTIONALIZATION

Institutionalization is a very general term referring to the multifarious processes by which individuals, groups, and other types of social units become organized. Whether attention is drawn to the organization of relations among a few interacting individuals or among large organizations and communities, the specific concepts brought to bear at either level of analysis denote a facet of the more general process of institutionalization. When phrased in this way, a "solution" to the problem of order will involve understanding the complex process of institutionalization. Sociological theorizing must therefore begin to develop an interrelated body of concepts organized into formats of theoretical statements

297

that can categorize, explain, and provide a sense of understanding of why and how institutionalization should occur.

Problems of Conceptualization

Because the concept of institutionalization is highly abstract and covers a wide spectrum of social phenomena, it is difficult to comprehend what classes of less abstract concepts will be necessary for building social theory. What is it that social analysts should look for? With respect to what general types of phenomena should theorists begin developing concepts? These are not trivial questions, since they ask theorists to consider the basic properties of the social reality that they purport to study. To phrase the matter differently: What is "out there" in the "real" social world?

At the most abstract level, ignoring for the moment the substantive diversity of social phenomena, it is argued that theoretical understanding of institutionalization will require concepts capturing variations in the following *general classes of social phenomena:*

1. individual humans,
2. social relations among individuals,
3. emergent patterns of collective organization among individuals,
4. social relations among different types of units of collective organization, and
5. emergent patterns of organization among diverse types of collective units.

This ordering of phenomena is intended to acknowledge that concepts denoting the nature of individuals will be necessary to an understanding of the process of institutionalization. In turn, as indicated by (2) above, concepts pointing to the processes through which individuals establish social relations will also be critical. Then, as emphasized by (3), another body of concepts will be necessary to denote the variable properties of the emergent patterns of collective organization which arise out of interaction among individuals. In turn, as interacting entities in their own right, these emerging collective patterns of organization can have variable types of social relationships among themselves, indicating the need for another body of concepts describing these processes (4). Finally, from processes establishing relations among collective units emerge various patterns of social organization, which will require still another body of concepts (5).

This sketch of the general types and classes of concepts critical to an understanding of the process of institutionalization is perhaps obvious. After all, have not sociologists advanced concepts about the nature of human personality as well as the organization of such phenomena as dyads, triads, primary and secondary groups, complex organizations, communities, institutions, and other types of micro and macro social systems? Quite properly, sociological theorizing has devel-

TABLE 16–1

Conceptualization of Institutionalization

Conceptualization of Various Classes of Phenomena	*Legacy of Concepts*
Nature of individual	High
Nature of relations among individuals . .	High
Nature of emergent patterns of collective organization of individuals	Low
Nature of relations among collective organizations	Moderate
Nature of emergent patterns of organization among collective units	Low

oped concepts pertaining to these general classes of social phenomena, but the concepts that have emerged from this effort have tended to emphasize some classes of social phenomena to the exclusion of other classes. As Table 16–1 represents, a body of concepts and propositions with respect to the nature of individuals, the types of social relations among individuals, and the types of relations among different types of collective units has accumulated. But, with respect to the nature of emergent patterns of collective organization among either individuals or various types of collective units, considerably less conceptual attention has been devoted by current varieties of sociological theorizing. Indeed, while sociologists distinguish such emergent phenomena as primary and secondary groups, different forms of bureaucratization, diverse social institutions, urban and rural communities, and primitive, premodern, and modern societies, they have failed to develop theoretical statements about which of these phenomena are *generic* and thereby distinguishable from each other in terms of certain *basic properties*. Definitions on primary and secondary groups, community, bureaucracy, social institutions, and other presumably emergent phenomena abound in sociological theorizing, as only a cursory reading of any introductory sociology textbook will attest. Yet, these definitions represent only guesses about which phenomena are generic, since they are rarely used to build specific concepts that are incorporated into abstract theoretical statements that would allow insight into just where a primary group ends and a secondary group begins; how a small bureaucracy is different from a large one; where a "small urban" community exhibits generic properties that enable one to distinguish it from a "rural" community; where political, legal, or economic institutions exhibit fundamental properties that allow them to be distinguished from each other and from other presumably emergent social units. Sociological theorizing has developed many concepts, and suggestive propositions—about such phenomena as symbolic interaction, role taking, role conflicts, role bargains, primary and secondary exchange, conflict-cooperation, dominance-submission, authority, power, and coalitions—to describe *relationships* among different types of social units. Comparatively few concepts about the *nature of the units* that stand in relationship to one another have accompanied this effort.

Few sociologists would deny the existence of emergent social phenomena. Even "reductionists" such as Homans do not contend that social structures are not real, but only that they can be explained by concepts describing the relationships among individuals. Similarly, symbolic interactionists do not view emergent phenomena as nonexistent, but only as explicable in terms the capacity of individuals for role taking and self-evaluation. Obviously, conflict theorists such as Dahrendorf, with his concept of "imperatively coordinated association," functionalists such as Parsons, with the concept of "the social system," or exchange structuralists such as Blau, with concepts like "macrostructures" and "substructures," do not ignore emergent patterns of organization. Yet, as will be examined shortly, the proponents of each of these conceptual perspectives rarely discuss the generic types of units that stand in relationship to one another. Rather, the nature of emergent patterns of social organization is typically glossed over by vague concepts like "joint action," "the social system," "imperatively coordinated associations," "macrostructures," "collectivity," "subinstitutional-institutional," "cultural item or unit," "subculture," "subsystem," and so on. None of these concepts denote what social phenomena are distinguishable from each other in terms of fundamental properties that could be described by a series of concepts incorporated into theoretical statements.

Surprisingly, the apparent concern with social relationships has not caused theorists to ask what would seem to be a natural question: Is not the type of social relationship affected by the nature of the units involved in establishing a relationship? A considerable amount of attention has been devoted to how the nature of individuals affects the types of social relationships that will emerge out of their interactions, but beyond this micro level of analysis, interactionist, functional, exchange, and conflict theories have virtually ignored the fact that the nature of the units in interaction, exchange, functional interdependence, or conflict will affect the types of relationships they establish.

These problems with current attempts at portraying the process of institutionalization are fundamental. Indeed, if understanding of how and why different patterns of social organization are possible is to be achieved, it is necessary to make a theoretical commitment to discovering the most basic emergent patterns of such organization. This commitment will involve more than enumerating simple, textbook-like definitions, since these do not indicate how one unit of collective organization operates under laws that enable it to be distinguished from another generic unit of collective organization. Without this ability to distinguish classes of emergent phenomena from one another, theory building in sociology will be, to say the very least, inefficient, since it will be difficult to know at what level of social organization a proposition describing a particular social process will hold. Will, for example, a proposition about relationships among individuals in a "primary" group hold for a more "secondary" group? Or, will a proposition about relationships within one organization hold for other types of organizations? These are the questions that current theorizing in sociology has difficulty answering, primarily because insufficient analytical attention has been paid to the conceptualizing the basic levels of social organization.

Strategies of Conceptualization

There are a number of strategies available to theorists for rectifying this theoretical oversight. Probably the most fruitful is also the most obvious: State conceptual arguments propositionally. Too frequently, theoretical schemes are not stated propositionally, with the result that much of what passes for theory in sociology is an ambiguous mixture of unstated assumptions and images of causal processes. Were arguments about a particular social phenomenon stated propositionally, they would more readily beg the question: In what situations do they hold true, and when do they have little utility for categorizing, explaining, and providing a sense of understanding of social events? When stated propositionally, theoretical arguments will be more likely to inspire empirical investigation; and when tested against available data, the range of phenomena to which a proposition pertains will become increasingly evident. As these types of propositional arguments accumulate, they will begin to "cluster" around the particular level of social organization to which they pertain, thereby giving some indication of the basic levels of social organization which exist "out there" in the external social world. For example, as verified propositions on phenomena vaguely denoted by the label "groups" accumulate in the research and theoretical literature, it will become more evident that some of these propositions hold only for small "face-to-face" groups, while others apply only to processes in larger interaction networks. Not only would propositions "cluster" in this way, but it is likely that conspicuous propositional "gaps" would emerge between accumulating inventories. These gaps could indicate areas of neglected conceptual and research effort, but they could also point to areas of transition between one level and another of emergent organization. Thus, should propositions about small face-to-face groups suddenly not hold for larger interaction networks, a *qualitative* and *generic* difference between the two phenomena could be hypothesized (until additional evidence dictates otherwise), indicating the point where a new emergent level of social organization, operating under its own principles, exists. Naturally, such gaps between accumulating clusters of propositions will rarely be as obvious as implied here, but it is argued that, were a systematic effort undertaken to phrase arguments propositionally and then to examine empirically the range of events to which they apply, sociological theorizing would understand more clearly the levels of social organization which exist in the external social world. And, of course, emerging from various propositional inventories may be propositions that cut across many levels of organization, allowing theorists to tentatively hold the proposition as a more general sociological "law." In this way, a more adequate theoretical solution to the Hobbesian problem of order would be possible.

As the matter now stands in sociology, social phenomena are studied more for historical-political reasons within sociology as a profession than for their relevance to unraveling the complex problem of emergent phenomena. Sociology has seemingly partitioned itself politically into such subfields as small groups, social psychology, complex organizations, stratification, deviance, various institutional specialities (such as educational and political sociology), urban sociology, rural sociology, social change, economic development, micro sociology, macro sociology, and so on. Introductory sociology texts, however, typically address what appear to be more generic phenomena, such as the individual, primary groups, secondary groups, associations, aggregations, collective forms of behavior, stratification systems, complex organizations, community and social institutions. Are these all distinctive phenomena operating under their own set of laws? Currently, the research and theoretical efforts of sociology's many subfields have yet to provide even a tentative answer to what seems an obvious question.[1]

Although political subdivisions within the field are not likely to cease to exist,[2] it is possible to utilize their various proponents' research and conceptual efforts to build theory, provided arguments are phrased propositionally. Without at least some effort in this direction, efforts to build a theory of institutionalization will continue to be thwarted. How, for example, is it possible to determine if a vaguely stated set of assumptions and causal images of political processes in a particular nation-state has implications for the understanding of political processes in general, to say nothing of the operation of what is probably a more generic social unit like social institutions, when the argument is not summarized propositionally? It would be difficult to build theory in any discipline under these circumstances; and it is for this reason that theoretical work in sociology has not been as productive as is possible.

---

[1] Even attempts at developing propositional inventories have fallen into the trap of mixing propositions about such specific subfields as educational, political, or urban sociology with what textbooks tell us are generic social units, including groups, complex organizations, and stratification systems, communities, and social institutions. See, for example, Bernard Berelson and Gary A. Steiner, *Human Behavior: An Inventory of Scientific Findings* (New York: Harcourt, Brace, & World, 1964).

[2] Perhaps this is only my own distorted impression, but I find that those subfields in sociology which are organized around what I would consider to be some of the generic levels of social organization—small groups, complex organizations, and stratification—seem to be the most theoretically advanced in terms of clarity of concepts and explicitness of propositions.

In fact, it is the unwillingness on the part of research sociologists to summarize their research findings propositionally and of theorists to translate their specific models and paradigms into propositions that has made "theory" in sociology a series of suggestive, but highly vague, conceptual perspectives. While functionalism, conflict theory, interactionism, and exchange theory offer a provocative series of concepts and, at times, propositions on various aspects of institutionalization, their utility in arriving at a theoretical "solution" to the problem of order is limited. In the absence of a widespread commitment among sociologists to phrasing theoretical arguments and research findings propositionally, it will be difficult to accumulate the vast inventories of theoretical statements which these general perspectives might help organize.[3]

PERSPECTIVES ON THE PROCESS OF INSTITUTIONALIZATION

As has been emphasized, the process of institutionalization requires that analytical attention be drawn to the formulation of concepts and propositions pertaining to several general classes of phenomena: (1) the nature of individual humans, (2) the nature and types of social relations among individuals, (3) the nature and types of emergent patterns of collective organization among individuals, (4) the nature and types of social relations among such collective units of individuals, and (5) the nature and types of emergent patterns of organization among various types of collectively organized units. The conceptual perspectives discussed in the earlier pages of this volume suggest a tentative list of concepts for understanding (1), (2), and (4), but with respect to the issue of emergent phenomena—(3) and (5)—current theoretical perspectives have remained strangely uninformative.

In reviewing just what the major perspectives in sociology have to offer in conceptualizing the process of institutionalization, it is useful to summarize the legacy of concepts that each has developed for these five general classes of phenomena.

The Nature of Individual Humans

Functionalism. In *The Structure of Social Action*,[4] Parsons borrowed the basic assumption from utilitarian economics that individual humans are decision-making organisms, who weigh and then select appropriate means in the pursuit of goals (see chapter 3). In pursuing goals, individuals must become oriented to a wide variety of "objects" in the environment, including cultural values and

---

[3] It should be emphasized that most sociologists would agree with the above statements, but when it comes to phrasing the findings of their own study or to translating their own conceptual model into a series of propositions, what is espoused and what is actually done in sociology diverge.

[4] Talcott Parsons, *The Structure of Social Action* (New York: McGraw-Hill Book Co., 1937).

norms, as well as ecological and physical parameters of the situation. To a very great extent these objects determine the goals that actors pursue—thus indicating that the direction of human behavior is highly circumscribed by culture, constraints of the environment, and the physical features of humans as biological organisms. Furthermore, not only were environmental objects viewed by Parsons as influencing the perception of goals, but also the means available to achieve them. Hence, as actors weigh various alternative lines of action, the alternatives they perceive as available to them and the means they eventually choose in pursuit of goals are greatly influenced by the world of objects they perceive to exist in their environment.

In subsequent discussions of the individual, Parsons has increasingly focused on the structure of human personality—a feature of the individual which was virtually ignored in *The Structure of Social Action*. Cultural objects and the physical features of humans as biological organisms have now become visualized as interacting in complex ways to affect the individual's need structure, which, in turn, influences the goals that are pursued. Furthermore, the complex ego functions of humans have been more thoroughly explored as Parsons has begun to recognize the significance of actors' perceptions of themselves as objects that can be interjected into any interaction situation—thereby affecting the perception of goals as well as the weighing of means and the eventual selection of a particular line of behavior.[5]

All of these internal psychological processes have become classified in terms of their consequences for meeting the four imperatives facing any action system: adaptation, goal attainment, integration, and latency. The biological energy necessary to mobilize and sustain individuals is now conceptualized as an adaptive process; the weighing and choosing of alternatives is visualized as a goal-attainment function; the invocation of cultural objects that circumscribe the goal-attainment processes of decision making is now conceptualized as a latency process; and the perception of situational objects in the environment, including the projection of oneself as object, and their reconciliation with adaptive (biological needs) and latency (culturally induced needs) processes, is viewed as an integrative function of the human personality.

For Parsonian action theory, then, the individual is viewed as a decision-making entity who approaches any interaction situation with a complex legacy of objects which affects the general orientation of the individual, the perception of alternative lines of conduct, and the selection of a particular line of behavior.

---

[5] Talcott Parsons, "The Position of Identity in the General Theory of Action," in *The Self in Social Interaction*, ed. Chad Gordon and Kenneth J. Gergen, vol. 1 (New York: John Wiley & Sons, 1968). See also Talcott Parsons, "An Approach to Psychological Theory in Terms of the Theory of Action," in *Psychology: A Science*, ed. Sigmund Koch, vol. 3 (New York: McGraw-Hill Book Co., 1958).

However, in each interaction setting, an individual must reconcile this legacy with new objects—whether values, norms, other persons, or reevaluations of himself. Thus, human individuals are, on the one hand, partially "programmed" as they approach a social relationship, while, on the other hand, they possess the capacity to "reprogram" their orientations and behavior as they encounter the particulars of a concrete interaction setting (see chapter 12 for the details of this argument).[6]

Conflict Theory. For Dahrendorf, the individual is conceptualized only as a member of an imperatively coordinated association. Through such membership, individuals are then viewed to possess the ability to become aware of their subordinate positions and to organize themselves into a conflict group in an effort to change this position.

For Coser, the individual is conceptualized only as an organism capable of intense emotional arousal and of becoming involved, as either an individual or as a member of a group, in conflict with other individuals or groups.[7]

Interactionism. From the role-theoretic perspective, the individual is conceptualized to possess the capacity to interpret the requirements of an interaction situation and then to execute, with varying styles of performance, the required behaviors. Because humans possess the capacity to create symbolic environments, composed of expectations from other individuals and groups not actually present in an interaction situation, the interpretation of the expectations in any situation, and the performance to meet these expectations, is usually a mixture of expectations from other individuals and groups both immediately present and symbolically invoked. Furthermore, since individuals also have selves, their interpretations of expectations and the style of their performances to meet them will be greatly influenced by both their more enduring self-conceptions and situationally derived self-images.

For symbolic interactionists, considerably more conceptual emphasis is placed upon the fact that humans create symbolic worlds of objects. Such objects can include cultural proscriptions, normative prescriptions, the demands of invoked or immediately present individuals and groups, and the enduring or transitory images of the self as an object. For all the "objects" created in a situation, actors have dispositions to act in certain ways, with the sum total of these dispositions constituting an overall "definition of the situation." Individual behavior thus reflects the particular world of objects constructed at any given time in an

---

[6] Mertonian functionalism is not addressed here, since it provides no explicit formulation of the nature of the individual. To some extent, Merton's implicit conceptualization of the individual corresponds to that to be discussed under the interactionist heading below.

[7] Obviously, then, conflict theory has little to say about the nature of the individual. Rather, analytical attention is drawn by proponents of this perspective to the nature of conflict relations among collectively organized units.

interaction setting. However, because individuals create symbolically these worlds of objects toward which they respond, they are also capable of inserting new objects, and hence new dispositions to act, into an interaction situation—thereby giving humans the capacity to alter their behavior.

Exchange Theory. For all varieties of exchange theory, the individual is visualized as a reward-seeking organism. Rewards are then defined in terms of their capacity to bestow gratification, or meet either innate or acquired needs. In seeking rewards, the individual is conceptualized as capable of making calculations about rewards, costs, and investments derived and expended in emitting a particular line of behavior. While these calculations are not necessarily conscious or rational, and are influenced by many forces, exchange theory places emphasis on the individual's capacity to (*a*) perceive alternative behaviors in any interaction situation, (*b*) weigh and assess, whether explicitly or implicitly, the cost to investment-reward ratio of each alternative, and (*c*) decide upon a course of action likely to yield an "acceptable" profit or reward.

Following Parsons's reformulation of utilitarianism, exchange structuralists such as Blau conceptualize the impact of cultural components like values and norms on perceptions of, assessments about, and decisions on alternative lines of conduct. Both structuralists like Blau and psychologically oriented exchange theorists like Homans conceptualize the significance of self-conceptions and self-evaluations in circumscribing the individual's cost-investment-reward calculations of alternative lines of behavior.

In summary, each of these dominant conceptualizations of the nature of the individual is intended to highlight the capacities that enable humans to form, maintain, and change social relationships. Sociologists are not concerned with developing a model or "theory" of human personality, per se, but only with the capacities of humans that affect, and are affected by, the course of their interactions with each other. Yet, each of the various concepts developed by sociology's dominant theoretical perspectives touches upon the components of personality that would have to be more thoroughly conceptualized in a "theory" of human personality.

Following Parsons's emphasis on the biological parameters of action, as well as the exchange-theoretic concern with human motivation to satisfy innate needs, sociological theory recognizes the relevance of biological forces in understanding various types of social relationships and emergent patterns of social organization. However, these biological variables have not been conceptualized extensively, nor have they been incorporated consistently into various portrayals of human interaction.[8] Rather, sociological theorizing has focused more upon the nature of

---

[8] In Wallace's excellent overview of sociology's dominant theoretical perspectives, this gap in current forms of theorizing is clearly acknowledged as "A Missing Viewpoint"; see Walter Wallace, *Sociological Theory* (Chicago: Aldine Publishing Co., 1969), pp. 13–58.

"acquired" needs and their impact on the course of interaction. Whether one follows the Parsonian, interactionist, or exchange-theoretic portrayal, it is clear that the human capacity to interpret the gestures of others and to engage in covert symbolic processes results in the "internalization" of various cultural values and other symbols that in turn "motivate" individuals to channel their behaviors in certain general directions. Furthermore, from the Parsonian and interactionist positions, this same capacity to interpret the gestures of others and use these symbols to visualize the self as object in an interaction situation leads to the individual's conception of himself as a certain type of person who must be responded to in specified ways and who must engage in only certain types of conduct. Thus, from the sociological perspective, the initial mobilization of the human organism to form social relationships is conceptualized as an unspecified function of biological needs, culturally internalized motives, and evaluational conceptions of self.

The capacity of the human organism to create symbolically worlds of objects is then conceptualized by Parsonian functionalism, interactionism, and, to a lesser extent, exchange theory to circumscribe the direction of behavior, once initiated. For Parsonian theory, considerable emphasis has been placed upon the "actor's" legacy of internalized value orientations, his perception of normative demands attending any interaction situation, the specific interpretation of the demands of "alters" (others), and the general ecological parameters of the situation. While Parsons[9] has recently begun to conceptualize the processes whereby the self as an object comes to influence the course of interaction, it is in the interactionist perspective that the most consistent analytical effort to understand the impact of self-related variables on interaction has been undertaken. From the interactionist perspective, the capacity to create the symbolic world to which he responds allows the individual in interaction to introject the self as an object requiring certain types of responses into any interaction situation. Such introjection can occur through a variety of abilities: (1) to read the gestures of others in the immediate interaction situation, to derive a self-image, and then to respond to the self-image; (2) to imagine the evaluations of others not present in the immediate interaction situation, to derive an image of self in their eyes, and then to respond to the imagined self-image; (3) to bring to an interaction situation a more permanent and enduring conception of self, to interpret what responses are consistent (or inconsistent) with this conception, and then to respond to the constraints dictated by this more permanent self-conception. From the position of both Parsonian functionalism and interactionism, the complex interplay among these self-related capacities, coupled with the human ability to bring a legacy of values to a situation, to interpret normative and interpersonal expecta-

---

[9] Parsons, "Position of Identity."

tions of that situation, and to perceive the ecological constraints of such situations, results in what interactionists are prone to call a "definition of the situation," or what Parsons simply labels an "orientation." However one prefers to label processes, the thrust of sociological analysis has been to conceptualize those variables that channel and give direction to the behaviors of mobilized and motivated human actors.

The actual emission of behavior has been most adequately conceptualized by Parsonian action theory and exchange theory. In the concepts of "definition of" or "orientation to" a situation, humans are visualized as being directed toward goals or ends, since each object symbolically introjected into the interaction situation can be visualized as an end toward which responses are to be organized. Whether the objects are value commitments, normative prescriptions, interpersonal expectations of others, or self-related demands, humans treat them as goals that they must meet. Parsons has provided one of the most important conceptualizations of the complex processes whereby humans organize their behavior with respect to goals or ends. Such organization takes the form of making "decisions" about alternative responses as individuals attempt to sort out various means and reconcile them with the varieties of goals they perceive in any situation. Similarly, in a less precise formulation, the interactionist tradition has emphasized the "covert rehearsal"—or, in Mead's terms, "imaginative rehearsal"—process during which individuals weigh various alternatives and then select behaviors yielding the most "satisfactory" reconciliation of the various components of their "definition of the situation."

Just what would constitute the most "satisfactory" reconciliation has probably been best conceptualized by exchange theory. Though fraught with operational problems, the concepts of cost, reward, and profit, and the propositions they have inspired allow for the decision-making processes of human actors to be conceptualized in terms of the respective "value" of "objects" that have been introjected into the interaction situation. While the general course of interaction is influenced by the complex interactions among self-related objects, as well as by values, norms, the interpersonal demands of different others, and various ecological parameters, the emission of overt behavior in any interaction will be a reflection of the capacity of humans to assess covertly the likely payoffs that will ensue from responding to each object. While the concepts of "value," "reward," "cost," and "profit" are not easily measured, they provide sociological theorizing with a means for conceptualizing the way individuals—within the limits of their general "orientations to" and "definitions of" situations—are capable of making decisions about how they will respond to the worlds of objects they create in each and every social relationship.

In sum, then, it is with these concepts that sociological theory now approaches the study of the individual and the process of institutionalization. Although this conceptualization of the individual has often suffered from imprecise theoretical definitions and difficulties of operationalization, as well as from a failure to argue propositionally, it appears that sociological theorizing does have a suggestive inventory of concepts. This inventory can serve as a crude beginning to understanding how the nature of the individual "fits into" a theoretical solution to the Hobbesian problem of order.

Social Relations among Individuals

Since it is with the capacities enumerated above that individuals enter social relationships, the nature of their interaction will reflect which of these capacities is given analytical emphasis. While there is considerable overlap and complementarity among the various conceptualizations of the individual, each theoretical perspective in sociology has come to emphasize a somewhat different facet of the interaction among individuals.

Functionalism. For Parsons, the individual is conceptualized as entering interaction with a set of "orientations." Such orientations are the outgrowth of processes in which individuals reconcile acquired and biological needs with a wide variety of "objects" in the interaction setting, including cultural values, normative prescriptions, conceptions of self, and, most importantly, the perceived orientations of others. Unfortunately, Parsons does not provide a more detailed description of the *processes* whereby two actors—"ego" and "alter" in his terms —actually adjust their orientations to establish various types of social relationships.

What Parsons does provide is an impressive conceptualization of the individual and a set of variables—the "pattern variables"—to describe the types of social relations emerging from what are somewhat mysterious processes of interaction among individuals. While he implicitly recognizes that the "objects" brought to the situation, the interpretation of the gestures of others in the situation, the covert assessment of alternative lines of action, and the "voluntaristic" decision to behave in a certain way, all shape the course of interaction and the resulting social relationships, these capacities of individuals are not further conceptualized into a set of more specific concepts and propositions on the processes through which social relationships are created. However, once social relationships are established, Parsons delineates some classes of variables that could describe, in part at least, the maintenance and change of such relations. Included in this list are such processes as subtle interpersonal gestures and sanctions, ritual activities, role segregation, safety-valve roles, and force or coercion.[10] Beyond this tentative list, the Parsonian scheme is noticeably devoid of specific concepts denoting the processes of interaction and the formation of social

---

[10] For examples of this analytical concern, see Talcott Parsons, *The Social System* (London: Free Press, 1951).

relationships. It is probably this failure to be more specific on interaction as a process that has opened Parsonian action theory to the charge of emphasizing "structure" at the cost of ignoring social "processes."[11]

Conflict Theory. For Dahrendorf, social relations are conceptualized almost exclusively in terms of super- and subordination. Just how this state of affairs emerges is never seriously discussed, since it is assumed that the unequal distribution of power, authority and other scarce resources is endemic to all social relations. Discussion then focuses on how one set of superordinate-subordinate relations are transformed through conflict into another set of such relations in a seemingly endless dialectic. In this analysis, few analytical clues are given about how individuals interact to form the conflict groups that will usher in new patterns of superordinate-subordinate social relations.

In Coser's scheme, a similar conceptual vagueness over the interpersonal processes causing various types of social relations to emerge can be noted. While psychological variables such as "emotional involvement" and "relative deprivation," as well as such structural variables as the degree of "integration" and "social mobility," indicate some of the conditions leading to the formation of certain types of conflict relations, the theoretical scheme clearly does not address the more generic question of how and why social relations among individuals are possible.

Interactionism. As its name would underscore, the interactionist perspective focuses primarily on the processes involved in creating, maintaining, and changing social relationships among individuals. Much like Parsons's conceptualization of "orientation," the interactionist concept of "definition of the situation" denotes the complex processes whereby "objects" are introjected into an interaction setting. And, as with action theory, these objects can include immediately present or invoked others, norms, self-images and conceptions, or any other "object" defined as relevant to a situation by an individual. Unlike action theory, interactionism introduces a crucial concept—"role taking"—to denote the process in which two or more individuals "read" or "interpret" each other's gestures to derive not only a self-image but also an understanding of the dispositions of various "others" in the concrete interaction situation. However, role taking is not conceived to be necessarily tied to a particular situation. Humans often assume the roles, perspective, and dispositions of other individuals and groups

---

[11] Again, Mertonian functionalism is not discussed, since it is difficult to discern in his work a clear theoretical position on relations among individuals. This is not to deny that Merton's work is filled with insightful contributions on the nature of individual adjustments to various structural situations. For example, his "Social Structure and Anomie" and "Bureaucratic Structure and Personality" must be considered two important contributions on the nature of adjustments of individuals (see Robert K. Merton, *Social Theory and Social Structure* [New York: Free Press, 1968]). Despite the suggestiveness of these and other essays, a clear consistent perspective on social relations among *individuals* is not presented by Merton.

not immediately present and use the judgments inputed to them to evaluate not only themselves as objects but also the other objects, including the norms, values, and dispositions of others that are perceived to exist in the interaction setting. On the basis of reconciling the dispositions to act toward this complex configuration of objects, various potential lines of activity are then mapped out and covertly rehearsed. Eventually, a line of behavior is selected that best reconciles the dispositions to act toward the various objects of the situation. But as soon as one sequence of behavior is emitted, an individual (a) reinterprets its consequences by role taking with both immediate and remote others, (b) reevaluates himself as an object on the basis of his performance, (c) maps out a next course of action, (d) rehearses it covertly, and then (e) selects the behavior that best "fits" the particular configuration of objects that are now perceived to exist in the situation. Human interaction is then a continual process of role taking, mapping, rehearsing, and selecting behaviors that allow humans to align and realign their behaviors. The nature of such alignment, and the frequency of realignment, depends upon whether individuals perceive themselves to have reconciled the demands of each other, the norms and values of the immediate situation, and their situational evaluations of themselves, as well as the demands of remote others, groups, norms, values, and the more enduring conceptions of self.

The course of interaction is therefore a function of the symbolic worlds participants create. Presumably, the nature of social relationships will be a reflection of how individuals cope with and reconcile their diverse dispositions to act toward the objects of this symbolic world. However, in elaborating upon the concepts that denote the process of interaction, the interactionist perspective has tended to neglect questions of *which types* of processes will lead to *what types* of social relationships. Currently, interactionism fills in the conspicuous omission in action theory on the processual nature of interaction, but it has yet to indicate very precisely how variations in these processes lead to the formation of various forms and types of social relations among individuals.

Exchange Theory.   For all varieties of exchange theory, social relationships are created by the perceptions and expectations of individuals that their interaction is likely to yield some material or psychological profit (rewards less costs/investments). For psychologically oriented theorists like Homans, the strength of the initial attraction in an interaction, the maintenance of a social relationship, or the change and termination of the relationship will occur in accordance with certain "psychological laws," which incorporate variables such as value, frequency, marginal utility, and distributive justice. For more structurally oriented exchange theorists like Blau, these basic "laws" are supplemented by a series of principles denoting the impact of sociocultural variables such as norms of "fairness" and "reciprocity," as well as variables denoting the problems of maintaining balance and harmony among multiple exchange relations.

What is unique to the exchange perspective is that the concepts used to describe social relations have been incorporated into a series of abstract theoretical statements. Given the capacity of humans to perceive and calculate the cost-reward/investment ratio for various lines of behavior in any interaction situation, the resulting interaction should then follow from the relationships specified in these abstract statements (see chapters 15 and 16). However, it has proven difficult to operationalize the variables in these statements, primarily because what is perceived by an individual as valuable and hence as a cost, reward, or investment is not easily discerned by investigators. Furthermore, exchange-theoretic propositions are noticeably lacking in specification of the classes of variables that are potentially "valued" in any interaction situation. For example, what are the "objects" of "value" that are likely to be subjected to cost/investment-reward calculations? How important is self? remote others? others immediately present? norms? values? and other groups? Interaction and action theory provide a suggestive list of the classes of variables that are likely to enter into the exchange calculations of individuals attempting to establish, maintain, alter, or terminate social relations. Thus, to make the full use of exchange-theoretic concepts and principles, it will be necessary to derive some lower-order theoretical statements from them which specify more concretely the *types* of "objects" in different *types* of interaction situations which are likely to enter into exchange calculations of "value" and hence affect the *types* of social relations that will ensue.

In sum, then, contrary to many of the recent polemics launched against sociological theorizing in recent decades,[12] considerable conceptual emphasis has been placed upon the processes that create, maintain, alter, or terminate social relationships among individuals. Action theory has provided a listing of concepts denoting how social relations among individuals who reveal certain capacities are maintained, but has been somewhat vague on how such relations emerge, change, or terminate. With the concept of "role taking," interactionist theorizing can correct for this oversight in action theory by indicating how actors or individuals can (*a*) interpret each other's dispositions and (*b*) adjust their behaviors to each other's dispositions, as well as to those of other "objects" symbolically introjected into the situation. Exchange theory adds to this body of thought a set of concepts and propositions that can, with considerably more refinement, provide some indication as to why objects are introjected into an interaction in the first place, why only some are eventually used as the basis for action, and thus, why social relations among individuals are created, maintained, changed, and terminated.

---

[12] For examples of these critiques, see Herbert Blumer, "Society as Symbolic Interaction," in *Human Behavior and Social Processes,* ed. Arnold Rose (Boston: Houghton-Mifflin Co., 1966); and Walter Buckley, *Sociology and Modern Systems Theory* (Englewood Cliffs, N.J.: Prentice-Hall, Inc., 1967).

Emergent Patterns of Collective Organization among Individuals

While sociological theory has a suggestive accumulation of concepts on the nature of individuals and social relations among them, the types of structures emerging from interaction have received comparatively little rigorous analytical attention. Many definitions about the nature of different types of groups, collectivities, aggregations, masses, complex organizations and other supposedly emergent patterns of collective organization among individuals can be found in the literature, but such definitions have yet to become organized into sets of clear concepts about what is, and what is not, a distinct and generic type of social unit that operates under principles of interaction which would separate it from other generic types of social units.

The concepts used to describe social relationships are apparently assumed to be transinstitutional, for rarely has an advocate of one of sociology's dominant conceptual perspectives indicated unambiguously that the concepts and propositions of a particular theoretical position apply to only some types of social units and not others. While Homans has at times argued that he is concerned only with the "subinstitutional,"[13] or face-to-face, relations of "men as men," in actual practice he has employed concepts to explain interaction in diverse types of social units. Even when generic types of emergent structures are distinguished, as in Blau's analysis,[14] it is not made clear at what level of collective organization additional concepts, such as "mediating values" and "secondary exchange," become relevant.

Thus, since at least the time of Durkheim, sociologists have felt confident that society is a real entity, *sui generis*. Yet, they have not pursued this insight into the nature of society by grappling with the difficult conceptual task of delineating the generic levels of reality that would require their own concepts and laws of explanation. If only impressionistically, it is apparent that a small group is different in terms of some rather fundamental properties from a secondary group; a secondary group, from a complex organization; a small organization, from a large one; an organization, from a crowd or mob, and so on. Yet, the dominant conceptual perspectives in sociology today do not provide much insight into how individuals' social relations affect, and are affected by, various generic patterns of emergent organization. Surprisingly, rather than addressing this fundamental issue, these perspectives discuss in more detail the processes through which such poorly conceptualized units as "ICAs," "social system," "subsystems," "groups," "institutions" and "subinstitutions" establish and maintain various types of social relations.

---

[13] See George C. Homans, *Social Behavior: Its Elementary Forms* (New York: Harcourt, Brace & World, 1961), chapter 18.

[14] See Peter M. Blau, *Exchange and Power in Social Life* (New York: John Wiley & Sons, 1964), chapters 10 and 11.

Social Relations among Collective Units

While there is a growing body of literature in various substantive fields on the nature of social relations among various collective units, the dominant conceptual perspectives in sociology have yet to be informed by, or to inform significantly, this literature. For example, such specific fields as labor-management relations, ethnic groups, organizational research and theory, interest-group theory, or international relations have developed a legacy of concepts denoting relations among specific types of social units. Unfortunately, developments in such substantive areas have not begun to resolve the more fundamental theoretical issue: Under what conditions are what types of relations among what types of generic social units to be expected? At present, sociological theorizing has avoided addressing this issue.

Functionalism. The Parsonian scheme presents a series of concepts that attempt to classify the relations among various collective units, usually denoted by the vague notions of "social system" and "subsystem." For Parsons, subsystem is a general concept indicating that units collectively organized into a social system reveal relations with other units within some more inclusive social system. Except for a few theoretical and substantive works,[15] Parsons does not indicate how the social relations among subsystems are influenced by organizational properties—such as size, degree of differentiation, forms of integration, and other variables—which would distinguish one generic level of organization from another. Instead, he discusses interrelations among subsystems primarily in terms of the more general concepts of a functional imperativist scheme. While Parsons is clearly aware of the fact that the process of institutionalization involves diverse levels of social organization, he has not employed his elaborate system of concepts in a way that has allowed for specification of different types of social relations between and among different types of generic social units.

However, the action-theoretic scheme does reveal considerable potential for achieving such specification. In the Parsonian scheme, any subsystem is a "social system" in its own right and is composed of constituent "subsystems," but to designate a particular social system as a "subsystem" emphasizes that it exists in a pattern of interdependence with other types of subsystems within a more inclusive system. Institutionalization thus involves a complex web of external and internal relations among various levels of subsystems. Because the relations of such systems constitute a fantastically complicated web, the primary analytical task is to develop a set of concepts that can describe the types of relations existing among subsystems. Initially, in the evolution of the action scheme, Parsons employed the "pattern variables" to denote the types of common values, norma-

---

[15] For example, see Talcott Parsons and Neil J. Smelser, *Economy and Society* (New York: The Free Press, 1956).

tive prescriptions, and decision-making processes of interrelated social units. At this stage in the development of action theory, different combinations of the pattern variables could be used to classify the relations among social units, whether individuals or some constellation of collectively organized subsystems, in terms of the kinds of values and norms circumscribing the decisions of each unit.[16]

As notions of system needs and requisites became more prominent in the action scheme, the interrelationships among subsystems could be further classified in terms of inputs and outputs across the adaptive, latency, or goal-attainment sectors of each system.[17] Furthermore, the general type of interchange for any cluster of systems was conceptualized to be circumscribed by the location of the subsystem in either the adaptive, goal-attainment, integrative, or latency sectors of a more inclusive system. For example, the types of interchanges among subsystems located within the adaptive sector of a system would differ from those for clusters of subsystems within the integrative sector. Additionally, interchanges among subsystems located in different sectors of a more inclusive system would involve different inputs and outputs by each system across their respective boundaries. This recognition has led Parsons to conceptualize the "generalized symbolic media" of exchange to account for the fact that distinctive media are utilized by different subsystems located within different sectors of a more inclusive system. As was noted in chapter 3, Parsons has yet to develop completely the concept of generalized media; but it is clear that he is attempting to emphasize that relations among system units are not only circumscribed by various patterns of values and norms, but also mediated by different types of symbolic media. Thus, the types of social relations among units within a more inclusive system are conceptualized by Parsons to be a function of the types of values and norms circumscribing decisions by any unit and the distinctive media employed by interacting units in different sectors of a more inclusive system.[18]

Conflict Theory.   The Dahrendorf model suffers from a lack of specification on different types of relations of authority within different types of ICAs. Dahrendorf simply defines ICAs as the organization of roles in terms of authority relations, and thereby, defines away the question of what distincitve types or levels of ICAs are to be found in the social world. Presumably, an ICA can range from authority relations in a small group to those inherent in the stratification system of an entire society. Within any ICA, polarization into conflict groups can occur under specified conditions, leading to conflict and reorganization of

---

[16] This was the analytical tack employed in his *Social System.*

[17] See Talcott Parsons, Freid Bales, and Edward A. Shils, *Working Papers in the Theory of Action* (Glencoe, Ill.: Free Press, 1953).

[18] Again, Mertonian functionalism is not discussed, since it has not developed an explicit body of abstract concepts to describe relations among "cultural items" and other social units.

relations of authority in a potentially endless dialectical process. Social relations are thus conceptualized in terms of unspecified types of authority that, under partially enumerated conditions, lead to conflict of unspecified degrees of violence and intensity, which, in turn, results in unspecified reorganization of authority relations in unspecified types of ICAs.[19] Hence, the Dahrendorf model avoids theoretical questions on both the nature of the emergent patterns of organization that form social relations and on the specific types of authority and conflict relations these emergent units are likely to develop.

The Coser conflict model suffers from a similar lack of specificity on the types of social relations likely to exist among different types of collectively organized units. While the intensity and duration of conflict relations among groups are visualized by Coser as influenced by such group properties as size, extent of primary relations among members, degree of centralized leadership, and degree of internal integration, his model does not indicate how these properties distinguish the generic types of units from one another. In turn, without this information, different types of conflict relations cannot be distinguished.[20]

Interactionism. The role-theoretic perspective embodies a set of concepts devoted primarily to explaining individuals' relations with each other and with various types of groups. Because of this emphasis on the individual, role theory has yet to develop concepts that have utility in explaining social relations among collectively organized units. But to the extent that relations between collective forms of organization involve individuals as representatives of such units in interaction, it appears that the concepts of the role-theoretic perspective could have some utility. Only in a few studies on "marginal men," caught between the demands of two groups, and on "role conflict" has the role-theoretic perspective explored the fact that social relations between collective units are often carried out by individuals in interaction.[21] Even in these studies, attention is usually drawn to the consequences of role playing for the individuals involved rather than to the social relations between the collectively organized units represented by individuals. Thus, despite the lack of anlytical attention by role theorists to conceptualizing social relations among collective units, the fact that individuals are often role-playing representatives of various types of collectivities should suggest an unexplored area of conceptual endeavor for role theory—an area that needs to be explored before an adequate theoretical answer to the problem of order can be provided.

Symbolic interactionism, as espoused by Herbert Blumer, has recognized more clearly the applicability of its concepts to the analysis of social relations among

---

[19] See chapter 6 for the details of this argument.

[20] See chapter 7, tables 7–1 to 7–4.

[21] For example, see studies included in Bruce J. Biddle and Edwin Thomas, *Role Theory: Concepts and Research* (New York: John Wiley & Sons, 1966).

collectivities. Like individual humans, organized groups of individuals define situations, map out alternative lines of action, and reach decisions about how to interact with other collectively organized units. Whether through organized decision-making processes within an organizational structure or through decisions by individual "leaders" or "agents," collectively organized units interpret each other's dispositions, assess and evaluate situations, and make decisions on how to act. Then, on the basis of feedback derived from the perceived consequences of action, collectivities reinterpret, reassess, and, perhaps, readjust and realign their actions. While Blumer[22] is certainly correct in emphasizing that "a human society consists of acting units" and that the "acting units may be separate individuals, collectivities whose members are acting together on a common quest, or organizations acting on behalf of a constituency," little analytical work has followed from this insight into how different types of "social units" in different types of "situations" will "act" in different ways and thereby "align" and "realign" in different types of ways their actions in an effort to form different types of social relations. Currently, these important theoretical questions have appeared secondary to assertions that society—in all its diverse and unspecified levels of organization—is indeed "symbolic interaction."

Exchange Theory. Both Homans and Blau have developed preliminary, and somewhat divergent, perspectives on the nature of exchange relations among collective units. However, the respective conceptualization of relations among more macro social units by these two theorists reveal some important similarities.[23] (1) For both, exchange relations among collectivities are viewed as mediated by commonly accepted norms and values. (2) In each perspective, these social relations are conceived to utilize "secondary reinforcers," such as money, in complex patterns of indirect exchange among a plurality of collectivities. (3) For both theorists, exchange among units at one level of organization is visualized as affected by the internal exchange relations among the constituent parts or subsystems of each unit. (4) For both, exchange relations eventually lead to the differentiation and integration of units in terms of power, or the ability to derive rewards. (5) Finally, both perspectives view all existing exchange relations as ultimately generating pressures for their reorganization and change.

Yet within the broad outline of these formulations, Blau and Homans employ divergent sets of concepts to explain social relations among collective units of organization. For Homans, there is only a vague distinction drawn between individual exchanges among "men as men" and the groups and organizations that emerge out of these interactions of "men." For example, in his discussion of institutionalization, Homans visualizes "leaders," who presumably are in-

---

[22] See Herbert Blumer, *Symbolic Interaction Perspective and Method* (Englewood Cliffs, N.J.: Prentice-Hall, Inc., 1969), p. 85.

[23] See Blau's *Exchange and Power*, and Homans's *Social Behavior.*

dividual men, as "investing" their "capital" to form new and more complex webs of social relations. To maintain these collective patterns of organization, these "men," or perhaps some collective of men (it is not made clear), introduce "generalized reinforcers," such as money, to provide standardization of the rewards of all those "individuals" (or is it subgroups?) participating in the new and more complex web of social relations. Because these generalized reinforcers allow further extension and elaboration of the emerging institutional patterns of collective organization, "rules" are implemented (by whom? or by what collective units?) to specify further what are now becoming complex and indirect exchange relations among social units (men? groups? organizations?) with varying degrees of access to rewards. This organizational base, utilizing generalized or standardized reinforcers and relying upon codified rules, allows for even further elaboration of exchange networks (among what kinds of units?), eventually resulting in the vast "institutional piles" (composed of what types of exchange relations among what types of units?) which go to make up "society." But to the extent that they do not meet the "primary needs" of "men as men" (what are "primary needs"?), then these institutional arrangements become vulnerable to change when another "leader" (a man or group?) presents an alternative that offers more payoff.

In Homans's model, then, it is never clear whether social relations are being analyzed in terms of exchanges among men, among collective units, or among men as representatives of collective units. Furthermore, except for vague references to "generalized reinforcers" and "codified rules," Homans devotes little attention to indicating what types of reinforcers and what types of "rules" would be utilized among what types of generic social units to form what types of exchange relations revealing what types of differentiation and potential for change. Thus, Homans's intellectual "orgy," as he phrased the matter, provides a suggestive framework within which the hard analytical work has yet to be done. At present, Homans's model has yet to confront the real theoretical problems in developing an understanding of the process of institutionalization.

In contrast with Homans, Blau makes a more extensive conceptual effort to distinguish elementary exchanges among individuals and those among macro social units. First, Blau presents what appear to be four generic levels of social organization: categories, communities, organized collectivities, and social systems. Second, exchange relations within and among such macro social units are viewed as mediated by different types of values, including particularistic, universalistic, legitimating, and opposition values. Third, each type of value is seen as facilitating the operation of the basic social processes that occur at all these levels of social organization: attraction (particularistic values), competition and differentiation (universalistic values), integration (legitimating values), and opposition (opposition values). Fourth, as exchange networks become regularized within and between levels of social organization, they are seen to rely upon different values for their continued maintenance, enabling their classification into integrative institutions (particularistic values), distributive institutions (universalistic values), organizational institutions (legitimating values), and counterinstitutions (opposition values).

Thus, in contrast with much social theory, Blau's theoretical perspective inititates the difficult analytical task of delineating how the nature of social relations among units is affected by the nature of the units themselves and the distinctive symbolic media they employ. Yet, as was emphasized in chapter 15, Blau's analysis suffers from his failure to conceptualize very precisely the generic social units that seemingly utilize different values to mediate different types of social relations. Indeed, concepts such as "organized collectivity" are so broad as to encompass what are most likely several different levels of social organization. Thus, in the end, Blau's scheme provides a taxonomy of different types of values that facilitate the operation of different types of basic social processes leading to various types of institutional arrangements within different levels of social organization. However, Blau's failure to indicate how different levels of social organization affect the nature of exchange relations makes the scheme only an elaborate and suggestive taxonomy of social relations, with the critical question left unanswered (different types of institutionalized social relations among *what?*).

Emergent Patterns of Organization among Collective Units

Sociological theorists have talked rather easily about levels of social organization without specifying just what distinguishes one level from another. While most sociologists would admit that emergent social units, such as groups, organizations, communities, institutions, and the like, reveal social relations that result in the emergence of various types of macrostructures, the dominant conceptual perspectives in sociology devote little analytical attention to the problem, preferring instead to address the nature of social relations among these poorly conceptualized units of organization. Thus, theorists have rather easily discussed systems and subsystems, micro and macro analysis, institutional and subinstitutional, individual and joint action, sociocultural items and social wholes, imperatively coordinated associations, organized collectivities, and the like without defining the different types of units encompassed by these vague terms.

The end result of the situation is for sociological theory to lack a clear conceptualization of what entities emerge out of social relations among units of collectively organized individuals. In turn, this conceptual failing inhibits understanding of how such emergent phenomena feed back to affect the social relations among their constituent subparts (whatever these may be). Until this conceptual oversight is rectified, it seems unlikely that the process of institutionalization will be fully understood by sociologists, thereby deferring even longer a theoretical solution to the Hobbesian problem of order.

THE PROBLEM OF ORDER: A CONCLUDING COMMENT

This chapter has attempted to provide an overview of the key concepts employed by functional, conflict, interactionist, and exchange theorizing to answer the problem of order. What is evident from this review is that sociology has made many promising beginnings to finding a theoretical solution to this most fundamental problem. Also clear is that these efforts have been partially thwarted by the failure of sociologists to address the critical question of emergent phenomena. Without a more precise understanding of sociology's generic units of analysis, concepts describing social relations will continue to be vague.

While most sociologists would not question the necessity for more complete insight into the nature of emergent phenomena, few have directly addressed the question: What are sociology's units of analysis? This chapter has attempted to document the failings of contemporary theorists to address this question. It is hoped that this documentation is not interpreted as yet another platitudinous cry for theoretical reform in sociology. Rather, this conclusion has been reached only after careful assessment of the dominant theoretical perspectives in sociology and is therefore not intended as a counterpolemic to the imputed analytical atrocities of some delinquent conceptual perspectives. Yet, if sociological theory is to come to grips with its most basic question and begin to provide a scientific answer, then it must attempt to isolate its generic units of analysis. Only in this way will the joint process of institutionalization and de-institutionalization become more clearly understood.

17

Ethnomethodology: An Alternative Theoretical Paradigm?

Common to all the dominant efforts among mainstream sociologists to understand society is the presumption that patterns of social organization are *real and external entities*, which can be described and studied through the use of various theoretical constructs and methodologies. Not at issue in the jurisdictional disputes and quibbles among proponents of the various conceptual perspectives in sociology is the presumption that society is "out there" and waiting to be studied. What is at issue are the concepts, theory-building strategies, and methodologies that will best capture the essence of "society."

All this perhaps seems so obvious and self-evident to most sociologists that it is rarely discussed. Recently, however, just this issue has been debated. Some scholars are now asking a fundamental and disturbing question: What should sociologists study? This is not a mere jurisdictional dispute over whether sociologists should develop theories of micro and macro processes; whether society should be viewed in terms of action, symbolic interaction, or exchange; and whether conflict-consensus and stability-change dominate the social scene. Rather, the question concerns whether sociological theory should continue to operate under the presumption that society is amenable to study by proponents of current theoretical perspectives. This challenge raises an alternative theoretical question: How do sociologists and other groups of humans create and sustain for each other the *presumption* that the social world has a real character.[1] A "more

---

[1] For the most extensive statements of this position, see Harold Garfinkel, *Studies in Ethnomethodology* (Englewood Cliffs, N.J.: Prentice-Hall, Inc., 1967; Harold Garfinkel and Harvey Sacks,

real" phenomenon for those who propose this question revolves around the complex ways people (laymen and sociologists alike) go about consciously and unconsciously constructing, maintaining, and altering their "sense" of an external social reality. In fact, the cement that holds society together may not be the values, norms, common definitions, exchange payoffs, role bargains, interest coalitions, and the like of current social theory, but people's explicit and implicit "methods" for creating the presumption of a social order.

Such is the challenge of the relatively recent sociological perspective, ethnomethodology.[2] For the ethnomethodologist, what is directly observable are people's efforts to create a common sense of social reality. The substance of this reality is viewed as less interesting than the *methods* used by groups of persons, whether sociologists or laymen, to construct, reaffirm, and alter a vision and image of what exists "out there." Since this ethnomethodological position has only recently begun to take on clarity, there are no well-formulated principles denoting just how communities of actors actively negotiate common images of reality. Yet, the implications of ethnomethodology are potentially revolutionary for sociological theorizing.

ETHNOMETAPHYSICS OR ETHNOMETHODOLOGY?

Ethnomethodology has often been misunderstood by sociologists. Part of the reason for this misunderstanding stems from the vagueness of the prose of some ethnomethodologists,[3] but perhaps a more fundamental reason derives from the fact that sociologists who have been steeped in the theoretical traditions outlined in chapters 1–16 have had difficulty recognizing a radical alternative to these traditions. Indeed, even with clear and readable sources now available, most sociologists would profess not to understand the ethnomethodological position—

"On Formal Structures of Practical Actions," in *Theoretical Sociology: Prespectives and Developments*, ed. John C. McKinney and Edward A. Tiryakian (New York: Appleton-Century-Crofts, 1970), pp. 337–66; Don H. Zimmerman and Melvin Pollner, "The Everyday World as Phenomenon," in *Understanding Everyday Life*, ed. Jack D. Douglas (Chicago: Aldine Publishing Co., 1970), pp. 80–103; and Don H. Zimmerman and D. Lawrence Wieder, "Ethnomethodology and the Problem of Order: Comment on Denzin," in ibid., pp. 285–95.

[2] There are a number of antecedents to the recent formulations of the ethnomethodological position. See, in particular, the works of Schutz: Alfred Schutz, *Collected Papers I: The Problem of Social Reality*, ed. Maurice Natanson (The Hague: Martinus Nijhoff, 1962); Alfred Schutz, *Collected Papers II: Studies in Social Theory*, ed. Arvid Broderson (The Hague: Martinus Nijhoff, 1964); and Alfred Schutz, *Collected Papers III: Studies in Phenomenological Philosophy*, ed. I. Schutz (The Hague: Martinus Nijhoff, 1966).

[3] See, for example, Garfinkel, *Studies in Ethnomethodology*. However, recent portrayals of the ethnomethodological position have done much to clarify this initial vagueness. See, for example: Zimmerman and Wieder, "Ethnomethodology and the Problem of Order"; Zimmerman and Pollner, "The Everyday World"; Garfinkel and Sacks, "Formal Structure"; Randall Collins and Michael Makowsky, *The Discovery of Society* (New York: Random House, 1972), pp. 209–13; and George Psathas, "Ethnomethods and Phenomenology," *Social Research* 35 (September 1968): 500–520.

perhaps indicating that their commitment to existing modes of theorizing operates as a set of intellectual blinders. In addition, even when authors assume to understand ethnomethodology, misinterpretations still abound.

One form of such misinterpretation asserts that ethnomethodology represents a "corrective" to current sociological theorizing by pointing to sources of bias among scientific investigators. From this position, it is assumed that ethnomethodology can serve to "check" the reliability and validity of an investigator's observations by exposing not only his biases, but those of the scientific community accepting his observations. While ethnomethodology might be used for this purpose, if one were so inclined, those who advocate this use have failed to grasp the main thrust of the ethnomethodological position. For the ethnomethodologist, emphasis is not upon questions about the reliability and validity of investigators' observations, but upon the methods used by "scientific" investigators and laymen alike to construct, maintain, and perhaps alter what each considers and believes to be a "valid" and "reliable" set of statements about order in the world. The "methodology" in the ethnomethodological perspective does not address questions about the "proper," "unbiased," or "truly scientific" search for knowledge; rather, ethnomethodology is concerned with the common methods people employ—whether scientists, housewives, insurance salesmen, or laborers,—to create a sense of order about the situations in which they interact. The best clue to this conceptual emphasis can be found in the word, ethnomethodology: *ology*, "study of"; *method*, "the methods (used by)"; and *ethno*, "folk or people."

Another related source of misunderstanding in commentaries on ethnomethodology comes from those who assume that this perspective simply seeks to use "soft" research methods, such as participant observation, to uncover some of the taken-for-granted rules, assumptions, and rituals of members in groups.[4] This interpretation would appear to transform ethnomethodology into a research-oriented variant of the symbolic interactionist[5] perspective. Such a variant of ethnomethods would now represent a more conscientious effort to "get at" actors' interpretative processes and the resulting "definitions of the situation." By employing various techniques for observation of, and participation in, the symbolic world of those interacting individuals under study, a more accurate reading of how situations are defined, how norms emerge, and how social action is controlled could be achieved. While ethnomethodologists do employ observation and participant methods to study interacting individuals, their concerns are not the same as those of symbolic interactionists. Like all dominant forms of sociological theorizing, interactionists operate under the presumption that com-

---

[4] For example, see Norman K. Denzin, "Symbolic Interactionism and Ethnomethodology," *American Sociological Review* 34 (December 1969): 922–34.

[5] For another example of this interpretation, see Walter L. Wallace, *Sociological Theory* (Chicago: Aldine Publishing Co., 1969), pp. 34–36.

mon definitions, values, and norms emerge from interaction and serve to regulate how people perceive the world and interact with each other. For the interactionist, concern is with the conditions under which various types of explicit and implicit definitions, norms, and values emerge and thereby resolve the problem of how social organization is possible. In contrast, ethnomethodologists are interested in *how* members come to agree upon an *impression* that there are such things as rules, definitions, and values. Just what types of rules and definitions emerge is not a central concern of the ethnomethodologist, since there are more fundamental questions:[6] Through *what types of methods* do people go about seeing, describing, and asserting that rules and definitions exist? How do people use their beliefs that definitions and rules exist to describe for each other the "social order"? Thus, again, the "methods" of ethnomethodology do not refer to a new and improved technique on the part of scientific sociology for deriving a more accurate picture of peoples' definitions of the situation and of the norms of social structure (as is the case with interactionists). For the ethnomethodologist, emphasis is on the *methods employed by those under study* in creating, maintaining, and altering their presumption that a social order, forcing certain kinds of behavior, actually exists "out there" in the "real" world.

Indicating what ethnomethodology is not goes a long way to revealing just what it is. Ethnomethodology is not a new research method; it does not seek to answer the question of how society is possible by introducing sociologists to new research techniques. Rather, ethnomethodology is concerned with the study of a phenomenon that has received little attention within the intellectual confines of traditional theoretical perspectives. It seeks to study this phenomenon by the use of many research strategies, including variants of observational and participant-observational methods. And, contrary to some of its critics' assertions, ethnomethodology is concerned with building a theory—formats of abstract and generic statements tied to verified research findings—of the phenomenon under study. What is unique about ethnomethodology, then, is its subject matter. Ethnomethodology calls for an alternative set of metaphysical assumptions about the nature of the social world:

1. In all interaction situations humans attempt to construct the appearance of consensus over relevant features of the interaction setting.
2. These setting features can include attitudes, opinions, beliefs, and other cognitions about the nature of the social setting in which they interact.
3. Humans engage in a variety of explicit and implicit interpersonal practices and methods to construct, maintain, and perhaps alter *the appearance* of consensus over these setting features.
4. Such interpersonal practices and methods result in the assembling and disassembling of what can be termed an "occasioned corpus"[7]—that is, the *perception*

---

[6] Zimmerman and Wieder, "Ethnomethodology and the Problem of Order."

[7] Zimmerman and Pollner, "Everyday World"; see also, Garfinkel, *Studies in Ethnomethodology,* pp. 3–4.

by interacting humans that the current setting has an orderly and understandable structure.

5. This appearance of consensus is not only the result of agreement on the substance and content of the occasioned corpus, but also a reflection of each participant's compliance with the "rules" and "procedures" for assemblage and disassemblage of this consensus. In communicating, in however subtle a manner, that parties accept the implicit rules for constructing an occasioned corpus, they go a long way to establishing consensus over what is "out there" in the interaction setting.

6. In each interaction situation, the rules for constructing the occasioned corpus will be unique in some respects and hence not completely generalizable to other settings—thus requiring that humans in each and every interaction situation use interpersonal methods in search for agreement on the implicit rules for the assemblage of an occasioned corpus.

7. Thus, by constructing, reaffirming, or altering the rules for constructing an occasioned corpus, members in a setting are able to offer to each other the appearance of an orderly and connected world "out there" which "compels" certain perceptions and actions on their part.

It is from these kinds of assumptions about human interaction that ethnomethodology takes its subject matter. Rather than focusing on the actual content and substance of the occasioned corpus and on the ways members believe it to force certain perceptions and actions, attention is drawn primarily to the *methods humans use to construct, maintain, and change* the appearance of an orderly and connected social world. These methods are directly observable and constitute a major portion of people's actions in everyday life. In contrast, the actual substance and content of the occasioned corpus is not directly observable and can only be inferred. Furthermore, in concentrating on the *process* of creating, sustaining, and changing the occasioned corpus, the ethnomethodologist could ask: Is not a more fundamental answer to the Hobbesian problem of order being provided? Indeed, is not the process of creating for each other the appearance of a stable social order more critical to understanding how society is possible than the actual substance and content of the occasioned corpus? Is there anything more to "society" than members' beliefs that it is "out there" forcing them to do and see certain things? If this fact is true, "order" is not the result of the particular structure of the corpus, but of the human capacity to continually assemble and disassemble the corpus in each and every interaction situation. These facts suggest to the ethnomethodologist that theoretical attention should therefore be placed upon the ongoing process of assembling and disassembling the appearance of "social order" and to the particular methods people employ in doing so.

This concern with the processes of assembling and disassembling the occasioned corpus represents a radical departure from traditional modes of sociological theorizing. Most theoretical perspectives, and certainly each of those covered in previous chapters, conceptualize the occasioned corpus itself rather than the processes of its creation, maintenance, and alteration. In contemporary sociological theorizing, analytical attention focuses on the norms, values, perceived exchange payoffs, definitions of the situation, and other features of interaction settings created by actors. In fact, from the ethnomethodological perspective, sociological formulations themselves represent a particular occasioned corpus among the members of a community called professional sociology. Each of the theoretical perspectives covered in Parts 1–4 of this volume can, from an ethnomethodological point of view, be analyzed as assertions about the nature of what is "out there" in the "real" world, with the result that the methods employed by sociologists to create, sustain, and change these assertions could be a fertile field of study for the ethnomethodologist.

It is little wonder that sociology has reacted somewhat defensively to ethnomethodology. Sociologists like to view themselves as "objective" scientists in pursuit of verified knowledge about the "real" social world. It is naturally disquieting to have this noble pursuit relegated to the status of a mere subject matter. Such dismay among sociologists is especially understandable in light of the fact that, from the ethnomethodological position, sociologists employ the same generic methods as do laymen in constructing conceptions of "social facts," and hence, are much the same as any other group of interacting humans.

To this conclusion, sociologists often present the counterargument that their "methods" are less biased and distorted than those of the common man. For the ethnomethodologist, however, the sociologist and common man are not different, since each uses a series of methods to support a presumption that there is an independent social order that is amenable to their description. The assumption of a natural social world is not unique to sociologists; the fact that they have canonized some (but not all) of their methods in research protocols and theoretical formats does not remove them from the everyday world of ordinary humans. All humans seem to assume a natural social order, and all humans attempt to make sense of this order to each other. At the most abstract level, then, the methods employed by sociologists and laymen will look the same.

CONDUCTING ETHNOMETHODOLOGICAL INQUIRY

The task of ethnomethodological research is thus to understand the way people go about agreeing upon the rules that they will use to construct the features of an interaction setting. However, to discern these rules is difficult, primarily because people are rarely conscious of them. These rules remain implicit, despite the fact that, in any social setting, much everyday activity among participants is devoted to establishing agreement over the rules of assemblage and disassemblage of an occasioned corpus. Since the rules used to construct the corpus are implicit, it is likely that they can be discovered only through research methods that allow investigators to penetrate a social setting, and thereby become attuned to the ways its participants establish agreement over the rules for agreeing upon the structure of an occasioned corpus.

At present, ethnomethodological research appears directed primarily at confirming its central assumption that there are indeed hidden rules for constructing, maintaining, and changing a sense of order in any situation. For example, Garfinkel and his associates[8] report a series of conversations in which student experimenters challenged every statement of selected subjects. The end result was a series of conversations revealing the following pattern:[9]

> SUBJECT: I had a flat tire.
> EXPERIMENTER: What do you mean, you had a flat tire?
> Subject appears momentarily stunned and then replies in a hostile manner:
> SUBJECT: What do you mean, "What do you mean?" A flat tire is a flat tire.
> That is what I meant. Nothing special. What a crazy question!

In this situation, the experimenter was apparently violating an implicit rule for this type of interaction situation and thereby aroused not only the hostility of the subject but also a negative sanction, "What a crazy question!" Seemingly, in any interaction there are certain background features which "everyone should understand," and which "should not be questioned" in order that all parties to the situation be able to "conduct their common conversational affairs without interference."[10] Such implicit rules appear to guide a considerable amount of everyday affairs and are critical for the construction of at least the perception among interacting humans that an external social order exists.

Other research strategies can also yield insights into the rules used by parties to an interaction for constructing the occasioned corpus. For example, Garfinkel and his associates[11] summarized the "decision rules" jurors employed in reaching a verdict. By examining a group such as a jury, which must—by the nature of its task—develop an interpretation of "what really happened," the ethnomethodologist might achieve some insight into the generic properties of the processes involved in agreeing upon the rules used in constructing a sense of "social reality." From the investigators' observations of jurors, it appeared that "a person is 95 per cent juror before he comes near the court," indicating that through their participation in other social settings and through instructions from the court they had come to accept the "official" rules for reaching a verdict. However, these rules were altered somewhat as participants came together in an actual jury setting and began the "work of assembling the 'corpus' which serves

[8] Garfinkel, *Studies in Ethnomethodology*, pp. 35–76.

[9] Ibid., p. 42.

[10] Ibid., p. 42.

[11] Ibid., pp. 104–15.

as grounds for inferring the correctness of a verdict."[12] Because the inevitable ambiguities of the cases before them made difficult strict conformity to the "official rules" of jury deliberation, new decision rules were invoked in order to allow jurors to achieve a "correct" view of "what actually happened." But in their retrospective reporting to interviewers of how they reached their decision, jurors typically invoked the "official line" to justify the correctness of their decisions. When interviewers drew attention to discrepancies between the jurors' ideal accounts and actual practices, they became anxious, indicating that somewhat different rules had been used to construct the corpus of "what really happened."

In sum, these two examples of research strategies of prominent ethnomethodologists are sufficient to illustrate the intent of ethnomethodological research: to penetrate natural social settings or create social settings in which the investigator can observe humans attempting to assert, create, maintain, or change the rules for constructing the appearance of consensus over the structure of the "real world." By focusing on the process or methods used to agree upon the rules for constructing the occasioned corpus, rather than on the substance or content of the corpus itself, research from the ethnomethodological point of view can potentially provide a more interesting and relevant answer to the question of "how and why society is possible."

CONSTRUCTING ETHNOMETHODOLOGICAL EXPLANATIONS

The goals of ethnomethodological research and theory-building strategy appear to be the same as those of conventional sociological theorizing: to construct a system of abstract statements, verified by a body of research findings, on social phenomena. Of course, the principal difference between ethnomethodological strategy and that of mainstream sociology is that the phenomena under study differ.

One of the theory-building problems encountered by ethnomethodology, and probably all forms of social theorizing, concerns the *interpretative* nature of human interaction: How are ethnomethodologists to develop *literal*—that is, intersubjectively verifiable—descriptions of human interaction when the course of such interaction is influenced by wide variety of past experiences, setting interpretations, and adherence to implicitly perceived rules? To penetrate social settings, the ethnomethodologist must often come to understand members' background assumptions and natural language; but, in so doing, his descriptions of members' interpretative processes will in themselves represent interpretations,

---

[12] Ibid., p 110.

which could differ from those of another ethnomethodologist studying the same social setting. For example, two ethnomethodologists analyzing even a "hard" piece of evidence, such as the transcript of a conversation, must attempt to understand some of the background assumptions of the participants and the connotations implied by various words and phrases.[13] But the act of attempting to understand these features of the transcript is itself an act of interpretation, with the result that the judicious reading of the same transcript can yield different conclusions by two investigators. Thus, there is no way to determine which is the "correct" or "objective" interpretation of the data. These problems are compounded when the ethnomethodologist enters natural social settings and attempts to interpret members' methods for constructing an occasioned corpus, because, in contrast with the transcript, the number of diverse stimuli affecting the investigator's interpretation of "what's going on" escalate to a point at which it would become even more difficult for two investigators to arrive at a similar description of the interaction setting.

Without descriptions of events which are agreeable to a community of scholars, working independently of each other, developing abstract theoretical statements becomes difficult. For it can be properly asked: How would one go about refuting the statement when investigators could not agree upon the events to which the abstract statement is supposed to apply? Thus, to the extent that ethnomethodology is committed to developing abstract and generic statements of its defined phenomena, it must overcome the methodological problems of an interpretative social world studied through similar interpretative processes of investigators. These problems are no more severe for the ethnomethodologist than for other sociological theorists operating under the assumption that human interaction is a mutual process of interpretation. Much like other theoretical strategists in sociology, ethnomethodologists must seek ways to describe ongoing social settings or concrete displays (such as a transcript) independently of the "meaning" imputed to the setting or display, despite the fact that interpretation of this meaning by investigators is necessary to make the description. In this way, the various interpretations of social settings and displays can be rigorously compared with each other and with subsequent interpretations by different investigators. Common elements in the descriptions can become the initial empirical base for abstract theoretical statements, while divergent descriptions can constitute a research problem to be studied further.

Only through this commitment to resolving the methodological problems involved in collecting evidence of peoples' constructions of the occasioned corpus can ethnomethodology become more than an intellectual and rhetorical pastime

---

[13] Example borrowed from Thomas P. Wilson's unpublished paper, "The Regress Problem and the Problem of Evidence in Ethnomethodology."

and move to providing an alternative theoretical paradigm to current modes of sociological theorizing.

ETHNOMETHODOLOGY AND THE PROBLEM OF ORDER: A CONCLUDING COMMENT

In chapter 1, the task of sociological theorizing was viewed as that of providing a "solution" to the Hobbesian "problem of order." This solution was visualized as documenting with verified abstract statements the conditions under which various patterns of social organization were created, maintained, changed, and broken down. The succeeding chapters have focused on the concepts, propositions, theoretical formats, and strategies of the functional, conflict, interactionist and exchange perspectives. Each of these perspectives was seen to hold to the assumption that there is a "natural order out there" existing independently of peoples' perceptions.[14] In fact, such perceptions and other forms of human cognition are in part structured by the real social order. Theory building and research are thus directed to discerning the regularities in the operation of this social order—thereby offering a scientific solution to how and why society is possible.

In contrast with these assumptions and theory-building strategies are the views of ethnomethodologists, which call into question the relevance of this pursuit. What is most readily observable, and hence real, are the attempts by interacting humans to persuade each other that there is an order to specific social settings and to a broader "society." What is "really real," then, are the methods people employ in constructing, maintaining, and altering for each other a sense of order—regardless of the content and substance of their formulations. While not all ethnomethodologists would go this far, it is a reasonable conclusion that "order" is not maintained by some society "out there," but by *peoples' capacity to convince each other* that society is out there. Furthermore, the substance and content of their visions of society are perhaps not as important in maintaining order as the continually ongoing *processes* of constructing, maintaining, and altering some kind of vision, whatever it may be. The ethnomethodological solution to the Hobbesian problem of order is thus radically different from that proposed by current theoretical strategies, since for the ethnomethodologist, efforts should be directed toward developing a body of abstract and verified theoretical statements on the generic properties of how actors go about invoking and using rules for constructing a "sense of social order." The "sense of order" is not what makes society possible, but the capacity of humans to *actively and*

---

[14] For an interesting discussion of this assumption that challenges the ethnomethodological perspective, see Bill Harrell, "Symbols, Perception, and Meaning," in *Sociological Theory: Inquiries and Paradigms,* ed. Llewellyn Gross (New York: Harper & Row, 1967), pp. 104–27.

continually create and use rules for persuading each other that there is a real world.

From an ethnomethodological point of view, the pages of this volume—including those of this last chapter—constitute a phenomenon for study. For, indeed, the author has attempted throughout to persuade the reader that there are preferable ways of conceptualizing the social world. Some of the rules that have been invoked to accomplish this task remain hidden, enabling the author to offer this book as data for study by ethnomethodologists.

Indexes

Name Index

Subject Index

339

This book is set in 10 point Electra, leaded 3 points, and 9 point Electra, leaded 2 points. Part numbers are in 30 point Scotch Roman italic and chapter numbers in 36 point Scotch Roman italic. Part titles are in 18 point Scotch Roman italic and chapter titles are in 18 point Scotch Roman. The size of the type page is 27 x 46 picas.